POSTAL PLEASURES

"Small boys must be prepaid."

Postal Pleasures

SEX, SCANDAL, AND VICTORIAN LETTERS

Kate Thomas

Oxford University Press, Inc., publishes works that further
Oxford University's objective of excellence in
research, scholarship, and education.

Oxford   New York
Auckland   Cape Town   Dar es Salaam   Hong Kong   Karachi
Kuala Lumpur   Madrid   Melbourne   Mexico City   Nairobi
New Delhi   Shanghai   Taipei   Toronto

With offices in
Argentina   Austria   Brazil   Chile   Czech Republic   France   Greece
Guatemala   Hungary   Italy   Japan   Poland   Portugal   Singapore
South Korea   Switzerland   Thailand   Turkey   Ukraine   Vietnam

Copyright © 2012 by Oxford University Press, Inc.

Published by Oxford University Press, Inc.
198 Madison Avenue, New York, New York 10016
www.oup.com

Oxford is a registered trademark of Oxford University Press

All rights reserved. No part of this publication may be reproduced,
stored in a retrieval system, or transmitted, in any form or by any means,
electronic, mechanical, photocopying, recording, or otherwise,
without the prior permission of Oxford University Press.

Library of Congress Cataloging-in-Publication Data
Thomas, Katie-Louise.
  Postal pleasures : sex, scandal, and Victorian letters / Kate Thomas.
    p. cm.
  Includes index.
  ISBN 978-0-19-973091-9 (cloth : acid-free paper) — ISBN 978-0-19-973116-9 (pbk. : acid-free paper)
  1. Letter writing—Great Britain—History—19th century. 2. Literature and society—Great Britain—
     History—19th century. 3. Postal service—Great Britain—History—19th century. 4. Scandals—Great
     Britain—History—19th century. 5. Letter writing recreations. 6. Homosexuality—Great Britain—
     History—19th century. I. Title.
  PR915.T37 2012
  820.9'355—dc22   2011011838

ISBN: 978-0-19-973091-9 (Hardback)
ISBN: 978-0-19-973116-9 (Paperback)

For Hilda Porter, "top girl,"
and
Frances Parfitt

Contents

List of Illustrations ix
Acknowledgments xi

Introduction: Victorians Go Postal 1

1. *Postal Digressions: Mail and Sexual Scandal* 39

2. *"This Little Queen's Head Can't Be Untrue": Trollope's Postal Infidelities* 70

3. *A Queer Job for a Girl: The Communicative Touch in Trollope, Hardy, and Lynn Linton* 99

4. *All Red Routes: Blood Brotherhood and the Post in Doyle, Kipling, and Stoker* 148

5. *Postscript: Henry James's Public Servant* 208

Works Cited 224
Index 239

List of Illustrations

Frontispiece   "Small boys must be pre-paid." An early satirical response to the introduction of uniform penny postage. John Leech, illustrator, 1841. ii
Figure 1.1   The Pneumatic Despatch Tube. *Illustrated London News* (London, England), Saturday, November 18, 1865. 3
Figure 1.2   The Penny Post Act! Comic song, 1840. 13
Figure 1.3   Penny Black Stamps, block of eighteen. Put to press 8 December, 1840. 15
Figure 1.1   The Postman's Knock. Songsheet. Composed by W. T. Wrighton with lyrics by L. M. Thornton. Published by Robert Cocks & Co, New Burlington Street, London. Undated, but dedicated to "Sir Rowland Hill, late of the General Post Office," which dates the song to after 1864, when Hill left the Post Office. 41
Figure 1.2   *The Illustrated Police News*, January 25, 1890. 47
Figure 1.3   The Boy Messengers' unsupervised locker room and kitchen, 1882. 55
Figure 4.1   Pears' Soap Advertisement, *Harper's Weekly*, July 2, 1898. 150
Figure 4.2   Envelope promoting Ocean Penny Postage. Published by Charles Gilpin of London, designed by Henry Anelay, a prominent member of the League of Universal Brotherhood. 152
Figure 4.3   Illustration on the back of an Ocean Penny Postage envelope. Designed and engraved by J. Valentine of Dundee. 152
Figure 4.4   The Mulready Envelope. William Mulready, illustrator. Issued 1 May 1840. 156
Figure 4.5   "The Rhodes Colossus Striding from Cape Town to Cairo." Edward Linley Sambourne, illustrator. *Punch*, 10 December 1892. 161
Figure 5.1   "Going in and coming out of the PO." William James cartoon, *Henry James Autobiography* 1956. 211

ACKNOWLEDGMENTS

I AM EXTREMELY GRATEFUL for the meticulous work of the librarians and archivists without whom this book would not have happened: Barry Attoe, Mark Dimunation, Anne Garrison, Marianne Hansen, Sally Jennings, Brenda Marston, Eric Pumroy, Deborah Richards, and Claire Woodforde. Thanks also to the other library staff at Dartmouth College, Bryn Mawr College, Cornell University, the British Postal Museum Archive, the Bodleian Library, the Public Record Office, and the British Library.

I have benefited from the academic communities and generous grant support of the following institutions: Cornell University, Oxford University, Oberlin College, Dartmouth College, Bryn Mawr College, the University of Maryland, Rutgers University, the Fulbright Program, and the University of Pennsylvania Humanities Forum.

To my D.Phil. supervisor, Kate Flint: many thanks for your clear-sighted guidance and companionship along the road. Thanks also to Dorothy Mermin and the other members of my M.A. committee, Reeve Parker and Neil Saccamano.

The following people have supported this book project and my progress toward it and I am most thankful to each of them: Rachel Ablow, Rodney Battle, Lucy Bending, Emma Bianchi, Francine A'Ness, Katherine Biers, Duncan Black, Louise Blanks, Colleen Boggs, Lynda Boose, George Boulukos, Michael Bronski, Laura Brown, Megan Brown, Rachel Buurma, Jane Caplan, Kim Cassidy, Virginia Chang, Kate Chedgzoy, Jonathan Crewe, Ann Cvetkovich, Cindy Davenport, Richard Dellamora, Michelle Elleray, Sos Eltis, Eleanor Farmer, Rebecca Farmer, Martin Favor, Amy Foerster, Mia Ford, Nancy Frankenberry, Elaine Freedgood, Elizabeth Freeman, Veronika Fuechtner, Claudia Ginanni, Jonathan Goldberg, Jody Greene, Alex Halasz, Ellis Hanson, Pim Higginson,

Mary Jacobus, Gillian Johns, Laura Hawley, Jen Hill, Sarah Kavanagh, Homay King, Karl Kirchwey, Joseph Kramer, Deanna Kreisel, David Kurnick, Elisabeth Ladenson, Lázaro Lima, Kathy Linehan, Peter Logan, Antonia Losano, Heather Love, Dana Luciano, Agnes Lugo-Ortiz, Tom Luxon, Camilla MacKay, Biddy Martin, Patricia McKee, Scott MacKenzie, Brigitte Mahuzier, Michelle Mancini, Cleopatra Mathis, Hamish Mathison, Anna McCarthy, Meredith McGill, Laura McGrane, Jodie Medd, Mandy Merck, Imke Meyer, Mara Mills, Rajeswari Mohan, Doug Moody, Wendy Motooka, Michael Moon, Lydie Moudileno, Anuradha Needham, Sarah Newstok, Scott Newstok, Jeff Nunokawa, Amy Ongiri, Daniel O'Quinn, Laura Otis, Monika Otter, Ash Pandya, Andrew Parker, Don Pease, Clare Pettit, Anat Pick, John Plotz, Beth Povinelli, Yopie Prins, Meredith Raimondo, Harold Riley, Hollis Robbins, Jen Roder, Juana Rodriguez, Jordana Rosenberg, Mark Rounds, Matthew Rowlinson, Jason Rudy, Lisa Saltzman, Eve Sandberg, Heidi Schlipphacke, Laurel Schneider, Pat Schneider, Paul Schneider, Peter Schneider, Rebecca Schneider, Ivy Schweitzer, Elliott Shore, Heather Sias, Brenda Silver, Nigel Smith, Rosi Song, Gustavus Stadler, Jessica Steele, Molly Stevens, David Thomas, Elizabeth Thomas, Michael Thomas, Pamela Thurschwell, Sasha Torres, Sharon Ullman, Ruth Vanita, Nancy Vickers, Amy Villarejo, Patty White, David Walker, Hansjakob Werlen, Barbara Will, Margaret Williamson, Theodore Wong, David Young, Sandy Zagarell, Melissa Zeiger, and Christina Zwarg.

My students at Bryn Mawr College helped me develop the ideas in this book as much as anyone else. I honor their intellectual tenacity and courage. I am grateful also for the comradeship of my colleagues in the Bryn Mawr English Department: Linda-Susan Beard, Peter Briggs, Anne Dalke, Jane Hedley, Gail Hemmeter, Hoang Nguyen, Katherine Rowe, Jamie Taylor, Bryn Thompson, Karen Tidmarsh, and Michael Tratner.

Thank you to Kim McLean-Fiander, Clare Mullaney, and Rachel Roepke for their invaluable help with manuscript preparation.

And to B: signed, sealed, delivered, I'm yours.

Introduction

VICTORIANS GO POSTAL

FROM EPISTOLARY TO POSTAL

The Post Office is a Victorian institution. Postal systems existed before this time, and in other places, but postage stamps, mailboxes, and, most important, the idea that all people in all places are connected by the mail can be traced back to the first years of Victoria's reign. The young queen's head on the Penny Black stamp, first issued in 1840, became the symbol of a vast communication network, and this network animated the British cultural imagination. Post-letters and soon telegrams became the texts that Victorians sent before themselves, after themselves, or instead of themselves, as their proxy or their go-between, and they enfolded the correspondents and their desires in envelopes stamped with the approval of the nation. Literature of that era began to explore what kinds of relations were engendered, not by the contents of the letters themselves, but by the enfolding. What happens when a postbag bulges with the communication of *all* sorts, communication unified by the engines of the national Post Office? The answer, which this book shall unfold, is that it produces commutable relations and intimate strangers.

The nineteenth century witnessed a grand falling-off from the epistolary form that had dominated literature of the previous century. By the time Victoria came to the throne in 1837, novels built from the contents of letters were defunct.[1] But for Victorians, who

---

[1] For accounts of the decline of the epistolary novel, see Mary Favret, *Romantic Correspondence: Women, Politics and the Fiction of Letters* (Cambridge: Cambridge UP, 1993); Nicola J. Watson, *Revolution and the Form of the British Novel, 1790-1825: Intercepted Letters, Interrupted Seductions* (Oxford: Clarendon Press, 1994); Godfrey Frank Singer, *The Epistolary Novel: Its Origin, Development, Decline, and Residuary Influence* (Philadelphia: U of Pennsylvania P, 1933); Bruce Redford, *The Converse of the Pen: Acts of Intimacy in the Eighteenth-Century*

experienced Post Office reform almost simultaneously with the crowning of the new queen, the postal took the place of the epistolary in the cultural imagination. Things that were ancillary to the letter—envelopes, stamps, postmarks, and even postmen's thumbprints—became narratively all consuming. Epistolary fiction, in other words, gave way to postal plots, in which literary interest lay not in the interiors of letters, but rather their outsides: the letter became inverted. Rather than thrilling the reader with intimate access to the contents of Clarissa's or Pamela's letters, postal plots found excitement in the distance, separation, delays, and precipitous deliveries that could skew the trajectory of a communication, or reveal how skewed any communicative trajectory always is. The epistolary literature of earlier generations had peddled motifs of treason and infidelity via dramatizations of the interception of private correspondence. The Victorians, however, produced fiction in which the posted letter is *always* "unfaithful," rendered promiscuous by being passed through the postal machinery and among its many workers.[2] Circulation through the state apparatus of the postal system interfered with the conceit that intercourse between two correspondents was direct, discrete, limited, or private. Instead it construed postal exchange and its attendant passions and fields of relation as always, and often deliciously, intermediated.

A dominant fantasy produced by the reform of the postal system was that when you posted a letter, that letter took you places otherwise out of bounds to you, in the close company of a vast miscellany of others. You extended yourself through the post-letter's exploits and got to experience an exuberant displacement of subjectivity. *Postal Pleasures* will describe these transporting and transformative effects of posting a letter in the nineteenth century. "Stick some stamps on top of my head; I'm gonna mail myself to you," sings Woody Guthrie in 1962, imagining the charms of being a piece of mail. Victorians saw the charm too, and I begin with a reminder of their peculiar capacity to produce adventure from the technologies of everyday life. In 1865 the Post Office unveiled an underground pneumatic dispatch tube, which ran from Euston Square to Holborn. "A number of scientific gentlemen" were invited to watch the carriages full of postbags be sucked through the mile-and-three-quarters-long pneumatic tunnel, and after seeing several trains disappear into and emerge from the "mouth" of the tunnel, some of these

---

Familiar Letter (Chicago: U of Chicago P, 1986). For some exceptions to the claim that the epistolary novel disappears in the nineteenth century, see Kathleen Ward, "Dear Sir or Madam: The Epistolary Novel in Britain in the Nineteenth-Century." PhD Dissertation, University of Wisconsin-Madison, 1989.

[2] David M. Henkin uses the same term, "promiscuous," when describing the effects of the postal age in America. Having argued, as I do, that the postal network laid the cultural foundation [...] for the experiences of interconnectedness that are the hallmarks of the brave new world of telecommunications" (Henkin ix), he writes: "From the earliest days of cheap postage, users exploited and emphasized the centrifugal, promiscuous, and anonymous features of a network that could bring any two people into direct contact" (Henkin 153). Moreover, Henkin makes it clear that these qualities of the postal system were generally recognized during the nineteenth century: there were, he writes, "popular associations between the post office system and sexual promiscuity" (Henkin 80).

FIGURE I.I The Pneumatic Despatch Tube.

gentlemen "expressed a strong desire to pass through the tube themselves."[3] *The Illustrated London News* reported the event, applauding the men's gumption:

> They were warned that the line was "not constructed with a view to passenger traffic," and that they might find the way "a little rough." The spirit of adventure, however, prompted them to take this strange journey, and each of the waggons had soon as many occupants as it could comfortably accommodate in the recumbent posture enforced by circumstances.

Playing at being a postbag, or a piece of mail, apparently produced some "not agreeable [. . .] sensations" as a result of the "suction" and "friction" and "here and there [in the tube] a strong flavour of rust was encountered" (496). The romance of this new technology, and of speedy communication systems turns these "scientific gentlemen" into giddy boys who "strongly desire" a "rough" ride and who bundle up together to experience being jostled around like parcels. This is a fantasy in which you lay aside your top hat (the accompanying illustration shows hatless travelers witnessed by a firmly hatted crowd) and stuff yourself into a canister with other men, for the sensations of suction and the taste of a tunnel (see figure 1.1). Traveling with, or as, the mail, these men lose the markers of class and status, and gain a thrilling and sensory association with other men possessed of the same daring desires.

---

[3] *Illustrated London News* (18 November 1865): 496.

FROM INTERMEDIATED TO QUEER

The fiction and prose I explore in this book recognize that invoking "everyone" as communicative subjects, and incorporating "everyone" into a network designed to connect that same "everyone" to anyone, produces some queer interfaces and reverberations. The phenomenon of a universal discourse system, provided by the state in order to facilitate circulation and intimacy, led many writers to connect the (promiscuous, democratic) intermediations of the mail with the intermediate sex. In a work titled *The Intermediate Sex* (1908), socialist and homosexual activist Edward Carpenter exercised this exact connection. *The Intermediate Sex* was the first generally available book published in English that promoted homosexuality (or Uranianism, as Carpenter called it here) as socially meaningful, rather than a pathological problem.[4] In the last essay in the book, Carpenter proposes that "the Uranian spirit may lead to something like a general enthusiasm of Humanity, and that the Uranian people may [. . .] transform the common life by substituting the bond of personal affection and compassion for the monetary, legal and other external ties which now control and confine society" (108-9). Concerned that readers may imagine Uranian "bonds of personal affection" consequently to be *too* uncontrolled and unconfined, Carpenter reassures them: "Instead of the wild 'general post' which so many good people seem to expect in the event of law being relaxed, one finds [. . .] that common sense and fidelity and a strong tendency to permanence prevail" (117). "The wild 'general post'" is a reference to the parlor game in which players who have been assigned the names of postal towns exchange seats at the bidding of calls such as "The post is going from Liverpool to London." As the couple whose town-names have been called sneak across the room to swap seats, a blindfolded "postman" tries to catch them.[5] Carpenter fields the idea, in other words, that if the "general enthusiasm" and "personal affection and compassion" of homosexuals are unfettered, they might be as promiscuous as a postbag, that jumble of correspondence in which Liverpool might rub against London and then Newcastle. Carpenter's earnest and wholesome pen, striving to write the homosexual into a civic future, counsels against this fear that gay men swap partners as easily and often as they might post-letters. This was not an arbitrary metaphor for Carpenter. By 1908 there was a very well-established link in the cultural imagination between postal exchanges and digressive sexual relations. The reformed Post Office

---

[4] The general availability of the book is reflected in its diction: the collection of essays uses the words "general" and "generally" over fifty times. Carpenter's mode is anthropological but integrative: he writes to point out that the intermediate sex "play[s] a considerable part in general society" (9).

[5] The OED reference for the term reads: "1889 K. GREENAWAY Bk. Games 63 General Post. One person is selected as 'postman' and blindfolded, the others all take the names of different places, except one, who is chosen the leader, and has a written list of the places chosen by the players. 1898 A. B. GOMME Games for Parlour & Playgr. 51 An occasional call of 'General Post' by the leader, when all players must change their seats, gives a good chance to the blind man."

brought everyone into connection with anyone: accessible, cheap, and anonymous, the post was almost immediately understood to engender queer interfaces.

In an earlier, privately printed essay entitled "Homogenic Love, and Its Place in a Free Society" (1894), Carpenter used another postal/homosexual illustration, this time positively. He argues the case for what we now call homosexuality,[6] petitioning that

> homogenic passion ramifies widely through all modern society [. . .] among the masses of the people as among the classes, below the stolid surface and reserve of British manners, letters pass and enduring attachments are formed, differing in no very obvious respect from those correspondences which persons of opposite sexes knit with each other under similar circumstances; but that hitherto while this passion has occasionally come into public notice through the police reports, etc., in its grosser and cruder forms, its more sane and spiritual manifestations— though really a moving force in the body politics—have remained unrecognised. (47)

This passage installs a conceit in which erotic and epistolary exchange serve, metaphorize, and substitute for one another. The idea of "correspondence" structures this passage, as Carpenter implicitly draws out the epistolary and sexual meanings of the term, and explicitly allies homogenic passion with epistolary communication. Both, he suggests, form networks that "ramify widely through all modern society," and flow freely under the conversely inanimate terra firma of British manners. His essay argues at length for the social usefulness of homosexuality, not defending it as marginal, but rather characterizing it as historically and culturally integral. His post/passion conceit furthers his argument for homosexuality as a "valuable social force" (49) and helps Carpenter make a quirky and audacious bid: that homogenic love is, like the Post Office, an *institution* that is ordinary, everyday, and even essential to what he repeatedly calls "national life" (50, 51). Unlike the police force, these institutions— homosexuality and the Post Office— are *amiably* and "comradely" civic.[7] Both value the "importance of a bond" (47) between people, and both are instrumental in cultivating attachments across differences, especially that of class.

It might seem catachrestic to interpret Carpenter's reference to "letters passing" as postal rather than merely epistolary, but a few pages earlier in "Homogenic Love," Carpenter sanctions this reading through quoting a passage from composer and author Richard Wagner's 1849 pamphlet *The Art-work of the Future*. In this passage Wagner

---

[6] Carpenter rejected the term "homosexual," generally attributed to writer and campaigner for the rights of homosexuals Karl-Maria Benkert (who later changed his last name to Kertbeny). Carpenter's stated objection was etymological and he characterized "homosexual" as a "bastard" word, formed of a Greek prefix and a Latin noun. He preferred the all-Greek word "homogenic."

[7] The entire essay is suffused and structured by the notion of comradeship, and comrade-unions. The opening sentence reads: "Of all the many forms that Love delights to take, perhaps none is more interesting (for the very reason that it has been so inadequately considered) than that special attachment which is sometimes denoted by the word Comradeship" (3).

praises Spartan same-sex comrade love for being based "in the noblest pleasures of both eye and soul," claiming that it is "not unlike our *modern postal* correspondence of sober friendship, half businesslike, half sentimental" (my italics, 168). The thrust of Wagner's claim is that "the love of man to man" is heterogeneous: both physical and spiritual, its elements cannot be separated. It is exultation in engulfing, ego-dissolving heterogeneity that leads Wagner to liken love between Spartan men to modern postal relations. Carpenter then cites Wagner's postal parallel to figure homosexuality as radically conjoining, and a means of overcoming divisions: between classes (very important to the socialist Carpenter); between business and sentiment; between bodies and souls. Carpenter asks his reader not to see divisions, but instead to see networks that ally and hold everyone, especially men, together.

Carpenter similarly challenges the reader not to "differ" between same-sex and opposite-sex passion. Not only does the postal conceit help him champion homosexuality as a "moving force" in society, but it also supports his claim that homosexuality is a cognate of heterosexuality. The letters and the relationships "differ in no very obvious respect" whether the lovers are same or opposite-sexed. You cannot look at a letter, he suggests, and determine the kind of sexual partnering of which it is a manifestation: they all look the same. There are no different postal signs for homo- and heterosexual letters; every piece of correspondence is passed, undifferentiated, under the same postmarks and through the same network. In *How to Do the History of Homosexuality* (2002), David M. Halperin turns to the cryptic symbols of the U.S. Post Office to question the power of undifferentiated signs. He opens chapter 3, on historicizing erotic subjectivity, with a consideration of the 1990-issued "LOVE" postage stamp, portraying two identical lovebirds. Characterizing his own queer reading of the image as the exception and not the norm, he meditates on how the stamp and its image are incapable of withstanding "the weight of heterosexual presumption" (83). It is a revealing moment in a study that grapples with the challenge, leveled primarily by Eve Kosofsky Sedgwick, that Halperin's historical constructionism does not, as he hopes, allow for "queer correspondences between past and present" (Halperin 17) but instead obscures "relations enabled by the unrationalized coexistence of different models" (*Epistemology of the Closet* (47). Sedgwick's critique holds, I would argue, when Halperin turns his attention to this postage stamp. His reading is a reading of the image alone; he does not engage what it might mean for it to be on a stamp and distributed through the mail. He cannot, therefore, see the stamp as a means toward "correspondence." His argument snags on the assertion that "neither the Postal Service, the public at large, nor lesbians and gay men" see the queer content (82), and that he alone—as hermeneut—is liberated from the "collective hallucinations" (83) and "powerful cultural magic" (84) that causes all others to read the image as heterosexual. Halperin's exercise is playful, and it performs essential critical work by insisting that erotic subjectivities are formed in the public square of quotidian life and through the more banal symbols we pass between us every day. I want to counter, however, with the proposal that the postal service—and others—can indeed recognize the image as queer.

The image is on a postage stamp. A postage stamp enables, signals, and—importantly—*validates* multiple correspondences. It ensures carriage of the contents of the mail, with relatively little regard to the nature of those contents.[8] And indeed even the imagery chosen by the bureaucracy to symbolize love—two identical lovebirds, facing each other—mobilizes a depiction of love that is not hetero, or even human, specific, and functions instead to take a broad range of affiliation under its wing. The democratic (and market) structure of the postal system dissolves the separations that Halperin erects between "the Postal service" and "the public at large" and "lesbians and gay men." In postal—not to mention post-structural—terms, the Postal Service, the public at large, and queers of all stripes are all potentially connective: givers, receivers, readers, and writers. Although it would be foolish to romanticize, or even trust, the idea that the Post Office's democracy of letters is always benevolent, its textual transport systems are as open to play as they are to policing. The queer subject can get caught up in and utilize the Post Office as well as any other subject and—further—the universal utilization of the Post Office may land *all* subjects in some queer company and interactions.

This is, indeed, the endpoint of Carpenter's logic: that passion is as uniform and unifying as the mail. There is, or rather should be, no difference between heterosexual and homosexual passions and relationships. His essay is, to be sure, polemical. But it is not naïve. Although letters and the postal system enable the expression and exchange of affection, Carpenter recognizes that this network can also be misused and that illicit infiltration of the postal system can destroy this democracy of letters; he goes on in the essay to decry the social evil of blackmail, which "has thrown a shadow over even the simplest and most natural expression of an attachment which may [. . .] be of the greatest value in national life" (*Homogenic Love* 50). He thus acknowledges that homoerotic letters—and the passions they convey—are in practice vulnerable to violent differentiation. The very lack of cryptic symbols or codes to distinguish between opposite-sex and same-sex correspondence was a source of great anxiety to those who disliked the idea that all types mingled together in the postal system. And the post was also threatening because blackmail and the fear of blackmail or judicial interrogation could reimpose life-destroying divisions. In the mid-nineteenth century a woman named Rebecca Hamilton sought

---

[8] The question of censorship, of course, modulates this assertion. And censorship of the mail has a more muscular history in U.S. culture than in Britain, thanks to the implausibly influential and tenacious Anthony Comstock, who managed to prompt Congress to pass the Comstock Law in 1873, which made the postal circulation of "obscene, lewd, or lascivious" material illegal. Although the postal system provided Comstock and others with a checkpoint from which to police so-called obscenity, Comstock's efforts, and indeed his successes, testify to the power of the postal system to enable and engender the exchange of such material. Comstockian censorship—or "Comstockery," as Bernard Shaw dubbed it—was part and parcel of the nineteenth-century "discursive explosion" around sex and sexuality as Michel Foucault describes it. And as Foucault emphasizes, to privilege censorship as separate from and antagonistic to its object would be a mistake: "I do not maintain that the prohibition of sex is a ruse; but it is a ruse to make prohibition into the basic and constitutive element from which one would be able to write the history of what has been said concerning sex starting from the modern epoch" (*History of Sexuality Volume 1* 12).

to produce a conjunction between homosexual scandal and the anonymity of the mail. She blackmailed businessmen via letters that instructed them: "on receipt of this you are to enclose a sovereign in a letter." If they didn't they would "at once be denounced as a sodomite yourself and Partner." Her scheme purposely sought to reframe business relationships as sexual ones, as she threatened to "accuse you of an unnatural crime with your assistant" and to whisper "throughout all the City you are a sodomite vagabond."[9] Hamilton understood that the postal system was a powerful engine of circulation, but she failed to understand that what goes around comes around: she was traced via the return postal address with which she had supplied her would-be victims.

The fiction that I examine in this book shows the postal network enabling a diversity of erotic interactions, construing human relations via the model of a web. Husbands and wives become entangled with other lovers, with people impersonating lovers, or with intermediaries. Though the stories often resolve by sweeping aside this web, reinstating limited and definable lines of relation between spouses, the clutter of polymorphous interactions proffered by the communication network nevertheless permanently troubles the marital bond. The circuit circumvents social strictures. As Katherine Stubbs describes it in her study of American telegraph fiction, "On the telegraph circuit, it was theoretically possible to misrepresent oneself, to engage in a covert form of masquerade, trying on a new body and a new social identity." Even when the plot returned its characters to heterosexuality or other sexual proprieties, she notes, "the circuit [...] permanently queered things."[10]

Postal circuits can produce "permanent queering" both because a universal communication system leads people to imagine the consequences of getting your wires crossed, and because it allows for queer interactions to be undifferentiated and unmarked from straight ones. The personal post-letter or telegraph is a text that is detached from the body that produced it, a text that travels and overcomes the distance between the bodies of the writer and receiver. The passage of these epistles—whether they get waylaid through the postal system or simply delivered—therefore enables shifts, confusions, or cross-identifications of gender and sexual desire along the way. These digressions from a single pathway reveal homosexuality and heterosexuality to be as performative and encrypted as each other. It was this equivalence of expressions of heterosexuality and homosexuality that excited Carpenter and other figures in the fiction I examine. A letter by Oscar Wilde about romance and telegraphy wittily illustrates my point and shows both heterosexuality and homosexuality being, and being seen to be, performative. On 22 January 1884, Wilde wrote to the American sculptor Waldo Story announcing his engagement to Constance Lloyd:

> We are of course desperately in love. I have been obliged to be away nearly all the time since our engagement [...] but we telegraph each other twice a day, and the

---

[9] See letters to Thomas Welsh (24 March 1857) and William Allingham, indictment, CCC Felonies, 11 May 1857. PRO CRIM 4/575. Harry Cocks also cites this case in *Nameless Offences* 129.
[10] "Telegraphy's Corporeal Fictions" 92.

telegraph clerks have become quite romantic in consequence. I hand in my messages however very sternly, and try to look as if "love" was a cryptogram for "buy Grand Trunks," and "darling" a cypher for "sell out at par." I am sure it succeeds.

(Wilde, *Letters* 225)

In this letter, Wilde, who a little more than ten years later would be accused of "posing" as a sodomite, performs the part of the heterosexual suitor to perfection and with a large measure of self-consciousness. His prefatory phrase "We are of course" makes it clear that he knows the role he is playing very well, and he knows very well it is a role. It is a marriage plot, after all, and he luxuriates in its conventions. It is in this heterosexual situation that he talks, however, of the closet—of "cryptograms" and "cyphers." He uses it as an occasion to fantasize about being forced into code. The telegraphic publication of his supposedly private (but generic) sentiments provokes Wilde to wish for a secret because a secret reorients the relations: his interaction with Constance is overtaken by his interaction with the clerks. Wilde wants to cause the clerk to *wonder* about him, rather than banally collude in the well-worn plot of the heterosexual romance. The actual content of the telegrams is irrelevant: it is the business of telegram-sending that is erotic. And as Wilde portrays it, telegraphic commerce generates some decidedly nonmarital, same-sex flirtatious interactions: between Wilde and the telegraph clerks, among and between the clerks who "become quite romantic in consequence," and between Wilde and Story.[11] This becomes a story about communication among men, a dynamic that is amplified because the story is communicated in a letter sent between men.

The telegraph office produces, in other words, queer effects. I borrow this idea from Jay Clayton's and also Eric Savoy's work on Henry James's 1898 novella *In the Cage*, a story I will discuss more fully in chapter 5. *In the Cage* traces the "queer extensions of experience" (284) that attend both the telegraphist and the readers of the tale. Developing Savoy's lead, I am proposing that these queer extensions derive from and contribute to the network structure of postal communication. The "cage" of James's story proves to be a structure that does not separate people or spaces from each other, but instead enfolds all members of the correspondence in a mesh of Deleuzian planar relations, where "alliance," "conjunction," and being "between" overwhelms social hierarchy and division.[12] The sending of any piece of correspondence allies the sender and receiver with a "universal" spectrum of correspondents and a web of poly-sexual connections, rather than keeping them on the straight and narrow.

---

[11] Wilde campily flatters Story that Constance "knows I am the greatest poet, so in literature she is all right: and I have explained to her that you are the greatest sculptor: art instruction can go no further" (Wilde, *Letters* 225–26). A few months later the American painter and friend of both Story and Wilde, James McNeill Whistler, sent a letter to Story with this deflation of Oscar's marital adventure: "Oscar is awfully fat and is to be married on Thursday" (20/25 May 1884). This dry, gossipy aside deems Oscar's marriage absurd, prosaic, and faintly traitorous—exactly how Wilde himself often portrayed marriage in his drama and fiction.

[12] Gilles Deleuze and Felix Guattari, *A Thousand Plateaus* 6–7.

"IN THE BEGINNING, IN PRINCIPLE, WAS THE POST"[13]

Postal Pleasures focuses on sex and sexuality in late-century texts emanating from a cultural era that had absorbed the effects of the rise of the communications network. But before we arrive at these late-century fictions—and, indeed, at the sex—we need to look back a few decades to the foment that produced the founding of a national Penny Post. In 1830 Postmaster-General Sir Frances Freeling declared: "The Post Office seems to be bound to *keep pace* with the wonderful improvements with which the present age abounds" (Browne 37, emphasis added). He was referring to developments in transportation; in that year a railway link had been opened between Manchester and Liverpool and for the first time royal postbags made their journey by rail. Sending letters by steam train meant transporting them at a speed of thirty miles per hour—a huge increase in comparison to the 10 miles per hour of which the old mail coaches had been capable.[14] But this sense of keeping pace was rejected in favor of a commitment to setting the pace in a pamphlet published in 1837 entitled *Post Office Reform; Its Importance and Practicability*. The author was a Benthamite businessman and schoolmaster named Rowland Hill, a reformer who insisted that improvement in the postal system should not merely be a matter of running alongside the latest transport innovation, but rather, that the time had come for distance and passage to be reconceptualized in terms of mass circulation.

In 1830 the post was very much the province of the wealthy few. It traced its roots to Henry VIII. A messenger system of "posts," where fresh horses and riders were ready to relay the royal correspondence, was set up throughout the country. Under Charles I, this system was made available to the public, and the royal couriers began to carry the correspondence of the wealthy alongside the royal postbag.[15] It was an expensive service, and the charges were paid by the recipients of the mail, not the senders. By the eighteenth century, the "General Post Office" was hardly "general" in the sense that it would become, after Rowland Hill's expansions and reforms. It was a revenue-raising arm of the treasury, and it was expensive to receive a letter. Royals, aristocrats, and eventually MPs were able to "frank" their mail. Such a person could sign his name across the back of the envelope, a gesture of dominion that meant that his letters traveled free of charge in the postbag. Needless to say, franking was a privilege that allowed for extensive and costly abuses.[16] The postal system that trundled into the nineteenth century was therefore an expensive and corrupt institution that served only the powerful and wealthy.

---

[13] Jacques Derrida, *The Post Card* 29.

[14] The mail coach itself was, however, a very significant development in its own day. Mary Favret describes the significance of the speed of the mail coach and its influence upon letter-writing for the eighteenth-century correspondent in *Romantic Correspondence: Women, Politics and the Fiction of Letters* 16–17.

[15] For a wonderful essay on the post and homosexuality in a Renaissance context, see the chapter titled "Rebel Letters: Postal Effects from Richard II to Henry IV" in Jonathan Goldberg's *Shakespeare's Hand* (2003).

[16] Two of the most notorious fraudulent frankers were the poets Percy Bysshe Shelley and Samuel Taylor Coleridge. They would approach MPs, pleading extreme poverty, and persuade them to sign the backs of their letters. Shelley also forged the signature of his own father, who was an MP. See Christopher Browne, *Getting the Message—The Story of the British Post Office* (Stroud and Dover, NH: Alan Sutton Publishing, 1993), 42.

Rowland Hill proposed that the Post Office become a "universal," rather than an elite service. If the price of postage were radically reduced, the routes expanded, and the system made healthy by the elimination of privileges, corruption, and inequality, then more people, particularly "the poorer and more numerous classes" (*Post Office Reform* 55), would write letters and use the mail more regularly. The role of the Post Office needed to be repositioned: it had to become the people's institution. Hill argued that the "natural cost of postage" (*Post Office Reform* 7) was less than a penny and that the distance that mail traveled did not increase this cost; therefore, there should be a national, uniform rate of one penny for all letters weighing one ounce or less. Furthermore, letters should be prepaid by the sender, instead of being charged to the addressee upon delivery, an innovation that made receiving a letter a boon to a person of little means, rather than a burden. The notion of a Penny Post was not new—by the turn of the century penny posts already operated within the city limits of Manchester, Bristol, Birmingham, Edinburgh, and Liverpool; but it was Hill's suggestion that this be a *national* service "for all" that was to excite and even play a role in constructing the public imagination. Once the rate was applied to the whole country, "uniform" could, reformers argued, simultaneously signify "unified." As both instrument and metaphor of unification, the modern postal system was part and parcel of the emergence of the nineteenth-century nation-state.

In May 1837 Robert Wallace, MP for Greenock, moved for the appointment of a Select Committee "to report on the present rates of postage, and especially to examine the improvements recommended, and the mode of charging postage proposed, in a pamphlet by Mr. Rowland Hill, with a view to the general reduction of postage duties" (Daunton 17). This committee, appointed in November of that year, sat for sixty-three days. The main debate was the principle of uniformity. Their final report, released in 1838, did not fully support penny rates because of a concern for the state of revenue; the committee did not believe that Hill's pennies could add up. Frustrated by the government's approach, postal reform enthusiasts established an independent Mercantile Committee in February 1838 to rouse public feeling on the issue and actively promote what they saw as the great commercial and social benefits of Hill's scheme. Besieged by appeals and a total of 2,007 petitions with 262,809 signatures (many single signatures on the behalf of societies and organizations), the Whig government found itself forced into passing the Penny Post Act in December 1839. On January 10, 1840, Universal Penny Postage for the whole country was implemented. On the first day, 112,000 letters were posted; all but 1,400 of them prepaid. Crowds took to the streets in celebration, and the police were called in to keep the highways open.[17] The thoroughfares, blocked by the celebrating masses, marked what was understood to be a liberating of the metaphorical routes of communication and circulation from a tyranny of expense and social differentiation. The fact that the new postal system was called "universal" to denote its *demographic*

---

[17] For an account of the public jubilation, see Colin Hey, *Rowland Hill Genius and Benefactor 1795–1879* 72.

application within Great Britain alone carried with it the suggestion of a much larger *geographic* scope and described the proto-imperial function of the reforms. Performing an enfranchisement of Victoria's poorer subjects and a uniting of citizens was to become an important way of imagining the expansion and mapping of empire, an aspect of postal reform that I discuss in chapter 4.

Expansion of the service to all was not only comprised of the lowering of postage costs; the Penny Post Act was followed by efforts to improve the range, frequency, and regularity of rural distribution. In 1841 Rowland Hill ascertained by a circular of inquiry that there were four hundred registrars' districts without a Post Office, and he immediately obtained sanction for the establishment of a Post Office in each of them. To his frustration, this was not achieved until the middle of 1842, even though these districts were in some of the largest and most densely populated areas and, when supplied with a Post Office, the number of people using the Penny Post swelled yet further.

Postal reform thus meant that hidden masses of people were literally becoming accounted for, together forming a nation of correspondents. A comic song called "The Penny Post Act" that was published around 1840 commemorates the mixed mood of exhilaration and condemnation that attended the idea that everyone and anyone could now use the post. The illustrated front cover of the song sheet satirizes the clamor unleashed by the Penny Post as devilry: the "running hand" that everyone will now have has a fork in its tail (see figure I.2).[18] The caricatured correspondents who crowd around the knock-kneed, beleaguered postman include an Irish workman, a black washerwoman, an indigent street-sweeper and two pointy-nosed, curly-haired dandies. The image proposes that the Penny Post gathers all these unlikely correspondents into a bizarre diversity and involves them in the business of literary and romantic exchange (more properly the province of the cupid and the jaunty, doublet-ed author who hover above). The first verse of the song pokes fun at the idea of a scribbling nation, with everyone a correspondent: "Thy grand invention Rowland Hill loud every subject hails / The Females are all full of it and so are all the *mails*" (verse 1). Not only will the two sexes write profusely, the lyrics warn, but the postmen will be beset by "every kind of writing" (verse 7) and the St. Valentine's Day mail will be so voluminous it will have to be shoveled like coal, billets-doux delivered by omnibus (verses 5 and 6): the post-letter has become polymorphous. The song concedes that this new postal service is representative of the era, which "may be called the 'Penny Age,' " musing "We've penny blacking, penny plays, penny mags, for information, / And now a 'Penny Post,' which proves we've lots of penetration."[19] The jingle's rhyming couplet mischievously charges the Penny Post with having mixed sex and media, providing cheap and easy access to both.

---

[18] "The Penny Post Act!" comic song sung by Mr. Buckingham at the Royal Gardens Vauxhall. Written by James Bruton, music composed by J. Blewitt. Published by T. E. Purday, cover design and lithograph by G. E. Madeley, 3 Wellington Street, Strand. John Johnson Collection, Bodleian Library, Oxford. Postal Folder 1. Music is housed in Post History Folder 2. Stanzas 2–3 are missing from this document.

[19] For this verse, verse 2, see the reproduction of the song in *The Royal Mail: Its Curiosities and Romance* 288.

Introduction 13

FIGURE I.2 The Penny Post Act!

The reformed Penny Post's single-penny charge broke the practice of calculating postage fees according to distance traveled, and the greater speeds of travel meant that it took much shorter time to cover ground. Therefore, while the post helped expand the politically significant population to include the poorer classes, this social extension was matched by an opening up of the land itself. Hill's reforms became widely regarded as ones that made distance immaterial or, to use the immensely popular contemporary phrase, "annihilated time and space."[20] For many, this was a great advance; for some, like Tory journalist J. W. Croker who wrote, "The gods must annihilate time and space before a uniform rate of postage can be reasonable and just," there was a fear that Hill's reform collapsed the very ground on which they stood (301). Both sides of the argument recognized that networking the country and its populace amounted to mapping a new outline for the nation. Lord Macaulay declared that "of all inventions, the alphabet and the printing-press alone excepted, those inventions which abridge distance have done the most for civilization of our species. Every improvement of the means of locomotion benefits mankind morally and intellectually as well as materially" (Macaulay 343). The Post Office was engaged not only in the business of locomotion, but in abridging distance and reconfiguring textual systems too. It had lettered the nation and inserted itself as the intermediary to whom all of the nation's mail was addressed.

Under such changes, signature and address, as indices of subjectivity and social position, became significantly altered. Rowland Hill's reforms had demanded a clamp down on all inefficiencies and fraud, the most significant of which was the removal of the power of franking from aristocrats and MPs. It was fundamental to both the economics and the metaphorics of the Penny Post that the system should be so cheap that no one would need to cheat it. Now, a name availed no one. The only passport to free passage was a Penny Black—the postage stamp (figure I.3). The postage stamp was a new invention. Backed with a "glutinous wash" that allowed it to be licked and fixed to the envelope, it marked prepayment (Hill, *Post Office Reform* 45). In celebration of the institution of the Penny Post, Queen Victoria renounced her own franking privilege. This was a remarkable move: an act, on a certain level, of abdication. By stripping her signature of the power to circulate her correspondence freely in her own dominion, she relinquished her royal privilege and symbolically joined the "poorer and more numerous classes." From this point on, cheap communication was to be the right of a nation of citizens, not of a royal household. Victoria's renunciation of the frank was an inspired piece of PR; her signature disappeared from its place on the back of the royal envelope but was replaced by her head and shoulders on the postage stamp on the front of each and every envelope that passed through the postal system. Her mail thus traveled alongside all of her subjects, and she traveled with each and every one of their letters, her head forming an imprimatur of their importance, and a guarantee of equality.[21] Queen Victoria's postal benevolence was advertised through a pamphlet written by postal reformer Henry Cole, which was

---

[20] In *The Railway Journey: The Industrialisation of Time and Space in the Nineteenth Century*, critic Wolfgang Schivelbusch attributes this cultural catchphrase to the railways. In fact, it was used in association with all kinds of transport and communication networks. The phrase acquired several other applications in the course of the century. Karl Marx, for example, writing in *Grundrisse* in 1857, described the self-destructive contradictions of capital thus: "While capital [...] must strive to tear down every barrier [...] to exchange and conquer the whole earth for its markets, it strives on the other side to annihilate this space with time" (538–39).

[21] See Frank Staff, *The Penny Post 1680–1918* (London: Lutterworth Press, 1964), 83. Victoria reportedly enjoyed how the post allowed her to feel like one of the public. One of the first Post Offices was opened in

Introduction 15

Figure I.3 The Penny Black (1840).

stitched into the thirteenth part of Charles Dickens's serialization of *Nicholas Nickleby*. This enclosure dramatized a "scene" at Windsor Castle in which the Queen exclaims against "Mothers pawning their clothes to pay the postage of a child's letter!" and advises the adoption of Rowland Hill's plans. As sentimental as any Dickensian school scene, this

---

1831 in Crathie, near Balmoral. Queen Victoria often walked across the fields from Balmoral Castle to chat with Crathie's postmaster, Charles Thomson, and to buy stamps and post her letters. When Thomson died and his son Albert became postmaster, the Queen personally paid his salary and for a new extension to the Post Office. See *Getting the Message* 94.

pamphlet was very popular and was reprinted in various forms. The Queen's sanctioning of Hill's Penny Post scheme established a new way of "one" representing the "many." The penny stamp was promoted as an emblem of emancipation for *all* British subjects, but the only signifiers on the stamp were the head of the monarch and "1d."— signaling the single-penny postage charge. All subjects sent their mail under the favor of one penny and one monarch: it was a supremely effective everyday way of forging the sense of being part of one unified nation between citizens who were geographically or socially disparate.

Hill and his supporters narrated the reform as a blow against the indignities of poverty; prior to this, the addressee, rather than the sender, paid for mail, and the expense involved could be crippling to a poor household. Hill remembered:

> I early saw the terrible inconvenience of being poor. My mother used to talk to me more than all the others together of our difficulties, and they were very grievous. She used to burst into tears as she talked about them. One day she told me that she had not a shilling in the house, and she was afraid lest the postman might bring a letter while she had no money to pay the postage. She had always been careful to save the rags [...]. I was always sent by her on such errands, and I got this time about three shillings for the rags.
>
> (Hill, *Life* 53)

The sentimental charge of this story is derived from the emphasis on the importance of the lowest common denominator; the simple pleasure of a letter prompts an impoverished mother's fearful tears because postage costs shillings rather than pence. It was a story that was repeated ad infinitum in both arguments for and celebrations of the Penny Post and was also a prominent banner under which supporters such as Harriet Martineau campaigned for the reform (2: v, xv, 425–26). The story was used both to explain Hill's interest in postal matters and show it to be in the interest of both the underprivileged and those who want to relieve their suffering. This story and many like it promoted the Penny Post scheme as an investment in ordinary people, one that could improve the quality of their everyday lives. Both the scheme and this story stressed the importance of good circulation. Hill's nostalgic narrative is of a bad circulatory model, in which the flow of letters, hindered by excessive cost, brings about the flow of tears. Postal reform promised to remove barriers to what it characterized as the *natural* circulation of both letters and the sentiment that they could carry and develop. Origin stories of tears, rags, and domestic economy sought to give a familial face to, or naturalize the development of the Post Office into a national machinery. Having a material and emotional interest in the postal system could consolidate feelings of being part of a nation; of having been made a

---

[22] Similar motivations extended later in the century to the practice of stamp collecting. By midcentury, philately came to be considered the most suitable of hobbies for a young boy, as a way of teaching him about geography and empire: another way in which postal service was cemented firmly in the center of "everyday" civic life. See, for example, Chas J. Phillips, *Fifty Years of Philately* 7.

cog in a benevolent machinery that administrated and united the nation.[22] In turn, Hill pointed out, postal reform would make expansion of the nation a more stable, naturalized process. Of reduction in postage costs there was, he claimed, "scarcely any measure which would tend so effectually to remove the obstacles to emigration, and to maintain that sympathy between the colonies and the mother country, which is the only sure bond of connexion" (Hill, *Post Office Reform* 61). The "connexion" of which Hill writes is a two-ply bond of postal lines and family ties; a paralleling of steam routes and "sympathy." Together they made the Post Office a finely tuned instrument of imperial control and a cherished emblem of the paper empire.

Hill's reform interwove the strengths of organization and organic strength. In *Post Office Reform* he writes repeatedly of the "natural" cost of postage, and he reshaped the service to use the nation's demographic bulk, harnessing an organic strength of numbers, a "numerousness," in order to produce a single, standard charge. Formulated and published in the wake of the Reform Act of 1832, which had failed to extend the vote to most citizens, Hill's invitation of the working class into the daily functioning of the nation and its colonies, embracing the population at large as the lifeblood of systems of information and communication, offered an alternative kind of franchise. As postage costs were technically a *tax*, postal reform invoked notions of citizenship and enfranchisement, and the supporters of the Penny Post attacked high postal charges as a tax upon knowledge and speech. It has been a matter of contention whether Hill's motives were truly egalitarian or simply economically pragmatic, but both sides of this debate demonstrate the degree to which the discourse of egalitarianism took hold. Victorian postal historian William Lewins's celebration of the Post Office's evenhandedness in *Her Majesty's Mails* is dramatic, but representative of periodical literature on the topic: "The Post-office is eminently a democratic establishment, conducted on the most approved fraternité et égalité principles" (266). Twenty years later, the opening lines of James Wilson Hyde's *The Royal Mail* echoed the same sentiment: "Of all institutions of modern times, there is, perhaps, none so pre-eminently a people's institution as is the Post-Office" (vii). Hyde also stresses that the postal system has a universal influence, and he characterizes its application as socially egalitarian: "Its services are claimed exclusively or mainly by no one class; the rich, the poor, the educated, and the illiterate, and, indeed, the young as well as the old, all have dealings with the Post-office" (vii). Hyde takes his theme of a postal democracy so far that he claims the Post Office's class-blind universality extends even to the "illiterate," those who are unlettered.[23]

It is a striking assertion, but it was one commonly made; either by arguing that cheaper postal services encouraged the illiterate into literacy, or that those who could not read or write could still use its services, with a little help from others. The postal system imaginatively re-sited reading and writing as a national enterprise. It mimed the lifting of the shackles of poverty and illiteracy from all British citizens, employing and redefining them

---

[23] For an account of how the definition of "illiterate" shifted from meaning "uneducated" to "unable to read," see Raymond Williams, *Keywords* 11. Williams dates this shift to the 1840s, making it concomitant with postal reform.

as subjects, and made sticking a postage stamp on an envelope an act of national correspondence. Such was the appeal of this fantasy, that many literate people took to helping the illiterate write their letters. In Archibald Bowie's *The Romance of the Post Office: Its Inception and Wondrous Development* (1897), a Professor Hounslow recalls that when he was Rector of Hitcham, he had assisted his illiterate parishioners in letter-writing: that "Penny Postage is an important addition to the comforts of the poor labourer I can also testify," he writes. "From my residence in a neighbourhood where scarcely any labourers can read, much less write, I am often employed by them as an amanuensis, and have frequently heard them express their satisfaction at the facility they enjoy of now being able to correspond with their relatives" (Bowie 47–48). This figure of the amanuensis, as a go-between, is akin to the postman, and both figures acquire desiring subjectivities in the nineteenth century. Rather than being represented as merely instrumental, those who write or deliver letters for others become part of the affective circuitry they enable. As a correspondent by proxy, Professor Hounslow becomes participant in the poor laborer's connective pleasures. Who is writing to whom and who mediates that communication becomes a pleasurably compound question . . . in terms of both class and also gender relations. In chapter 1 I describe how titillating this question would be by the century's end, and in chapter 3 I show Thomas Hardy bluffing his way out of the gender problems attending the postal amanuensis.

These nineteenth-century shifts in the role of the amanuensis derive from the "universal" accessibility of the post. Communication was no longer limited to government officials and nobility but now incorporated the general population and their quotidian lives. The postal system is certainly not figured by Professor Hounslow as the instrument of social upheaval—his observation instead forms something of a postscript to his celebration of how the postal system circulates the latest knowledge in agricultural science to the landed gentry of his county—but the principle of the right to unimpeded circulation does indeed apply to all. Trade unionist and politician Gravenor Henson argued before the Committee on Postal Reform in 1838 that many of the working class, who at one point had learned to write, subsequently forgot how to because lack of practice and high postal rates were impeding the progress of their education ("Minutes" 213–16). In a report of Assistant Commissioners of Popular Education, made in 1861, the opinion of a curate from Devonport is cited that "the cheapness of the postage now causes all to desire to learn to write and keep up the art" ("Further Reports" 116). Like Professor Hounslow, Henson's and the curate's appreciation of the reformed mail's boons stem from the idea that knowledge, sentiment, and literacy itself must be engaged in a continual flow. As I will further explicate in chapter 4, the model is that of the body's circulation of blood: blood must keep pumping throughout the entire body, even to its extremities, if the body as a whole is to stay healthy and none of its parts wither and die.[24]

---

[24] Unsurprisingly, there is evidence that the claims that the Penny Post was a spur to literacy were mere wishful thinking. For a historical analysis of literacy in relation to the claims and rhetoric of the postal reformers, see

It is in the portrayal of Britain as a cohesive, corresponding nation, as the sum of its citizens—both those who own and those who work the land—that we can see the roots of a bureaucratized expansionist state. Figuring the illiterate subject within what was specifically a *system*, a *circulation* of textual matter, was a way of gesturing toward the eradication of their shortcoming and a subsequent strengthening of a sense of nationhood. Hyde's jovial hailing of the Post Office's principles of "fraternité and egalité" left the reader to infer that "liberté" must result from this epistolary republicanism. Epistolary republicanism was seen by most as infinitely preferable to the real deal. The postage stamp banner under which liberty, equality, and brotherhood were delivered to the British public was hardly revolutionary in the French sense; rather it was resolutely royal, a point that is important to my argument about the evidentiary status of the post-letter in chapter 2. In the British postal revolution, the Queen was still separated from her head, but her disembodied noggin on the Penny Black asserted the centrality of the monarch's benevolence to the welfare of her citizens and inaugurated the development of state structures that would encourage national and imperial, rather than local (and internecine) thinking.[25]

The postal reformers had both demographic and geographic expansionist ambitions. Not only did postal reform aspire to make the illiterate and the laboring classes into correspondents, but it also reached to the farthest, most remote regions of the country. No one was too ill-equipped, badly located or eccentric to be embraced in its folds, and there was even an office to make sure of it: the Blind Office. Illiterate or inexperienced users of the postal service would have had their mail sorted by one of the Post Office's "blind officers" who deciphered obliterated, partial, and orthographically puzzling addresses—efforts made before an entirely illegible letter would be passed to the Dead Letter Office, the final resting place of the undeliverable. Hyde describes the blind officers' job: "To facilitate this special work, the blind officers are furnished with a series of gazetteers and other books containing the names of gentlemen's seats, farms and the like, throughout the country, and many a letter reaches hands of the person addressed through a reference to these books" (196–97).

It was not just the illiterate who had trouble with addressing their correspondence; the notion of an address was a recent one and was brought about by postal reform. Postal reform induced the birth of the address and alphabetized space. Just as the features of the Queen's head on the stamp—"familiar to all her people" (Smyth 199)—signified the topography constituting "Britain," the country had to be made familiar to all its people, by becoming mapped, addressed, and indexed, so that the land itself could be "read."

Mitch's *The Rise of Popular Literacy in Victorian England: The Influence of Private Choice and Public Policy*, in which he concludes that lower postage rates could only have been a very marginal factor in the growth of literacy (66).

[25] That a Penny Black bore relation to the "beheading" of a Queen was noted by *Punch* on the retirement of Rowland Hill. A cartoon showing Britannia crowning Hill with a laurel wreath was accompanied by a caption that read "Should Rowland Hill have a statue? Certainly, if Oliver Cromwell should. For one is celebrated for cutting off the head of a bad Queen, and the other for sticking on the head of a good Queen" (*Punch* 19 March 1864).

Before the spread of the postal system, there had been little requirement for streets to be named and houses numbered. As the postal service expanded, that changed rapidly and the Post Office found that not only did it need to introduce systematic naming and numbering, but it also needed to produce its own maps of towns and counties, featuring details never before represented cartographically.[26]

The rhetoric of citizenship and the metaphorics of a republic that countersigned Rowland Hill's postal reforms were a trajectory from the principles of democratic self-government he established as headmaster in his boys' school. Hill favored self-supporting systems and in *Post Office Reform* his focus is the "motive force" and self-perpetuating nature of circulation systems. It is by means of this thematic bridge of motive force that he suggests a connection between financial and cultural currency:

> The loss to the revenue is, however, far from being the most serious of the injuries inflicted on society by the high rates of postage. When it is considered how much the religious, moral, and intellectual progress of the people, would be accelerated by the unobstructed circulation of letters and of the many cheap and excellent non-political publications of the present day, the Post Office assumes the new and important character of a powerful engine of civilization; capable of performing a distinguished part in the great work of National education [...].
>
> (Hill, *Post Office Reform* 8)

As a schoolmaster, Hill was renowned for taking his pupils out of the classroom to learn about the world around them; here he describes a machine that brings the benefits of the classroom into the world. Hill's campaign against the unreasonable "tax on the transmission of letters" was closely allied with another project committed to lowering the expense of communication. This was the Society for the Diffusion of Useful Knowledge set up in 1826, of which Hill was a founding member, along with Henry Brougham and Charles Knight. The emphasis of the above passage upon liberated circulation and dissemination was central to the campaign; they argued that a free flow of information and

---

[26] A review article on the *First Report of the Postmaster-General, on the Post-Office* (1855) details the problems of "faulty nomenclature" of streets and offers this anecdote to illustrate the irregularity and anomaly in the numbering of houses: "On arriving at a house in the middle of a street, I observed a brass number 95 on the door, the houses on each side being numbered respectively 14 and 16. A woman came to the door [...] she said it was the number of a house she formerly lived at in another street, and it (meaning the brass plate) being a very good one, she thought it would do for her present residence as well as any other. If," continues the Inspector, "the removal of such anomalies could be effected, there can be no doubt that the service and the public generally would be materially benefited" (*LQR, 1855* 176). This anecdote is gleefully and repeatedly recounted in a number of contemporary journals, as stories of such postal "curiosities" and "eccentricities" often were. The *London Quarterly Review*, for instance, printed it in October 1855 (176) and then republished it as a review article on the *Ninth Report of the Postmaster General, on the Post Office* in October 1863 (221).

affections would invigorate and speed the growth of a nation. Hill's scheme was shaped by a paradigmatic microeconomics, which argued that the strongest revenue was made up of the *locomotion* of many pennies and likewise that many informed Englishmen made a great Nation. Rowland's oldest brother, Matthew, wrote in the *Edinburgh Review*:

> That the Post Office ought to be open to all in practice, as well as in theory, is now felt to be as necessary to our progress in true civilisation as the liberty of the press, the representation of the people in Parliament, public education, sound law reform, the freedom of commerce, and whatever else we require to maintain our "high prerogative of teaching the nations how to live."
>
> (Hill, *Post Office Reform* 7)

The radical expansion and extension of the Post Office's services immersed and incorporated masses of people into its circulation. The "poorer and more numerous classes" were to be enfranchised by the Penny Post, but their passions and persons, national and statistical, were incorporated and regulated by the same system. Its goal was not to be "for" them, but to undifferentiate them and make them part of a republic of letters governed by a muscular self-discipline, an order generated by its own civic machinery.

In *A History of England During the Thirty Years' Peace* (1849), Harriet Martineau describes the genesis of postal reform in Britain:

> Mr. Rowland Hill, when a young man, was walking through the Lake district, when he one day saw the postman deliver a letter to a woman at a cottage door. The woman turned it over and examined it, and then returned it, saying that she could not pay the postage, which was a shilling. Hearing that the letter was from her brother, Mr. Hill paid the postage, in spite of the manifest unwillingness of the woman. As soon as the postman was out of sight, she showed Mr. Hill how his money had been wasted, as far as she was concerned. The sheet was blank. There was an agreement between her brother and herself, that as long as all went well with him, he should send a blank sheet in this way once a quarter; and thus she had tidings of him without expense of postage. Most people would have remembered this incident as a curious story to tell: but Mr. Hill's was a mind which wakened up at once to a sense of the significance of the fact. There must be something wrong in a system which drove a brother and sister to cheating, in order to gratify their desire to hear of one another's welfare.
>
> (2: 425)

Rowland Hill did drastically lower postage costs; he did introduce prepayment of letters and expand the range of the postal service both geographically and demographically. He did not, however, perform the act of misguided benevolence that Martineau recounts. The incident was real, but it was Samuel Taylor Coleridge who had been the magnanimous young man: the hero was a poet, rather than a postman. Martineau's misattribution (which she corrected in later editions of the work) was understandable; many other authors of articles, memoirs, and histories that celebrated the liberating effects of the Penny Post similarly miscast the gallant gentleman of the tale. The story of Hill's inspirational encounter was so widely "believed and amplified" that a friend of Hill's visiting the Lake District found himself being shown to the room in which "Hill had first thought of penny postage."[27] While it might be considered a natural mistake to make, given Hill's role as the inventor of postal reform, there were other ways in which this particular switch was—to use an oxymoron—a natural cultural slip. From the late 1830s to the turn of the century, the figures of the poet and the postman were more easily mistaken for each other than the twenty-first-century reader might imagine.

In *Victorian Scrutinies*, Isobel Armstrong describes the status and position of the poet in the early nineteenth century. She writes of how the poet was seen as the mouthpiece of "universal sympathies" and of "fellow-feeling," emotion that was "common to all."[28] This idea of commonality is central to Harriet Martineau's dramatic portrayal of the reformed Post Office as a means of enfranchising the "vast multitude of the lower orders" (426). The postman figures in her account as the angel who delivers the country from "a terrible blank of enforced silence" (425). Fellow-feeling, sympathy, and common emotion are by definition produced through structures of mutuality: they stem from corresponding emotional ties and expression. The assertion of these ties and the exchange of their expression not performed in person require a communication system and across the nineteenth century, the Post Office was seen as an instrument through which "universal"—by which was meant national, imperial, and Anglo-American—sympathy or cohesion could be attained. "Sympathy," clarifies Armstrong, "was the faculty of sharing and understanding the situation of another person by being able to change places with him in imagination" (9). Both the poet and the postman could —through the texts they put into circulation—enable a reader to experience correspondence with someone or something outside of themselves, to imagine themselves in another place or time, or to feel the feelings of someone else.

The reformed Post Office invited each and every household and citizen to imagine themselves as part of a national discourse network which, in turn, provided a way of citizens understanding themselves as one of many, as in correspondence with each other and as part of a circulation system in which citizens could exchange information, sentiment, and imaginative place with each other. With the birth of the modern postal system, the citizen became disseminated. The cultural discourse that figured the Post Office as an instrument of dissemination developed the idea that a body—and the discursive reflection of a body—in motion ceased to be discrete. The very "universalism" of the postal network, with its unlimited range of intersections, and the way its wires, channels, and routes could literally and imaginatively crosshatch the globe soon exceeded the bounds of nationalist and increasingly imperialist rhetoric.

---

[27] *The Life of Sir Rowland Hill and the History of Penny Postage* 1: 240.
[28] Isobel Armstrong, *Victorian Scrutinies: Reviews of Poetry, 1830–1870* 8–10.

In chapter 4 I look at fictions of universalism that show, through their emphasis on the idea of the reunion of the United States and Great Britain, that by late century, universalism was synonymous with white imperialist federation. And expansion of the Penny Post and the telegraph system was regarded as a crucial tool in this process of racial federation. The Anglo-American imperialism found in late-century fiction was held together by the wires, offices, and timetables of communication networks. Drawing a line between the Penny Post and the Imperial Penny Post charts a metamorphosis in the language of scale and relation; the word "universal" is used for both. Upon inception, the 1840 Penny Postage Scheme had been called "Universal Penny Postage." In 1898, the then Colonial Secretary, Joseph Chamberlain, petitioned for Imperial Penny Postage, arguing that England "should be quite ready to make any sacrifice of revenue that may be required in order to secure a *universal* penny post throughout the Empire" (emphasis added, Potter 178). In the same year, Sir Spencer Walpole, Secretary of the Post Office, opposed Imperial Penny Postage because he feared that "Imperial Penny Postage would necessarily lead to Universal Penny Postage."[29] Their slips between national, imperial, and global illustrate that it was not clear what parts and populations of the globe were designated by the term "universal." The multiple and variant applications of the word were a symptom of the difficulties in agreeing on and determining what and who constituted "Great Britain." Both the designations "universal" and "Great Britain" entangled questions of class, geography, politics, and race: did they include all of the population within the British Isles, those within the colonies and ex-colonies, or other allied Anglo-populations and nations? The empire was a geographical miscellany and as Imperial Penny Postage was being called upon to aggregate and unify the empire, it opened for question what lay behind its aggregation and what could maintain its unification: Did this responsibility fall to religion? To the English language? To whiteness? The "All Red Routes" of telegraph wires and postal routes on the world map traced a white, British diaspora. If they marked the dissemination of British culture and information, they also traced and symbolized British blood and its diffusion.

The material I explore in chapter 4 speaks variously of "English-speaking" or "Anglo-Saxon" races. It is important to remember that these are both fictions—and they are fictions that ignore their own hyphenations, pretending homogeneity across the patent hybridity of both race and language. In this midst of late-century reunion fever, there were some dissenting voices that objected to the racial imprecision and prejudice of the term Anglo-Saxon. A remarkable article debunking the myth of Anglo-Saxonism appeared in *The North American Review* in 1898 in which the author, Professor Charles Waldstein, calls the term "Ethnologically Chauvinist" and warns that it is merely an "inaccurate and misleading figure of speech [that] may offend the feelings of great masses of people and thus cripple or stultify or misdirect action" (225). This problem of terminology was accompanied by the less abstract problem of the considerable nonwhite, non-Anglo-Saxon presence

---

[29] In 1905, Conservative MP and postal enthusiast J. Henniker Heaton set up a League for Universal Penny Postage. The league pressed for a penny rate to the United States and France.

in America: how did these "others" fit into the model of reunionism? But if a proponent of Anglo-Saxonism acknowledged this at all, it was to dismiss it as an irrelevance. The industrialist Andrew Carnegie—who had himself started life as a telegraph messenger-boy[30]—spoke for many when he claimed that "the amount of blood other than Anglo-Saxon and Germanic which has entered into the American is almost too trifling to notice, and has been absorbed without changing him in any fundamental trait" (*Reunion* 9). The fiction that reunionist thinkers drew from the United States was one of domestic and transatlantic racial homogeneity.

At the end of the twentieth century, postcolonial theorists turned to the Post Office to explore the position of the postcolonial writing subject. In "Today, the Balance of Stories," Chinua Achebe points out with unprecedented clarity that Salman Rushdie's oft-repeated metaphor of the "empire writing back" is a "metaphor of postal correspondence" (105). Achebe's essay reads the "post" in "postcolonial" as "postal" and thus finds the perfect, "rather pedestrian" (75) metaphor for the path to attaining "the balance of stories" of his title.[31] Many of the British writers I address revel in the idea of life lived "within easy *walking* distance of the General Post Office," (Sims 1) and Achebe also uses the peripatetic term "pedestrian" to characterize the proximity afforded by the Post Office. He uses both this term and the Post Office itself to emphasize that the structure of imperialism is found in that which is ordinary, everyday, and is therefore supremely able to penetrate the imaginary. "Our town's participation in a network of imperial transactions," he writes of his childhood life, "was made manifest in the daily coming and going at our post office" (Achebe 76). Achebe's essay goes on to attack "those who believe that Europe and North America have already invented a universal civilization" (Achebe 104), and his essay makes it clear that universality is itself an imperial fiction: often himself praised for his universality, he rejects this as any praise at all: "I should like to see the word 'universal' banned." Michael Hardt and Antonio Negri concur that communication systems and the praise of universality are often evilly twinned, noting that "communicative production and the construction of imperial legitimation march hand in hand, communication systems and the "imperial machine [...] pretending to put forward a project of universal citizenship" (34). As Achebe's essay points out, however, the imperial missives distributed through the postal machine bear a return address. When Achebe advises young writers working in the "remote" places of the world, he tells them not to move to London or New York, but to write where they are and to "take it down that little dusty road to the village post office

---

[30] For an account of his days as a telegraph messenger-boy, and then telegraph operator, see *Autobiography of Andrew Carnegie* 36–70. Carnegie writes, "From the operating-room of the telegraph office I had now stepped into the open world" (65). Carnegie attributes his career in railways to an incident in which he dealt with a train accident by running the "trains by telegraph" (70), telegraphically impersonating his supervisor in the process (71–72).

[31] Edward Said puts it succinctly: it matters which stories get told, or get through, because "stories are at the heart of what explorers and novelists say about strange regions of the world; they also become the method colonized people use to assert their own identity and the existence of their own history" (xii). If nations are narrations, we need to pay attention, as Achebe does, to the system that circulates and delivers them.

and send it!" (97). In his youth, he and his village saw the postman as a "licensed killer" (99). Now, he can—"wryly"—enjoy the idea of the postman as a healer (99). When people write from where they are, the postman is part of the empire writing back, can "balance a diversity of things" (97). This is what Arthur Conan Doyle and other late-century writers had feared during the late-century crises in British imperialism. Their fiction about the special routes between the United States and Britain sought to backtrack on the project of universalism and delimit it to a white British diasporic population. The model of the network had turned threatening, and the fictions of communication that it enabled proved too diverse for comfort.[32]

Toward the end of the century, it was exactly the communication network's capacity for expansion, extension, and plurality that began to be understood as a potential for sexual and gender deviation. The birth of the network engendered narratives of indiscreet or undiscriminating exchanges of passion through which national, imperial, and sexual identities became conjoined. As I discuss in chapter 1, in the last quarter of the century a series of scandals, along with their ensuing criminal trials, directly connected the postal system with sexual impropriety, particularly homosexual. These scandals implicated the correspondences circulated by the post office—letters, their envelopes, telegrams and, later, postcards[33]—and also the postal machineries that did the circulating. The metaphors that allied postal communication with diffusion of information and freedom of human exchange, at this time also likened and allied that epistolary exchange to erotic transaction. A variety of late-century literatures depict the postal system as a network that engendered diversity and divergence, and the exchange and circulation of erotically charged post-messages produced queer cross-identifications.

DEAD LETTERS

Although this study focuses on late-century writers, I want to turn briefly here to Thomas De Quincey and Elizabeth Gaskell, two midcentury writers who set up some of the coordinates that I trace in later fiction. De Quincey wrote a memorial to the English mail coach in 1849. "The English Mail-Coach, or the Glory of Motion," is a lament for the lost mode of postal transport (revolutionary in its day), and for the time when it was the speedy new conveyance of the old, aristocratic post. The new mail trains might "boast of more velocity," De Quincey writes, "but not however as a consciousness, but as a fact of our lifeless knowledge" ("English Mail-Coach" 193). De Quincey's complaint is built on a

---
[32] The mail also played an important role in accruing the subjectivity and citizenship denied to the enslaved in America. For an account of how slaves used the mail to outwit slave-masters and the infamous case of a slave mailing himself to freedom, see Hollis Robbins, "Fugitive Mail: The Deliverance of Henry 'Box' Brown," *American Studies* (2009).
[33] The plain postcard was first introduced in October 1869 in the Austro-Hungarian empire. The first British postcards were released for sale on 1 October 1870. They were plain buff and printed on one side in purple was the royal coat of arms and a halfpenny stamp with the Queen's head.

fine distinction: although he deplores the plodding regularity of mass communication, he commemorates the way in which the mail coach engendered, as critic John Plotz puts it, the "public homogenization of all minds into one population" (*The Crowd* 104). De Quincy's anxiety about the train versus the mail coach in his essay is tied to an anxiety about the insides and outsides of letters themselves, under the new supervision of the national Post Office. The preeminent symbol of the new mass communication was the penny stamp, invented by Roland Hill and introduced alongside the Penny Post in 1840. This stamp heralded the principles of accessibility and equality by which the Penny Post was promoted. No longer could MPs or even the monarch herself sign the backs of envelopes to get free passage of their mail; the penny stamp was the symbol of mass, undifferentiated "national correspondence." Rowland Hill repeatedly called his invention a "tell-tale stamp." One of De Quincey's own letters reveals that De Quincey was wary of how Post Office stamps and symbols "told tales" on the individual letter-writer. On 30 March, 1854, De Quincey wrote to a friend who had not dated his last letter. De Quincey used this secretarial oversight to muse on the Post Office markings on the letter's envelope:

MY DEAR SIR—This morning I received, and with very great pleasure, your letter dated—not at all; that is, not dated by yourself, but by the motherly old Post Office [...] dated thus

> GLASGOW
> MAR. 29 H
> 4

I am sure it must be secret spiritual consolation to every gentleman who in his race and strife with Brandy knows how easily he may be *overtaken* by the dreadful potentate, that in such a case his own errata and oversights will be corrected and supplied by the benign old lady in Glassford Street. A good creature she really is— but also a mysterious creature. For mark those deep cryptical symbols, held aloft like blazing cressets to some distant corresponding scoundrel —H close after the 29—and underneath the whole, as the basis of some inconceivable knavery, that tetragonic numeral or digit 4. What is the first impulse on finding oneself *under*written [as they say at Lloyd's], and *over*written [as they say—in no rational place that I am aware of], and round-about-written [as they never will say]—in short, *super*scribed, *subter*scribed, *circum*scribed— what, I ask, is the first, the earliest impulse? Why, this—Like the faithful slave in the *Forty Thieves* [what is her name—is it Margiana?], one seeks to indorse H and 4 upon all the letters of one's friends; so that, if one has no chance of being symbolic anywhere else, he might indulge it here, and rely on the motherly old Post Office to be more specific as it suits her.

(*De Quincey Memorials* 2: 184–85)

De Quincey is playfully anxious that the Post Office's codes, which are legible to the Post Office, but "hieroglyphic"[34] to him, are a means of surveying and limiting his correspondence. The "cryptical symbols" intrigue him, make him worry that he himself gets no chance to be "symbolic" (reigned in, as he figures it, by a domineering "mother"): he imagines running amok with postal marks to cause a little social chaos.[35] The slave-girl in *Forty Thieves*— actually called "Morgiana"— saves her master's life by her proliferation of unintelligible signs. Murderers mark her master's door with a chalk cross in order to know which house to attack when they return to kill him. Although Morgiana doesn't know of the plan, she thinks that no good can come of such a mark, and she makes identical crosses on the doors of the houses to the right and left of their house, which does indeed confuse the assassins and thwarts their intentions. Morgiana overwhelms the murderers' sign system, detaching address from persons. De Quincey worried that the reformed mail was deadening, and this letter toys with the idea that addresses can kill. But De Quincey learns from Morgiana and escapes through ebullient "knavery." The Post Office does not smother him with its maternal bosom, nor leave him lifeless; rather, being "*super*scribed, *subter*scribed," and even "*circum*scribed" shows him how to practice dissent from within a system, and escape into the crowd. In light of Carpenter's observation that "letters pass and enduring attachments are formed, differing in no very obvious respect from those correspondences which persons of opposite sexes knit with each other under similar circumstances," De Quincey's fascination for the possibilities of "same-signs" postal play paves the way for thinking about "same-sex" postal relations. A postal bureaucracy and its regularizations can counterintuitively allow for some productive, playful, and queer undifferentiations.

The second midcentury author who thinks about dead letters and their queer effects is Elizabeth Gaskell. Her 1851 novel, *Cranford*, contains a chapter called "Old Letters," which aggregates and animates the whole tale. Richard Menke has ably described this chapter as an "extended exercise in intratextual nostalgia" (251) and traces how important postal delays are to the text, but my interest is the very specifically *queer* displacements that Gaskell shows the postal system enabling. The novel is narrated by Mary Smith, who "vibrates" (Gaskell 211) between Cranford and her hometown of Drumble. In between her visits to Cranford she had "several correspondents who kept me *au fait* as

---

[34] Many commentators on the reformed postal services were animated by the idea of the "hieroglyphics" of envelopes, though most applied the term not to the Post Office's codes, but to the handwriting of letter-senders. In one of his several articles on the Post Office, published in *Household Words*, Charles Dickens writes of the "hawk eyed gentleman" at the Dead Letter Office whose job it was to use "hieroglyphic powers" to decipher addresses (*Household Words* 30 March 1850).

[35] De Quincey not only preached but also practiced irregularity in matters postal. Alexander Hay Japp points out that De Quincey's own correspondence was characterized by "errata and oversights"; he regularly ignored the epistolary conventions of date and signature, as if, Japp writes, "his sign-manual lay so indubitably dispersed through the whole tenor of the letter that there was no necessity to gather it up in full-beaming individuality at the end" (2: 183–84). The Post Office and its codes, then, punctuated the correspondences that De Quincey often so recklessly "despatch[ed] [...] with no winding-up whatever, as though his correspondence was meant to be continuous, and one epistle just to be tacked on to the end of the other" (2: 183–84).

to the proceedings of the dear little town" (Gaskell 50–51). At the end of the paragraph in which Mary mentions the possibility that she has blood connection with the interesting Cranford family, the Jenkynses, she concerns herself with quite another lost family tie, that of Matty's lost brother. Mary determines to "make the account given by the signora of the Aga Jenkyns tally with that of 'poor Peter,' his appearance and disappearance" (Gaskell 170). The long-awaited "word or two about myself" thus becomes a word or two about the mysterious cross-dressing Peter, who is lost to his family, Cranford, and England; as a result of his queer "posing," to borrow a phrase from Wilde's trials, Peter has literally fallen off the map and out of correspondence with his family. Written by the "treacherous" (Gaskell 180) light of the candle that she is forbidden to use under Miss Matty's strict candle economy, Mary mails the letter to Peter, with a little help from Cranford's token "foreigner"—the signora—who Mary also binds to secrecy. Some critics have suggested that this episode amounts to a wheeling-in of the romance convention of the lost brother[36] but it is also a wheeling-in of an epistolary-turned-postal structure; Mary's letter to Peter is a response to a letter she encountered much earlier in the novel. Mary's quest is in part an attempt to reunite a dispersed family, and in the grand style of epistolary novels, the contents of the letter in question are deeply affecting. But more than this (since only Miss Matty remains of the family), Mary's intervention is about completing a postal delivery. It is an attempt to conclude an aborted delivery of mail. Mary's search for Peter effectively mends family connections, gaps in Cranford history *and*, importantly to this study, the postal network itself.

The letter to which Mary is responding is that of the now-dead Mrs. Jenkyns to Peter, written years ago just after he had run away, and imploring him to return home. It is the only letter in the novel that is reproduced, rather than quoted, complete with its address to "My Dearest Peter," and it is arguably the most moving passage in the novel. Its powerful emotive force is a result not only of the epistolary words on the

---

[36] Coral Lansbury, for example takes this view in *Elizabeth Gaskell: The Novel of Social Crisis*. In *Nineteenth-Century Literary Realism*, Katherine Kearns writes: "As if to bring this point [that currency may change] home quite literally, Gaskell shakes Cranford to its core with the bank failure that ruins Miss Mattie Jenkyns; *Cranford*, so devoted to the ordinary, the daily, and the non-hyperbolic as to become emblematic of realism's modest purview, must turn to the devices of romance—the long-lost and exoticised brother—for rescue" (9). While the Peter Jenkyns whom Mary Smith conjures up (his return is narrated as a dramatic consequence of Mary's letter reviving his "odd vehemence") can be seen as a thoroughly romantic figure, who tells "more wonderful stories than Sinbad the Sailor" (*Cranford* 211) and feeds Mary Smith herself narratives "like Baron Munchausen's" (*Cranford* 208), he does not exactly "rescue" Miss Matty from her crisis. Neither Miss Matty nor Cranford is devastated by the bank failure; when the Cranford ladies band together, they form a consortium that effectively underwrites the risk taken in the joint stock. Similarly, Miss Matty's tea-selling is successful, both in keeping her financially afloat and because her only objections to the plan in the first place were because "she distrusted her own powers of action in a new line of life" (*Cranford* 197). She proves herself quite capable at this new life, however, before Peter delivers her from it. Nor does Mary Smith write to Peter because of the loss; she makes it quite clear that she had been planning to write to him before the whole affair and it had merely hastened her to action. Although Gaskell employs romance devices of the long-lost brother, financial disaster, servants' romances, and railway accidents, they are not wholesale imports and serve primarily to recall the genre to which they belong, namely serial fiction.

page, which are themselves charged with love, pain, and incomprehension. The words in the letter are given a tragic twist by the postal history of the letter's travels, as we learn that the letter was misaddressed and never delivered, but was "returned [. . .] unopened; and unopened it had remained ever since" (Gaskell 100). Mary Smith is the first one to open it, years and years after its return, and she is the person who reads those most personal and painful of words *in place of Peter* himself, and she reads it in the place to which he was begged to return: Cranford. Mary plays a game of "General Post" with Peter. The letter written by a woman in Cranford and addressed to Peter never makes it to him, and is instead returned to its origin where many years later it is read—by a woman in Cranford. This explains Mary's sense of intimacy with his story and why, when she begins to write a "few words about herself," she ends up crossing wires between his life and her own.

It also explains why the letter is not simply quoted from, but is presented unmediated, prefaced only by the stark "This is it." It is one text that has not been subject to readings, or even the labelings and filings of Miss Jenkyns, as it was "inadvertently put by among other letters of that time" (Gaskell 100). Why doesn't it belong with them? As a letter that did not reach Peter *in time* (or in the right space—it is mis-addressed), it becomes a letter that is somehow *out of time*, or not "of that time," just as it is *out of place* in Miss Jenkyns's otherwise rigidly organized archive. The passing and dislocation of time is the focus of Mary Smith's postscript commentary to the letter:

> But Peter did not come back. That spring day was the last time he ever saw his mother's face. The writer of the letter—the last—the only person who had ever seen what was written in it, was dead long ago—and I, a stranger, not born at the time when this occurrence took place, was the one to open it.
>
> (Gaskell 100)

Shot through with dashes, Mary's words go into shivers of realization about the tricks and slips of time and space and postal systems that resulted in those ghostly words reaching her eyes only. The letter wrongly addressed to "the house of an old schoolfellow, whither [his mother] fancied he might have gone" (Gaskell 100) ends up from beyond the grave addressing the wrong person. Mary Smith recognizes the disjuncture between how distant she is, "a stranger, not born at the time," and yet how directly the letter delivers its emotive message to her, the "wrong" reader, a mere intermediary. When we remember that the intended recipient was a young man and a son who cross-dressed first as a townswoman and then as his own sister, the queer effects of this misread and temporally misplaced letter are fully amplified. When Mary reads that letter *in place of Peter*, the gender and kinship relations that the letter intended to realign become fully inverted. Peter becomes a woman (again) while Mary becomes a young man. Fully invested now in Peter's story, Mary procures Peter's address in India and writes him a letter:

> At last I got the address, spelt by sound, and very queer it looked. I dropped it in the post on my way home, and then for a minute I stood looking at the wooden

pane with a gaping slit which divided me from the letter but a moment ago in my hand. It was gone from me like life, never to be recalled. It would get tossed about on the sea, and stained with sea-waves perhaps, and be carried among palm-trees, and scented with all tropical fragrance; the little piece of paper, but an hour ago so familiar and commonplace, had set out on its race to the strange wild countries beyond the Ganges!

(Gaskell 182-3)

Gaskell is emphatic: this post-letter is "very queer." It is a transitive missive. It transports both Mary and Peter, and Gaskell's prose becomes most poetic about imagining transportation itself. It becomes a haptic instrument that will produce touch between those who are "out of touch," and it can yoke the supreme domestic familiarities of the village of Cranford with "strange wild countries." This is a postal plot, rather than epistolary: Gaskell draws our attention to the marks of passage that the letter will accrue: stains and scents. And Mary not only posts this letter, but also in so doing becomes like a postal functionary herself. Sending the letter is a way of Mary playing a go-between role, postman-like, to recover a lost relationship. As an intimate stranger and a postal functionary, she is positioned to arbitrate between two siblings lost to each other because of the self-destructive sexual and gender proprieties of their blood-family. In this way, her role is much like that of the postman Bagwax in Anthony Trollope's *John Caldigate*, which I discuss in chapter 2. However, the letter not only mediates, but also ends up transporting Mary herself. After posting it, she gazes at the "gaping slit," the "divide" between her, her letter, and other worlds of which she can only dream. This divide prompts her to a romanticized vision of diverse geographies, narrated as if she herself had been sucked into that gaping slit and was being tossed about on foreign seas and breezes. It is a meditation on how the queering effects of the Post Office can intermix the "familiar and commonplace" with that which is "strange" and "wild."

Peter leaves Cranford for India because of a cross-dressing prank, which confounds gender and blood relation. Having already fooled his father with an impersonation of a lady who admires the Reverend Jenkyns's sermons, Peter dresses up as his sister Deborah Jenkyns and parades, pretending to carry a baby, in front of the villagers. Even though Peter gets demonized for his queer behavior, Gaskell suggests that everyone in the community has some connection to cross-gender pleasures. In each instance Peter explains his impulse to dress as a lady by saying that he wanted to deliver narrative pleasure to Cranfordians. Miss Matty remembers, "He used to say, the old ladies in town wanted something to talk about; but I don't think they did. They had the *St James's Chronicle* three times a-week [. . .]. But, probably, school-boys talk more than ladies" (*Cranford* 94–95). The emphasis here, underscored by the reference to the triweekly newspaper,[37] is on the pleasures of

---

[37] The *St. James's Chronicle* was an established newspaper, founded in 1760, which represented the views of the church and the court. That Miss Matty equates its dignified news with gossip about a cross-dressed Reverend's son is both a joke at the expense of Miss Matty's infamous prudery and a way of showing that —like Dickens's fiction and Johnson's letters—one can discriminate between them on content, but they are nonetheless both serial fiction: literatures of circulation.

circulated news, and how proprieties of gender get lost in that process of circulation. In *Cousin Phillis*, Gaskell describes how letters can bring a "whiff of foreign atmosphere into [a] circumscribed life" (288). This is what Peter wants to do; he sees Cranford life as circumspect and circumscribed, both fearful and desirous of scandal, and he wants to create spectacle that will feed its pleasures (and, it could be supposed, fulfil his own). He embodies, or rather, performs the decidedly postal function of someone who is both foreign and queer. When Mary Smith finally meets him, she notes his "out-of-the-way foreign" clothes and the "odd" and "peculiar" look about his eyes. He also drums his fingers on the table "just for all the world as [his disapproving sister] Miss Jenkyns used to do" (*Cranford* 206). Peter demonstrates that people exist within a looped spectrum of gender roles and codes; he was forced to travel "all the world" because he consciously impersonated his sister, and now he returns to Cranford and unconsciously replicates her somatic habits. The game of "General Post" is a game of swapping places, of being blindly touched and sent again to the origin—a game of circuitry. There is always a return address.

EXISTING POSTAL SCHOLARSHIP

Critics such as Alexander Welsh who have written on correspondence and interception commonly work from the premise that public and private became "opposed principles" in the nineteenth century[38] and that communication was fraught with sexual and class anxiety, because "private" postal correspondence was exposed to the public servant.[39] The reformed Post Office, such work suggests, was a threat to the boundaries between public and private that the nineteenth century had erected. Such a premise reiterates the terms of the repressive hypothesis, which, according to Michel Foucault, erroneously posits that in the nineteenth century veneers of reputation and respectability made sex secret and silenced sexual expression. Foucault replaces this seductive fiction of repression "back within a general economy of discourses on sex."[40] The Post Office is something of an overlooked state apparatus by those working broadly within a Foucauldian tradition: medical, legal, juridical, and even educational institutions have taken priority over this more banal and benign-seeming civic structure. But this is an ironic oversight: if we are to pursue discourse analysis, we should study the institution that existed to facilitate the circulation of discourse. Studying the Post Office also helps to counter, again, the notion that Victorians policed a definitive border between public/private and interior/exterior binaries.

Not only did the postal system aggregate the broadest miscellany of textual expression, as Wagner and Carpenter pointed out, but the civil servants who administered the dissemination of these texts were "discourse functionaries" who intermediated all postal exchanges. When it came to correspondence public and private were intermixed, intermediated.

---

[38] Alexander Welsh, *George Eliot and Blackmail* 63–64.
[39] See, for example, Eric Savoy, " 'In the Cage' and the Queer Effects of Gay History."
[40] Michel Foucault, *The History of Sexuality: An Introduction* 10–11.
[41] Anita and Frank Kermode, *The Oxford Book of Letters* xix.

Imagining a break between the "history" of letter-writing and the e-mail technology of today, Anita and Frank Kermode assume that in the past "privacy [was] a natural condition of letter-writing."[41] While this is an assumption that this book strongly disavows, their subsequent claim that e-mail is a "public" technology that "fosters promiscuous communication" is revealing. The Kermodes stage, in the twentieth century, the same moment of communication technology disrupting the private "nature" of correspondence that Welsh claims occurred in nineteenth-century culture. More intriguing still is their constitutive pairing of sex with publicness. The Kermodes employ a sexual metaphor to describe the public nature of the correspondence engendered by e-mail; technological disruption of the "privacy" which is a "natural" condition of writing makes correspondence, they claim, public and therefore negatively sexualized ("promiscuous"). Like Welsh, and for that matter Edward Carpenter, the Kermodes find a sexual metaphor at their fingertips when expressing fear of mass communication, and a metaphor of mass communication when expressing fear of sexual promiscuity. *Postal Pleasures* concurs that mass communication produces sexual metaphors but argues that this is because sex is construed via—rather than imperiled by—dissemination, circulation, and public imaginaries. Circulation through the state apparatus of the postal system interfered with the conceit that intercourse between two correspondents was direct, limited, or private. Instead it construed postal exchange and its attendant passions and fields of relation as always intermediated.

Thomas Richards's work on the imperial archive elegantly articulates many of the thematic and theoretical issues that I encounter in my analysis of the nineteenth-century rise of the network.[42] Addressing the common mistake of understanding the empire as a monolithic, invincible entity, he claims that most Victorians were aware that their empire was "something of a collective improvisation" (3) and goes on to describe how "the nineteenth century had seen time collapsed and space contracted as never before. Technologies like the railway, the steamship, the telegraph, and the telephone made it possible for people to imagine knowing things not sequentially but simultaneously" (5–6). Richards does not apply this to the question of the postal reforms (even though the cover design shows Britannia flinging stamped envelopes marked "Colonial Penny Post" to the four corners of the earth), but I would argue that correspondence—the etymology of which implies "answering simultaneously"—was the point of reference for these technologies and how they and their function were understood. Richards writes, "Seen from the perspective of our own information society, however, the Victorian archive appears as a prototype for a global system of domination through circulation, an apparatus for controlling territory by producing, distributing, and consuming information about it" (17). The language of the literature I examine confirms that the postal system did, by circulating information through, over, around, and about British and British-controlled lands and nations, achieve precisely this. It is important, however, to realize that this is not only a twentieth-century, postcolonial interpretation—the postal network was described *at the time* as a

---

[42] Thomas Richards, *The Imperial Archive: Knowledge and the Fantasy of Empire*.

"machine" or "instrument" designed for this purpose; to be "an engine of civilisation" that could penetrate all parts of the globe and be employed for the administration and edification of colonial territories.

As a study of institutional effects, *Postal Pleasures* makes few distinctions between post-letters and telegrams. There were some important differences between the forms of correspondence, to be sure. The primary one was of cost and therefore class: Henry James writes, for example, about the class who "wired everything, even their expensive feelings" (*In the Cage* 237). And in one of his abusive letters to his son Lord Alfred Douglas, the Marquess of Queensberry says he tore up telegrams as soon as he saw they were from him, adding "You must be flush of money to waste it on such rubbish" (Holland 217). Post-letters, too, made a more material journey than telegrams, and acquired the marks of their passage on them as they traveled. But in other regards, once it acquired monopoly of the existing private telegraph operations in early 1870, the Victorian Post Office made surprisingly little distinction between telegrams and post-letters. A Post Office bylaw even asserted that there was no institutional distinction between post-letters and telegraphs.[43] Although telegraphs could travel almost instantaneously, post-letters were delivered, on average, six times a day, and they arrived almost as fast. Postal communication and telegraphic communication were regarded as equally instrumental to modernity. Writing to an American friend in 1859, Elizabeth Barrett Browning berated the United States for not following the example of Britain in accepting a national Penny Postage:

> Why will you not as a nation embrace our penny post scheme, and hold our envelopes in all acceptation? You do not know—cannot guess—what a wonderful liberty our Rowland Hill has given to British spirits, and how we "flash a thought" instead of "wafting" it from our extreme south to our extreme north [. . .] I recommend you our penny postage as the most successful revolution since the "glorious three days" of Paris.
>
> (1:135)[44]

Barrett Browning's electrified language ("flash") is of interest because although it might seem she is referring to telegraphic communication, her letter makes it quite clear that she is talking about the Penny Post. Her language shows that although discourses about speed and communication fueled and were fueled by technological development, technological development did not force or happen at the same time as developments in discourse. Telegraphy offered the possibility of instantaneous communication (though it still needed

---

[43] The Telegraph Act of 1869 states: "Every written or printed message or communication delivered at a post-office for the purpose of being transmitted by a postal telegraph, and every transcript thereof made by any person acting in pursuance of the orders of the Postmaster-General, shall be a post letter within the meaning of an Act passed in the first year of the reign of Her present Majesty, chapter thirty-six" (Carmichael 108).

[44] Barrett Browning's literary reference is one that is found repeatedly in periodical literature about the Post Office. The idea of communication "wafting" is from Alexander Pope's "Eloisa to Abelard." Doomed lover Eloisa wishes that Abelard might "speed the soft intercourse from soul to soul, / And waft a sigh from Indus to the Pole" (111).

a uniformed delivery boy to trot it over to the recipient's house, as I discuss in chapter 1), but the Penny Post had already been established in the public mind as a marvel of speed and mechanization. To the nineteenth-century mind, there was less difference between a post-letter and a telegram than there is to a twentieth- or twenty-first-century mind. New technologies grow out of or share the same discourses as those that precede them, and the technologies themselves neither produce change alone, nor line up precisely with the cultural change that enables and reflects them.[45] It is also important to theorize the institution and the technology together, to avoid casting either as totalizing or determinist. Raymond Williams recognized this when he pointed out that it is wrong to assume "that it is only with the coming of 20th-century technologies that communication has been at once systematised and mechanised. [...] communication systems have never been as it were an optional extra in social organization or historical development."[46]

When I propose that the Post Office was a desiring machine, my figuration is drawn in part from the work of theorists of systems like Herbert Marcuse, Bruno Latour, and Felix Guattari. In "Machinic Heterogenesis," Guattari ascribes both psychic subjectivity and a consciousness of fracture to the machine, which he describes as "haunted by a desire for abolition. Its emergence is accompanied by breakdown, by catastrophe, by the threat of death" (40). Latour's study of an institution (that, in this case, failed to be born), the Aramis guided-transportation system intended for Paris, brings Aramis to life and has it declare itself: "We are—ah! what are we? Whirlwinds, great loops of retroactions, troubled crowds, searching, restless, critical, unstable, complex, yes, vast collectives" (296). Breakdown is, in this account, the symptom of desire and this correlates with the swathes of periodical literature detailing the Post Office's Dead Letter Office, the misaddressed mail, and the curiosities that people misguidedly send through parcel post. In "Some Social Implications of Modern Technology," Herbert Marcuse suggests "the mechanical contrivances which facilitate intercourse among individuals also intercept and absorb their libido." Marcuse believes that that this interception and absorption "thereby divert[s] it from the all too dangerous realm in which the individual is free of society" (47). The materials I analyze suggest that communications networks can indeed disperse this libidinal power but can also readdress and redeliver it.

If the "discourse network," as Friedrich Kittler terms it,[47] can write back, it can also blend forms: conjoining bodies with machines, or novels with telegrams. Over the last twenty-five years, scholars have been exploring the effects of nineteenth century connectivity. Gillian Beer's 1983 *Darwin's Plots* broke critical ground by showing how literary interest in "webs of affinity" grew in the wake of Darwin's evolutionary theories of interconnection. In his 1988 study, *Circulation: Defoe, Dickens, and the Economies of the Novel,*

---

[45] This point is made in the introduction to an excellent collection of essays on literature and communication systems: *Language Machines: Technologies of Literature and Cultural Production* (eds. Masten, Stallybrass, and Vickers), xi. See also *Rethinking Media Change: The Aesthetics of Transition* (eds. Thorburn and Jenkins): "The essays in this book [...] conceive media change as an accretive, gradual process, challenging the idea that new technologies displace older systems with decisive suddenness" (*Rethinking Media Change* 2).

[46] Raymond Williams, *Contact: Human Communication and Its History* 15–16.

David Trotter linked the circulation systems of plague, money, and the post, emphasizing (as Wagner and Carpenter did) how the post stood for heterogeneity: "The post was exciting not only because of its scope and efficiency, but also because of its mixed content of ideas and emotions, commercial data and private confidences. For the health of the nation depended on the flow of information *and* the flow of feeling" (Trotter 103). Like Trotter's claim that in a postal age, data and feelings conjoin, David F. Bell equally stresses that bodies and messages become commensurate with each other, conflated by new technologies of velocity. In *Real Time: Accelerating Narrative from Balzac to Zola* (2004), he notes that the "speed of movement of passengers" went hand in hand with "the speed of message exchanges" (Bell 2). Bell says that technologies of acceleration made literary style more telegraphic: "Time is short, movements need to be accomplished quickly, embellishments are out of place" (Bell 3). Bell's study is of French literature, and the French postal system has a very different history due to its role in revolution, but his work on speed and communication finds English precedent in the work of Mary Favret, who in her 1993 book, *Romantic Correspondence: Women, Politics and the Fiction of Letters*, argued that the speed of the mail coach made people write faster and more frenetically. Laura Otis takes up the notion of "wired thoughts" (1) and shows how the trope of the network intertwined telegraph wires with nerves, revealing that "we are all telegraphers" (Otis 226). Most recently and comprehensively, Richard Menke has argued, "The age of the postage stamp and the electric telegraph decisively altered the meaning of the old technologies of writing and print" (Menke 3). In this age, he claims, literature comes to look like media and vice versa: "An informatic history of literature also offers a literary history of information" (Menke 4). For Menke, Victorian literary realism posited the same "multifarious networks of relation" (Menke 6) that its authors and readers found on stepping into a Post Office.

CHAPTER OUTLINES

Chapter 1, "Postal Digressions: Mail and Sexual Scandal," takes as its touchstone the 1889 Cleveland Street Affair that turned post-boys into rent-boys and suggested an institutional likeness between the Post Office and the brothel. This chapter notices that while the Cleveland Street Scandal has been much analyzed in gay histories, its postal implications have gone unmarked. Governmental investigations into the goings on at the Cleveland Street brothel revealed that this was no isolated incident: the Post Office had been aware for some time that the young boys in their employ regularly turned tricks, and that the specific conditions of postal employment made them desirable and available. The pleasures of procuring and buying the sexual services of these doubly employed boys, in other words, was specifically bound up in their status as uniformed postal deliverers —intermediaries between both hetero- and homosexual interlocutors. The Cleveland Street Affair was prosecuted under the Criminal Law Amendment Act of 1885, notorious in gay historiography.

---

[47] Friedrich Kittler, *Discourse Networks 1800/1900*. Trans. Michael Metteer with Chris Cullens. (Stanford, CA: Stanford UP, 1990).

This was the same Act that framed Oscar Wilde's trials ten years later. The chapter ends with an examination of the way letters—and envelopes—featured in Oscar Wilde's downfall, and this chapter argues that Wilde found erotic postal pleasures from out of the midst of blackmail.

Chapter 2, " 'This Little Queen's Head Can't Be Untrue:' Trollope's Postal Infidelities," examines the gender and sexual fallout from Anthony Trollope being both a novelist and a postal inspector. I show that postal work made Trollope specifically vulnerable to charges that as a novelist he was effeminate and promiscuous. Analysis of Trollope's descriptions of his Post Office work in his *Autobiography* shows that he himself allied his postal service with textual agility and sexual mobility. His portrayal of himself as a "beneficent angel"—the idea of postmen as angels is a common motif throughout *Postal Pleasures*—reflects his understanding that facilitating the circulation of post-letters could counter stagnant and painfully differentiating social structures. I center my argument on Trollope's racy but under-studied novel *John Caldigate* (1879), which features both a bigamy plot and a postman hero. This chapter focuses on the shift from epistolary to postal plots, and the effects of narratives turning on the importance of stamps and postal markings. In chapter 1, the figure of the intermediary who queers the lines of postal connection was the desiring and desirable figure of the pretty telegraph boy. Here, that intermediary is the heroic and romantic postman who vanquishes the sinister intermediating figure of the blackmailer.

Between 1877 and 1881, Anthony Trollope, Thomas Hardy, and Eliza Lynn Linton published stories which all portray women companions who are "more like lovers than girl and girl." The women are also all telegraph operators or Post Office employees. Chapter 3, "A Queer Job for a Girl: The Communicative Touch in Trollope, Hardy, and Lynn Linton," explores why working with postal technologies goes hand in hand with these women's "predilection" for women. In search of independence, these heroines all set up home with their female companion: these are fictions that imagine what domestic relations might look like for the unmarried, middle-class woman who chooses a working life. This chapter proposes that the telecommunicative nature of this work, which situates the women as part of a communication matrix, or a civil service, proffers sexual alternatives, the trope of the network replacing the rule of the family tree. This chapter and chapter 5 are the only ones to deal directly with lesbianism. Chapter 3 is the only chapter to engage a female author: until this point *Postal Pleasures* is about the postal commerce between men. The argument could be made, however, that even this chapter about women is still about postal traffic between men. Hardy and Trollope are both clearly titillated by thinking about girl-on-girl telegraphic exchanges and Eliza Lynn Linton was a notorious antifeminist who wrote her autobiography in the voice of a man, Christopher Kirkland. The importance of women here, though, is that they step into this project as characters *through being postal workers*. Both being postal and being workers relieves them somewhat from the restraints of their gender, and even writing about them produces some cross-gendered effects. Trollope has to write about telegraph girls because he feels he can't write about sexually suspect telegraph boys, and Hardy has to admit that he's impersonated women through the mail. In this sense, this chapter about women is not an anomaly within *Postal Pleasures,* but rather forms a kernel to the book's overarching thesis that becoming postal can detach subjects from gender and sexual subjectivities that then reattach to queer effect.

The British Empire was made of colonies marked red on the map, an infamously disparate geography that was governed at a distance. These colonies were linked by a vast web of telegraph and postal routes known as the "all red routes." This trope turned the language of blood ties into a prosthetic familial relation, appropriate given that the militarized bureaucracy of empire was in large part held together by mobile homosocial bonds. Chapter 4, "All Red Routes: Blood Brotherhood and the Post in Doyle, Kipling, and Stoker," focuses on America as the "lost boy" of the British Empire. America is the forgotten character in current understandings of Victorian imperial narratives, yet it played a defining role in the way that Victorians thought about the consequences of expansion. The late-century Anglo-American reunion movement ran a prominent campaign for an Imperial Penny Post under a rhetoric of brotherhood that was fueled by conjoined fantasies of homosocial alliance and racial continence. I read Arthur Conan Doyle's "A Study in Scarlet" (1881), poetry and fiction by Rudyard Kipling, and Bram Stoker's *Dracula* (1897) through contemporary queer theorizations of military brotherhood and the kinds of comrade love embodied by pacifists such as Walt Whitman and Edward Carpenter and imperialists like Cecil Rhodes. Before dying in his arms, Cecil Rhodes's lover reportedly whispered to him "You have been father, mother, brother, and sister to me" (Rotberg 195). And Bram Stoker says of Whitman that he is "a man who can be if he wishes father, and brother and wife to his soul" (Traubel iv: 185). This polysemous mode of address, which aggregates the variously gendered roles of the traditional family into the figure of the homosexual beloved is, *Postal Pleasures* contends, a postal formulation. It is through constructing an index of all relation, listing all means of address and all kinds of affective relations, that men can translate these many forms into the one "unspeakable" love, and thus commute the kinship denied them into gay relation.

Chapter 5, "Postscript: Henry James's Public Servant," concludes the book with a reading of the female civil servant as a queer agent in Henry James's 1898 novella *In the Cage.* I take James's central trope of "queer extensions" of experience and self and read it alongside his own postal practices. I show that although there has been much excellent recent queer scholarship on this novella, it has been foreshortened by its emphasis on blackmail and the threat that the postal worker could expose gay male subjectivity. This emphasis on peril and masculinity has contributed to an inability to see the postal exchange as erotically charged, and the girl telegraphist as herself queer.

CONCLUSION

The nineteenth-century literary tendency to ally the Post Office, as Henry James did, with what he called "the diversity of human relations" (*Partial Portraits* 122), derived from and fed back into this powerful, emergent cultural model of the network. *Postal Pleasures* tenders a critical bid that there is a structural and historically constitutive relationship between the Victorian postal network and queer theoretical frameworks, proposing that Victorian "postal fiction" was able to portray and imagine structures of human relation built on virtual associations. The rise of the network as a prominent cultural metaphor helped enmesh the stiff and limited lineages of marriage and blood descent in a web comprised of many forms of human relations. As Shawn Rosenheim describes the effects of telegraphic technology, "The Newtonian unities of being are replaced by the prosthetic extension of the self over a network of wires."[48] Unity of being became a hard sell in a world that claimed to have annihilated time and space. The metaphorics and rhetorics of blood and family that were used to describe the development of the postal system labored to explain a system that was by definition *not* based on blood or kinship. It was not based on subject positions at all, but on a circulation that metaphorically and literally enabled myriad relationships and interactions. And, furthermore, the model of a circulation system revealed that all relationships and interactions implied this myriad. In an interview published in 1981, called "Friendship as a Way of Life," Michel Foucault elaborates on his tenet that homosexuality is not an ontology: "Homosexuality," he explains "is a historic occasion to reopen affective and relational virtualities, not so much through the intrinsic qualities of the homosexual but because the 'slantwise' position of the latter, as it were, the diagonal lines he can lay out in the social fabric allow these virtualities to come to light."[49] Foucault's language is that of the network; the homosexual lays "diagonal" lines across the rigid warp and weft of a social fabric that only allows limited, sanctioned heterosexual subject positions to be visible. The "slantwise" orientation or discursive position of the homosexual disavows these limitations and "reopens" possibilities or "virtualities." Foucault goes on to describe that the exchange of queer "affection, tenderness, friendship, fidelity, camaraderie and companionship" threatens a society that fears "the formation of new alliances and the tying together of unforeseen lines of force."[50] *Postal Pleasures* catches up the threads of this way of describing relations as disseminated, showing the way in which the Victorian postal system, as an organized miscellany of "lines of force," was instrumental in the articulation of *all* forms of relation as built from alliance and misalliance. *Postal Pleasures* parts ways from Foucault's critical legacy in that it is a portrait of queerness as neither resistive nor subversive to the institution, the establishment and dominant social norms, but rather as emanating from within one of the more staid of State facilities, and becoming necessary to it. The postal system is the most quotidian of networks, one whose logic of "anyone, everyone, everywhere" construes all subjects as thoroughly intermediated and transactional, and thus potentially queer, a queerness which is useful to its bureaucratic function. *Postal Pleasures* proposes that together the post and queer subjectivity forgo identity for interaction. Both invoke structures of human relation that are dispersed, infinitely relative, prosthetic (yet affective and affecting) associations.

---

[48] Shawn Rosenheim, *Cryptographic Imagination* 91.
[49] Michel Foucault, *Ethics: Subjectivity and Truth* 138.
[50] Michel Foucault, *Ethics: Subjectivity and Truth* 136.

1

Postal Digressions

MAIL AND SEXUAL SCANDAL

TAILORS AND TELEGRAPH BOYS

In 1890, the *Scots Observer* published a review of Oscar Wilde's *The Picture of Dorian Gray* that attacked Wilde for "grubbing in muck heaps" and "writing stuff that were better unwritten."[1] It concluded: "Mr. Wilde has brains, and art, and style; but if he can write for none but outlawed noblemen and perverted telegraph boys, the sooner he takes to tailoring (or some other decent trade) the better for his own reputation and the public morals" (4: 181).[2] The author, with the sneer of a schoolmaster, threatens Wilde through sexual and class shame. If Wilde must insist on writing literature that panders to those who indulge in cross-class, homosexual affairs, then he should put down the pen—and class privilege—and pick up the tailor's chalk instead. The slur corrodes the very distinctions it sets up: the picture it conjures of Wilde on his knees hemming men's trousers, or taking inside leg measurements, makes it quite clear that taking up the trade of tailoring would be no solution to Wilde's love of rough trade.

Tailoring, then, is easy enough to connect to homosexuality, but why are telegraph boys—specifically—used to attack Wilde in this review? Why infer a connection between pornography and the postal service? In 1889, one year before this review appeared, telegraph boys were the protagonists in a real-life homosexual scandal; Boy

---

[1] Unsigned review, *Scots Observer* (5 July 1890): iv, 181. The authorship of this review is disputed; for a note about the debate, see Karl Beckson, *Oscar Wilde: The Critical Heritage* 74.
[2] This section of the review was read aloud to Wilde in the first of his trials. See Holland 77.

Messengers, as the Post Office called its young deliverers of telegrams, were found to be simultaneously employed as sex workers in a West End brothel. This scandal, known popularly as the Cleveland Street Affair (sometimes known as the West End Scandal), was one of the most notorious of late-century sexual scandals. It was by no means the first time that Post Office telegraph boys were implicated in prostitution; trouble had been brewing for nearly twenty years, with minor scandals erupting across the 1870s. But the Cleveland Street Affair was big news. It entailed three trials and a forced expatriation, and it endangered the reputations of the Prince of Wales and the Prime Minister.[3] Not only was it—due to the efforts of journalists eager to expose aristocratic deviancy—a national sensation, but it also occasioned the first high-profile prosecution under Britain's first ever law against homosexuality: the Criminal Law Amendment Act, Section 11. This law, which was passed in 1885, was the same law under which Wilde would be prosecuted ten years later. The 1890 reviewer in the *Scots Observer* was therefore eerily on target: there would prove to be a connection between telegraph boys and Wilde's sexual persona. That connection would be juridically imposed, but it was also, as I will show, sexually desired. In the late nineteenth century, the telegraph boy featured in a number of homoerotic texts, texts that recognized and explored the structurally erotic potential of that job in particular and the Postal Service in general.[4] A telegraph boy disseminated mail. Not only did he appear on your doorstep himself (male) along with the message (mail), but he was also a uniformed reminder that in a postal age, all correspondence is mediated by a vast network of functionaries (see figure 1.1). The Cleveland Street Affair dramatized what many had already realized: Post Office employees were entangled in the correspondence they distributed. Disseminators diffuse themselves along with the thing they carry. Michael Moon defines the concept of dissemination through the poetry of Walt Whitman (who, as I discuss in chapter 4, had a telegraph boy lover). Moon writes, "Texts and persons [can] stand in more than merely analogic relation to each other."[5] Whitman's "own body *can* be successfully projected through, and partially transformed into, his printed text, and his readers in turn *can* engage in contact with the actual physical presence of the author, at least in liminal terms, as they read" (Moon 69). Letters are the quotidian version of the poetic body-in-text. When this fusion between body and text is then disseminated by a pretty Boy Messenger, that

---

[3] For a full account of the affair, published soon after the Home Office papers on this case were finally opened, see H. Montgomery Hyde, *The Cleveland Street Scandal* (New York: Coward, McCann and Geoghegan, 1976).

[4] The association of telegraph boys with homosexual availability was still lively in the 1920s. Matt Houlbrook documents the experiences of teenage messenger-boys with a Post Office customer they called the "bum Major." See Matt Houlbrook, *Queer London* 180.

[5] Michael Moon, *Disseminating Whitman: Revision and Corporeality in Leaves of Grass* 69.

FIGURE 1.1 The Postman's Knock.

messenger becomes a complicating, potentially titillating other body, a uniformed instrument and symbol of interchangeability.

The Cleveland Street Affair has received attention from historians of sexuality because it was a case that publicized homosexual sex, under the new "Section 11" legislation, and it has thus proved a useful lens through which to debate the "invention" of the homosexual.[6] The postal nature of the scandal has largely been portrayed as incidental, but this moment of "becoming homosexual" is just as much a moment of "going postal." In the first place, it was the federal structure of the Post Office that turned the scandal into national news, and the boys' status as civil servants was what prompted the government to take legal action.[7] In the second place, "mail" intersected with "homosex" to produce metaphoric relations between them. That the Cleveland Street Affair was named via an address must be read symptomatically: it is both an anxious attempt to contain the potential of dissemination and an aroused locating of illicit (but deliverable) pleasures. The address served to provide literal directions to one homosexual brothel and also to imply that many more might be strewn through the postal directory. The scandal derived its force from the disclosure that sexual deviance was not contained in a single residence or street, but rather circulated as widely and easily as the post, and indeed, with the post.[8] The Cleveland Street Affair revealed a relationship between the postal system and homosexual desire that was analogic, metaphoric, *and* instrumental. The crux of the matter was

---

[6] The first stirrings of scholarly attention begin with H. Montgomery Hyde's 1976 *The Cleveland Street Scandal* and Colin Simpson, Lewis Chester, and David Leitch, *The Cleveland Street Affair* (Boston and Toronto: Little, Brown, 1976) and include Jeffrey Weeks, *Sex, Politics and Society: The Regulation of Sexuality Since 1800* (1982). For more recent adjudications of the significance of the case, see William A. Cohen, *Sex Scandal: The Private Parts of Victorian Fiction* (Durham, NC: Duke UP, 1996); H. G. Cocks, *Nameless Offences: Homosexual Desire in the Nineteenth Century* (London: I. B. Tauris, 2003); Matt Cook, *London and the Culture of Homosexuality, 1885–1914* (Cambridge: Cambridge UP, 2003); Sean Brady, *Masculinity and Male Homosexuality in Britain, 1861–1913* (Basingstoke, UK: Palgrave Macmillan, 2005); Morris B. Kaplan, *Sodom on the Thames: Sex, Love, and Scandal in Wilde Times* (Ithaca, NY: Cornell UP, 2005).

[7] Mark Seltzer has written on the twentieth-century phenomenon of "going postal" by killing serially. He observes: "Mass murder in America has had two popular sites: the fast-food system [...] and the postal system [...]. On these sites systems, numbers, and bodies collide. Personal communications, in the postal system, are the property of the impersonal clerks of the system" (21). But the phenomenon of "going postal" is due not to proportionally more postal workers becoming mass murderers, but instead a consequence of the Post Office being a federal network: occurrences of violence among its workforce must be made public and must be made national news. Numbers, systems, and bodies do indeed collide, but not to frustrate individuation to the point of homicide. Seltzer's is a reading that presumes alienation is a consequence of impersonality (rather than a consequence of pressurized labor practices, bad management, and inequity in the workplace). Seltzer turns to the Jack the Ripper case to draw a connection between the "series of torn and opened bodies of too public women" and the "series of more than 300 letters (none authenticated) mailed to the London press, signed Jack the Ripper. In such cases, the boundaries come down between private desire and public life, along with the boundaries between private bodies and the public media. Letters and bodies, word counts and body counts, go together from the inception of serial murder" (9). For Seltzer's project, "going postal" is a way of "reconnecting what [...] the information society disconnects: private desire and public life" (18). But in the era of Jack the Ripper, all participation in postal communication already rendered "private" bodies less private and the "public" media less public.

[8] Some news reports made the same point. The editor of the penny-paper *Modern Truth*, for example, printed letters applauding his efforts to document the scandal, and wrote on 21 December 21 1889: "And now one word more. Hitherto the whole interest has been centred on the history connected with the one house in Cleveland-street." He theorizes that this has led people to believe that "this spot was the one foul blot in all London, and that the scandal contains within itself all that is scandalous in this modern Babylon. Let nothing of the sort be imagined" (DPP1/95/2).

that both looked like unfettered, undifferentiating systems of exchange. Earlier century rhetoric extolling the benefits of the reformed Post Office had emphasized the circulation of mail as the lifeblood of the nation. One journal representatively declared, "Letter-writing is a circulation of moral, intellectual, and commercial blood; every postman's bag is a ganglion of social nerves that maintains the vitality of the body politic."[9] The problem attending this metaphor is that nerves, even social ones, transmit pleasure and sensation along with vitality. The Cleveland Street scandal revealed that the public facility of the Post Office, an institution dedicated to making epistolary association accessible to all, had enabled the "wrong" kinds of sexual association and this fact sensationalized systems of association per se. In reporting the affair, *The Referee* expostulated: "Is it not wonderful, and terrible as well, to hear that at the West-end there are not mere individuals, but *associations*, so tired of every natural enjoyment this world possesses, that they *band themselves together* for the exact purpose of doing that which is unnatural?" [my italics].[10] Horrified at the idea that an organized collectivity structured the scandal, the paper nevertheless reports that news of it has reverberated through the acceptable "clubs and pubs" and will soon be "flooding our households." In other words, the paper admits that media itself functions through a combination of circulation and congress, thus mirroring the very social choreography of perverts with postal preferences.

THE CLEVELAND STREET BOYS

The events comprising the Cleveland Street Affair came to light because of an irregularity in another circulation system: currency. On 4 July 1889, one of the General Post Office's internal policemen, P. C. Luke Hanks, interrogated a fifteen-year-old Boy Messenger named Charles Swinscow who had been found with an amount of money disproportionate to his meager wages as a telegraph delivery boy. There had been a theft in the Central Telegraph Office, then situated in the General Post Office West in St. Martin's-Le-Grand. On the trail of a thief, the suspicious Hanks asked Swinscow to account for his possession of 14 shillings. But Hanks caught a different fish altogether. Swinscow, it turned out, was not a thief, but a rent-boy. He had the unusual amount of money because he had been working as a prostitute in a West End brothel, on Cleveland Street. His tale thoroughly implicated the Post Office. Not only was Swinscow one of several Post Office boys involved in the brothel,[11] but they had also been procured, and some of them even had sex, on the Post Office premises. Swinscow himself had been seduced on the Post Office premises by another Boy Messenger called, aptly, Newlove. Interviewed by a senior officer

---

[9] *The Atlas* (12 February 1853).
[10] *The Referee* (Sunday, 24 November 1889). Archived in the Public Record Office, file DPP1/95/1–7.
[11] The authorities believed that many other boys were involved in similar sexual activities. A Scotland Yard report of 18 July 1889 reads: "I have not deemed it prudent to interrogate other boys employed at the Post Office but I have every reason to believe that a large number of them have been defiled at this house" [HO 144/477/X24427].

in the Confidential Inquiry Bureau, John Phillips, Swinscow described how: "Soon after I got to know him he asked me to go into the lavatory at the basement of the Post Office building—we went into one water closet and shut the door and we behaved indecently together—we did this on other occasions afterwards."[12] Though clearly stilted by the vocabulary of the police official ("behaved indecently"), this interview makes the topography of the sexual encounter quite clear: it was initiated in the basement of the Post Office building and this initiation led Swinscow directly to the Cleveland Street brothel. Water closets merge with the subterranean bowels of the Post Office, which lead to the West End address—to which, presumably, some of these boys would have delivered mail while on official duty. Having a postal route takes on a new meaning. Henry Newlove persuaded Swinscow to go to the Cleveland Street house where the proprietor, Charles Hammond, sent him to bed with a customer. Swinscow gave the names of two other Boy Messengers involved in the brothel: George Alma Wright and Charles Ernest Thickbroom (another implausibly diverting name), who were both seventeen. Wright's story is another tale of seduction by Newlove:

> He persuaded me on several occasions to go to the lavatory in the basement with him. It was about 4 months that I first made his acquaintance. We used to go into the water closet together and behave indecently. On one or two occasions certainly more than once, Newlove put his person into me, that is to say behind only a little way and something came from him. I never did this to him. One afternoon I met him in the corridor of the Post Office during my dinner hour he said to me "I know a gentleman I go with sometimes and if you like to come I will shew him to you. He wants to have a game at spooning about with you.[13]

Wright's account, structured by the banalities of dinner hours and lavatories, makes it quite clear that the Post Office provided boys with a domestic life that was homosocially alternate to that of the family. The boys not only worked, but also lived with each other, sharing meals and lodging. These young men's accounts are accounts of association, alliance, and acquaintanceship as much as they are tales of sex. Wright introduces Newlove to Thickbroom, who tells a similar tale of passage to the brothel, and sexual encounters, that he calls "play," all brought about while he was clothed in his Post Office uniform.[14] The interrogations, in other words, revealed the homosexual network they needed in order to pursue prosecutions, but this network uncomfortably overlapped the much-lauded network of the postal system itself.

The testimonials reverberate with redefinitions of the concept of the *public facility*. Initiated in water closets, facilitated in the passageways of the Post Office building, these sexual encounters redefined the tenor of these uniformed boys' status as "public servants,"

---
[12] DPP1/95/3, 106.
[13] DPP1/95/3, 95–97.
[14] DPP1/95/3, 102–3.

and suggested that in serving the public, they serviced a diversity of needs. In his essay "Tearooms and Sympathy, or, The Epistemology of the Water Closet," Lee Edelman describes "the men's room" as "a site at which the zones of the public and private overlap with a distinctive current of psychic charge."[15] He notes that this charge is intensified "when the bathroom in question is a public or institutional facility" (Edelman 561) and argues that the "men's room" holds out the promise of sexual difference as determinate and knowable, but simultaneously engages a heterosexual anxiety that in fact this sexual difference might not be recognizable or avoidable. Epistemological crisis ensues. What happens when the bathroom in question is not only in a public institution, but also in a public institution that disseminates private mail? When Edelman describes a bathroom under Grand Central Station, he notes that the "cloaca of the city" links the sewer with the intestines, in a relation of abjection (Edelman 563). Edelman argues that the continent self can be threatened by collapse into itself, and its "internal space of difference" (Edelman 563). We could also, however, read the sewer system in destabilizing relation to the connectivity of train tracks, or postal routes, to argue that further threat derives from the distention and dispersal of the self through a material, extra-bodily, communal network. Attention to these technologies of removal might, in fact, also be in pursuit of the logic of the abject. Abjection refers to that which is expelled or thrown off; in Julia Kristeva's definition it disturbs the fixity of identity by throwing off preconscious multiplicities of self. It involves the loss or detachment of self, followed by partial, in-process incorporations and thus can be linked to the mulchy aggregation of dispersed selves that occurs in cesspools, postbags, and railway-station waiting rooms. Drains, telegraph wires, postal routes, train tracks, extrude and then connect all bodies—indiscriminately—servicing their base circulation needs. This network relation threatens culturally policed fixities of difference not only between persons (differences of class, gender, race, sexuality), but also between persons and systems. A person can become an address.

The Cleveland Street scandal and the homophone it produced between "mail" and "male" collapsed the distinction between post and person, reminding correspondents that the bodies and sexual desires of postal functionaries intermediated all correspondence. Moreover, the number and nature of intermediaries could not be known: your correspondence might be conveyed from the Post Office by a messenger-boy, or it might be conveyed by a messenger-boy who detoured through the promiscuous relations of a brothel on the way to your door. A postal relation balanced between the seemingly determinate coordinates of the sender and the addressee, but the mediating stretch *between* the sender and the addressee rendered that relation thoroughly indeterminate.

The force of the Cleveland Street Affair was that the deviations it highlighted appeared to be sanctioned. The boys' servicing of brothel patrons didn't look so different from their

---

[15] Lee Edelman, "Tearooms and Sympathy, or, The Epistemology of the Water Closet," in *The Lesbian and Gay Studies Reader*, ed. Henry Abelove, Michele Aina Barale, David M. Halperin (New York: Routledge, 1993), 553–74, 561.

servicing of the general public. The Post Office's royal insignia functioned unwittingly as an imprimatur to the goings on at Cleveland Street and other deviations of the mail. Even more significantly, this sanction and this imprimatur was an essential part of the erotics that the scandal showcased. The Cleveland Street clients had sex with messenger-boys who were *in their Post Office uniforms.* The telegraph boy was considered, as some have described it, a particular catch because of his "smart new uniform" and the official status and civic position it signaled. Having sex with a telegraph boy was a way of having sex with Queen and country, with officialdom. The post was a public facility that enjoyed a peculiarly public presence. It was not sequestered in barracks, or closed off behind governmental office doors: rather, it had full roam of the public space. Indeed, its addresses and its house numbers and its postboxes organized public space. Public spaces have, as Lisa Duggan, Michael Warner, and others have amply demonstrated, long formed the arena of the queer subject.[16] And the marginalized gay male subject has a particular history of forging private spaces out of public ones: the cubicle of the public toilets, the shadows of a park, the darkness of a cinema, or the recesses of a museum. The public facility offers the flux, anonymity, and sociability via which a queer subject might find sex and sexual relation.[17] The Cleveland Street Affair brought the network of the mail and mail delivery into relation with cottaging. Part of the frisson of the affair was that it eroticized the kind of duty and civic service that routinely materialized on every household's doorstep in the form of a uniformed postman or telegraph boy. Less distant than the armed forces and less disciplinary than the police, the postal worker was a more widely circulating, domestic, and available figure.

THE LAW AND THE MAIL

It is clear from the Home Office files that the Cleveland Street case was understood to have national ramifications. When the Post Office officials turned the investigation over to the Metropolitan Police Force, it was put in the high-ranking hands of Inspector Frederick G. Abberline, who was simultaneously heading the Jack the Ripper investigation. It transpired that the patrons of the brothel included the Earl of Euston, Lord Arthur Somerset (who was Assistant Equerry to HRH The Prince of Wales), and possibly even "Eddy," Prince Albert Victor (who was son of the Prince of Wales and Heir Presumptive to the throne (see figure 1.2). When the police discovered that these notable figures were implicated, the investigation papers were sent, on 25 July, to the Director of Public

---

[16] Michael Warner describes the erosion of what he calls "sex publics" as a result of the erosion of "a democratic public sphere" (162)—the phenomenon that Lisa Duggan calls "the incredible shrinking public," see *The Incredible Shrinking Public: Sexual Politics and the Decline of Democracy.*

[17] For an evocative description of the attraction between the homosexual and the railway, as a public facility, see Henning Bech, *When Men Meet: Homosexuality and Modernity.* Trans. Teresa Mesquit and Tim Davies. 1987. (Cambridge: Polity Press, 1997), 158–59.

FIGURE 1.2 The West End Scandal, Sketches at Bow Street.

Prosecutions, Sir Augustus Stephenson. A fraught and complex battle ensued about whether or not the scandal should be suppressed.

It was a battle that pivoted on notions of publicness and publicity: the press and the Home Office furiously debated whether giving publicity to these crimes would be in the public interest and whether public men should be protected. The crucial question, however, was, who are the public men? There were three possible answers: the patrons of the brothel (public because they were aristocrats), the homosexual (typed as always public by the law), the telegraph boys (public because they were civil servants). The legislation under which the Cleveland Street defendants would be tried was the infamous Section 11, or "Labouchère" clause, of the 1885 Criminal Law Amendment Act.[18] The clause reads:

> Any male person who, in public or private, commits, or is a party to the commission of, or procures or attempts to procure the commission by any male person of any act of gross indecency with another male person, shall be guilty of a misdemeanour [...].
> (Section 11, Criminal Law Amendment Act)

Following the lead of Michel Foucault, many scholars have regarded the passage of this law as a defining moment in the history of homosexuality in Britain. This body of scholarship

---

[18] The clause was named after its "author," Henry Labouchère, MP and editor of *Truth*. Implemented on 1 January 1886, the 1885 act's full title was "An Act to make further provision for the Protection of Women and Girls, the suppression of brothels, and other purposes" (Session 48 and 49 Victoria, chapter 69).

argues that prior to Section 11, laws against sodomy were not gender (or even human) specific. This new clause, instead of legislating against a specific sexual act, criminalized any kind of sexual interaction between men, thus inventing a homosexual "type."[19] As Ed Cohen summarizes this scholarly perspective, the legal focus shifted from viewing sodomy as a "criminally punishable sexual *act*" to construing it as "a defining characteristic of a type of sexual *actor* (the 'sodomite')" (127). Legislating against a type, rather than an act, was not the only consequence of the epistemological shift that this law produced, however. Legal historian Leslie J. Moran points out that the five words "in public or in private" declared the annihilation, for the homosexual "type," of the public/private distinction:

> Perhaps the most important aspect of the Labouchère reform relates not so much to the inauguration of a new offence through the introduction of the phrase "gross indecency" into the law but in the reference to "in public or in private" […]. Through this phrase the law declares its unbounded operation.
>
> (211, n.25)

The realm of the law (and its "unbounded operation") in general is, Moran goes on to explain, almost without exception that of the public rather than the private sphere. Section 11 of the Criminal Law Amendment Act departs from this framework, robbing those who engage in homosexual sex of a "private" life and making them ultra-public subjects, subject to the full force of the law.

More recent work in "new gay history" has taken issue with these Foucauldian-led accounts. Scholars such as H. G. Cocks, Matt Cook, and Sean Brady have argued that 1885 was less of a turning point than previously imagined: they reach backward to show that gay sex had not enjoyed the protection of privacy prior to 1885, and they reach forward to show that subsequent to the passing of the bill, it did not fully succeed in typing gay men.[20] As Joseph Bristow has articulated in his overview article "Remapping the Sites of Modern Gay History: Legal Reform, Medico-Legal Thought, Homosexual Scandal, Erotic Geography,"[21]

---

[19] In *The History of Sexuality*, Michel Foucault declares: "The sodomite had been a temporary aberration; the homosexual was now a species" (43). Jeffrey Weeks's *Coming Out: Homosexual Politics in Britain from the Nineteenth Century to the Present* explains that the abandonment of the death penalty for buggery, which had been tacitly abandoned by 1836 and removed from the statute books in 1861 (1889 in Scotland), "was a prelude not to a liberalization of the law but to a tightening of its grip" (14). The 1885 legislation was followed, he explains, by "the Vagrancy Act of 1898 [which] clamped down on homosexual 'soliciting.' These two enactments represented a singular hardening of the legal situation and were a crucial factor in the determination of modern attitudes" (Weeks, *Coming Out* 14–15). Weeks expands this analysis in *Sex, Politics and Society* in chapter 2, "The Construction of Homosexuality." Ed Cohen's work on the power of representation on public and queer imaginaries in *Talk on the Wilde Side* also describes how the "wide publicity" given to the Oscar Wilde trials effected an "epistemological shift" in which the concept of the male homosexual replaced the figure of the sodomite (97–99).

[20] Harry G. Cocks, for example, argues that the phrasing of Section 11 "has led to the misleading assumption that hitherto, private acts had been legal" (37). He points out that even prior to 1885, sexual acts that took place in "private rooms or similar locations, were on the same legal footing as those taking place in the street or the park" (37)—the acts merely needed the testimony of witnesses. Cocks does concede that police practice, however, reinforced distinctions of public and private (74).

[21] *Journal of British Studies* 46 (January 2007): 116–42.

this new gay history kicks against accounts of grand epistemic change that seem to privilege medico-juridical discourse over and above "thick descriptions" of everyday life. But as Bristow observes, this work does not stand in opposition to, but rather on the shoulders of scholars like Michel Foucault and Jeffrey Weeks. If we reread Weeks, we find he makes it plain that the results of the "significant shift in sexual meanings" (Weeks, *Coming Out* 14–15) he describes were "uneven," as old models lingered and became "inextricably entangled" with emergent, scientific theories and new taxonomies were compromised by "vagaries of application."[22] And as Eve Kosofsky Sedgwick cautions, in her critique of David Halperin and Michel Foucault's historiography, it is important to remember that intervening models of sexuality are not necessarily "supervening" models (*Epistemology* 47).

The problems of when and what public and private meant did not originate with twentieth-century theorists and historians of sexuality. The officials in charge of deciding whether or not the Cleveland Street case should be brought to trial were very troubled by the overlap between old and new definitions of public and private. In the Director of Public Prosecution Sir Augustus Stephenson's memos, we find him chewing over the problem of publicness and publicity. Initially, Stephenson was of the opinion that Lord Arthur Somerset should not be prosecuted. On 29 July 1889, he wrote to the Chief Commissioner of the Police, referring the Commissioner to a correspondence between the Home Secretary and the Commissioner of Police "in the year 1880 and 1884 and to the conferences which are referred to therein" (DPP1/95/1). In these papers he "urged on the grounds of public policy the expediency of not giving unnecessary publicity to cases of this character" and recommended not referring such cases to the Director of Public Prosecutions (DPP1/95/1). What is curious about Stephenson's referral of the Commissioner to 1880 and 1884 discussions is that they took place *before* the passing of the Criminal Law Amendment Act in 1885. By the time of the Cleveland Street case, the "whether in public or private" clause of Section 11 of this Act had supposedly annihilated any possibility of swathing homosexuality in privacy.

There is no firm evidence in the Public Prosecution papers to suggest that Sir Augustus Stephenson subsequently realized the ways in which the legal implications of Section 11 affected his stance, and as the new gay historians have argued, the very existence of debate perhaps shows that Sir Stephenson's authority trumped any bombastic "innovations" of legislation. "Whether in public or in private" might have remained the melodramatic "democratic" righteousness of New Journalism, with little effect on how the establishment, in the form of the Home Office, actually operated. The Director of Public Prosecutions could simply choose not to prosecute—as it first seemed he would. But the new law, with its potential for "unbounded operation" through the "whether in public or private" clause, was now on the books, and was at least a sleeping giant. Sir Stephenson considered allowing the giant to snooze on for the protection of an aristocrat, a public figure, but then he decided to allow it to be awakened—by the competing public figure

---

[22] Jeffrey Weeks, *Sex, Politics and Society* 103–4.

of the telegraph boy. On Sunday, the fifteenth of September 1889, Sir Stephenson wrote an impassioned memo in which he reversed his original decision to protect Somerset and sent it to the Attorney General, Sir Richard Webster:

> Whatever may be said, and much may be said—as to the public policy of allowing *private* persons—being full-grown men to indulge their unnatural tastes—in private—or in such a way as not necessarily to come to public knowledge—in my judgement; the circumstances of this case demand the intervention of those whose *duty* it is to enforce the law and protect the children of respectable parents taken in to the service of the public, as these unfortunate boys have been, from being made the victims of the unnatural lusts of full-grown men—and no consideration of public scandal—owing to the position in society or sympathy with the family of the offender should militate against this *paramount duty*.
> (DPP1/95/1)[23]

This memorandum is riven with the fractured and diffracted meanings of the terms "public" and "private"; Stephenson uses the words repeatedly and with a number of different inferences. Phrases such as "in private—or in such a way as not necessarily to come to public knowledge," which suggests that sexual acts could be "public" but not "public knowledge," make it clear that public and private are not cleanly opposed principles when it comes to legal adjudications of sex in the late nineteenth century. Stephenson also tries to negotiate differences between concepts of "duty" and "law." He writes not of an absolute or inevitable authority of the law but of the governmental decision about whether or not to apply the law to Somerset. The "intervention" of which he speaks is not the unquestioned intervention of the law, but rather the intervention of those whose *civic duty* it is to enforce the law. His language very much reflects the cultural foment out of which Section 11 emanated: he echoes the paternalist call to protect the vulnerable from the supposedly unbounded lusts of "full-grown" men.

If Stephenson catches up the spirit of the law, he is much less certain about the letter of it, and particularly troubled by the public/private distinction it invokes. This was a new law, and indeed the transcripts of the Cleveland Street trial make many references to the "innovation" of Section 11 and the changes it brought.[24] Stephenson suggests that "much may

---

[23] This memorandum, dated Sunday, 15 September 1889, was sent via Stephenson's Assistant Director, Hamilton Cuffe, who later became Director of Public Prosecutions and in this capacity initiated the criminal proceedings against Oscar Wilde.

[24] The transcript for Wednesday, 18 September 1889, for example, records Mr. Poland, acting for boy-messenger Newlove, reminding the judge "section 11 gives your Lordship very full powers" (DPP1/95/1). Mr. Gill, appearing for Veck (one of the men accused of procuring the boys) talks of "the offence created by section 11" and points out that his client has "never had a charge against him before; he simply pleads guilty to the offence under the new Statute" (DPP1/95/1). While these comments are clearly, in part, a rhetoric employed to plead for leniency for their clients, the Recorder, Sir Thomas Chambers QC, also prefaced his sentencing of the boys thus: "You have pleaded guilty to these offences, all of them offences created by a recent Statute, making such acts as these misdemeanours" (DPP1/95/3).

be said" against the logic of this law and that there are advantages to allowing homosexual practices to remain under the cover of privacy. The reason Stephenson gives for overriding these advantages, overturning his original decision, and deciding to prosecute is one that effectively dismisses the issue of whether or not homosexual sex should be public or private. The passion of the memo builds to this point: Stephenson asserts that it is the nature of the boys' occupations that has prompted him to reconsider his decision; he subordinates all his misgivings to the fact that the boys involved in this affair were public servants employed by the Post Office. As postal workers, the boys were employees of the State, "taken in to the service of the public." Stephenson portrays the Post Office as a custodian; answerable to the "respectable parents" for whom it stands in, and he links the public nature of the boys' service to the duty of civil servants to disregard the shame prosecution would bring on members of the nobility. To do otherwise would make the Post Office look not like a custodian, but rather a pimp. The state would have taken these boys from their "respectable parents" and prostituted them to the "service of the public." The redefinition, then, produced between Section 11 and this memo, is a redefinition of who gets to be classed— and protected—as a public man. The Home Office's decision to prosecute performatively subordinated the fate of the socially eminent to that of the civil servant.

Stephenson's deliberations were under significant pressure from New Journalism. New Journalism crusaded loudly and particularly against aristocratic abuses of the poorer and, as it characterized them, morally vulnerable classes.[25] The press had got wind of the Cleveland Street story and cast the messenger-boys as victims of Britain's deviant nobility. On 12 September, the *Pall Mall Gazette* challenged Stephenson to defend why the aristocrats should "be allowed to escape scot free," warning him: "There has been too much of that kind of thing in the past. The wretched agents are run in and sent to penal servitude; the lords and gentlemen who employ them swagger at large and are even welcomed as valuable allies of the Administration of the day" (35). The *North London Press* published a column headed "Our Old Nobility" on 28 September 1889. The column covered one story about Lord Galloway sexually molesting a ten-year-old girl and also reported on the Cleveland Street Affair, under the heading "Noblemen Concerned in an Unspeakably Gross Case in the West End Are Allowed to Escape While Their Panders Are Mildly Punished" ("Our Old Nobility" 3). That one of these cases concerned homosexual sex is almost eclipsed; the paper portrays homosexual sex as the symptom of the broader crime of aristocratic degeneracy. *Reynolds's Gazette* commented similarly on the Cleveland case, deploring that there was "one law for

---

[25] As H. G. Cocks describes it: "Anti-aristocratic abuse of this kind borrowed extensively from a language of social purity that not only attacked the alleged aristocratic involvement in seduction and White Slavery, but also defined sexual depravity of all kinds as a form of dissipation, excess and cruelty" (92). This yoking of antiaristocratic rhetoric with attacks on homosexuality is a reminder that spectres of sexual and racial degeneracy were called up by the Left, albeit the bourgeois Left. As Foucault describes it, anti-Semitism and other doctrines of racial degeneracy were monstrously birthed from left-wing fanaticism. See Michel Foucault, "The Confession of the Flesh," in *Power/Knowledge: Selected Interviews and Other Writings 1972–1977*, ed. Colin Gordon, trans. Colin Gordon, Leo Marshall, John Mepham, and Kate Soper (New York: Pantheon, 1980), 222–24.

the rich and another for the poor" (29 September 1889 3). The report which appeared on 9 November in *St. Stephen's Review* makes a particularly fascinating parallel to Stephenson's memorandum: "Where public men are concerned in such a crushing accusation we have not only a right, but a duty, to demand an instant explanation, and as the matter is in the hands of the Government, the Government, for its own reputation, must see to it at once [...]. Our national boast is that we possess one and the same law for both rich and poor. This honoured boast is undergoing a very severe test indeed just now, and I trust it may come safely through the trying ordeal" (9 November 1889 4). Stephenson also decides that where public men are concerned the government has a duty to provide explanations, but with a crucial twist. Whereas *St. Stephens' Review* uses the term "public men" to mean the aristocrats, for Stephenson, the "public men" for whose sake there should not be a cover-up, are the boys, the *public servants* employed, he emphasizes, by the Post Office.

THE IMPORTANCE OF BEING IN "THE SERVICE"

By the late 1880s, the Post Office was well on its way to being the single largest employer in the country.[26] It had offices in the smallest villages and its insignia had become part of the landscape, on the "iron stumps" of pillar-boxes (invented, as I will describe in chapter 4, by Anthony Trollope) and on the uniformed bodies of its employees. The Post Office put a vernacular face on civic duty, and many referred to it simply as "The Service."[27] So when Simpson refers to the government as having a duty to protect its young employees, he is rearticulating the New Journalist idea that the overprivileged, degenerate few should not violate the many who better serve the nation and more properly represent the civic self. Henry Labouchère, author of Section 11, made a speech in the House of Commons on the scandal, and similarly emphasized the boys' occupation, in order to characterize them as victims of the men who ran the brothel:

> I know that evidence of informers is generally tainted, but the evidence of the boys is not nearly so tainted as would have been the evidence of one of these professional wretches. These boys were employed at the Post Office. They have been more sinned against than sinning, and it is not likely that they would have identified Lord Arthur Somerset unless they honestly believed he was the man who tempted them.
> (H. M. Hyde, *Cleveland Street* 28)[28]

---

[26] See Daunton, *Royal Mail* 193–94.
[27] See Simpson, Chester, Leitch, *The Cleveland Street Affair* 86.
[28] The "professional wretches" to whom Labouchère refers are Mr. Veck and Mr. Hammond, who were instrumental in procuring the boys. Veck was himself an ex–Post Office worker, who had been dismissed from the service for "improper conduct with telegraph messengers" and at the time of his arrest, lived with an eighteen-year-old man (H. M. Hyde, *Cleveland Street* 25). For more on the low status of the professional "Mary-ann" and the relative privilege of the part-time telegraph boys, see Morris B. Kaplan, *Sodom on the Thames* 189 and 202–3.

As in Stephenson's memorandum, it is the institution of the Post Office itself that influences Labouchère's reading of the boys' agency and innocence. His reference to the boys' occupation is simply stated, seemingly disconnected from the preceding or the following sentences; he does not explain why the nature of the boys' employment testifies to their character; rather, he invokes the Post Office as an unquestioned standard of trustworthiness. The Post Office functions as guarantor of the truthfulness of the messenger-boys' testimonies because Labouchère casts it as a place of public service, in contrast to the world of commerce implied in the phrase "professional wretches."

But the Post Office was not able to act the outraged parent very effectively. If the question of the boys' youth and vulnerability was used by political and newspaper commentators to absolve them from homosexuality, that same youth and vulnerability also reflected badly on the Post Office which, brothel-like, "procured" young boys into its service. A Cleveland Street case witness and Irish sex worker, John (also known as Jack) Saul, even testified that "a gentleman named Captain Le Barber used to visit […] and bring boys with him. He used to get the boys situations in the Post Office service."[29] Not only, then, were boys procured, but the Post Office jobs themselves were subject to procurement by pimps. The Post Office itself was thereby structurally implicated in the exploitation of boys. Boys were taken on by the Post Office and employed as messengers, but not trained for any other work. Instead of being apprentices, preparing for a permanent career, they were "boy labourers employed for their immediate commercial utility" and were dismissed upon reaching manhood (Daunton 202). Post-boys were the civil service's Peter Pans. In a dictionary of heterodox English, slang and phrases, *Passing English of the Victorian Era*, the entry for "boy" reads: "'Boy' (Bolton). Man. There are no men in Bolton—all are boys, even at ninety. This quality they share alone, throughout England, with post-boys—who never grow up" (Ware 46). Post-boys "never grew up" because for the most part they were shunted out of the Post Office, unskilled at the age of sixteen.[30] A constant stream of youngsters filled the jobs and thus the Boy Messenger was bound to a standardized prepubertal and early adolescent existence. He was similarly standardized through the Post Office uniform that he wore. The Post Office, which did not provide for the welfare of

---

[29] DPP1/95/4, 36.

[30] Oscar Wilde's Dorian Gray, the preeminent example of a young man who never grew up, was named after John Gray, a friend and lover of Wilde's, who was, for the six years immediately prior to meeting Wilde, a postal clerk. See Ellmann 307. The perennial youthfulness of post-boys had also struck others to cast it in a supernatural light. Earlier in the century, Charles Dickens had, in *The Pickwick Papers* (1836–37), rehearsed the notion that post-boys never die: "'Wos you ever called in,' inquired Sam, glancing at the driver, after a short silence, and lowering his voice to a mysterious whisper: 'wos you ever called in, ven you wos 'prentice to a sawbones, to wisit a postboy?' 'I don't remember that I ever was,' replied Bob Sawyer. 'You never see a postboy in that 'ere hospital […] 'No,' replied Bob Sawyer. 'I don't think I ever did.' 'Never know'd a churchyard were there wos a postboy's tombstone, or see a dead postboy, did you?' inquired Sam, pursuing his catechism. 'No,' rejoined Bob, 'I never did.' 'No!' rejoined Sam, triumphantly, 'Nor never will.'" Sam reminds his listener that "some wery sensible people" assert that postboys (and donkeys) are "immortal" and if that's not the case, they do at least "just rides off together, wun postboy to a pair in the usual way" (*Pickwick Papers* 810–11).

grown Boy Messengers, was not actually beneficently in loco parentis as Labouchère and Stephenson imagined. And the boys, who simultaneously "engaged in the carriage of Her Majesty's mails" and engaged in prostitution, simply, easily, and regularly conflated service to the civic state, which valued them for their youth and bearing alone, with service within a homoerotic economy that had an eye for exactly the same qualities.

The Post Office struggled for many years against the problem of Boy Messengers prostituting themselves. In his history of the Post Office, M. J. Daunton reveals that prostitution among telegraph boys had been a concern of the Post Office long before the Cleveland Street Affair. Daunton cites the papers of the Controller of the London Postal Service who in 1881 looked back with nostalgia to the days when postmen had been recruited as young men direct from the country, "with a fine physical constitution, somewhat blunt in manners, though sound in morals" (203). In place of these country innocents, he feared that "contaminated sources" and a "bad source of supply for Telegraph messengers," coupled with the failure "to ascertain the antecedents of the boys before admitting them to the Service," had caused this problem (Daunton 203). It was exacerbated, in his view, by the lack of supervision, frequent bouts of idleness and "the naturally demoralising influence of a street life on juvenile character" (Daunton 203). His language of impurity and contamination, all suggestive of "bad blood," resonates against metaphors of circulation, common in periodical fiction about the postal system, which figured the General Post Office as the nation's pumping heart.

All of the Post Office papers dealing with this subject struggle with the fact that the demands they placed on their own post-boys created the conditions for prostitution. The Cleveland Street Affair was prefaced by much smaller-scale scandals in the late 1870s around telegraph boy prostitution and in 1877, action was urgently demanded when the Post Office discovered that the boys had "a willingness to prostitute themselves even for very small sums. They had no particular liking for the vice, as a vice, but whatever dislike they had for it was entirely and easily overborne by the money which was tendered to them by their seducers" (Daunton 203–4).[31] On 17 December 1880, the Controller of the Circulation Department, Mr. T. Jeffery, wrote to the Secretary of the Post Office about recent incidences of drinking, gambling, and theft among Telegraph Messenger Boys, again linking this "tendency to the bad rather than the good" to the "source of our supply of force" (Post 30/468, 46391/88). Jeffery's letter makes it clear that he sees two issues at stake: first, the safety of the mails and second, the confidence of the public. He concludes that while the terms of employment for Boy Messengers are "economical in a pecuniary sense," the boys also cost the Service dearly as they are "attended by many evils, and lack that respectability without which not even a Government Department will long secure the confidence of the public" (Post 30/468, 46391/88). The report makes repeated reference to finding good "sources" of Boy Messengers and the importance of obtaining

---

[31] For originals, see Post 30/1924, E1976/1911; Post 30/468, E15611/1884, file III; Post 30/1052, E22956/1903, file I in the London Post Office Archives and Records Office.

FIGURE 1.3 Sketch of the Boy Messengers' domestic life at the Post Office..

a "superior class" of boy. As I shall explore at length in chapter 3, one of the best ways of obtaining a "superior class" of boy was to employ a girl, but the practical measures instigated to deal with the problem of the boys' degenerate behavior makes it clear that the Post Office interpreted "source" to mean "family." Jeffery's report notes that many boys came from households that only had "but one parent or none at all," and the Post Office subsequently appointed inspectors who could make random visits to the boys' homes and lodgings. They also employed "Matrons" for the boys' kitchens and leisure rooms at the Post Office (see figure 1.3). By trying to reconstruct a domestic household for the boys and instituting moral guardian figures who had jurisdiction over both work and home lives, the Post Office attempted to reinforce in the Boy Messengers a sense of duty and made the boys' moral welfare their responsibility. Were Boy Messengers employees, rent-boys or state-adopted sons? The Post Office was engaged in a complicated struggle to define the very thing it had played a great part in creating: the public servant.

DRESSED FOR THE JOB

In all of the interviews with the boys involved in the Cleveland Street case, police took great pains to establish whether or not the boys had been wearing their Post Office uniforms while they had sex. Some of them had. This not only threatened to disgrace or devalue the Queen's liveries, but also caused concern about whether the uniform affected the way that the boys and their bodies had been read. The uniform's purpose was to standardize the boys and make them easily identifiable as public servants. The principle of uniformity that had shaped Post Office reform from the early century onward was also applied to personnel; Post Office procedures imposed a strict standardization upon the bodies of the Boy Messengers.[32] When boys put on their uniforms, they were expected to remove all personal belongings, even tobacco, from their persons and leave them in the locker room. This was intended to ensure that the blue uniform functioned as a "badge of honesty" and marked the boys as now "engaged in the carriage of Her Majesty's mails"; every postal worker had to be "clean," and this rule was stringently enforced with routine spot checks.[33] It was one of these spot checks that had sparked the entire Cleveland Street Affair; the messenger-boy Swinscow was questioned after such a check revealed that he was carrying an irregular amount of money on his person. In 1890, in the aftermath of the Cleveland Street Affair, the newly formed Postal Telegraph Clerks Association pressed for the improvement of their conditions. In sharp contrast to their usual slow response to worker agitation,[34] the Post Office acted immediately—workers' wages were raised and the messenger-boys also received "smart new uniforms." The Postmaster-General, H. C. Raikes, said of the new outfits: "It should be impressed upon the boys that, wearing as they do the uniform of the Queen, they are under an obligation to conduct themselves in a manner which shall never bring that uniform into disrepute" (qtd. in Browne 124–25).

Somewhat endearingly, the Post Office utterly failed to realize the currency of "smart new uniforms" within a homosexual economy of desire. In "Your City Cousins," a poem published in 1892, the "Uranian" poet John Gambril Nicholson describes love for young uniformed boys, writing "Smart-looking lads are in my line; / The lad that gives my boots a shine, / The lad that works the lifts below, / The lad that's lettered G.P.O." (27). Just as the admonishing Raikes had emphasized that the boys' uniforms were the Queen's uniforms, this verse draws similar attention to the Royal insignia borne by the post-boys. The other boys provide services easily read as sexual—they "shine" or "work the lift below"; the Post Office messenger is simply "lettered" with his employers' initials, a pun playing on the "letters" he bears. The pun conflates the boy—and Nicholson's desire—with his delivery work and the institution that employs him; his role as deliverer is enough to mark him as sexually available. Nicholson was not the only admirer of the uniforms. Similar appreciation was expressed in an unsigned essay titled "On the Appreciation of Trifles" that appears

---

[32] Post Office records note that in 1870, when the GPO absorbed the private sector telegraph companies and their employees, the boys were called "Telegraph Messengers," a nomenclature which held until 1908, when their title was changed to "Boy Messengers" (*Post Office Circular* [1908] 316). Throughout both the Cleveland Street materials and other Post Office papers relating to these boys, however, the term "Boy Messenger" is used from 1870 onward. The persistent use of this term emphasized how these boys' youth was as much a mark of their trade as their uniform. It is also indicative of employment low in both class and payment, as "boy" was the term generally used of a laborer, regardless of age.

[33] For the regulations and concerns about boys' uniforms, see Colin Simpson, Lewis Chester, and David Leitch, *The Cleveland Street Affair* 16–17.

[34] For an exhaustive account of labor disputes and the repressive conditions of work in the General Post Office, see H. G. Smith's *A History of Postal Agitation: From 50 Years Ago Till the Present Day* (1900).

in the single-issue, Oxford-published 1894 magazine *The Chameleon*—the magazine that was invoked as evidence of Oscar Wilde's degenerate literary tastes in his trials. One of the "trifles" that the author deeply appreciates is the post-boy. He thanks the Post Office for supplying these boys, writing, "I am sure that we must all constantly feel that we are under the deepest obligations to the Government officials connected with the Post Office, for filling our streets with the graceful neatly uniformed figures of those that bear our messages and our telegrams" (58).[35] Just as Postmaster-General Raikes had used a language of indebtedness and written of the boys' "obligation" to the Queen, the *Chameleon* "queen" writes of being "obliged" to the government for filling the streets with uniformed boys. Both the postmaster and the magazine writer point to the same conjunction exemplified by the uniform: obligation and duty. The question is, whom do the boys serve? Their uniformed bodies become a site for a game of tug-of-love. The boys, the *Chameleon* writer claims, "bear our messages." This expression of ownership forms a conscious shunt between the homosocial, the heterosexual, and the homosexual, referring at once to everyone's messages and the messages of *Chameleon* readers in particular. The subject-position designated by the word "our" functions much like what Eve Kosofsky Sedgwick calls the "treacherous middle stretch" between the obviously homosexual and the obviously heterosexual, attaching itself to both "the British people," generically, and homosexual *Chameleon* readers, specifically. Sedgwick describes how the middle stretch produces "homosexual panic"—the fear of being "misrecognized" as homosexual. The *Chameleon* writer recognizes such a middle stretch when he sees one, and—writing for a coterie audience—engages the ambiguity of "our," campily conjuring pleasure in the place of panic. The hauteur of the conceit being, of course, that the heterosexuals are the infiltrators and that queers own the place.

This is the queer coterie taking over the town square. When the homosexual assumes the pronouns "us" and "our," they stake a claim in the grammar of the social. Henry Abelove explores this notion in his introduction to *Deep Gossip*. He parses the Allen Ginsberg line from which the title *Deep Gossip* is taken. Ginsberg memorializes Frank O'Hara as having had "a common ear for our deep gossip" (xii). "Our": the word is allowed to splay wide open. Abelove's intrigue fixes on Ginsberg's use of the pronoun "our" to find it emphatically possessive: he notes that "illicit speculation, information, knowledge" form "an indispensable resource for those who are in any sense or measure disempowered." Jeff Nunokawa highlights a similarly playful use of the word "our" by a gay writer in his essay "'All the Sad Young Men': AIDS and the Work of Mourning." Nunokawa analyzes a line in James Merrill's 1988 elegy for David Kalstone that makes reference to "'our' Venetian tailor." Nunokawa comments: "'Our' tailor is, *mutatus mutandis*, the Italian designer who caters first to a gay coterie, and whose clothes eventually enwrap unsuspecting heterosexuals in an unspoken embrace that has supplied generations of homosexuals

---

[35] Richard Ellmann writes of *Chameleon* that it "attracted adverse comment in *To-Day* on 14th of December from Jerome K. Jerome [...]. *To-Day* recommended police action. More important, the *Chameleon* fell into the hands of Queensberry, who [...] was still more inflamed" (428).

a certain passing amusement" (318). Merrill, Nunokawa, and the *Chameleon* author enjoy the notion that the public at large not only contains, but also provides for gay subjects. The government officials who fill the streets with attractive young men are unwitting, and the straight customers of the Venetian tailor are "unsuspecting." These writers joke that the world was designed for homosexuals. And of course, both passages do indeed turn around design in the form of clothes: the Italian suiting and the "graceful, neat uniform" that distinguishes telegraph boys. As messengers, the boys literally traverse the "treacherous space" of public streets, delivering both "our messages" and their own uniformed bodies to the doorsteps of, among others, *Chameleon* readers.[36]

The *Chameleon* author writes in straight drag, impersonating the lofty tones ("deepest obligations") of propriety. The author, as well as the boys, traverses a treacherous space; treacherous because he flirts with the Establishment, as much as with the mail boys themselves. He portrays himself as bound, "obliged," to the "Government officials," thus reminding the reader that the uniform so admired on the boys is *Her Majesty*'s uniform. In other words, the author imagines his illegal desires to be state sanctioned and sponsored, bearing the ultimate stamp of legitimacy—the Queen's livery. This piece of literature, published almost ten years after legislation that criminalized homosexuality, playfully flaunts the radical interconnectedness of "transgressive" desire with the discourse and institutions that deem that desire transgressive.[37]

The flirtatious and performative ambiguities of homoeroticism were not exclusive to a homosexual coterie. It is important to assert that a constitutive component of homosexual panic and anxiety was titillation and pleasure. D. A. Miller's work on "Secret Subjects,

---

[36] The *Chameleon* author's humorous conceit that his readers are "provided for" also emphasizes a class distinction between the humble messenger-boys and the higher-class, university-educated *Chameleon* readers. This returns us to the *Scots Observer* barb that I cited in the introduction to this chapter, through which it is implied that the "unnaturalness" of homosexuality bridges, matches, or even incurs the unnaturalness of cross-class association between lowly telegraph boys and noblemen. An earlier nineteenth-century text similarly pairs civil servants and noblemen under the umbrella of effeminacy. Gustave Doré and Blanchard Jerrold's 1872 publication *London a Pilgrimage* cast both as dapper flâneur-figures who mingle in public places; "gentlemen who live at ease, amble to and fro the early burst in the park; and Her Majesty's civil servants honour the pavement, each looking as though he had just stepped out of a band-box, and protested somewhat at the stern duty that compelled him to emerge before the day was aired—to use Beau Brummel's delightfully whimsical phrase" (115–16).

[37] Diana Fuss elegantly articulates this interrelationship, between heterosexuality and homosexuality, the illegal and the structures of legality: "The difference between the hetero and the homo, however, is that the homo becomes identified with the very mechanism necessary to define and defend any sexual border. Homosexuality, in a word, becomes the excluded; it stands in for, paradoxically, that which stands without. But the binary structure of sexual orientation, fundamentally a structure of exclusion and exteriorization, nonetheless constructs that exclusion by prominently including the contaminated other in its oppositional logic. The homo in relation to the hetero, much like the feminine in relation to the masculine, operates as an indispensable interior exclusion—an outside which is inside interiority making the articulation of the latter possible, a transgression of the border which is necessary to constitute the border as such" (Fuss 3). The anonymous admirer of the Post Office boys plays with precisely this function of homosexual desire, both to uphold the established order and hint at its never acknowledged complicity.

Open Secrets," which lies at the heart of Sedgwick's later, fuller articulation of the open secret in *Epistemology of the Closet*, touches on this issue of pleasure. Miller reminds us that Basil Hallward in *The Picture of Dorian Gray* declares to Lord Henry that he has "grown to love secrecy. It seems to be the one thing that can make modern life mysterious or marvelous to us" (qtd. in D. A. Miller 195). Although Miller does not follow the quote further, the ensuing conversation between Hallward and Lord Henry reveals how the pleasures of secrecy are common to many, including married persons. Lord Henry says that "the one charm of marriage is that it makes a life of deception absolutely necessary for both parties [...]. My wife is very good at it" (Wilde, *Dorian Gray* 26). Marriage works if the two "parties" purposely miscommunicate. Through Lord Henry, Wilde proposes that heterosexual social formations are salvaged through the machineries associated with homosexual living: deception and secrecy. The secret, in other words, is not always "homosexuality," but the media of secrecy is always homosexually informed.[38]

To illustrate the importance of queer media to stories of heterosexual transgression, I turn to another exchange in which the depravity of telegraph boys is encoded, and the coding itself functions as flirtation—this time between straight men. In January 1877, Anthony Trollope visited the telegraph office in the main Post Office building at St. Martin's-le-Grand and observed the women who staffed it at work transmitting telegrams. I discuss Trollope's take on these girls in chapter 3, but the telegraph boys interested him as well. In a letter to Donald Macleod, editor of *Good Words*, Trollope wrote:

> Some weeks since I went to see these young women at work and composed a little story about one. This, when written, seemed to be nice, and I took it to Ludgate Hill [...]. Then Mr. Isbister suggested (on hearing my description of the girls work and of the excellence of their conduct) that I should give some such description in a separate article [...]. I think you will be gratified at the success of this branch of female employment.
>
> (*Letters* January 1877, 2: 705)[39]

William Isbister, an editor who later bought the publishing side of *Good Words*, subsequently suggested that Trollope write another piece about the telegraph boys working at

---

[38] This assertion is distinct from that which James Eli Adams makes in his 1995 study on styles of Victorian manhood. He writes: "It is of course the case that male-male desire throughout the Christian West has tended to be cloaked in secrecy, but this does not entail—as a good deal of recent literary and cultural criticism tends to assume—that secrecy always speaks of homoerotic desire" (Adams 13). While rightly claiming that we should not assume an equals sign between "secrecy" and "homoeroticism," and that secrecy can always contain more than homoeroticism, he does not allow homoeroticism to contain more than secrecy. Adams's thesis that "gender deviance in Victorian culture [...] is a social category more inclusive, and more complex, than the assignment of transgressive sexuality" (13) ultimately relies upon a model of homosexuality as marginal and exclusive: not, in the end, either "inclusive" or "complex."

[39] Both the factual article, entitled "The Young Women at the London Telegraph Office" and the fictional story, called "The Telegraph Girl," were published in *Good Words* later that year.

the General Post Office. On 9 February 1877, Trollope wrote to Isbister saying: "I will look into the boys and see what can be made of it" (*Letters* 9 February 1877, 2: 715).

A couple of months later, he wrote to Isbister again, refusing the commission on the basis of what he had found when he "looked into" the boys: "When I made inquiry I found that [the telegraph boys] were as unsatisfactory as the girls were the reverse" (*Letters* 17 April 1877, 2: 718). He does not give details, writing instead that he had called by the office one day to tell Isbister about his findings, but Isbister had not been there. Three days later, he sent Isbister another letter, one which is notable for its diversion from business-speak into humor: "Some time when I am passing Ludgate Hill I will look in and tell you about these wicked little boys. I hope they did not learn their bad manners when engaged on your premises" (*Letters* 20 April 1877, 2: 719). Trollope will not write about the boys, and he says he will only explain his decision to Isbister in person. This is not the consequence of sober discretion or the proprieties of epistolary practice, however; the tone of Trollope's second letter is flirtatious. This letter stages and plays upon the difference between what can be written and what can be told in person and in doing so, gets away with a sizeable innuendo.[40]

The "wickedness" to which Trollope refers is homosexual sex. As I've mentioned, the trouble with telegraph boys came to a minor head in 1877, when an internal inspectorate of the General Post Office had demanded urgent action regarding the prevalence of prostitution among telegraph boys. Like the later Cleveland Street scandal, this inquiry placed great weight on the cross-class relations that this homosex revealed: three telegraph boys were found to have been sexually "corrupted" by a socially prominent man of high class and political connection.[41] This man, James Smith, himself emphasized the boys' lower class when he petitioned the Home Secretary that the "testimony of lads who admitted having allowed themselves to be defiled for five shillings" needed more corroboration. His solicitor had informed him that "the crime for which I am sentenced has been very prevalent amongst the Telegraph lads and that many have been found out and dismissed in consequence and that the authorities were determined to prosecute me [...] as a warning to others."[42] Smith's appeal (which failed and he was jailed for life) invokes

---

[40] Trollope's innuendo is even more impressive because he had in the past encountered problems with the suitability of his material for *Good Words*. Trollope's work had gone unprinted in *Good Words* on one earlier occasion. In 1863 the magazine's editor, Norman Macleod, had asked Trollope for a novel. Trollope protested that his work was too worldly for *Good Words*, a magazine that characterized itself as having a "distinctively Christian spirit." "Worldly" is a word that the devout Mrs. Bolton in *John Caldigate* glosses as meaning "ungodly" (*JC* 577). Trollope himself, however, believed that amusement was not incompatible with a godly life, and his narrative voice elsewhere gently suggests the unreasonableness of such a view: "The Babingtons were worldly [...]. But if worldliness and religion are terms opposed to each other, then they were not worldly" (*JC* 149). Pressed by Macleod, Trollope reluctantly submitted *Rachel Ray*. Macleod did, however, eventually decide against printing it. Sally Mitchell points out that the magazine became less restricted as the century progressed, but Trollope, ever astute to the literary marketplace, still modified his language for this magazine (Mitchell 145–49).

[41] As in the Cleveland Street Affair, the 1877 scandal concerned the so-called sexual corruption of telegraph boys by a socially prominent man of higher class. For more on this case, see Brady, 89–90.

[42] James Smith, First Petition to the Home Secretary, April 1877, PRO HO 144/20/58480

that particular relation of "one to many" that is so postal. Smith appeals by saying that lots of the telegraph boys do this, but he fears he will be singled out to pay for their crimes. And the idea that he would serve as a warning to "others" means, in turn, that there are lots of James Smiths in the world. Boys become johns and johns become boys ... echoing the way that Trollope, scared off by homosex, turns post-boys into post-girls. Trollope's references to the messenger-boys' "wicked conduct" are clearly allusions to the discovery of this "vice" among them. Trollope's letters to Isbister stage and manage the (non-)disclosure of a secret. They simultaneously tell and do not tell. It might appear from the 17 April letter that Trollope is unwilling to use the medium of the post to discuss the homosexual adventures of the Post Office delivery boys. Trollope's coy claim that he can only reveal the wickedness *in person*, at Isbister's *office*, however, can also be read as sexually suggestive, especially in light of Trollope's subsequent suggestion, in the 20 April letter, that Isbister took advantage of the proximity of the workplace to initiate boys into deviant ways. Since this entire correspondence occurs in the context of Trollope's and Isbister's shared understanding that the piece would not be appropriate for publication in the Christian-oriented magazine, it is in the end, a shared joke about the necessities and nature of discretion. D. A. Miller's theorization of the open secret is again a useful model:

> We [...] inevitably surrender our privileged position as readers to whom all secrets are open by "forgetting" our knowledge for the pleasures of suspense and surprise [...]. In this light, it becomes clear that the social function of secrecy [...] is not to conceal knowledge, so much as to conceal the knowledge of knowledge.
>
> (206)

Although Miller's comments are about novel reading, it can be argued that Trollope's letter-writing performs the pleasures of secrecy in much the same way. Trollope actively participates in the concealing (nonpublication) of the knowledge of the knowledge, but he also delightedly dabbles in homoerotic revelation. Like the "Appreciation of Trifles" author, Trollope forms a homoerotics around both the noun and the pronoun of "our messages."

ALIAS WILDE

A pronoun is a part of speech that is thoroughly relational, intelligible, and instrumental only because it stands in the stead of the noun. It takes the place of the noun and marks that place. It is by its location—its address—that it is understood. A pronoun enables us to "designate an object without naming it" (OED), and this capacity of the pronoun brings to mind the construction that came to denote homosexuality: "The love that dare not speak its name." Wilde's lover, Lord Alfred Douglas, first used the phrase in his poem "Two Loves," which was also published in that single issue of the *Chameleon*, alongside "On the Appreciation of Trifles." The phrase is uttered by the second of two youths, who answers "What is thy name?" with the reply "My name is Love." The first youth protests, "He lieth, for his name is Shame, But I am Love" whereupon "said the other, 'Have thy will, / I am the love that dare not speak its name.'" The poem's topos of interchangeable, indeterminate, or disavowed nomenclature fits precisely with the *name* of the magazine in which the poem was printed: *The Chameleon*. The chameleon is a creature that can change hue to match contiguous objects or its environment. The magazine underscored its invocation of morphed and relational identities through its subtitle: "A Bazaar of Dangerous and Smiling Chances," a line that is taken from Robert Louis Stevenson's 1885 story *The Dynamiter*, co-written with Fanny Van De Grift Stevenson.[43] The dynamiter of the title, who describes himself as "nameless by day" (Stevenson/ Van De Grift 115), has traveled under many aliases, "Yet that which I most prize, that which is most feared, hated, and obeyed, is not a name to be found in your directories; it is not a name current in post-offices or banks [...] by night, and among my desperate followers, I am the redoubted Zero" (Stevenson/ Van De Grift 116. *The Dynamiter* is a story of passing; passing that is achieved first through the infinitely plural indexes of "post-offices or banks" and then under the protection of a "nothing" ("zero") name. Through assuming the "anyone" of the post office and bank lists, the dynamiter seeks to become "no-one," to un-name himself. The nothingness of this name, this non-name, is a source of power and commands fear and obedience.

But being unnamed also produces peril. Oscar Wilde was accused, in his 1895 trials, of being the author of a story, published anonymously in *The Chameleon*, entitled "The Priest and the Acolyte." The prosecution was attacking Wilde by scrutinizing his literary works for signs of homosexuality, and they turned from works published under his own name to this story, charging him with its authorship—which Wilde vigorously denied. The story was signed only with an "X" and despite Wilde's scornful repudiation of the text, his name was reiteratively drawn into association with it. The prosecution tried to build a case for Wilde's alliance with the story by arguing that Wilde had contributed to the same magazine, that he knew the editor very well, that he had himself been an Oxford undergraduate and the magazine was made by and circulated between Oxonians. The prosecution, in other words, pursued a theory that might be called proximate authorship. The publication's dispersed signature made in the form of the anonym, the "X" that is itself a proxy and stands for "anyone" (even, of course, the illiterate), allowed the prosecution to put a return address on the story and send it back to Wilde. The story was in fact written by Oscar Wilde's friend, and the editor of *The Chameleon*, Jack Bloxam, though this was not revealed during trial proceedings. The defense team's attempts to pin authorship on Wilde were attempts to make Bloxam's anonym "X" be read as "Wilde," be read as "homosexual." But if the defense wanted to damn Wilde through proximate authorship and guilt by association, this associative "guilt" was exactly the erotic thrill sought by Wilde and Bloxam themselves as they played with the "dangerous and smiling chances" of pronouns set adrift

---

[43] Stevenson uses it to refer to "the pavement of the city" 37.

among addressers and addressees. The "X" with which Bloxam signed the scandalous essay not only conceals, but also reveals his identity because it is the letter buried in the middle of his name: he takes the universal anonym and reinscribes himself through it, making it his own private joke. Wilde, too, had also interwoven Jack Bloxam's first and second names into his play about naming and the significance or insignificance thereof: *The Importance of Being Earnest* (1895). Jack/John Bloxam became Jack/John Moncrieff and "Lady Bloxham" who is, pointedly, a *renter*...of one of Jack's properties in Belgrave Square. These switched names and occupations of a temporary address are the floating signifiers through and between which a homosexual way of life can be both hidden and construed.

The Importance of Being Earnest explicates the benefits of identity confusion and obfuscation through Algernon's practice of the art of Bunburying: the invention of a fictional friend whose needs call one away from relatives and other unpleasant social commitments. Christopher Craft has described how Bunburying dances a merry jig amidst the constrictions of the "technically unspeakable—*non nominandum inter Christianos*."[44] Craft claims that Wilde refuses "to chafe under this stricture against representation" and instead "inverts it by inserting Bunbury into the text behind the ostentatious materiality of an empty signifier, a name without a being, a pure alias." Thus the gay male body becomes what Craft calls "an atopic body, a body constitutively 'somewhere else at present'" (117–18). My interest is the explicitly postal mechanism by which Wilde achieves this "pure alias" that allows for a gay "atopic body." It is the signaling technology of the telegraph. When Aunt Augusta requests that Algernon come and witness married love at a dinner party, a telegram conveniently intervenes:

> ALGERNON. It is a great bore, and, I need hardly say, a terrible disappointment to me, but the fact is I have just had a telegram to say that my poor friend Bunbury is very ill again. (*Exchanges glances with JACK.*) They seem to think I should be with him.
>
> (36)

Telegraphy provides the anonymous authority that can trump the formidable Aunt Augusta's thrusting heterosexuality: "they" think that Algernon should be at the bedside of Bunbury. As in "our messages," the pronoun "they" procures social respectability and then pimps it out, with a wink and a nod ("*Exchanges glances*"), to fellow homosexuals. Jack receives the signal and amplifies it, later killing off his own version of "Bunbury," his imaginary brother Earnest. Once again, it is a telegram that delivers the blow:

> JACK He died abroad; in Paris, in fact. I had a telegram last night from the manager of the Grand Hotel.
>
> (55)

---

[44] Christopher Craft, *Another Kind of Love: Male Homosexual Desire in English Discourse, 1850–1920* (Berkeley: University of California Press, 1994), 117.

The invented character who allowed Jack to roam abroad dies abroad, and the news of his death is conveyed by the technology whose name means "writing at a *distance*": *tele*-graphy. The telegraph exchange is the sine qua non for the production of aliases and atopicality.

Stevenson's dynamiter protects his criminalized self and procures mobility through an "empty signifier" in the form of his alias "Zero." This no-name is not his only cover. He *also* finds the facility of an empty signifier through the crowd of commerce and correspondence: by day he adopts *any and all* of the names "current in post-offices or banks." In a postal age, the systematization of persons and their addresses can be used as routes for a criminalized identity. Generating multiple identities can allow one to navigate social codings that require certain kinds of self at certain moments and places. The art of "Bunburying" is less about disguising a real self and more about producing, chameleonlike, the self appropriate to the place and moment.

The etymology of "alias" shows that the term has roots in the notion of the version or the variant: it means "at another time, in another way" (OED). The characters in *Importance*, and indeed the play itself, get away with inversion by being what Craft calls polytropic—generating multiple, adaptable versions of themselves. "Bunburyism releases a polytropic sexuality," Craft observes, that is mobile, evanescent, and "traverses, Ariel-like, a fugitive path through oral, genital, anal, and aural ports" (119). In Wilde's play, the self becomes what Lady Bracknell calls a "Terminus," a place that is itself no-place, but rather a ganglion of ports, arrivals, departures, exchanges, and wanderings.[45] A terminus facilitates and bureaucratizes passing and self-invention. When Gwendolen solicits Jack's country address and asks, "There is a good postal service, I suppose? It may be necessary to do something desperate. That of course will require serious consideration. I will communicate with you daily," (47) Algernon is quietly writing the address on his shirt-cuff. He then picks up the Railway Guide to plan his sylleptic passage to the Hertfordshire home, and another identity. A postal address permits Algie the homosexual meanderings he calls Bunburying and it also permits meanderings through heterosexuality: Gwendolen inquires about the postal service in order to perform cartoonishly heterosexual poses. Postal and train routes function as thoroughfares that both metaphorize and literally enable the production of alternate selves and alternate erotics. To be delivered by post or train is to be rendered removed from oneself and made subject to myriad possible encounters with other subjects.

POSTMAN'S KNOCK

The Cleveland Street scandal had shown that the postman could be entangled sexually, and he could also be addressed romantically, imagined—as Gwendolyn describes it—as a constitutive part of bearing love-letters. The parlor game "postman's knock," in which letters are paid for by kisses, was prefigured by music hall songs featuring

---

[45] Joseph Bristow (ed.), *The Importance of Being Earnest and Related Writings* 77. All subsequent references pertain to this edition.

handsome postmen knocking on doors with romance twinkling in their eyes (see figure 1:1).[46] Several years later, Giles Lytton Strachey, while writing his last literary work, *Elizabeth and Essex* (1928), sent passionate verse to the man with whom he'd fallen in love, hailing the postman who would deliver it by inscribing the envelope:

> Deliver this to SENHOUSE (Roger)
>   I prithee, postman debonair!
> He is the handsome upstairs lodger
> At number 14 BRUNSWICK SQUARE.[47]

The coy deflection of affection through the "postman debonair," making him the rhyming partner of the beloved's address, elaborates and amplifies the flirtation. This amplification is achieved in part by decorating the postman's duty with the curlicues of pleasure and bequest ("prithee"). The postman is duty bound to deliver the note, but how much more pleasurable would the exchange be if that duty was made to blush and tingle.[48] The messenger is thus the message.

If the messenger is the message, then half the pleasure is that of the sanctioned public exposure of the message. The "secret" of homosexual desire struts through the street in natty official attire ("smart new uniforms") and knocks on the doors of those to whom the secret is addressed. The Cleveland Street trial did not intimidate everyone with an eye for a handsome telegraph boy—instead it ushered the figure more fully into the gay male vernacular. Just four years after the scandal, Aubrey Beardsley wrote to Oscar Wilde's closest friend, Robert Ross, archly joking:

> I suppose you've heard all about the *Salomé* Row. I can tell you I had a warm time of it between Lane and Oscar and Co. For one week the numbers of telegraph and messenger boys who came to the door was simply scandalous.
> (Wilde, *Letters* November 1893, 574).

Salomé was beset by disputes about the obscenity of Beardsley's drawings and the question of how Lord Alfred Douglas's name should appear on the play. In Beardsley's letter,

---

[46] The Oxford English Dictionary has a 1927 entry for "postman's knock" that makes it clear the game was already very well known. See OED entry for "postman's knock." "Paying" for mail with kisses is itself a romance of a past era: the pre–Penny Post era when letters had to be paid for by the receiver, rather than the sender.

[47] H. Montgomery Hyde, *The Love That Dared Not Speak Its Name: A Candid History of Homosexuality in Britain* (Boston: Little, Brown, 1970), 195–96.

[48] A later, American, and anxious example of the relation between the postal functionary and the homosexual can be found in Tennessee Williams's 1941 play *Auto-Da-Fe*. The protagonist, a young postal worker called Eloi, obtains a "lewd photograph" by intercepting mail sent from a university student to an antique dealer in New Orleans. Eloi decides to visit the student to warn him about sending such materials in the mail but panics when the student becomes "suggestive." Once again, the gay *male* delivers himself in place of the *mail*.

however, these potentially sexually scandalous problems are waved aside in favor of the delicious conceit that Beardsley was inundated with suitors in the form of telegraph and messenger-boys and/or the correspondents they served. In the wake of the Cleveland Street Affair, this *was* indeed scandalous, and Beardsley enjoys it as such. Even Oscar Wilde himself, after serving his sentence in Reading Gaol and writing from miserable exile in France, indulges in a similar postal tease. Oscar writes to Robert Ross mentioning that he had not received a copy of "Bosie's latest success" even though he knew it had been sent. Out of this failed correspondence with his faithless—indeed, treacherous—lover, Wilde finds wry solace in the notion of a poetic postal functionary: "Some lyrical postman stole it, I suppose."[49]

"DID YOU WRITE HIM ANY BEAUTIFUL LETTERS?"

That Wilde was able to joke about a thieving, amorous postman is particularly poignant given that much of the evidence used against him in his trials was letters that came from what Henry James referred to as a "nest of almost infant blackmailers."[50] During the first of Oscar Wilde's three 1895 trials—the prosecution for libel brought by Wilde against the Marquis of Queensberry—courtroom tension surrounding Wilde's letters to Lord Alfred Douglas ran high. Both prosecution and defense used the letters in their opening addresses, aiming to establish resoundingly different readings of Wilde and his "nature."[51] For the defense to succeed in typifying Wilde as a sodomite, it was essential that they should characterize the letters as the natural productions of a sodomitical man.[52] The ground over which the prosecution and defense fought was whether the letters were private correspondences intended for an audience of one or public texts written for a mass of readers. Wilde and his barrister Sir Edward Clarke attempted to deny the correlation of the letters to Wilde's sexual nature, arguing that the most romantic of them was not in essence a letter, but rather a prose poem—and one which had been submitted for publication in the *Yellow Book*. This was an effort to sabotage the argument they knew the defense would try to establish—that Wilde's "extraordinary" (Holland 104, 110) letters were textual evidence of extraordinary sexual practices.

---

[49] *Letters*, 3 July 1899, 1157.

[50] Henry James, *Letters* 291–92.

[51] Oscar Wilde's trial has recently been the subject of exhaustive studies, despite the disappearance of the official trial transcripts; any quotation of the courtroom exchange is therefore approximate, but now as fully documented as possible. My references to the courtroom cross-examinations are taken from Merlin Holland's *Irish Peacock & Scarlet Marquess: The Real Trial of Oscar Wilde* (London and New York: Fourth Estate, 2003).

[52] The term "homosexual" was not used in the trial. I generally use the term "homosexual" both in recognition that this term was in development at the end of the nineteenth century, and for clarity's sake. For succinct histories of the terminology ranging from "inversion" to "homogenic" to "heterosexual," see Ed Cohen, *Walk on the Wilde Side* 9–14; Chris White, *Nineteenth-Century Writings on Homosexuality: A Sourcebook* 1–6; and Jeffrey Weeks, *Sex and Society: The Regulation of Sexuality Since 1800* 96–121.

In his opening speech, defense counsel Edward Carson attacked Clarke's "refer[ring] to the letter which has been called a sonnet" as "a thinly veiled attempt to cover the real nature of this letter" (Holland 262). Both Carson and Clarke, therefore, worked on the seemingly paradoxical understanding that to publish a text, to expose it to a reading public, could be a way of "covering" or hiding its nature.[53] Carson's subsequent questions tried to establish norms of epistolary practice. He pressed Wilde about whether his letters were "exceptional," "ordinary," or "the kind of letter that one man writes towards another man" (Holland 110). Carson based his questioning on analyses of style and form. He established that Wilde considered it a "beautiful" and "exceptional" letter, and asked if Wilde often wrote letters of this kind. Carson was to use these letters throughout the trial as a typological tool, a means for characterizing Wilde's relationships with young men as having the "stamp" of perversity: he repeatedly punctuated his cross-examination with the refrain, "Did you write him any beautiful letters?"

Carson's rhetorical reiteration of this question turned "writing beautiful letters" into a euphemism for homosexual relations and sought to establish that Wilde's deviance was both unmentionable by the virtuous and deliberately encoded by the perpetrators and their type. Furthermore, the reiteration suggested that Carson, and the court, had broken this code, revealing the public significations of a private language. Wilde and his counsel resisted this construction by "sonnetizing" the letter. They sought to give the correspondence the garb of public Art, not only presenting its desires and emotions as a fiction, but also arguing that a text as accessible as a published sonnet cannot have the enclosed meaning—in this case, homosexual sex—of the private text that has gone astray. Prosecution and defense counsels concurred that the question of whether the text was a letter or a published poem fundamentally changed how it should be read and absolutely changed whether or not it reflected Wilde's sexual self. The point turned, therefore, on a seeming paradox: publication—the printing and distributing of a text to a (theoretically) wide audience concealed, rather than revealed the "meaning" of the text as Carson construed it. Public exposure was no exposure at all, but, conversely, a cover for the text's "real nature."

It could be said that Wilde's downfall was precipitated by lack of an envelope. Wilde initiated libel proceedings against the Marquis of Queensberry because of the calling card Queensberry had left at Wilde's club that read "Oscar Wilde posing Somdomite [sic]." For a charge of libel to be brought, the so-called libelous statement has to be published.

---

[53] Clarke and Carson's exchange over the sonnetized letter calls to mind, of course, another nineteenth-century story of a stolen and disguised epistle: Edgar Allan Poe's 1844 "The Purloined Letter." The letter in Poe's story, stolen from a bedroom, is famously concealed from the diligent, methodical police through being openly displayed on a letter-rack. Just as Carson sought to find the "real nature" of the private Wilde, the police in Poe are intent upon revealing interiors. They relentlessly probe the insides of cushions, chair legs, and tabletops before Dupin reveals that the thief had "deposited the letter immediately beneath the nose of the whole world, by way of best preventing any portion of that world from perceiving it" (Muller and Richardson 20). The letter is further disguised by having been "turned, as a glove, inside out, re-directed, and re-sealed" (22). In other words, the letter is, like Wilde and his sonnetized letter, inverted.

It has to be made in a public venue. The marquis had made plenty of accusations by letter before, but this time he left the card at Wilde's club, and he left it unsheathed and readable. As Richard Ellmann points out, this method of accusation left "no hope of confining the matter to private correspondence" (438).[54] In the first trial, the club's porter, Sidney Wright, was called to the stand to testify. Wright recalled:

> He handed me the card [...] on which he had written in my presence: "For Oscar Wilde ponce and somdomite." [...] On the card was printed "Marquis of Queensberry." He said, "Give this card to Oscar Wilde." On the back of the card I wrote the time and date on which the card was handed to me. I put the card in the envelope [...] and addressed it to "Oscar Wilde Esq." I did not seal the envelope.
> (Holland 4)

Much attention is paid in the trial to Wright having placed the card in an envelope (see, for example, Holland 44 and 20). Wright claims that he looked at the card "but I could not understand what was written on it" (Holland 44)—a not unreasonable claim given Queensberry's splenetic handwriting and lousy spelling—but more likely (given that he can recite the message in court) a cover for the awkward fact that he was the publishing agent, the reading "public" through whom a calling card was transformed into libel. He also provided the card with a proto-postmark, in the form of the time and date that he marked on the card. Wilde's own counsel calls Wright "a very sensible man" for having put the card in an envelope (Holland 37). The sensible envelope was, however, too late. And when Carson derides Wilde for claiming his "my own boy" letter to Lord Alfred Douglas was a sonnet, Carson asks:

> CARSON: Did it go as it is there, by itself in an envelope?
> WILDE: Yes, in an envelope—not torn, of course.
> CARSON: No, and perhaps not so soiled? (Holland 104).

The enveloped letter presented in court as evidence is torn and soiled because of its sub-postal, irregular circulations by blackmailers. Carson tries to reduce this "beautiful letter" to its grubby materiality, inferring that a dirty envelope contained shameful secrets (Holland 58). Wilde tosses his head at Carson's attempt to open a door that is already open: he retorts that he only writes for publication (Holland 58). Carson tries again to imply that Wilde's postal practices are perverse, this time accusing Wilde of "constantly communicating [...] by telegram" with young men not of his own class (Holland 158, see also 174 and 116). Carson professes bafflement at what such a mismatched couple of men

---

[54] Ellmann also describes the confusion—still reflected in critical studies—about whether the card said "posing Somdomite" or "ponce and Somdomite." The confusion derives both from bad handwriting and the legal shuffles made to make his accusation stick.

could possibly talk about: "What was there in common between you and this young man of this class?" (174). He prods further: "Do I understand that even a young boy that you would pick up in the street would be a pleasing companion to you?" (175). Wilde replies, with Whitmanian homo-democracy, "Oh, I would talk to a street Arab if he talked to me, with pleasure" (175).[55]

Taylors, telegraph boys, and street Arabs: we find Wilde in correspondence with them all, professing delight in their company and conversation. As Wilde's interrogators pursue the logics of purloined letters and privacy disturbed, Wilde strides out into the street into the pleasurable company of the passing traffic of young boys. The conversion from passionate epistle to "police report" that Edward Carpenter deplored in *Homogenic Love* (quoted in my introduction) was one that tried to lift queer correspondence out of the routes of undifferentiated intercourse. Like the Cleveland Street scandal a few years earlier, Wilde's trials were animated by an interrelation between gay panic and postal promiscuity. The prosecution hoped, in skewering the marvellously multiple Wilde, to contain the "wide ramification" of queer passion that Carpenter portrays as supported and even engendered by the communication network: with postal help, "letters pass and enduring attachments are formed" (47).

---

[55] Less than ten years earlier, a *Pall Mall Gazette* article titled "Walt Whitman at Camden" had described the pleasure Whitman took in watching the daily traffic of delivery men and telegraph boys: "He takes great delight in frequent gifts of simple flowers brought by the milkman as he comes from the country, or the butcher or the telegraph boy as they pass his house" (*Pall Mall Gazette*, London, England. Thursday 23 December 1886; Issue 6793).

2

"This Little Queen's Head Can't Be Untrue"
TROLLOPE'S POSTAL INFIDELITIES

ANTHONY TROLLOPE WROTE twenty-one of his forty-seven novels while simultaneously holding down a full-time appointment in the General Post Office.[1] The GPO was more than a day job for Trollope—while there, he also invented that ubiquitous sign of the postal facility, a now vernacular piece of civic furniture: the pillar-box.[2] To many critics, Trollope's postal work (1834–67) is incidental to his literary career; to his detractors, his connection to this most everyday of bureaucracies explains a lot: is he not the *dullest* of novelists—"as insipid as yesterday's newspaper," moaned Virginia Woolf's father, Leslie Stephen.[3] In reviews of Trollope's work, Henry James repeatedly lodged the same objection and after sharing a cross-Atlantic trip with Trollope, complained—with the kind of weary grandiloquence fostered by the confinement of an ocean liner—"he is the dullest Briton of them all."[4] The young James wrote several reviews of Trollope's novels and repeatedly slammed him for his dogged pursuit of the quotidian.[5] The "sayings and

---

[1] Trollope began his thirty-three-year Post Office career as a clerk in London in 1834. His 1841 appointment to a position as an assistant surveyor necessitated a move to Ireland, where he mostly lived until 1859. Continuing to rise in Post Office ranks, he established, improved, and inspected postal routes throughout Great Britain and was entrusted with the negotiation of global postal treaties. He retired in 1867.

[2] Biographer Victoria Glendinning acknowledges that Trollope is popularly credited with this invention, but tempers the claim: "Anthony Trollope is commonly credited with the introduction into Britain of pillar boxes for posting letters. It would be more truthful to say that it was his persistence and enthusiasm that resulted in their adoption" (197). In his autobiography, Trollope has no such hesitation, calling himself the "originator" (*Autobiography* 2: 118).

[3] N. John Hall (ed.), *The Trollope Critics* (Totowa, NJ: Barnes and Noble, 1981), xv.

[4] Letter sent to the James family, 1 November 1875. See Leon Edel (ed.), *Henry James Letters Volume I 1843–1875*. (London: Macmillan, 1974), 486.

[5] For a description of the unlikely but generative relationship between Trollope and James, see Elsie Michie, "The Odd Couple: Anthony Trollope and Henry James."

doings" of automaton-like characters, James laments, "are registered to the letter and timed to the minute. They write a number of letters, which are duly transcribed; they make frequent railway journeys by the down-train from London; they have cups of tea in their bed-rooms."[6] Such associations of Trollope with newspapers, letters, railway journeys, and cups of tea ally him with regularity, predictability, and the media of the everyday. He's not an artist, they argue, he's an observer. The thrust of the insults is clear: Trollope is more of a postman than he is a novelist.

In an 1888 pen-portrait of Trollope, however, an older and mellower James proposes that Trollope's postal work not only influenced his novel writing, but also awakened in him some curious and quirky predilections. James describes how "no contemporary story-teller deals so much in letters" as Trollope, and he gives this description of Trollope's love of epistolarity:

> Trollope was familiar with all sorts and conditions of men [...] his work is full of implied reference to the whole arena of modern vagrancy. He was for many years concerned in the management of the Post-Office; and we can imagine no experience more fitted to impress a man with the diversity of human relations. It is possibly from this source that he derived his fondness for transcribing the letters of his love-lorn maidens and other embarrassed persons.[7]

James still maintains that Trollope "overworked" his imaginative gifts, but this passage is firmly framed by a discussion of what Trollope does "very well," indeed, uniquely well. Here, James characterizes Trollope as an author whose knowledge of human "sorts" and "relations" is as broad as the postal service is comprehensive.[8] James is crediting Trollope, and by extension the Post Office, with something more than diligence. James's insistent anyone-and-everyone formulation underscores that in the Post Office and in fiction there always is a place for the seeming misfit—indeed, both the Post Office and fiction need the seeming misfit. Victorian periodical literature about the Post Office repeatedly explored the idea that the postbag constituted an expansive archive, bringing together the correspondence of "all sorts," figuring it as a site of indiscriminate congress. The postbag taught, in other words, that diversity entails—is indeed comprised of—divergence from norms, deviance even. James's review of Trollope implies and celebrates a sexual and gender deviance that James recognizes as postal. Trollope, he tells us, enjoys (has a "fondness" for) impersonating not merely the feminine sex ("love-lorn maidens"), but also "other embarrassed persons"—those who are stigmatized or shamed. James is

---

[6] *Anthony Trollope: The Critical Heritage* 255.
[7] Henry James, *Partial Portraits* 122. Quoted in *Anthony Trollope: The Critical Heritage* 539.
[8] Another early reviewer of Trollope, Michael Sadleir, writing in 1927, also portrayed Trollope as invested in a heterogeneity that produced queer effects. "It takes all sorts to make a world," Sadleir imagines Trollope saying, noting that he builds his books from "multifarious trivialities" which produce a "queer sense of the absorbing interest of normal occupations" (*The Trollope Critics* 36–37).

not alone in noting that Trollope eagerly assumes the position of the subjugated, the passive—he was notorious for subordinating his own authorship to the will of his characters, characterizing himself as in their hands.[9] Trollope's choice of compromised subjects, James implies, stands in relation to how Trollope compromises his own authorial practice: he does not, in James's formulation, *author*, rather he *transcribes*. He is, James is reminding us, a copyist, a clerk, a postal functionary. He is a faithful postman. But the very "faithfulness" of Trollope's transcriptions implies that he is unfaithful to the business of authorship.

Being unfaithful and even disgraceful may not, however, be altogether a bad thing. In an 1865 review, James had signaled that Trollope facilitated the yoking of *pleasure* with indignity, "We have long entertained for Mr. Trollope a partiality of which we have yet been somewhat ashamed" (*Trollope Critics* xv). Using the first person plural that I described behaving so queerly in chapter 1, James suggests that although it might be somewhat shameful to enjoy reading Trollope, Trollope's plain style repels the literary pretensions often used to install regimes of taste and shame. In *Partial Portraits* James proposes that Trollope "has no visible, certainly no explicit care for the literary part of the business; he writes easily, comfortably, and profusely" (Smalley 540), and he favorably compares Trollope with French realist novelists who are full of theories on the novel and realism. He points out how writers such as Gustave Flaubert, Emile Zola, and Alphonse Daudet are "more at home in the moral world" (Smalley 540) whereas Trollope "is so occasional, so accidental, so full of the echoes of voices that are not the voice of the muse" (Smalley 539–40). For James, Trollope is guided neither by moral nor literary spheres, but instead by the reverberations of chatter. It is a characterization that once again turns Trollope from an author into a postman. The postal system is a system "full of the echoes of voices," distinctly non-muse-like: its "occasional […] accidental" texts are produced as part of a network, not a privileged, singular relationship between author and a lone muse. Meditating on Trollope, James becomes interested in the liminal nature of the voices that can only be heard when the domineering muse is quelled and the writer thrills

---

[9] It was a commonplace that Trollope didn't even really write his books—they wrote him. Trollope himself embraced this idea. Fellow novelist Amelia Edwards recalls: "'Why *did* you let Crosbie jilt Lily Dale?', I asked Anthony Trollope one day. 'Why did I "let" him?', he repeated, 'How could I help it? He *would* do it, confound him!' This was not said in jest. It was earnest." Cited in R. C. Terry (ed.), *Trollope: Interviews and Recollections* (New York: St. Martin's Press, 1987), 102. Margaret Oliphant makes and expands a similar point about Trollope's noninterventionist, indiscriminate approach: "His mind did not concentrate upon any individual view of existence, nor was there that relation between the different parts of his work which some great novelists have aimed at. We might almost say that his selection of subjects was accidental and that he took whatever came uppermost with a general sense of capacity to deal with what he took up, rather than a particular impulse within to search into the depths of human motive, or to discover its endless discrepancies and shortcomings. He was a storyteller rather than an analyst or moralist, although no man ever took more pains to show the way in which the mind justified to itself a certain course of action. Where he held his lantern there came into light with its circle a little world, a microcosm, with everything going on in little which goes on at large in the universe" (*Interviews and Recollections* 103–4).

instead to the jabbering of a network of mortals. Trollope's unauthorly, unmanaged polyphony admits characters who are not deemed worthy by more literary literature. James approvingly notes, "For Trollope the emotions of a nursery-governess in Australia would take precedence of the adventures of a depraved *femme du monde* in Paris or London" (Smalley 539). The *femme du monde* might well produce and inspire texts of many kinds. A nursery-governess's textual production, however, could only occur for and through the mail.

We might initially imagine that James is contrasting Trollopian innocence with continental depravity, but this is not the case. James immediately turns to *The Vicar of Bullhampton* (1870) and Trollope's compassionate portrayal of a "castaway": a fallen woman named Carry Brattle who takes up prostitution. He cites Trollope's preface, which defends Carry by proposing that novels should cater to young people of both sexes. James remarks that the French realist school would mock such a goal—but James himself is compelled by it. If Trollope's express intention is to appeal to a mixed gender readership, he is similarly capable, James notes, of finding heterogeneity within gender categories. Trollope has, James points out, "presented the British maiden under innumerable names, in every station and in every emergency of life, and with every combination of moral and physical qualities" (Smalley 542). Trollope famously declared, "I am realistic,"[10] but did so while critiquing the division commonly made between realism and sensationalism. "A good novel should be both" (*Autobiography* 2: 42), Trollope asserts: his genre—or type—is plural. For James, this means that Trollope does not fix and reiterate the woman as the limited and limiting "depraved *femme du monde*"; rather, he attends to "all sorts and conditions [...] the diversity of human relations." James, in short, ends up finding literary virtue in the very numerousness of voices for which he originally attacks Trollope.[11] Trollope's ability, he theorizes, to inhabit and represent diversity derives from being prolific, and from working in an institution devoted to prolific textual production, circulation, and exchange: the Post Office. James comes full circle: having stigmatized Trollope for his excessive production, he recognizes that this output allows Trollope to write about all sorts, for all sorts, and this very indiscriminate inclusiveness enables him to portray the *outcast*. When James praises Trollope's novels for being uniquely "spacious" (Smalley 539), he is linking Trollope's postal perambulations with his affording of space to characters who have suffered sexual and gender stigmatization.

---

[10] Anthony Trollope, *An Autobiography*, 2 vols. (Edinburgh and London: William Blackwood and Sons, 1883), 2: 41.

[11] George Eliot who, along with her partner G. H. Lewes, enjoyed a long friendship with Trollope, had other concerns relating to Trollope and proliferation. When Trollope retired from the Post Office, she feared that having more time to write more ("led to excessive writing") might have adverse effects. In fact, Trollope wrote less after his retirement. See N. John Hall, *Trollope: A Biography* 312. Eliot and Lewes had directly benefited from Trollope's postal employment: Trollope had helped Lewes to procure a Post Office position for his son, Charles Lee (*Biography* 202).

PRODUCTIVE, REPRODUCTIVE

In the early reviews, James had written of Trollope's "fertility," calling it "gross, importunate."[12] Other reviewers who exhibited distaste for Trollope's mode of production as preternaturally rapid and prodigious routinely employed the metaphor of excessive sexual reproduction. An 1859 *Spectator* review uses a reproductive figure of speech to rebuke Trollope: "The fact is he writes too fast. An average six or eight months is too short a time for the *gestation* and production of a first-class novel" (Smalley 91, italics mine). The *Saturday Review* hammers the point home in 1859: Trollope's writing is not "pregnant with genius" (Smalley 96). An 1858 review in the *Saturday Review* had made a similar objection with an extended reproductive metaphor that comes complete with Malthusian limits:

> Those who care for the interests of literature […] cannot but feel a considerable degree of uneasiness at the rapid multiplication of his progeny. A man must have a very long purse, and an extraordinary fund of philoprogenitiveness who would not feel a little cross if his fruitful vine were to plant three olive branches round about his table in the course of a single year. Nature prevents the material nursery from being stocked quite so fast as that; but Mr. Trollope's brain is so prolific that he will soon be the father of as many Minervas as would relieve the Muses and the Graces, too, from their functions.
>
> (Smalley 75)

Just as James had disassociated Trollope from the Muses, this review similarly casts him as too prolific to need a Muse: his prodigious output requires no input. He appears autoreproductive, as he is described not only fathering but also giving birth: Minerva was said to spring from the head of Jupiter, and this reviewer casts Trollope's head as similarly uterine and (multi)parous. Trollope's capacity for multiplicity and cross-gendered production that James attributes to postal work turns, in this trope, to sexual reproduction that is diverse not only in its productions, but also in its mode of production: Trollope can, hermaphroditically, both spread his seed *and* be pregnant and give birth.

Remarkably, Trollope himself engaged the trope. In his *Autobiography* (1876), he recognized that he had "crowded [his] wares into the market too quickly" (Smalley 141) but countered that

> the work which has been done quickest has been done the best […] the rapidity has been achieved by hot pressure, not in the conception, but in the telling of the story […]. I have been impregnated with my own creations till it has been my only

---

[12] 'Anthony Trollope,' *Partial Portraits* (1888), 97–133. First published in *Century Magazine* (New York: July 1883): 385–95. Reprinted in Donald Smalley (ed.), *Trollope: The Critical Heritage* (London: Routledge and Kegan Paul, 1969), 525–45.

excitement to sit with the pen in my hand, and drive my team before me at as quick a pace as I could make them travel.

(Smalley 142)

In *The Ethics of Reading* (1987), J. Hillis Miller points out that this passage makes "the sexual metaphor latent in the terminology of the 'conception' of character" extraordinarily manifest (Miller 94). The initial allusion to the "conception" of character unfolds into a description of auto-insemination, excitation, and exhilarating exertion. Just as James praised Trollope for his ability to write women characters, Hillis Miller admires how Trollope "plays within himself the role of both male and female" (Miller 94) and argues that Trollope is "an island of heterogeneity which cannot be measured by publicly accepted standards of value" (Miller 95). Trollope evades these public standards of value, Hillis Miller theorizes, because "his novels are too secretly like himself" (Miller 95). Hillis Miller himself capitulates to the need to explain Trollope's excessive literary production, and he does so through a model of internalized anxiety and lack: Trollope's "secret motivation" for his "obsessive writing of novels" was to finally produce "a novel which would assuage his need for a written ascertained moral law" (Miller 98). Hillis Miller argues that Trollope, too, like his characters, sought "secure possession of the grounds of moral decision" (Miller 98). His literary promiscuity and incontinence, in other words, is paradoxically a symptom of Trollope's drive toward monogamy and continence: Trollope doesn't really want to be a trollop. I will return to Hillis Miller's resolution of Trollope via the notion of the secret obsession, but first there is more to be said about how Trollope's gender and sexual status relates to transitivity.

Trollope was commonly regarded as a feminine writer, to his detriment. As Nicola Thompson has investigated in her article "Gender and the Literary Reception of Anthony Trollope," from the late 1860s, Trollope's reputation suffered from "increasingly feminized associations made with his writings."[13] Thompson ably articulates, however, that such feminization sat side by side with appreciation of Trollope's often-noted bluff manliness: "Despite critical perceptions of Trollope the man and Trollope the writer as intensely masculine, many critics, paradoxically, also felt that Trollope's writing had many feminine qualities" (Thompson 157). Once again, heterogeneity seems to be the defining term. And it is a heterogeneity that is allied, specifically, with circulation. Trollope's domestic realism made him, as a *Times* critic wrote in 1859, an author "*of the circulating library sort*" (my emphasis).[14] This reference to a circulating library groups Trollope with women writers like Jane Austen, and Thompson notes that it was "a critical commonplace to compare Trollope with Austen" (Thompson 165). In his autobiography, Trollope invokes his decision that "Pride and Prejudice was the best novel in the English language"

---

[13] Nicola Thompson, "'Something Both More and Less than Manliness': Gender and the Literary Reception of Anthony Trollope," *Victorian Literature and Culture* 22 (1994): 151–71, 153.
[14] [E. S. Dallas], "Mr Anthony Trollope." *Times* (23 May 1859): 12.

(Trollope, *Autobiography* 1: 55) as evidence of a flair for the literary. Although he points out that he switched allegiance to the (much more masculine) Scott, Trollope immediately sutures himself even further to the feminized communicative, circulating, and diurnal literary arts, by asserting that:

> I could write a letter. If I had a thing to say, I could so say it in written words that the readers should know what I meant [...]. Early in life, at the age of fifteen I had commenced the dangerous habit of keeping a journal, and this I maintained for ten years. The volumes remained in my possession, unregarded—never looked at—till 1870, when I examined them, and, with many blushes, destroyed them. They convicted me of folly, ignorance, indiscretion, idleness, extravagance, and conceit. But they had habituated me to the rapid use of pen and ink, and taught me how to express myself with faculty.
> (*Autobiography* 1: 55–56)

Trollope here describes himself as an efficient correspondent and a blushing diarist—feminizing attributes—but Trollope finds within these feminine arts the exercise of rapidity. And if there's something Trollope admired, and to which he tuned himself, it was speed.

Trollope developed stratagems of efficiency and speed for literary production. He realized that if he traveled by rail instead of by horse, he could use the hours on a train to write, and he had a writing tablet designed that functioned as a portable desk for railway carriage production. In later years, he applied the same principle to ocean travel and had carpenters fit writing desks in his cabins.[15] Not only did he write while traveling, but he also (in)famously wrote to strict quota, timing his production in tandem with the travel. Many reviled Trollope for such "mechanical processes,"[16] but Trollope himself reveled in what he called his "mechanical genius" (Trollope, *Letters* 329) and in the idea that he transcribed and delivered industriously, rather than authored through inspiration. In his *Autobiography*, published posthumously in 1883, Trollope merrily described how he would allot himself not only a word quota for each work session, but also a precise word quota for each novel that he would neither under-, nor overshoot. Brushing aside critiques that his methods, which he calls "appliances," are "beneath the notice of a man of genius" (Trollope, *Autobiography* 1: 160), he rejects the very term "genius" and advises young men who want to be authors "to seat themselves at their desks day by day as though they were lawyers' clerks;—and so let them sit until the allotted task shall be accomplished" (Trollope, *Autobiography* 1: 163). This is a very striking image of production, saturated by iteration. Not only does Trollope argue that to produce a book you must keep writing *day after day*, but also his use of the plural emphasizes the iterative—he envisions not a single man, but instead *rows* of clerks. Trollope's emphasis in the *Autobiography*'s scenes of

---

[15] See N. John Hall, *Trollope: A Biography* 143.

[16] The phrase is Henry James's. 'Anthony Trollope,' *Partial Portraits* (1888), 97–133. First published in *Century Magazine* (New York: July 1883): 385–95. Reprinted in Donald Smalley (ed.), *Trollope: The Critical Heritage* (London: Routledge and Kegan Paul, 1969), 525–45.

writing is unapologetically upon the same things he valued in his postal work—repetition, speed, and the all-important "considerable circulation" (*Autobiography* 1: 203). His alliance of himself, and by extension others, with the "circulating library" starts to look not like the feminized, domestic spaces of an Austen parlor, but rather like the civic spaces of law courts and Post Office departments. In his postal work, Trollope exercised a specific ambition to widen the public sphere and civic conveniences. The pride he took in "inventing" and promoting the pillar postbox was about bringing the facility of a vast communications network to street corners and rural isolation. In his *Autobiography* he wrote of his sense of mission to integrate the domestic with the public:

> That the public in little villages should be enabled to buy postage stamps; that they should have their letters delivered free and at an early hour; that pillar letter-boxes should be put up for them (of which accommodation in the streets and ways of England I was the originator, having, however, got the authority for the erection of the first at St. Heliers in Jersey) [...] these were the matters by which I was stirred to what the secretary was pleased to call energetic performance of my duties.
>
> (Trollope, *Autobiography* 2: 118)

Trollope had not initially fared well in his Post Office employment, when he was confined to the drudgery of an office and his bad spelling and lack of diligence were marks against him. But when his work took him out and about, he became animated and dedicated by both his own circulation and the circulation of correspondence that he saw himself enabling. He was "stirred" by the idea of cheap and accessible postal facilities for the most far-flung of citizens.

BANALITY, ANALITY, AND COBBLER'S WAX

> I was once told that the surest aid to the writing of a book was a piece of cobbler's wax on my chair. I certainly believe in the cobbler's wax much more than the inspiration.
>
> (Trollope, *Autobiography* 1: 162–63)

Trollope passed on this writing advice about the nubble of cobbler's wax at an 1871 luncheon hosted by George Eliot and G. H. Lewes, which was attended by a cadre of literary luminaries. Trollope reputedly made George Eliot "quiver" by describing his prolific production schedule, and when Eliot said there were days when she could not produce a line, he self-deprecatingly replied that "with my mechanical stuff it's a sheer matter of industry. It's not the head that does it—it's the cobbler's wax on the seat and the sticking to my chair!"[17] Was it Trollope's industry or his averred organ of industry—his backside—that made Eliot "quiver"? Another account of the evening describes Trollope connecting

---

[17] Donald Hall, *Trollope: A Biography* 363.

the industry and the organ with graphic emphasis; he enacted his point "with an inelegant vigour of gesture that sent a thrill of horror through the polite circle there assembled" (363). The cobbler's wax that fixes Trollope's backside to his chair conjoins anality and productivity, and it shocks with its banality—its "inelegance." Trollope insists that writing is, for him, (b)anal. It is a *service* (the term "banal" derives from the concept of feudal service); it must deliver. That Trollope's adhesive of choice is cobbler's wax is not arbitrary. Trollope repeatedly likened the novelist to a shoemaker—on at least five occasions in the *Autobiography* alone —and the image derives figurative power from the notion that you sit still in order to make shoes for those who will perambulate in them. Stasis serves circulation, or, he also serves who only sits and waits.

Trollope's dedication to the desk, complete with cobbler's wax smeared on the seat of his trousers, has something of the besmirched and deviant schoolboy about it. This quality leads me to believe that when Trollope shocked his luncheon companions by attributing his literary success to his rump, slapping it (it is inferred) robustly, he produced a somatic echo of his schoolboy days at Harrow, where he was repeatedly flogged. Perhaps the literary circle was shocked in part because Trollope's gesture was both hearty and effeminizing? Richard Dellamora brilliantly pursues a similar hunch in an article titled "Stupid Trollope." Dellamora contends, "The politics of male homosociality, as experienced when Trollope was a schoolboy, later shaped his politics, leisure and fiction" (Dellamora 22). What Trollope experienced as a Harrow schoolboy was a regime of corporal punishment, under which Trollope perceives himself as slow, stupid, and dirty. Dellamora reads Trollope's account of a particular incident of "nameless horror" (Trollope, *Autobiography* 1: 7) perpetrated by some "curled darlings of the school" (Trollope, *Autobiography* 1: 7), for which the ever "disreputably dirty" (Trollope, *Autobiography* 1: 6), nonangelic Trollope is blamed. Harrow enjoyed a particular reputation as a hotbed of public school sexual antics, and Dellamora observes that the "first of his body parts to which Trollope refers in the *Autobiography* is his bum" (Dellamora 23). Trollope refers to it via a memory that Dellamora likens to a "bad dream" (Dellamora 23). The headmaster stops the young Harrovian in the street and

> asking me, with all the clouds of Jove upon his brow and the thunder in his voice, whether it was possible that Harrow School was disgraced by so disreputably dirty a boy as I! Oh, what I felt at that moment! But I could not look my feelings. I do not doubt that I was dirty;—but I think that he was cruel. He must have known me had he seen me as he was wont to see me, for he was in the habit of flogging me constantly. Perhaps he did not recognize me by my face.
> (*Autobiography* 1: 5–6)

By what bit of the boy's body *would* the headmaster recognize him? Once again Trollope gestures toward, but does not name, his backside. The namelessness of the body part suggests a connection between it and the "nameless horror" for which Trollope is beaten, and Dellamora draws out the suggestion that Trollope's behind is harassed not only by the repeated attentions of the Headmaster, but also by—at least the fear of the accusation of—anal sex. Dellamora's reading delicately balances Trollope between his heterosexual bluffness and his childhood proximity to shamed and punished homosexuality. Isolated by his stupidity, "an ultimate line of defense lay in Spartan stoicism" because he could bear the pain of the floggings, Trollope compensated for it in adulthood through his passion for fox-hunting "which permitted him an endless opportunity to act out the sado-masochistic binds of his school days" ("Stupid Trollope" 24).

Much as J. Hillis Miller argues that the "secret motivation" for Trollope's "obsessive writing of novels" "was an attempt to write a novel which would assuage his need for a written ascertained moral law" (98), Dellamora turns finally to the same language of obsession, arguing that Trollope "obsessively sought substitutes for [...] sexual desire, fear and violence impressed upon him as a schoolboy" ("Stupid Trollope" 26). I greatly admire both Hillis Miller's and Dellamora's readings—not least for their insistence that the category of the sexual be part of the "social" that forms such a dominant and often defensive term in Trollope scholarship—but I want to ask if there is an alternative to this shared, final term of their argument. Their critical turn—to the obsessive, *personal* self—sidelines one of the critically compelling consequences of Trollope having answered the question "What is an Author?" with the reply "an author is a postman or a clerk or a cobbler." Trollope's answer theorizes novel writing as *impersonal* production.[18] While Hillis Miller and Dellamora resolve their readings through the personal, I want to propose that Trollope's row of clerks writing novels stages instead the "anonymity of a murmur" (Foucault, "Author" 222) that Foucault hopes, in his 1980 essay "What is an Author?," will displace the name of the author, and replace the questions about authenticity, originality, and whether an author has revealed "part of his deepest self" (Foucault, "Author" 222).

Trollope's *Autobiography*, a text that we might reasonably expect to reveal some of this "deepest self" (Foucault, "Author" 222), explicitly and repeatedly rehearses the trajectory toward being a novelist as a series of disidentifications. He begins by describing a lonely childhood, of how other boys did not identify with him: "As a boy, even as a child," he writes, "I was thrown much upon myself [...] other boys would not play with me. I was therefore alone, and had to form my plays within myself" (*Autobiography* 1: 56–57). This might sound like a scene of suffering offered up as a key to understanding his adult life, but Trollope is very careful to enunciate that what it teaches is that everything is invention: "Play," he emphasizes "of some kind was necessary to me then, as it always has been" (*Autobiography* 1: 57). The alienation of the schoolyard prompts Trollope to further

---

[18] I am not the first to regard Trollope's *Autobiography* as a theoretical text. In *The Novel-Machine: The Theory and Fiction of Anthony Trollope* (Baltimore, MD: Johns Hopkins UP, 1980), Walter Kendrick observes that although it "does not look like a book of theory, and none of Trollope's traditional critics has taken it for one" (3), it is all about how to write, how to read, and how to relate literature to life. I differ from Kendrick in his understanding that what Trollope theorized was a realism in which writing is a "medium without a message" (6). I am instead advocating that we understand media and messages as structurally informing all Trollope's writing, and that his pronouncement "I am a realist" be read performatively, as an address.

alienate himself, causing him "to live in a world altogether outside the world of my own material life [in which] I myself was of course my own hero. In after years I have done the same—with this difference, that I have discarded the hero of my early dreams, and have been able to lay my own identity aside."[19] If this is a story of displacement and alienation, Trollope doubles the alienating effect in the retelling, by parodying his own childish self-centric self-mythologizing: "I myself was of course my own hero" (*Autobiography* 1: 57). He may retain a taste for self-aggrandizement (and autobiography), but he has detached himself enough to show it is a fiction. The passage persists with its theme: describing how turning childhood play-acting into the adult profession of literature-making entailed yet further disidentification: he "lays [his] own identity aside." What is striking about this passage is that this is no sacrificial gesture, nor is it a story of repression—Trollope presents the art of laying identity aside as triumphant and forcefully generative.

Trollope (and, indeed, James) scholarship has been particularly animated around the question of consciousness. Whether they knew what they were doing, and whether others knew what they were doing is a debate that has been methodologically rangy —taken up by psychoanalysis, or strains of Marxist-derived criticism that appeal to the social. It is a debate that has been productive in its own right, but if we add the insights of theories of performativity, we can step back a little and regard this critical fixation on the question of whether Trollope knew what he was doing[20] as a symptom of how thoroughly he stages and theorizes the impersonal. Rachel Ablow has recently argued that Trollope was constructively comfortable with the notion of the split self. Whereas Marx recoiled from any suggestion that alienation could be generative, maintaining that it is "monstrous" because it painfully splits the laborer into work and home selves, for Trollope, Ablow proposes, "alienation is very nearly worth celebrating."[21] A split self offers benefits because it can "interrupt the potentially narcissistic relation between the writer and her or his work" (Ablow 134). Alienation renders "personality, interiority, and belief [. . .] irrelevant" (Ablow 134), and Ablow argues that Trollope's "commitment to the impersonality of labor" (Ablow 135) can be perceived in his repeated and strenuous objections, to merit-based promotions. Nicholas Dames has similarly proposed that, for the careerist Trollope, "'career' is a mediating [. . .] figure for social energy" (248). I would

---

[19] The rest of the quote reads "Such is a necessity of castle-building. But I never became a king, or a duke—much less when my height and personal appearance were fixed could I be an Antinous, or six feet high. I never was a learned man, nor even a philosopher. But I was a very clever person, and beautiful young women used to be fond of me" (Trollope, *An Autobiography* 1: 57). His reference to Antinous is particularly intriguing: Antinous was the beautiful young lover of the Emperor Hadrian. He was known for his beauty, sharp wit, and—importantly for Trollope—hunting prowess. Once again, Trollope sits proximate to homosexuality and denies that this is *his* identity. As Dellamora pithily puts it, "Trollope assures the reader that Anthony is not an Antinous" ("Stupid Trollope" 24).

[20] Admittedly Trollope's titles could be said to incite such a critical fixation on consciousness: *He Knew He Was Right*; *Can You Forgive Her?*; "Not If I Know It." (Anthony Trollope, *Later Short Stories*).

[21] Rachel Ablow, *The Marriage of Minds: Reading Sympathy in the Victorian Marriage Plot* (Stanford: Stanford UP, 2007), 134.

add that one of the mediations it produces is impersonality and this impersonality retains the traces of mediation itself.

Trollope's reflections on how he lays his identity aside in order to write his novels accords with James's portrayal of him as a transcriber. It also accords with James's alliance of Trollope with "embarrassed persons"—Trollope describes his youth as fraught, isolated, and, emphatically, shameful. In a striking passage in the *Autobiography*, he describes the "first twenty-six years of my life [as] years of suffering, disgrace, and inward remorse. [. . .]. There had clung to me a feeling that I had been looked upon always as an evil, an encumbrance, a useless thing—as a creature of whom those connected with him had to be ashamed" (*Autobiography* 1: 79). Eve Kosofksy Sedgwick has written of shame (through a reading of Henry James) as a response to the "loss of feedback from others [. . .]. Shame," she writes, "floods into being as a moment, a disruptive moment, in a circuit of identity-constituting communication" (*Touching Feeling* 36). (That she is using communication as more than a casual metaphor is made clear when she further theorizes shame in relationship to adjacent affective structure— "shyness"—to be shamed or to be shy is to be out of the conversation.) Sedgwick's language of "communication," "correspondences," and "disrupted circuits" figures shame as a breakdown of the postal system.

And, indeed, Trollope's *Autobiography* proposes a similar correlation between the post and states of shame. He describes the opposite of shame, pride, when he writes of his work in repairing and improving the communication circuits of the rural postal system. In his descriptions of his (nonclerical) Post Office work, he transforms from a "shamed creature" into an exalted meta-messenger. "I was," he writes "a beneficent angel to the public, bringing everywhere with me an earlier, cheaper, and much more regular delivery of letters" (*Autobiography* 1: 121). His portrayal of himself as a "beneficent angel" recalls and recompenses his shaming and punishment at the expense of the "curled darlings" at Harrow (*Autobiography* 1: 7). Once tortured by pampered cherubs, he is now himself a rebel angel. Trollope dates the beginning of his proud and passionate life to his twenty-sixth year.[22] He was twenty-six years old when he left his family and moved to Ireland to be a Postal Surveyor's Clerk. Trollope's narrative is very clear: the Post Office appointment is what allows him to throw off disgrace. His *Autobiography* narrates it as a shocking shift: suddenly all the crippling doubts about not fitting in, about social and economic embarrassment and his intense self-consciousness about his slovenly, ungainly physical body fall out of the narrative. "I began my manhood at a desk in the Post Office," he declares (*Autobiography* 1: 10). What does a Post Office appointment give him? He tells us: it gives him the *pleasures* of *dissemination*; of making deliveries. He facilitates a rapid, free-flowing circulation of post-letters that counters the stagnant and painfully differentiating structures of silence that characterize his youth. The Post Office did what many jobs can do. It removed Trollope from his tortured family life and the failures of that structure

---

[22] The publication of *John Caldigate* had similarly uplifting effect for Trollope. Despite now being considered a minor work, it marked a turning point for Trollope's literary reputation, a "turn upwards" in his novelistic fortunes, as biographer N. John Hall puts it (*Trollope: A Biography* 458).

and replaced that home with employment that enabled economic independence, social and sexual mobility, and a network of alliances much broader than the family. But the postal nature of his work made that change explicit; Trollope was lifted out of personal and social stasis into movement and community, *and* he literally opened up closed communities, by extending the postal network and facilitating the circulation of letters.

Trollope could have told the story differently. He could have narrated this shift as a finding of self, or the location of a newfound sense of purpose or dignity. But he does not trade shame for dignity, and disidentification for realized selfhood. Instead he emphasizes that the job allows him to play and hunt (he calls hunting "a passion […] one of the great joys of my life"), live the sexually unfettered life of the "altogether jaunting jolly bachelor," and travel around. What I am suggesting here is that there is a relationship between the Post Office and the post-structural. Trollope emphasizes the subject as a site rather than a center and repeatedly portrays relationships to categories of identification as mediated and contingent. As Ablow puts it, Trollope believes that "subjectivity *can* be produced through relations with others" (33). The James quote with which I opened this chapter uses the same term—"relations"—to trace Trollope's success back to his work at the Post Office. In the *Autobiography*, Trollope shows us that employment in the Post Office reanimated his childhood understanding of the importance of cross-identification and the transformative effects of structures that allowed a persona to imagine extending themselves and take the place of another—*any* other. As James's quote suggests, Trollope thereby has a capacity for a queer kind of sympathy. I use the term "queer" not to categorize Trollope's own sexual identity, but to emphasize, along with James, that Trollope's literary and postal careers both begin from and lead him into queer structures of alliance. That is to say: the very capaciousness and diversity of the Trollope oeuvre produces nonfamilial, nonmarital relations that can encompass the stigmatized subject, engage divergent sexual roles, and allow for transitive selves. In *The Novel and the Police*, D. A. Miller notes that Trollope's characters always display "mixed motives" (Miller 124) and that Trollope treats his characters with notable "evenhanded detachment" (132). It was his capacity for detached heterogeneity that made Trollope as commodious as the pillar-boxes he claims to have invented.

TELLTALE STAMPS

The reformed and expanded Post Office was recognized and promoted as an institution that used an impersonal machinery to facilitate all kinds of communication, including the deeply personal. Its regularizing effect could accommodate all sorts of irregularity, and through its mass application, it could cater to the single (smallest, poorest) patron. These kinds of institutional "mixed messages" made it, I am arguing, a stimulating figure for fiction. The kind of fiction it produced was overwhelmingly interested in the exterior, rather than the interior of letters, and this fiction prizes post-letters for their material ability to document human interaction by bearing traces of their own origin and passage. These traces overwhelm the importance of the letter itself; the letter is emptied of signification, as postmarks, telegram forms, envelopes, addresses, smudges, and stamps are shown to tell their own tale. Trollope makes many an aside in many of his novels about the wonders (and shortcomings) of the post,[23] but one of his novels is entirely structured by a postal plot: the 1879 *John Caldigate*. In *John Caldigate* the survival of the protagonist's marriage and good name hinges on a postal worker's ability to read the clues on a single envelope. It is an example of a novel that seems to be devoted to a marriage and its restoration, but by complicating the marriage plot with a postal plot, Trollope crosses and double-crosses these marital lines of relation until they lose their discrete and privileged narrative status. *John Caldigate* stages the literal and metaphorical potential of the postal system to sustain queer and irregular structures of alliance.

The protagonist of the title, John Caldigate, loses his wife, child, and reputation and is wrongly thrown into jail for bigamy. His misadventures begin when he turns from his family, hometown, homeland, and future bride (Hester Bolton) to pursue a wayward course of fortune seeking in Australia.[24] While there, John has an affair with a widowed actress named Euphemia Smith. Making a name into a label is one of Trollope's favorite comic turns, and Euphemia's first name signals that she employs "euphemism," or the co-option of a reputable name.[25] Her last name, Smith, is the sexually suspiciously generic name used in boardinghouse registries.[26] Her two names, which imply correctly that she goes by hoards of other names, tip off readers that she's double trouble. When Caldigate returns to his hometown, marries his fiancée and has a son with her, Euphemia shows up. She claims that they had been married in Australia and accuses him of bigamy, producing a post-letter with which she proceeds to blackmail Caldigate.[27] The envelope

---

[23] See R. H. Super, *Trollope in the Post Office* (Ann Arbor: University of Michigan Press, 1981).

[24] That this bigamy novel takes place partly in Australia (Trollope traveled there twice, in 1871 and 1875), indicates the importance of theorizing the relationship between colonial and sexual politics. As studies like Christopher Lane's *The Ruling Passion* and Robert Aldrich's *Colonialism and Homosexuality* show in depth, Other places allow Other kinds of sexual relation. Victorian intellectuals noted this too. Tracing the history of monogamous bourgeois marriage, Friedrich Engels noted: "The trend of these changes is to narrow more and more the circle of people comprised within the common bond of marriage, which was originally very wide, until at last it includes only the single pair, the dominant form of marriage today" (*Origin* 96). He goes on to emphasize that "all forms of sexual life" are found in the animal world (*Origin* 98) and that the idea that primitive societies enjoyed promiscuity has recently "become fashionable to deny" because of the ignominy of it: "Humanity," he derides, "must be spared this 'shame'" (*Origin* 97). Engels's two primary case studies of primitive kinship systems are Aboriginal Australia and pre-Columbian America; Australia and America figure large in Trollope's own "New World" experience.

[25] This is not the first time that Trollope uses this curious name, nor is it the first time he links it with gender and sexual transitivity. In May 1866, in the *Fortnightly Review*, he published a tale called "The Gentle Euphemia," subtitled "Love Shall Still Be Lord of All." In this story Euphemia is adored by Lord Mountfidget, who gets wounded by a poisoned arrow. Euphemia follows him, disguised in male attire as a page, and saves his life.

[26] She also, we learn across the course of the novel, goes by the names Mademoiselle Cettini and Mrs. Salmon.

[27] Euphemia's blackmail, the accusation of bigamy, and the backdrop of Australia all indicate that when Trollope wrote *John Caldigate* (in 1877, between 3 February and 21 July), he had the infamous Tichborne claimant in mind: an imposter who returned to England from Australia to claim the Tichborne inheritance. The Tichborne trials were held in 1871 and 1873. Trollope most fully engaged the case in his 1878 novel, *Is He Popenjoy?*, which he wrote between October 1874 and May 1875.

of that letter is addressed, in John Caldigate's handwriting, to her as "Mrs John Caldigate." Although Caldigate did use the name in play, the two were never formally married. Euphemia is lying when she claims to be his wife, but the postmark on the envelope makes it strong evidential status. Enter the enjoyably unlikely hero: a postal clerk named Samuel Bagwax who uses his knowledge of postal stamps, impressions, perforations, and codes to show how the Post Office "hieroglyphics" (*JC* 452) on the envelope are fraudulent, proving that the mistress is guilty of libel and disproving the accusation of bigamy.

Bagwax is described as a clerk with a "post-office mind" (*JC* 451), fired by a passion for his job. His name recalls the cobbler's wax that Trollope said he stuck to his backside in order to be able to write efficiently, and this adhesive is diacritical, indicating once again a bond between the postman and the novelist. Critics might have doubted that a postman makes a good novelist, but in *John Caldigate,* Trollope allows Bagwax to save the day and gratify the author too. Trollope told periodical editor John Blackwood, "There was a touch of downright love in the depicting of Bagwax. Was I not once a Bagwax myself?"[28] If Trollope's creation of a postal-clerk hero gave him pleasure, Bagwax too is principally animated by the "delight" he takes in "showing how important to the world was a proper understanding of post-office details" (*JC* 450). What kind of "touch of love" is this? It is the love for the ungainly, overlooked, besmirched but passionate character. The novel's plot rewards such a character. Bagwax's nerdy attachment to detail and duty will take him to Australia, and this travel practically turns him into one of the post-letters he loves so dearly: it fulfills his "long[ing] to overcome great distances—to feel that I have put illimitable space behind me" (*JC* 505). Prior to this opportunity, we learn, Bagwax has only been to Boulogne and Ostend, achievements of which he is touchingly proud (505). His pride is others' shame: Ostend is the city in Belgium to which the Trollope family fled to escape creditors. In his autobiography, Trollope describes how he became a "Pariah" (*Autobiography* 1: 12) with the other students when school stopped credit being extended to him because his father was not paying his bills. It is through his loving crafting of Bagwax as a humble hero that Trollope can recast his own social exile. That he can laugh while doing this (Bagwax remains a figure of affectionate fun), recalls the ironic detachment of "I was, of course, my own hero" (*Autobiography* 1: 57).

It is hard to overemphasize how much of the drama of the novel is displaced onto Bagwax. Trollope stages a David and Goliath battle; John Caldigate is convicted and imprisoned for bigamy by the state and Bagwax single-handedly fights to secure the evidence necessary to overturn this sentence. Instead of being shown the heart-wrenchings that attend Caldigate and his separated wife, we are shown the drama of Bagwax's mediations of that position. It is Bagwax who feels "every moment I pass with that envelope before my eyes I see the innocent husband in jail and the poor afflicted wife weeping in her solitude" (*JC* 499). If his sentimental sympathy is for the divided heterosexual

---

[28] Hall *Letters* 2: 815.

family, we mustn't lose sight of the envelope in this scene—as the object of his passion. His struggle in the novel is to make his beloved postmarks as legible as other narratives. And he runs up against the problems of signification—specifically the inability of others, blinded by marriage, to understand competing significations.

Bagwax's province is the "crosses and letters and figures upon which so much of the civilization of Europe depended" (*JC* 453), but he finds himself trapped between competing signs of civilization. He has to pit his postal markings against "an impassive emblem of sovereign justice" (*JC* 466); since John Caldigate is already sentenced, Bagwax has to fight for a "Queen's Pardon." He finds himself caught between what the Queen's head on his postage stamps tells him—that Caldigate is innocent—and what the queen's crowned head, representing the law, has decreed—that Caldigate is guilty. Bagwax's evidence demonstrates that the postage stamp on the envelope was not yet issued at the time when the letter was dated, and that the postmark was obtained by fraud and stamped on the envelope at a later date.

The mock-heroic Bagwax feels called to arms by this clash of symbols and emblems, adopting as his own the motto used by another national hero—Nelson: "Duty! Duty! England expects that every man [this day shall do his duty]" (*JC* 516).[29] This motto was communicated at the battle of Trafalgar via semaphore, another language of "crosses and figures" peculiar to a national institution, the Navy, rather than the Post Office. Nelson's motto invokes masculinity in the service of nation building; here the "honest, manly" (*JC* 541) Bagwax epitomizes selfless service to his queen and country. His impassioned mantra of "Duty! Duty!" is shown to be vital in the face of the impassive law and its administrators; he restores justice and thus public confidence in the justice system, and he reinstates John to his rightful, landed position of Squire of Folking.[30] Bagwax succeeds in his task of deciphering the meaning of the queen's head on the postage stamp and makes his postage stamp queen's head prevail over that of the impassive law. He rescues

---

[29] Trollope's choice of motto for Bagwax is extremely apposite. Nelson was a highly romanticized paradigm of duty in the nineteenth century. Samuel Smiles, in his 1880 book *Duty: With Illustrations of Courage, Patience, & Endurance*, writes of Nelson: "He felt that it was his business and his duty to watch over the very existence of England [...]. His life was a romance. His weaknesses were as remarkable as his gifts and qualities" (169).

[30] Bagwax's heroism is also a means by which Trollope can critique the perception held by "the popular newspaper, the popular member of Parliament, and the popular novelist—the name of Charles Dickens will of course present itself to the reader who remembers the Circumlocution office" (*JC* 452) that civil servants are "idle, dilatory, supercilious and incompetent" (*JC* 547). Instead, Trollope protests: "It is the nature of a man to appreciate his own work [...]. The policeman is ambitious of arresting everybody. The lawyer would rather make your will for gratis than let you make your own. The General can believe in nothing but in well-trained troops" (*JC* 452). For Trollope, such zeal as Bagwax's was a manifestation of "manliness." As I explore further in chapter 4, Trollope valued work as a source of "manly independence" and praised "the obedience of the workman to his work. That obedience which should induce a shoemaker to make his shoe well, even though the wearing of that shoe should bring him no personal credit" (*Four Lectures* 14). This concurs with Samuel Smiles's notion of duty as something that is "self-devoted" and transforms the smallest into the greatest: "The sphere of Duty is infinite. It exists in every station of life. We have it not in our choice to be rich or poor, to be happy or unhappy; but it becomes us to do the duty that everywhere surrounds us. Obedience to duty, at all costs and risks, is the very essence of the highest civilized life" (Smiles 2–3).

Caldigate from jail and happily restores him to the bosom of his family—reuniting him with his wife and child. In one sense, Bagwax's role in the story is one of alignment; he clears away the clash and clutter of symbols and adjudicates competing narratives in order to reveal, restore, and even replicate the straight lines of marital relation. Bagwax's obsessive deciphering of the envelope's codes produces a vision of the married couple, and his job entangles him in the structures of marriage to the ultimate degree: his restoration of the Caldigate marriage prompts his own progress into marriage with a fellow postman's daughter, Jemima Curlydown. Bagwax's reuniting of John and Hester Caldigate thus rouses in him twinned passions for postmarks and Jemima; both his postal job and marriage share similar schematics of duty and contract.

There are problems, however, with reading this novel, and the function of Bagwax, as overridingly restorative and regulating. One of the problems derives from the novel's bigamy. There are other ways to disrupt marriage—why does Trollope choose bigamy? Nancy Bentley has analyzed bigamy's spectral function in the domestic novel, arguing that more than adultery which "breaks the marriage contract […] the spectre of bigamy hints that marriage may not really be a contract at all" (Bentley 341–42). I think Bentley is right and that it is bigamy's—polygamy's—reiterative quality that makes it such a troublemaker. It doesn't break the marriage vow so much as baffle it.[31] The marriage vow works through iteration across a population, but when the reiterations are bigamous, issuing from the mouth of a single man, they crowd out the belief in the transformative power of the vow. Like Morgiana baffling the murderers and De Quincey imagining baffling the Post Office (see introduction, page 27), the multiplication of signifiers can stump the system. As I proposed, (see page 16), the penny stamp similarly reformulated the relation of "one" to "many." That this novel's marriage plot hinges on a postage stamp, as a sign of bigamy (one wife or many), amplifies that claim: the anonymity and scale of a mass communication system could allow correspondents to inhabit plural selves.

I also want to suggest that the very materiality of the postage stamp and postmarks that Bagwax uses to clear Caldigate's name and reunite him with his wife and child trouble the transcendency of the marriage plot, because their power in the narrative derives more from irregularity than it does from regulation. There are two features of the envelope and its postmark in *John Caldigate* that Bagwax uses to clear Caldigate's name. First, he observes that the postmark is too perfect, too clear-cut: "Letters in the post-office," he explains to the court, "are hurried quickly through the operation of stamping, so that

---

[31] Trollope was given the brush-off by the most famous of polygamists when returning from an 1872 trip to Australia that he'd made in order to see his son. He returned via America and attempted to see Brigham Young: "I came home across America from San Francisco to New York, visiting Utah and Brigham Young on the way. I did not achieve great intimacy with the great polygamist of the Salt Lake City." Young had kept Trollope in the doorway, refused to invite him in, and clearly had no idea who Trollope was (*Autobiography* 2: 204). It is a charmingly queer joke: the author of plots about infidelity is curious to meet the great father of polygamous living, but Trollope's own (embarrassing) obscurity prevents him enjoying "intimacy" with him.

one passing over the other while the stamping ink is still moist, will to some extent blot and blur" (*JC* 402). The absence of such blots and blurs reveals the studied and designing hand of an individual, rather than the disinterested, impersonal machineries of the postal clerks. Once again I am arguing that deviation from uniformity is the norm. And it is deviation that turns the postage stamp into a "tale-telling" device.

Uniformity was the trademark of the universal Penny Post and its related systems. The postage charge was made uniform, and so was the postage stamp; Queen Victoria's head was established as a single, recognizable sign of regulated, cheap postal passage. This whole question of the role of deviation in the significatory power of the Queen's profile comes to a climax in the courtroom when the prosecutor Sir John Joram, looking at the postage stamp on the envelope, exclaims, "Surely this little queen's head here can't be untrue" (*JC* 511). As both barrister and knight, he looks to the image of the Queen's head for guarantee of his legal authority and social position. It is a symbol that he needs to be stable and secure. But he is a bad reader of symbols. In fact, he can't see symbol at all. When he elides the gap between the symbolic and the literal (he doesn't call it a "stamp" or an "image," but rather a "head"). Bagwax and Trollope reveal that Joram's mistake is to look to the image for its faithfulness. Indeed his fixation on faithfulness makes Joram a bad reader. He turns the question of whether Caldigate has been faithful or true to his wife into a question of the faithfulness of the Queen, and neither question is the question to ask. Bagwax teaches Joram that the Queen's head signals no one truth. In fact, its usefulness as evidence derives not from its *faithfulness*, rather the opposite. It is the unfaithfulness of each copy, the deviations of its reproduction (*and* the fact that it is a copy, rather than the real deal that Sir John Joram seems to imagine), which allow it to be used as an instrument of justice. Trollope tells a story in which the symbol of the queen's head is important not for the "truth" that it can bear or represent, but for the irregularities and the relativities of the system that it can disclose.

The "meaning" of the queen's head is dismissed. Just as the contents of the letter are set aside in favor of this all-important envelope, and just as the sexual transgression is set aside in favor of a narrative that pivots not on sex or passion but on the legal formulation of the marriage contract. The letter itself makes it quite clear that Caldigate had a premarital sexual relationship (with Euphemia) while engaged to his future wife (Hester). Caldigate's lack of sexual purity is not, however, Trollope's focus, and he palms this narrative, delaying and subduing the revelation of it to his readers, with the result that it is no kind of revelation at all. This narrative delay is an antimoralist move. Instead of judging Caldigate's sexual adventures, or defining his fidelity sexually, Trollope's postal plot adheres to and highlights the legal framework of marriage, judging it as a contract, by the terms of its own contractual function.

Marriage is itself, Trollope emphasizes, network-like. The postal plot highlights the legal framework of marriage over and above romance, and the notion of the contract involved in both personal relationships and letter-exchange is an important element of the novel and one that was particularly topical in the 1870s. Trollope makes it clear that although John has not committed bigamy, he *is* guilty of breach of promise— the breaking off of an engagement.[32] In May 1879, the same year that *John Caldigate* was serialized and then published, the House of Commons vigorously debated whether or not breach of promise should continue to be an indictable offence, and a book detailing several recent breach of promise cases that had "appeared already very prominently before the public" was published later in the same year (MacColla 65). Personal letters were used in court to prove or disprove breach of promise cases. In his study of the offence, Charles MacColla quotes the affectionate opening of a love-letter and urges his readers not to feel that it is wrong to read it, reassuring them that such epistolary trespassing has become the order of the day: "The reader must not be burdened with the letter. In the cases given a few pages further on he can peruse letters such as this, which have had 'a world-wide circulation,' or 'the largest circulation in the world,' and so on" (MacColla 50). He elaborates on this question of circulation and readership, suggesting that while some people fear "the reading to the world of those two trunks of coloured letters" (MacColla 51), the "usual sample of female plaintiffs" wanted their letters to be read in court (MacColla 39). Such plaintiffs sought to have their intimate relationships validated and legitimated by the evidence of their letters. Once again, the letter features as more than a vehicle for the expression of sexual or romantic passion; MacColla describes the exchange and circulation of a letter as being like the sexual interactions of which the letters are a manifestation. The plaintiffs *desire* to have their private letters circulated and read just as they desire the men who are deserting them.

Trollope litters John Caldigate's life with potential breach of promise claims. When John's uncle, Humphrey Babington, helps John clear his debts, Babington's wife Polly subsequently expects John to marry their eldest daughter Julia. She "got him into her own closet upstairs, where she kept her linen and her jams and favourite liqueurs, and told him that his cousin Julia was dying in love for him" (*JC* 8). She then thrust Julia into his arms and "when he left the linen-closet the two ladies understood that the thing was arranged" (*JC* 8). Aunt Polly's trapping of John amidst her stock of conserves and alcohol, succinctly reflects the nature of her intentions; John is to be stored at Babington, put away like a preserve until he matures and inherits his family fortune, upon which he can marry and move into his father's house.[33] He emerges from the closet subject to a decidedly nonwritten and more-or-less unspoken covenant in which he has taken no active part. "He never said that he would marry her" (*JC* 8), but Caldigate has a nagging worry that he might be considered engaged, and he has to write a letter to his aunt extricating himself from

---

[32] After reading the manuscript of *John Caldigate*, Trollope's publisher, John Blackwood, wrote to Trollope pointing out how close the plot came to bigamy: "You are no doubt aware that Caldigates [*sic*] proceedings with the female adventurer would have made a marriage in Scotland" (Trollope, *Letters* 2: 730). Blackwood was himself Scottish, and his observation further emphasizes that marriage is contractually and culturally dependent and variable.

[33] For another example of a breach of promise case in which letters associate with comestibles, see James Greenwood, "A Tale of a Breach of Promise": "The love correspondence was contained in a tin biscuit box" (115). In *A Queer Showman and Other Stories* (London and New York: Ward, Lock), 1885.

this possibility. This episode comes to nothing and serves merely to establish Caldigate as inclined to stray, lusty but hapless ("he had not kissed Julia more than her sisters" *JC* 8), into breach of promise territory. It also serves to foreshadow the more serious situation that Caldigate ends up in with Euphemia Smith.

At a point when Caldigate is separated from and out of love with Euphemia, he recalls his promise to write to her: "He had promised that he would [write], and he must keep his word" (*JC* 107). Although he "would so fain have forgotten her," he remembers his words to her: "'I shall hold you as engaged to me,' he had said, 'and myself as engaged to you'" (*JC* 106–7). He therefore writes a letter to her, "squatting down just within the tent on a deal case which had contained boxes of sardines, bottles of pickles, and cans of jam" (*JC* 107–8). The detail of the preserves recalls the scene in Aunt Polly's linen and jam closet, and the situation is very similar; in both instances, John allows himself to become contracted, engaged to marry a woman whom he does not love. Trollope's explanation of Caldigate's decision to write to Euphemia links "shame" with the public, contractual nature of the "promise":

> It shames no man to swear that he loves a woman when he has ceased to love her; — but it does shame him to drop off from the love which he has promised. He balanced the matter in his mind for a while before he would send his letter. Then, getting up quickly, he rushed forth, and dropped it into the post-office box.
>
> (*JC* 108)

It might seem that "swearing" and "promising" are two similar speech acts, but Trollope asserts that false swearing in the name of upholding a promise is not shameful. The fact of the promise, the engagement to marry, alters or inflects all subsequent communication between the two people—and can completely invert the meaning and consequence of the utterance "I love you." Once again, love or sexual passion is not the end point of Trollope's narrative; he focuses rather on the contractual framework of love relationships and on the impersonal, social network of which heterosexual romantic relationships are but a part. Thus it is Caldigate's relationship with a public, with those who would shame him, rather than his relationship with "a woman," on which the scene focuses. And the post-letter is the agent in the scene. It will decide whether Caldigate will be shamed or not. In the above passage, the decision to write the letter is not dramatized or even represented. It is the decision to post the letter that is suspended, agonized over, and then done precipitously: "He rushed forth." Trollope understands the expansive potential for drama contained in the banal act of letting a letter slip from your fingers into a pillar-box, and he dramatizes the moment in several of his novels. In *The Eustace Diamonds* (1873), for example, Trollope emphasizes the moment of relinquishing a love-letter to the "iron stump" that he himself had invented (*ED* 1: 122). Frank Greystock has made his romantic feelings clear to Lucy Morris, expressing his love, but not sealing it with a proposal of marriage. He agonizes about whether or not he should propose to Lucy and eventually writes a letter in which he does ask her to marry him. He then agonizes further whether or not he should post the letter, but eventually, "He walked out of the Temple with it in his hand, and dropped it into a pillar-box just outside the gate. As the envelope slipped through his fingers, he felt that he had now bound himself to his fate" (*ED* 1: 122). Meanwhile, Lucy is tormented by the uncertainty of her relationship to Frank and the narrator remarks: "If only Lucy could have known of the letter, which was already her own property though lying in the pillar letter-box in Fleet Street [...]!" (*ED* 1: 132). The language of this passage is that of law and contract; Frank is "bound" and the letter is Lucy's "property."

Legal scholar Simon Gardner has researched the law of contract as it applied to post-letters.[34] Gardner explains that early nineteenth-century postal reforms provoked "a radically new perception of the nature of the post" by establishing in the public imagination an "equation of the posting of [a] letter with its delivery" (Gardner 180). He suggests that the prepayment of letters, the instituting of both door-front and street letter boxes and the much-lauded reliability of the service, all meant that the public imagined that a letter posted was a letter received. This perception, Gardner posits, may have influenced the courts to judge in 1869 that a contract became effective upon posting, rather than upon delivery. Gardner also argues that this was no obscure "legal curiosity," but something that "correlated with a general public consciousness about the post" (Gardner 184).

Gardner's focus is commercial contract law, but if we consider his general conclusions alongside the legislation surrounding contracts of marriage, then it is clear that the act of posting a love-letter was doubly charged. The moment in which the letter containing a proposal "slipped through his fingers" (*ED* 1: 122) into the pillar-box was indeed a "binding" moment; an offer of marriage was a legal contract, and the mailing of an offer activated that legal contract. The site of the law was the post-letter—the letters, if complete with the postmarks that were considered to transform the letter into a published text, were the evidence of such contracts. This legal shift was huge because it made the postal clerk who sorted or delivered the letter into a *reader*—though their eyes may not actually scan the page, when a letter passed through their hands, they became the site of its publication—and as such they could be brought onto the stand in a trial. They could be named as a *correspondent* in divorce or breach of promise cases. Juridical and literary characterizations of the postal functionary as a reader meant that all letters could be imagined as unfaithful to their senders and their addressees. The letters became promiscuous by being passed through the intermediating postal machinery.

Diverse and deviating lines of both communication and threads of human relation together form what Trollope calls "the web of our story" (*JC* 610). What Bagwax pulls out from this web is merely the straightened-out narrative configuration that is legible to

---

[34] See Simon Gardner, "Trashing with Trollope: A Deconstruction of the Postal Rules in Contract." For another account of Trollope's twinned interest in epistolarity and the laws of contract, see Coral Lansbury, *The Reasonable Man: Trollope's Legal Fiction* 202–3. Lansbury's study proposes that not enough scholarly attention has been paid to Trollope's written reports for the Post Office and their influence upon his novel writing. She makes an important link when she notes, "The Post Office under Francis Freeling and Rowland Hill was noted for its speed, efficiency, and handsome annual profits. When Trollope spoke of his virtues as a novelist he used the same terms in his own praise" (x).

the discourse of law. The fact that he almost doesn't pull it off discloses that the "straight" narrative is actually the exception rather than the rule of both postal and sexual communication. Trollope's postal plot reveals that the marriage plot is a relatively arbitrary narrative configuration. It is only through a master narrative of law that the network of human relations is reducible to simple paths of relation, and even then the traces of deviation remain; there are no moral highroads in this story. Trollope despised the hitching of the novel to morality, and this belief hitches him to some progressive views on gender. In an 1877 letter to American writer Kate Field, Trollope declaims the moralist's plots as conspiracies: "Who is the man of the world who exclaimed that 'a lecturing woman is a disgrace to her sex'? It is like the good little books which say that Tom told a lie and broke his leg, whereas Dick spoke the truth and was at once made a lord. There is no evidence of the facts but the statement of the writer."[35] What makes Trollope the mouthpiece of proto-women's rights here? Because elsewhere, his politics stiffened by discursive sobriety, he expresses quite different sentiments: "[…] we cannot alter the law [of the family arrangement […]. The necessity of the supremacy of man is as certain to me as the eternity of the soul."[36] When Trollope writes to Kate Field decrying "good little books," we should be attentive not only to the seeming political content of the lines, but also to their form: Trollope is flirting. Sociologist Georg Simmel theorized flirting as a way of imagining social leveling. He differentiated between sociability and the social, describing the "democratic nature of sociability," and observing that sociability can suspend social hierarchies, producing illusions of equity.[37] Flirting is a way of stylizing the sexual self that can sometimes, through its performativity, reimagine ones relationship to sex and gender limitations.[38] It is when Trollope *flirts* with a woman that he can express outrage at sexual politics that seek to keep women in their place. Just as Henry James drew a connection between Trollope's unfaithfulness to the art of the novelist and his capacity for representing lovelorn maidens, here sexual infidelity prompts Trollope to express an attraction to gender equity.[39]

---

[35] Bradford Allen Booth (ed.), *The Letters of Anthony Trollope* (London: Oxford UP, 1951), 362.
[36] *Letters*, 821.
[37] Georg Simmel, "Sociability" in *The Sociology of Georg Simmel* 47–48. See also Georg Simmel, "Flirtation," in *Georg Simmel: On Women, Sexuality, and Love* 133–52.
[38] For more on the indecisive erotic and Victorian flirting, see Richard A. Kaye's study, *The Flirt's Tragedy: Desire Without End in Victorian and Edwardian Fiction*.
[39] Trollope's biographers, N. John Hall and Victoria Glendinning, portray Trollope as caught between two paradigms regarding the emancipation of women. This ambivalence was most cartoonishly illustrated by Trollope's suggestion that women exercise the vote in alternate years with men! (*Trollope: A Biography* 339). Hall notes that Trollope both admired and opposed women who worked, but in his fiction was "highly sensitive to wrongs done to women by society's rules and conventions. When writing fiction he seems able to detach himself from his opinions" (340). Moreover, Trollope contributed gratis two stories to collections published by Emily Faithfull, who had established a feminist publishing house staffed entirely by women, called the Victoria Press. Hall notes that one of the tales has a Kate Field–like heroine and explains Trollope's generosity to the feminist press: "He seems to have regarded doing so as a kind of friendly lark, done chiefly for the sake of Emily Faithfull herself" (340). If we accept this description, it bolsters my reading of Trollope's correspondence with Field: "friendly larks" must not be overlooked as saucy overpasses to better gender politics.

The punch line to this flirtation is that Kate Field was a lesbian. Once again, Trollope's heterosexual perambulations land him in a queer position. Sharon Marcus has documented Field's erotic life with women, and specifically discussed its effect on her friendship with Trollope. Marcus cites Trollope's "confusion" (Marcus 230) at Field's romantic and domestic choices, but notes that Trollope (protected by masculine, heterosexual privilege) nevertheless maintained friendships with Field and other lesbians who were abandoned by feminist friends when the threat of sexual scandal gathered over them.[40] Trollope's fondness for "love-lorn maidens and other embarrassed persons" (*Partial Portraits* 122) was "postal" in the sense that he understood sexual identification as built from dispatches, relays and—above all—rovings. Trollope stood by sexual relations that went astray.

THIS LITTLE QUEEN'S HEAD

John Caldigate is a pro-sex novel. Not only does Trollope refuse to moralize or sensationalize Caldigate's premarital affair and "jolly"[41] bachelor years, but he also makes Caldigate's promiscuity a desirable attribute. He does this by pitting it against the sexual puritanism of Hester's mother, the evangelical Mary Bolton who lives, pointedly, at *Puritan Grange*. Mrs. Bolton is the figure who is most scorned in this story and who is perhaps the most extreme and scorned of all the low-church fanatics in Trollope's novels. Even before she knows of John Caldigate's entanglement with Euphemia she doesn't want Hester to experience sex or the world: "all sensual gratifications were wicked in her sight," Trollope writes, and "on behalf of her child, she desired seclusion from the world" (*JC* 172). "Sensuality" and "the world" are synonymous for Mrs. Bolton, who seeks to delimit Hester's circulation, while John Caldigate circulates freely. Her desperate desire to preserve her daughter's sexual continence is mocked by the narrator and also by her own husband, Robert Bolton, whose profession as a banker gives him authority on matters circulatory: when his wife denounces brides who adorn themselves in "gold and pearls" and "go out into the world," he defends material and sexual dissemination as "evidently intended" (*JC* 177). The standoff between Mary Bolton and the rest of her family is configured as a question of faithfulness. Mary Bolton is too faithful—possessed of a self-righteous sexual puritanism that leads her to lock up her daughter (literally), while Caldigate's sexual unfaithfulness—his infidelity—appears as plainly preferable.

Not only does infidelity appear preferable, but it is also, I would argue, theorized by Trollope as integral to marriage. Mrs. Bolton seeks to lock up her daughter before she knows anything of the slur of *bigamy* because she conceives of the *exogamy* of marriage as an infidelity to the home. When Hester takes her marriage vows, Mary Bolton makes a doubling, variant vow: "The mother standing up in the dark corner of her pew heard her daughter's silver-clear voice as she vowed to devote herself to her husband. As she heard

---

[40] Sharon Marcus, *Between Women* 229–32.
[41] This is the term Trollope uses repeatedly about his own bachelor years. See *Autobiography* 1: 67, 86, 91.

it, she also devoted herself. When sorrow should come as sorrow certainly would come, then she would be ready once again to be a mother to her child. But till that time should come the wife of John Caldigate would be nothing to her" (*JC* 197). Mary Bolton's vow, which is both a malediction—a disowning—and an affirmation of maternal duty, forms what Eve Kosofsky Sedgwick calls "a permanent shunt across the marriage proscenium" (*Touching Feeling* 74). Mary Bolton's utterance displaces the speech act being performed by her daughter and, along with Euphemia, she joins a long cast of women in this novel who complicate the marriage utterance. Noting how hard it is to make heterosexuality visible, Sedgwick shows that heterosexuality makes totalizing claims on history or romance, using what she calls the "institutional pseudonyms" of "Inheritance, Marriage, Dynasty, Family, Domesticity, and Population" (*Tendencies* 10-11). In *John Caldigate* Trollope investigates marriage as a pseudonym. He interrogates the pseudonym (via "euphemism," for example) and in so doing makes it evident that marriage is all about names. Through Bagwax, he pits the performative speech act of "just by telling me that I am" against the performative speech act of the marriage ceremony. Postal devices come into play in the plot by doing their own "telling." Both the novel's plot and the courtroom are concerned only with the question of whether or not Caldigate had been legally married to Euphemia. The sexual contents of the letter are set aside, almost unread, in favor of the "reading" of the envelope. Its mode of address ("*Mrs.* Caldigate") and the postmarked date are the details that, in the words the judge later uses, are "very material" (*JC* 461). The postmarks on the envelope both date and validate it as evidence; as Bagwax later explains, "a letter sent regularly by the post—that would be real evidence" (*JC* 503).[42]

The postage stamp began its career as a "telltale." In 1839, the Post Office reformer Rowland Hill held a competition to come up with a way of marking that a letter had been prepaid. He rejected every one of the 550 entries and modestly declared himself the winner, with his own design of the postage stamp, the now familiar adhesive label featuring the Queen's head. He called this penny stamp a "tell-tale device" (*Post Office Reform* 38), a quirky phrase that blends intimations of the schoolyard, courtroom, and peep show. A telltale has an irregular relationship with the disciplinary institutions that stand for the regulation of knowledge. The taleteller also benefits, gaining profit or even pleasure from the disclosure. Hill's curious description reveals key elements of the complicated role that the Post Office, as a state institution that both incited and legislated the circulation of knowledge and information, would play across the course of the nineteenth century. In *John Caldigate*, Trollope emphasizes that names, addresses, initials, and Post Office "hieroglyphics" (*JC* 452) can all tell tales. They are all textual systems that have the

---

[42] Trollope's knowledge of both Post Office and the law meant that he understood how significant a postmark could be and how it altered the nature of the missive that it accompanied. The postmark showed that a letter had passed through the postal system and simultaneously signaled that the letter had passed from being a private document to being a public one. According to *Roscoe's Digest of the Law of Evidence in Criminal Cases*, "If a letter containing a libel have the post-mark upon it, that is *prima facie* evidence of its having been published" (674).

capability to signify, and signify more, in fact, than the letter they helped transport. The media itself—when interpreted by the intermediary Bagwax—becomes a protagonist in the tale of tangled sexual relationships. The network is, to use Edward Carpenter's phrase, a "moving force" in the business of marriage and extramarital relationships.[43]

In this narrative, Bagwax defends that which is *marital* through his expertise in the postmarks that are, in the words of the trial judge, "very *material*" (emphasis added, *JC* 461). Throughout the novel Trollope examines the ways in which private transactions and personal relationships get misconstrued from actions and the accounts of others and material pieces of evidence that "tell." Chapter 29 of the novel is entitled "Just by telling me that I am." John has just determined against paying his blackmailer, fearing that making a payment might "tell" against him, and that it might suggest that the accusations of bigamy were true:

> The evidence against him, already named, was very strong, but they had been put in possession of other, and as they thought more damning evidence than any to which he had alluded in telling his version of the story to Robert Bolton. The woman had produced […] the envelope of a letter addressed in John Caldigate's handwriting to "Mrs. Caldigate, Ahalala, Nobble," which letter had been dated inside from Sydney, and which envelope bore the Sydney post-mark […]. The letter itself she also produced but it told less than the envelope.
>
> (*JC* 280)

The dismissal of the letter as "immaterial" is surprising; it is a letter that makes it quite clear that Caldigate and Euphemia Smith had a sexual relationship. Sex, however, is not "material" here. Caldigate becomes, briefly, a radically public persona as the open secret of his supposed bigamous marriage with a woman in Australia gets interrogated in the courts:

> When it would all come out in the dreaded trial he would be quite unable to defend himself. […] And yet—and yet there had been nothing which he had not dared to own to his wife in the secrecy of their mutual confidence, and which in secret, she had not been able to condone without a moment's hesitation […]. The story would be very bad as told in Court, and yet he had told it all to his wife!
>
> (*JC* 380)

Caldigate is appalled that the secrecy to which he believes marriage has entitled him can be shattered when the law suspects that his marriage is illegal. Rescuing Caldigate from the public eye requires a superhuman effort by the postal clerk, and it is a rescue that can only be achieved by this clerk's single-mindedness and his utter indifference to the deflecting, moral question of extramarital sex. Bagwax can restore the privacy of marriage

---

[43] See introduction, p. 5.

precisely because he is not interested in sexual morality but is instead only interested in postage stamps. It is the contractual, not the sexual, status of the marriage that matters.

DRESS AND ADDRESS

I want now to outline a series of identifications and cross-identifications that vex the seeming stability of the name in this novel that has a name for a title. The first vexed identification is patrilineal. *John Caldigate* opens with direct and explicit descriptions of the inadequacies of the father-son relationship between Squire Caldigate and his son John—stern, peculiarly paternal estrangements that recall those which Trollope suffered at the hands of his own father who habitually "knocked me down with the great folio Bible" (*Autobiography* 1: 20). If the young Anthony suffered at the hands of the Law of the Father, he gets his say in this novel, as the rifts between Squire and John Caldigate beget multiple denouncements of primogeniture, entails, and patrilineal legal orders in general.[44] In *Tendencies*, Eve Kosofksy Sedgwick diagnoses the violence that the young Trollope experiences at the hands of his father as *marital*, noting that the boy was "Left by his mother *in the mother's place*" (*Tendencies* 212).[45] Like John Caldigate whose mother and sisters die when he is in adolescence, twelve-year-old Anthony was abandoned by his mother and sisters when they headed off for America to try and make the fortune that Thomas Anthony Trollope seemed unable to build or keep.[46]

John Caldigate is a remarkably unstable character. He spends the duration of the novel shuttling between wives, households, contracts, continents, and states of legality and illegality, reputation and shame. Even the way that the title seems to privilege him, figuring him central to the text is misleading: Trollope shifted the title of the book back and forth between *Mrs. John Caldigate* and *John Caldigate's Wife* before finally settling on simply *John Caldigate*.[47] These draft titles help reveal that *John Caldigate* is less a declarative

---

[44] Before a bout of nostalgia for the soon-to-be-lost scenes of childhood, John ruminates upon how "there had seemed to him to be something ridiculous in the idea of a permanent connection between the names of Caldigate and Folking. It was absurd that, with so wild and beautiful a world around him, he should be called upon to live in a washy fen because his father and grandfather had been unfortunate enough to do so" (*JC* 20). Although his nostalgia, which enlists him in service to "the hearths of many generations of Caldigates," might seem to undo such recognition of the absurdity of the patrilineal, the trace remains. As I shall explore, the novel proceeds to open up the legal fault lines in family and fatherhood. The twinned law of the father and law of the land too nearly prevent Caldigate from assuming his position in this lineage to remain themselves entirely unscathed.

[45] Eve Kosofsky Sedgwick's essay "A Poem Is Being Written" (echoing Freud's "A Child is Being Beaten") links the "severe economy" (184) *Tendencies,* 177-214) of poetic meter with that which disciplines the youthful body—the slap of the parental hand. The essay cites Sedgwick's own "half-written novel-length narrative poem with a Victorian setting," (178) *The Warm Decembers,* coming to rest on a section about Anthony Trollope's violent childhood. Sedgwick's project throughout this chapter is to comprehend the power of sexual identifications that refuse to align with adult "pseudolinearity of differentiated gender and identity formation" (211).

[46] Trollope consolidates his identification with his character by noting that John attends Harrow, as he himself did.

[47] See N. John Hall (ed.), *The Letters of Anthony Trollope* 2: 724–31.

identity than a site of relativity—an address. This address is not only used as evidence of bigamy, but it also underscores the gender transitivity inherent to marriage: marriage is one way a "John" can be a "Mrs." or a "Wife."

If Trollope notes the complex choreography of identification and gender roles through his title, this theme is amplified because the blackmailing, would-be Mrs. John Caldigate, Euphemia, has a career on the stage. I have been arguing that this novel posits a relationship between being a postman and being a novelist. It also, and relatedly, posits a relationship between being a novelist and being an actor—or, more precisely—an actress. The novel pays close attention to the power of dress, and costume is repeatedly deployed as a mode of dress-up, disguise, and betrayer of identity—and furthermore, as a means of producing gender, class, and sexual transitivity. Caldigate plays at being a miner by dressing as one. Caldigate's bosom buddy Dick Shand, whom we first meet when his mother is sewing buttons onto his "thick woolen drawers" (*JC* 33), is known by his bright yellow trousers. Dick's mother fretfully charges John to make sure that Dick wears underwear, warning that appearances are not everything and that her son is not as strong as he looks. The wicked Trollope reports: "Our hero who had always regarded his friend as a bull for strength of constitution generally, promised that he would be attentive to Dick's drawers" (*JC* 33). John is not only attentive to Dick's drawers, but also to the Dick in the drawers: at the end of the novel we are told: "One of the few things which Caldigate did before he took his wife abroad was to 'look after Dick Shand' " (*JC* 612) whose "yellow trousers and the manners which accompanied them" (*JC* 612) had made life hard for him in England. Caldigate sees that Dick is shipped off back to Australia to live his yellow-trousered life there, financed by Caldigate money. Dick becomes, in other words, John Caldigate's mistress.

While it is roaringly plain that Trollope's wit about Dick and his knickers is self-consciously homoerotic, it is not the only sexual horse- or role-play that John gets up to. Having promised to make Dick wear his underwear, the Shand "females" turn their attention to John's undergarments. At first "somewhat modest" about handing them over, "that feeling soon wore off, and the markings and mendings, and buttonings and hemmings went on in a strictly impartial manner as though he himself were a chick out of the same brood" (*JC* 34). Surrounded by women determined on alterations, John becomes a "chick," cross-dressed and thoroughly part of the feminine cluckings. This is not the only incidence of matters sartorial producing cross-gender identifications. Later in the plot, when Caldigate is brought to hear the deposition of Euphemia, the scene parallels the Harrow headmaster recognizing Trollope not by his face but by his backside: "The woman was closely veiled, so that he could not see a feature of her face; but he knew her figure well" (*JC* 279). The closeness of this parallel might well lead us to extend Trollope's claim "Was I not a Bagwax myself?" to "Was I not a Euphemia myself?" Trollope extends himself, and his extensions are no respecter of boundaries.

The result? The trope of a tangled web, to which Trollope repeatedly turns. Forms of personal communication are the threads that form what Trollope calls "the web of our story" (*JC* 610) and from early on, the novel hones in on the problems of miscommunication, noncommunication, and interference. Caldigate's early troubles in life are caused by broken and undeveloped lines of communication. When trapped in the linen closet, Trollope informs us: "Had he been more communicative, he might perhaps have saved himself from that scene" (*JC* 10). "That scene" takes place because of John's inarticulacy with both his aunt and his father; the father-son relationship had broken down partly because the squire was "silent unless when he had something to say" and John "lent him a very inattentive ear" when he did (*JC* 1–2). Later in the novel Trollope movingly describes how Caldigate's relationship with his father, which had brought such "crushing troubles upon each of them" in Folking (*JC* 1), is mended by a long-distance correspondence between them. "John had promised to write [to his father]. The promise had not been very enthusiastically given; but still, as the months went by it was constantly remembered" (*JC* 116). Squire Caldigate receives monthly letters from John, "which came to be expected at Folking, till each letter was regarded as the rising of the new sun" (*JC* 119). These letters both document and bring about the rising of a new *son*; not only has John begun to make his fortune, but he has also learned how to have a relationship with his father and begun to understand himself as belonging in or to Folking. At the outset of the novel, John "hated Folking. He was certain that any life would suit him better than a life to be passed as squire of Folking" (*JC* 13), but during the course of correspondence, John's letters received by his father in Folking began to be *sent* from Folking: subsequent to finding gold, John names his claim after his hometown. In a neat illustration of the colonial goals of postal expansion—to make everywhere England, and annihilate time and space—a Folking in England and a Folking in Australia are connected by the post. And the heartiness of Trollope's plot and sensibility suggests the aural play: "fucking" in England and "fucking" in Australia are connected by the post.[48] This epistolary tautology also signals how completely John has replaced himself in his father's title and affections; after three years of regular correspondence, "there had come to be a complete confidence between him and his father" (*JC* 119). Travel and distance, bridged by the postal system, proves more binding than physical proximity, and John's relationships with both his father and his wife and son are restored and reinvigorated through a separation mended by postal correspondence.

Communication and lines of communication are not straightforward, but rather tangled and capable of both manipulation and mending. Trollope's sympathy toward John Caldigate's wayward ways and tangled love affairs is a manifestation of Trollope's understanding of the postal system as a discursive machinery that can be used to police human relation, but only through disclosing the ways in which, as James suggested, diversity and deviation are fundamental to human relations.

---

[48] For more on Trollope's taste for double entendre see Mark Turner, *Trollope and the Magazines* 183–221.

POSTMEN AND VAGRANTS

To end this chapter, I return to James's 1888 reflections on how Trollope's postal work made him a queer sort of novelist and draw out one further implication of that passage. James writes: "Trollope was familiar with all sorts and conditions of men [...] his work is full of implied reference to the whole arena of modern vagrancy." What does James mean by that striking phrase "modern vagrancy?" Trollope was a *traveling* inspector for the Post Office, and he himself described his postal career causing him to write his novels under "vagrant conditions" (*Autobiography* 1: 168). Novels happened on the go, as a sideline, moonlighting even. Trollope's mode of novel-production retains the scent of something illicit, something unfaithful or promiscuous. I am suggesting that James's reference to "modern vagrancy" cements the connections I have described both him and Trollope building between circulation and queerness.[48] The historian of sexuality Jeffrey Weeks has noted that late-century "vagrancy" acts were acts that were used to target homosexual cottaging.[49] This legislation consolidated a trope of vagrancy as sexual deviation, figuring the homosexual and his passion as perambulatory or circulatory, and, crucially vice versa. To worry about the homosexual as a wandering, circulating subject is to worry that circulation itself installs or enacts deviance. It was in this way that the homosexual and the post-letter were imagined to have similar operations: both circulating, instituting digression, engendering queer interfaces, and—to return to Carpenter's phrase—ramifying widely through modern society.

---

[48] Another Trollope text that clearly establishes this relation between homosexuality, vagrancy, and circulation is his 1869 short story "The Turkish Bath." This story traces the relationship, inaugurated in a Turkish bath on Jermyn Street, between a magazine editor and a down-and-out writer named Molloy. The Jermyn Street baths, which Trollope himself frequented, were all male and became known as a cruising ground. I have been arguing that Trollope is a trollop, and in this story it is clear that Mr. Malloy plays the part of a "Molly," that is to say a prostitute or fag. For more on this story and its sexual tension, see Mark Turner, *Trollope and the Magazines* 201–7.

[49] Jeffrey Weeks, *Sex, Politics and Society* 85, 87, 106.

3

A Queer Job for a Girl

THE COMMUNICATIVE TOUCH IN TROLLOPE, HARDY, AND LYNN LINTON

BETWEEN 1877 AND 1881, Anthony Trollope, Thomas Hardy, and Eliza Lynn Linton[1] published stories which all portray women companions who are "more like lovers than girl and girl" (Hardy, *Laodicean* 50). The women are also all telegraph operators or Post Office employees. This chapter explores why working for the Post Office or with postal technologies goes hand in hand with these women's "predilection" (Hardy, *Laodicean* 113) for women. These are fictions that ask what work and domesticity might look like for the unmarried, middle-class woman who chooses a working life. Their answer is that these workers, workplaces and households look lesbian: Anthony Trollope's 1877 short story "The Telegraph Girl," Eliza Lynn Linton's 1880 novel, *The Rebel of the Family*, and Thomas Hardy's 1881 novel *A Laodicean* all depict their heroines in passionate relation to another woman and trace how these couples set up same-sex domesticity. The heroines eventually leave behind both same-sex partnership and postal work, as the plots each resolve into heterosexual marriage and female non-employment. The traces of queer erotics and financial independence remain, however. Having figured the women as part of a communication matrix and civil service, this fiction finds it hard to completely vanquish the alternatives that those networks allowed the women to glimpse, or indeed, touch. Post Office work and lesbian partnership may be just a phase, but the hasty heterosexual marriage plots with which each story ends are overhung with remnant, affective threads which loop the women back around to lives and loves precursive to marriage. Communications work,

---

[1] These writers were all known to each other. Anthony Trollope corresponded briefly with both Eliza Lynn Linton and Thomas Hardy, and Lynn Linton and Hardy were in lengthier communication with each other beginning in 1888.

and "communicative" girls out-trammel the trammels of marriage, with the consequence that unidirectional vectors of desire and attachment can no longer be guaranteed.

The heroines' subjectivities are formed by working with circulation systems that literally and metaphorically engage practices of *passing round* and *writing back*. The women work in what Jean Baudrillard has described as a "universe of communication," made up of "connections, contact, contiguity, feedback, and generalized interface" (1983). Baudrillard's essay is useful because it characterizes interface culture as entailing erotic sprawl, and is indeed titled (in translation) "The Ecstasy of Communication." But Baudrillard condemns the erotics he describes, claiming that communicative ecstasy has numbed us even to alienation (and thus its revolutionary potential). He extends the metaphor of sexual depravity, decrying the "*promiscuity* that reigns over the communication networks" (my italics 131) and what he calls the "*pornography* of information and communication" (my italics 131).[2] Baudrillard's call to resist the orgy of an overwired world is made from the perspective of late capital, animated by a fear of playwrights becoming automatons, and the rest of us similarly enslaved to our computer terminals.[3] In Baudrillard's late-twentieth-century dystopia, sex and the communication network together dissolve public space and subjectivity.

But the nineteenth-century fiction I will explore in this chapter does not figure the worker as privatized, made into a "pure screen, a switching center for all the networks of influence" (153). Instead, it explores the very public role and public spaces given to the communications worker in the nineteenth century, asking how these public aspects of the employment affect the woman worker who is entering civil service for the first time. She, too, of course, must be understood to be at risk of being consumed by the machinery of capital, but loss of subjectivity is not new to the female character, and the ways she gets lost within the communication network sometimes appear generative, or at least, alternative to more conventional forms of female disappearance. The noise and the feedback of the network can act as useful amplification devices, and the prosthetic relations they engage—putting women in relation to each other, to supervisors, to customers and myriad correspondents—function as a stent that can relieve some of the pressures of unelected subjectivity. The practice of achieving female subjectivity through a marital attachment to a single, oppositely sexed partner is not, in the stories I explore, compelling or concluding. The resultant marriages are instead fretted by recognition of the other

---

[2] This conflation of sexual and communication excesses, along with a mistrust of both, is to be found throughout Baudrillard's work. When he writes of the subject being "seduced" by the object, the root sense of the word "seduce" is being "led astray" by excess of signs and meanings. This is unlike De Quincey's Scheherazade who proposes that overwhelming the hostile sign with a plethora of signs is a good way of confounding the enemy (see introduction).
[3] Baudrillard briefly addresses the otherwise antisex consequences of his metaphors, when he proposes that obscenity has itself changed—that "the hot, sexual obscenity of former times is succeeded by the cold and communicational, contractual and motivational obscenity of today. The former clearly implied a type of promiscuity, but it was organic. [...]. Unlike this organic, visceral, carnal promiscuity, the promiscuity that reigns over the communication networks is one of superficial saturation" (151–52).

options they have foreclosed. Postal routes allow these women access to alternate erotic and social routes, and these routes play against the marriage plots.

Sedgwick has proposed that many a Victorian novel finds the climax of its sexual plot in what she calls "periperformative refusals, fractures, warpings of the mobile proscenium of marital witness" (*Touching Feeling* 73). The periperformative is, she explains, not itself an utterance as we derive the concept from J. L. Austin, but rather something that surrounds and troubles and even un-utters the utterance. The end of Trollope's "The Telegraph Girl" demonstrates peri-performativity to a T: how his heroine "became as good a wife as ever blessed a man's household, need hardly here be told" ("TG" 385). It is an acknowledged paradox that the Victorian marriage plot rarely shows you the marriage toward which the entire novel has driven, but Trollope's story ends with a double omission, a negating formulation that specifically shuts down the "telling"—I won't show you the marriage, and I won't tell you about it either. The other two stories also end with troubled utterances: Hardy's heroine closes out her story with a sigh and a wish that her husband were more like her female lover, and Lynn Linton tempers an otherwise didactic concluding engagement scene by allowing her heroine to wonder what has become of her lesbian suitor (*Laodicean* 397). Sighs, silences, and regrets constitute interference—noise on the line—that scrambles the univocality of the vow "I do."

CIVILLY SERVICING

The three stories I will examine were published in the immediate wake of women entering the civil service and during a time of vigorous debate about whether the sex and marital status of the civil servant, itself an emergent identity, had a relationship to the work they did for the state. The three heroines all look alike: the descriptions of their physical appearance, as workaday and decidedly unromantic looking, are remarkably similarly expressed. Lynn Linton's Perdita Winstanley is "unlovely" (*RF* 6) and "plain" (*RF* 10), and Trollope's Lucy Graham is characterized by a "serviceable" and "pervading brownness" ("TG" 356). In *A Laodicean*, Thomas Hardy's heroine, Paula Power, has an "imperfect" face and she, too, is predominantly "brown" (*Laodicean* 17). Brown like wrapping paper and twine, these heroines' plainness equips them all the better for public service. They fiercely desire to find meaningful work or position in the public world, and their struggles for self-definition turn upon the question of whether they are destined for the workplace and public life—an ending each author portrays as lesbian—or for the enclosure of marriage.

The Post Office was the gate through which women first entered the civil service. Women workers were admitted into the Post Office workforce in 1870 as a so-called "daring experiment" (Post 33/3213) by the authorities.[4] Their employment was in fact not daring at all, but rather a side effect of nationalization. The 1869 Telegraph Act, which

---

[4] In *Women in English Life: From Medieval to Modern Times*, Georgiana Hill also cites the Postmaster-General of 1871 using the term "experiment" to apply to the employment of women clerks (2: 179).

was implemented on 5 February 1870, had handed over complete control of the telegraph system to the Postmaster-General. The government purchased the separate, privately owned businesses that dealt with inland telegraphs prior to this time and thereby simply inherited the services of the women operators who already worked for these commercial companies. Thus, as civil service historian Hilda Martindale explains, "By this act women for the first time became civil servants" (15). The "experiment" was a notable success; the Post Office soon became the largest single employer of women in the country and, as I shall explain later, women soon came to be regarded as ideal Post Office workers specifically *because* of their gender. In turn, the Post Office was commonly seen as a spouse or guardian of these women. The institution offered women what Anthony Trollope called "tender surveillance" ("YW" 378); the government department was imagined to provide for and protect the unmarried women workers in place of a father or husband.

It was also a homosocial environment in which the women's sensory organs, their "fingers, eyes, ears and intellects" (Trollope, "YW" 377–84), mediated and disseminated the public's personal messages: mail passed through large rooms of women whose job it was to transmit and translate feeling. They turned vibrations into messages, and together they formed what might be called a homo-sensorium. Moreover, the work of mediating and disseminating messages had hermeneutic potential: the meaning and status of the post-letters or telegrams was changed by being passed through the women's workers' interpretative bodies. Not only could the women "read" the letters that they processed, becoming a third party to private correspondence, but also the relationships between the women workers could interact with and entwine the messages they sorted. In short, the trajectory of a post-letter or telegram was anything but straight. The organization that enabled its swift, cheap, and regular distribution was enabled by a complex material network that prompted the public to imagine the postal system as an instigator of an infinite variety of human interfaces.[5] The girls' mediations of human intercourse fired the cultural imagination and produced fictional accounts of the impassioned bonds between "communicative" (Hardy, *Laodicean* 32) girls.

The Post Office specifically recruited well-educated, middle-class women for their workforce. The relationship between work and marriage for middle-class women was in the second half of the nineteenth century generally undergoing change. Middle-class girls and women started to be sent to schools and colleges and were encouraged to take up philanthropic work. Although many reformers viewed female education and charitable work as a means of strengthening the moral, home-focused life of women and the nation, education and charity work nonetheless introduced young women to public, institutional life and notions of civic duty. Elaine Showalter has pointed out that although unmarried women were regarded as a social "problem" across the nineteenth century, there was a simultaneous, growing awareness of the "unmarried woman as a new political

---

[5] The word "interface," which the OED traces back to the 1880s, is a term that often appeared in periodical literature about postal communication from midcentury onward.

and sexual group, not just an absence or cipher in the social body, but a constituency with potential opportunities, powers and rights" (21). "Constituency" is an appropriate term: unmarried women entered the social body via largely female communities like school and philanthropic societies that offered an alternative social network to that of the family. Showalter's use of the word signals how nineteenth-century middle-class women's move into the public sphere was an important means to acquiring political agency. Working women, in other words, had begun to acquire a civic profile.

In the second half of the nineteenth century, discussion of the "woman question" homed in on the ostensible problem of what W. R. Greg and others called "redundant" women, for whom there would be no chance of marriage. Reaction to this "problem" sedimented out into debates about separate spheres which pitted the middle-class domestic home against the public arena.[6] The premise that society was burdened with superfluous women who were not contained in marriage, however, concealed a demographic sleight of hand. The debate centered on middle-class women, but its prompt, the results of the 1851 census, had specifically referred to *working-class* women.[7] Separate sphere rhetoric was driven not only by concerns that middle-class women who worked would become equivalent to, or like men, but also by concerns that they might become confused with working-class women. The later nineteenth century was haunted by the spectre of middle-class women whose primary companions were other working women and whose class positions were vulnerable because of their wage-earning status in the public sphere.

The admission of women into the postal workforce occurred in the midst of this intense debate about the sexual and class status of the woman worker. It also occurred at a time when general definitions of the civil service and the role of the male civil servant were similarly contested. As early as the 1850s, there had been growing discontent in the Post Office workforce, and this escalated across the last quarter of the century into full-scale worker disputes. Wages were low and were lowered further on several occasions; fines for misdemeanors were imposed; workers who campaigned for better conditions were imprisoned; strikes were busted and union organizers were put under surveillance. Ironically, postal workers suspected of unionizing activity had their own mail and telegraph messages intercepted. These struggles threw into relief the eccentric civic position of the civil servant; he served a citizenry of which he was not allowed to be fully part. Most notably, he was not allowed to vote until a long-awaited "Bill of Rights" was carried in Parliament "in despite of formidable opposition" in

---

[6] See W. R. Greg, "Why Are Women Redundant?" 434–60. Greg was a liberal manufacturer, and a regular contributor to periodicals, whose concern with the remedy of social ills found full expression when he cofounded the eugenics movement with Francis Galton.

[7] See Elizabeth K. Helsinger, Robin Lauterbach Sheets, William Veeder, *The Woman Question: Social Issues, 1837–1883* 2: 134. This is a compendious three-volume study of the woman question in nineteenth-century Britain and America. For further studies of women and work in the nineteenth century and the separate spheres debate, see Martha Vicinus, *Independent Women: Work and Community for Single Women 1850–1920* and Lee Holcombe, *Victorian Ladies at Work: Middle-Class Working Women in England and Wales*.

1868. This lack of franchise was a relic of the eighteenth-century method of recruiting postal workers through patronage. Patronage could leave employees open to demands for political allegiance to the patron and in 1782, postal clerks had petitioned for the removal of their franchise rights in order to protect themselves from coercion. In the nineteenth century, after postal reform, nationalization, and the dissolve of recruitment by patronage, the demand for the franchise for civil servants was the cornerstone of a drawn-out crisis in the definition of citizenship: how were public servants to understand themselves? Did they, as Sir Stevenson Blackwood, who headed the commission investigating Post Office labor disputes claimed, "forfeit the privileges of English citizenship by entering the public service"? Blackwood remarked that workers' "private lives" were severely compromised by their "public service" and he condemned the Post Office for allowing its workers fewer rights than the British subjects whom they served (Donald 13).[8] This argument highlighted once again that the postal worker occupied a thoroughly median position; not only did he materially mediate the textual exchanges of others, but he also held an intermediate position in terms of civic constructions of public and private.

The conflict over the male workers' civic status also entangled their sexual status. The Post Office was repeatedly accused of emasculating its workers; to be intermediate was, many feared, to be effeminate. Trollope articulated this connection between civic and gender/sexual status in a lecture about allegiance, obedience, and authority that he delivered to postal workers in 1861 titled "The Civil Service as a Profession." Trollope equates "manliness" with the nature of the profession: "Then as to the independence, or what I may call the manliness, of our profession! [...] Manliness, a spirit of independence, grows quickly with a man, as does a deficiency of that spirit" (Trollope, *Lectures* 12). The connection between masculinity and the obligations involved in civil service work was a persistent concern of Trollope's. In his autobiography, the only Post Office reform of which he voices approval is civil service examinations, suggesting that it might bring the public servant "in closer connection with the real master who pays him—the public" (Trollope, *Autobiography* 12). He also warns against treating civil servants like machines, emphasizing that "the first and chief obedience required is that of a workman to his work [...] an obedience which is Godlike in its nature, and which is the very source and fountain spring of manly independence!" (Trollope, *Autobiography* 14). The crux here is the relationship between the master and the servant; Trollope wants the master of postal workers to be either the work itself or a communal body, "the public." He approves of civil service examinations because they replaced appointment through patronage—a system that left the civil servant beholden to a man of higher rank. Otherwise, he believed that manliness had been endangered by the increased bureaucratization of the Post Office, and in 1870 many others, including Union organizers, saw the employment of women as

---

[8] See A. K. Donald, *Why There Is Discontent in the Post Office*. For a full account of the lengthy and complex worker disputes for which the Post Office became notorious, see H. G. Swift, *A History of Postal Agitation from Fifty Years Ago Till the Present Day*.

both sign and cause of the increased erosion of the status, rights, wages, and masculinity of male postal workers.[9]

For many, women laborers were, as the professional antifeminist Eliza Lynn Linton put it, "a proof of a barbarous and imperfect civilization," and working women therefore seriously threatened the "community or nation" ("Queen Bees" 576).[10] "Civilization," "community," and "nation" were the foundational principles of the reformed Post Office. From the late 1830s onward, the Post Office had been seen as a "civilizing engine" (Hill, *Post Office Reform* 7) that promoted national and imperial unity. The reformed Post Office's "universal" invitation to each and every household and citizen to imagine themselves as connected to each other and as part of a national discourse network stumbled over the idea that the discourse functionaries themselves could be "universal"—women as well as men. Not only was there opposition to the Post Office employing women because of the effect of employment upon middle-class womanhood, but the terms of this opposition suggested that working women would erode the national and imperial ideals of the postal mission.

Nonetheless, in 1871 the Postmaster-General, Mr. Frank Ives Scudamore, extended the employment of women as telegraph operators, also appointing them to clerical work. His description of the rationale behind this move and the general desirability of women employees for the Post Office is worth quoting at length because it shows very clearly that middle-class women were not preferable to all male employees, but preferable to a certain *class* of male employee:

> In the first place, they have in an eminent degree the quickness of eye and ear, and the delicacy of touch, which are essential qualifications of a good operator.
> In the second place, they take more kindly than men or boys do to sedentary employment, and are more patient during long confinement to one place.
> In the third place, the wages, which will draw male operators from but an inferior class of the community, will draw female operators from a superior class.
> Female operators thus drawn from a superior class will, as a rule, write better than the male clerks, and spell more correctly; and, where the staff is mixed, the female clerks will raise the tone of the whole staff.
> They are also less disposed than men to combine for the purpose of extorting higher wages, and this is by no means an unimportant matter.

---

[9] Trollope's autobiography also makes a connection between civil service work, manliness, and authorship. He was anxious to impress that he regarded one of his greatest achievements as having raised the "style of writing official reports" and that it was much more important to him that a report be well composed than neatly copied out. He claims that "it is hardly manly that a man should search after a fine neatness at the expense of so much waste labour [he] should send [the letters] out as written by himself, by his own hand, with his own marks, his own punctuation, correct or incorrect, with the evidence upon them that they have come out from his own mind" (*Autobiography* 2: 129). Trollope desires to see the Post Office clerk not as a nameless cipher, but as someone with an institutional profile who leaves his imprint on paperwork.

[10] See Lynn Linton's "Queen Bees or Working Bees," published in the notoriously antifeminist *Saturday Review*, which later hired her as a full-time journalist.

> On one other ground is it desirable that we should extend the employment of women. Permanently established civil servants invariably expect their remuneration to increase with their years of service, and they look for this increased remuneration even in the cases, necessarily very numerous, in which from the very nature of their employment they can be no more use of value in the twentieth than in the fifth year of their service [...]. Women, however, will solve these difficulties for the department by retiring for the purpose of getting married as soon as they get the chance. [...] On the whole, it may be stated without fear of contradiction that, if we place an equal number of females and males on the same ascending scale of pay, the aggregate pay to the females will always be less than the aggregate pay to the males; that, within a certain range of duty, the work will be better done by the females than by the males, because the females will be drawn from a somewhat superior class; and further, that there will always be fewer females than males on the pension list.
>
> (qtd. in Martindale 17–18)[11]

This memo asserts that middle-class women were physically, socially, economically, and temperamentally the ideal employees for the public institution of the Post Office. Scudamore's directive clarifies a particular worker profile that appears repeatedly in literature concerning women postal workers. Women represented economic value for the civil service: while there were regular queries made about whether or not women's various frailties would offset these savings, at base the authorities realized that the work would be done better and at less cost with female staff.[12] Gender thus served to rearrange the relation of wage to class; the Post Office could pay women less money, but employ a higher *class* of women than they could men. The class superiority of women employees was important not only to Post Office managers, but also to proto-feminist writers. Lady John Manners, who was the wife of the Postmaster General, published essays that encouraged women to work and she urged the reassessment of gender distinctions in the workplace. In her book *Employment of Women in the Public Service*, Lady Manners assured her readers that women employees' class positions would be maintained: "their future prospects shall not be compromised, nor their social position affected" (22).

Assurance about workers maintaining social distinctions was particularly important precisely because the postal technologies themselves were often represented as having the potential to erase or at least blur markers of gender, race, and class. Communication that was cheap, accelerated, universal, and accessible increased the potential for

---

[11] See Hilda Martindale, *Women Servants of the State 1870–1938: A History of Women in the Civil Service*.

[12] W. R. Greg also considered cost effectiveness as reasonable grounds for making an exception to his objection to women having "industrial careers": "Women and girls are less costly operatives than men: what they can do with equal efficiency, it is therefore wasteful and foolish (*economically considered*) to set a man to do" (456).

[13] In *When Old Technologies Were New: Thinking about Electric Communication in the Late Nineteenth Century*, Carolyn Marvin details a case in America where a couple married over the telegraph, never having seen each other (93–94). The technology obscured the fact that the bride was white and upper-middle-class and the groom was a black barber. The courts annulled the marriage.

social intercourse that crossed these boundaries.¹³ The "discourse functionary" therefore needed to be ultra-ordered and ordering: the class and conduct of the postal workers who mediated the public's intercourse was of great concern to the Post Office. The "raising the tone" of which Mr. Scudamore writes is a reference to the importance of sexual and moral propriety. In the same year that his directive was produced, the Post Office investigations into homosexual prostitution among boy-workers that I examined in chapter 2 had concluded that the boy's low wages had driven them into part-time renting. The hiring of women was in part a response to this problem and was seen as a way of avoiding the low wages/sexual immorality equation.

TROLLOPE'S TELEGRAPH GIRLS

Whereas the Post Office had, by many accounts, "turned" messenger boys to prostitution, many regarded Post Office employment as a way to save women from the same fate. Anthony Trollope represented work in the Post Office as a way for women to avoid both prostitution and the sexual exploitation to which women working in private households could be vulnerable. In 1877 Trollope visited the new Post Office headquarters at St. Martin's-le-Grand and shortly afterward published an article called "The Young Women at the London Telegraph Office," followed by a short story titled "The Telegraph Girl," both printed in the popular, Christian-oriented magazine *Good Words*.¹⁴ "The Telegraph Girl" opens with the heroine of the title, Lucy Graham, "[finding] herself alone in the world" (Trollope, "TG" 354). The sudden death of her brother, with whom she had lived, means that unmarried Lucy is forced to rearrange her life. The tale charts how Lucy establishes her own household, independent of blood family. Significantly, however, the death of her brother and the opening of the tale are not coincident with her becoming a telegraph girl. Even before her brother's death, Lucy's "life had been full of occupation" and she had worked at the telegraph office to "earn her own bread" (Trollope, "TG" 354). Trollope's tale, in other words, focuses on the beginning of Lucy's quest for domestic, as opposed to financial, independence.¹⁵

The problem that Lucy faces after her brother dies is her lack of social context or household. While the telegraph office provided for women workers in many ways—ways that Trollope's story and article go on to praise and promote—it was not a job that situated

---

[14] "The Young Woman at the London Telegraph Office" was published in *Good Words* 18 (June 1877): 377–84. "The Telegraph Girl" was published in *Good Words* 19 (January 1878): 1–19.

[15] Alfred Austin, campaigning for a "masculine" literature, saw something odd in a male author putting himself so squarely in a woman character's shoes. He accused Trollope of being a "feminine novelist, writing for women in a womanly spirit and from a woman's point of view" (464). Austin concludes that literature has been "ruined" by women, women's issues, and the female perspective. Though a somewhat hysterical essay, Austin's comments serve to remind us that Trollope's narrative perspective in this story is firmly cross-gendered and displays active—to many minds, unseemly—concern with the domestic plight of the unsupported woman.

the woman in a domestic household, a necessity for the middle-class Victorian woman. Consequently, "it was suggested to [Lucy] that she had better abandon the Telegraph Office and seek the security of some household" (Trollope, "TG" 355). Trollope explains that "seeking the security of a household" ordinarily means looking for a job as a nursemaid, nursery governess, or servant; these jobs would make Lucy an adjunct to a family and give her lodging in a private home. The suggestion that Lucy find this kind of work, however, is both anonymously cited and constructed in the passive voice, prompting the reader to imagine it as the voice of social pressure. Lucy recognizes that employment in a private household would compromise her freedom and make her "subject at all hours to the will of others" (Trollope, "TG" 355). Trollope demonstrates a similar concern for her that he'd expressed about male workers who were made beholden to men with more power. "Her spirit," Trollope writes, "rebelled against the counsel" ("TG" 355) and she rejects the pressure to find this kind of security. Defiant and proud, she commits herself to employment in the telegraph office and sets about fashioning her own household, forging a domestic partnership with fellow telegraph girl Sophy Wilson. This partnership mimics a heterosexual marriage: "It was as though," Trollope tells his reader, "she had consented to marry" ("TG" 358). All marriage is, of course, mimetic. The power of the wedding vow derives from its referral to past and future reiterations.[16] Elizabeth Freeman has described the wedding as a fundamentally allegorical mode, and a ritual that has alternative kinships systems and repudiated Others "congealed" within it (*Wedding Complex*, 38). There is therefore a reverberation produced by a partnership that is described as resembling marriage: that "Other" partnership is already rattling around within the structure of the wedding, so when it is likened to marriage it is tautologically referred back to itself. When Trollope proposes that Lucy's relationship with Sophy is like a marriage, his simile is a reminder that "I do" is a noisy speech act.

Just as her relationship with Sophy is described through simile, Lucy styles herself in a similarly antiphonal manner. She had "taught herself to despise feminine weaknesses," and she identifies with a masculine role, explicitly reiterating a masculine gender to herself: "She must begin life after what seemed to her to be a most unfeminine fashion—'just as though she were a young man,'—for it was thus that she described to herself her own position over and over again" (Trollope, "TG" 355). "*As though*"—this is the same simile-based mechanism through which Trollope describes Sophy and Lucy's "marriage." It calls up other forms, other types to which Lucy refers herself. She rejects several other kinds of roles she could be, priding herself on being singular and unlike other women. Prior to her brother's death, we learn that she had always determined not to be "feckless, helpless, and insufficient for herself as had so many females" (Trollope, "TG" 355). She is wary not only of being "helpless," but also of being a mere helpmeet. She had rejected one suitor, a widower looking for a "second mother for his children" (Trollope, "TG" 357) and imagined spending her life not in a marriage, but in a different kind of partnership: a business

---

[16] See J. L. Austin, *How To Do Things with Words* 14–15.

partnership with her brother. Lucy's brother was a bookseller, as was the spurned suitor; it is thus made quite clear that Lucy rejects marrying the trade in favor of working in it. After her plans for commercial partnership with her brother are dashed by his death, sturdy brown Lucy teams up with the "startlingly pretty" young Sophy Wilson, and she cares and provides for Sophy as if she were her husband. Just as Lucy wanted employment that would make her "bound of course to her work at certain hours, but so bound only for certain hours" (Trollope, "TG" 355), her relationship with Sophy enables her to express a kind of devotion that she can imagine as mutual:

> From the first Lucy Graham made up her mind that it was her duty to be a very friend of friends to this new companion. It was as though she had consented to marry that widowed bookseller. She would then have considered herself bound to devote herself to his welfare. It was not that she could say as yet that she loved Sophy Wilson. Love with her could not be so immediate as that. But the nature of the bond between them was such, that each might possibly do so much either for the happiness, or the unhappiness of the other!
> (Trollope, "TG" 358–89)

As the story unfolds, Sophy proves herself increasingly unworthy of the devotion expended on her by Lucy. Sophy is Lucy's inverse; she is pretty, primped, and eager to be married. Sophy seeks to entrap a husband, and she takes both her job and propriety lightly. The extent to which Lucy considers herself "bound to devote herself to [Sophy's] welfare" is striking—depriving herself of money and food, in order to support the wasteful girl. In consequence, the principal term here is that of the "bond"; Lucy contracts herself, devotes herself to both work and a spouse. Sophy's shortcomings are emphasized in order to showcase the depths of Lucy's sense of duty.

In 1877, the year in which Trollope published "The Telegraph Girl," the question of women postal workers' sense of duty had come under Post Office and public scrutiny. More specifically, the question concerned how women's sense of duty to the workplace—and thus to the State—corresponded to their marital status. Women postal workers' employment was conditional upon their celibacy; when they married they were required to leave the service. There were no such requirements or considerations with male workers.[17] In 1876, however, this regulation was brought into question and became the subject of both public debate and a Post Office inquiry. Some argued that "in steadiness and attention to duties, the service rather gains than otherwise by the presence of married women" (Daunton 219). Others, including the Post Office Secretary, believed: "Directly they get married, other and high duties devolve upon them, and it is not […] for their own good nor for the good of their husbands, children or society, that they should be

---

[17] The only equivalent situation was that of Boy Messengers who were required to vacate their positions at the age of sixteen, the age at which they were considered to have reached manhood.

encouraged to neglect those duties" (Daunton 220). Both sides of the argument surrounding the celibacy requirement emphasized that for women postal workers, their job was a quasi marriage, demanding duty and devotion in the same way that a marriage did. Both sides insisted on the same terms and the same equation: that the institutional nature of the Post Office was comparable with the institution of marriage.

The central term in Trollope's fiction and the legislative materials concerning women civil servants is duty. Whether it adhered to a husband or to the workplace—and I am arguing that marriage and work were imagined as somewhat interchangeable terms—duty was a surprisingly malleable abstraction. Although it was a discourse of governance and discipline, it could be variously inflected and discursively transferred across a range of occupations and, indeed, a range of kinds of relationships. It is through, not despite, a discourse of duty that Lucy enters into a marriage with Sophy. That duty can have a creative, as well as a legislative, quality calls to mind Michel Foucault's theorization of the coincidence of regulation and desire. "Pleasure and power," he writes, "do not cancel or turn back against one another; they seek out, overlap, and reinforce one another. They are linked by complex mechanisms and devices of excitation and incitement" (*Sexuality* 48).[18] Foucault's implied metaphor is of the technologies of amplification and resonance. In a similar way, I am arguing that this fiction's exploration of same-sex partnerships between unmarried Post Office women workers proposes not a conflicted, but rather a *constitutive* link, or plane of contiguity, between public duty and same-sex partnership and passion.

Martha Vicinus has shown how, in the second half of the nineteenth century, nonmarital bonds of duty began to form substitutes for familial blood ties for women: she writes that the "more pervasively disciplined life" of schools, sisterhoods, and societies "meant simultaneously a breaking down of the division between public and private and the encouragement of an emotional life dependent upon distance and discipline," and that "sexuality found expression [...] through a disciplined love" (187). Scholars of masculinity and sexuality have identified the ways in which the homosociality and homoerotics fostered in the disciplined institutions of public school and the armies not only equipped a boy for public life, but also were a cohesive force in the imperial endeavor.[19] Their work demonstrates the interrelations of "private" sexual desires and "public" duties, complicating any impulse to see them as opposed principles. As more women entered institutional and civic life, grammars of discipline and duty, like those that had long applied to men, similarly fueled and were fueled by homosocial bonds and contexts.

---

[18] The original French confirms a metaphor of amplification (overlap, relaunchings): "Plaisir et pouvoir ne s'annulent pas; ils ne se retournent pas l'un contre l'autre; ils se poursuivent, se chevauchent et se relancent. Ils s'enchaînent selon des mécanismes complexes et positives d'excitation et d'incitation" (*Histoire de la sexualité* 66–67).

[19] See, for example, *The Ruling Passion: British Colonial Allegory and the Paradox of Homosexual Desire*, in which Christopher Lane provides a comprehensive account of how many imperial administrators, who appreciated the combination of homosexual impulses and duty to empire, "considered the vigilant internal discipline of passions as a valuable quality for export" (16).

The trope of the bond or covenant dominates "The Telegraph Girl." Lucy Graham does not depend on her looks or dress, but is earnest, honorable, and actively seeks what Trollope repeatedly calls "bonds" of affection and duty. The story is similarly dominated by an emphasis on how much she works: both with and for Sophy. Her work brought about her partnership with Sophy and her partnership with Sophy brings about more work. I would like to read the bond of *work* as something more than an incidental occupation, or a casual connection between the two women. When Katherine Bradley and Edith Cooper, who wrote under the name Michael Field, characterized themselves as "poets and lovers" (*Underneath* 79), they radically conflated their sexual relationship with their professional relationship. They pair work and same-sex marriage in a similar way to Trollope's Lucy Graham. In a letter to Havelock Ellis in 1886 the Fields used the language of the marriage service to describe their professional partnership: "As to our work, let no man put asunder what God has joined" (qtd. in Sturgeon 47). It was a powerful conflation and one that they reiterated. In their journal, titled *Works and Days*, they describe themselves as "closer married" than the Brownings, explaining that although both Robert and Elizabeth Barrett wrote, they wrote alone and "did not bless or quicken one another at their work" (Field, *WD* 16). These references have formed an important basis for recent scholarship on both the Fields and the field of lesbian studies more generally, and are used to note, as Chris White does, that "marriage was an available metaphor or conceptualisation for both women to apply to their relationship" ("Poets and Lovers" 202–3).[20] The critical focus has been upon the Fields' invocation of marriage to describe a lesbian relationship. I would suggest that *work* was at this time an equally available, equally connotative metaphor for lesbianism. The very audacity of the Fields' invocation of the marital metaphor, and the comparison of their love to the Brownings, that "famous benchmark of marital passion," as Emma Donoghue reminds us (43), has blinded us to the other term in the equation: work. At each point that the Fields use the language of marriage, they are writing of their work. Work and marriage, and the implied interchangeability of these two occupations, each signifies the closeness of their relationship: that unnameable fact of same-sex love between women.

The bond of work is similarly something more than an incidental occupation, or a casual connection between Lucy Graham and Sophy Wilson. Lucy is determined to have an "independent" (Trollope, "TG" 354) life outside of marriage, and this independence entails both professional work and devotion for another woman; the work and the same-sex partnership are coincident. They imply and engage each other. Lillian Faderman makes a similar point about the lesbian characters in the 1903 German novel by Aimé Duc, *Sind Es Frauen?* In this novel, Faderman notes, the "other life" of the women "takes its shape not primarily through love but through work" (249). The combination of Lucy's same-sex domestic bond on the one hand and her job as a functionary of the General

---

[20] For more on marriage as a way of describing lesbian relationships, see Sharon Marcus, *Between Women*.

Post Office on the other gives her a personal autonomy: "During a third of the day she was, as she proudly told herself, a servant of the Crown. During the other two-thirds she was lord—or lady—of herself" (Trollope, "TG" 355). Trollope establishes Lucy's decision in precise and charged terms; she rejects the duties of a servant in favor of those of a civil servant. Instead of serving a private household, either as a wife, or as an employee, she serves the government and achieves a personal dominion that gives her both gender and class mobility—she could be "lord—or lady" through the beneficence of the General Post Office. The story progresses toward Lucy being courted by Abraham Hall, an engineer at a printing factory who strikes up a friendship with the two girls. At Hall's proposal of marriage, the Post Office recedes into the background as a place that had developed and proved Lucy's sense of duty. Her service there enabled her to reject the loveless marriage in which she would have become little more than a servant and allowed her instead to develop a moral self-sufficiency that Trollope portrays as the basis of a sound marriage. Disappointed by Sophy's personal shortcomings as a companion, Lucy loses her masculine impulses and begins to desire "a mode of life more fitting to her feminine nature" (Trollope, "TG" 383).

Trollope's story is something of an exemplum. It was a common assumption in late-century periodical literature that working for the Post Office was an excellent precursor to a sensible marriage. I am going to show how lesbian relationships emerge in these coming-of-age as a telegraph girl stories, as an equally excellent (if ultimately reviled) precursor. The Crown provided a guardianship that allowed women to (just) sustain themselves economically,[21] keeping them safe from the lure of prostitution or from sexually predatory private employers. Lucy is acutely aware of the proximity between financial and sexual transactions; when her soon-to-be suitor Abraham Hall asks why he should not give her and Sophy money, "her answer was ready. 'We are both girls.'" Hall pauses and realizes that she means that "for a young woman to accept money from a man seemed to imply that some return of favours would be due" (Trollope, "TG" 375). This little scene would be quite generic—an unmarried girl refuses money from a man because to do so would imply prostitution—were it not for the way Lucy includes Sophy in her refusal. "We are both girls," Lucy says when she rejects his charity. Lucy is not a prostitute because she is a telegraph girl and because she is a telegraph girl she is a lesbian; accepting money from the State keeps Lucy free from sexual obligation to a man, *and* accepting money from the State allows Lucy to live in a marriage-like relation with

---

[21] In *The Education and Employment of Women* (1868), Josephine Butler laments the fields of work to which women are "refused admission" and approvingly notes that "as a favourable symptom of the last few years [...] 1822 women are returned as employed by the Post-office. 213 women returned as telegraph-clerks." But she warns that Post Office wages have dwindled to reprehensibly low levels: "It is instructive to note the way in which the salary of these women telegraph-clerks has fallen. When the telegraph companies were first formed, the pay of a female clerk was eight shillings a week, to be increased by a shilling yearly, until it reached fourteen shillings a week. So great, however, has been the competition of women for these situations, that the pay has been reduced to five shillings a week, a sum on which a woman can scarcely live unassisted." Conveniently available and qtd. in Bradshaw and Ozment, eds. 706–7.

another woman. Her employment and her queer marriage are mutually constitutive, and both exclude Abraham Hall from the equation. She must leave both her employment and her relationship to Sophy before he can expect "some return of favours" from her.

I have shown, in chapter 1, how the causal relationship between work at the Post Office and homosexual prostitution scandalously troubled the employment of Boy Messengers. Here we see lesbianism also produced through labors at the Post Office, the opposite of and indeed the answer to the prostitution that seemed to loom as the alternative to postal employment. If girls who are employed by the Post Office would otherwise be prostitutes (and as I will show, their labor of passing messages indiscriminately was understood to be sexually charged), how can their labors in the public sphere and in the business of passing indiscriminate messages anywhere and everywhere be framed as something other than promiscuous? How can postal work make them into good wives?

The Post Office had trouble pitching itself as a wholesome work environment for young women; positions at the Post Office were unlike other jobs that seemed naturally feminine. Martha Vicinus points out that a devotion to teaching "represented the best combination of public service and motherhood" (168). Devotion to careers in nursing, social, and church work preserved femininity by being hitched to the notion that although this work was conducted in the public sphere, it iterated the maternal or sisterly roles of the private family (Vicinus 168). But working for the Crown is a national, rather than a familial or sexual, duty. An article titled "Civil Service Examinations" in *The Woman's Gazette*, a publication for women about work, tries to argue that it is duty that makes Post Office employment ideal for girls:

> [...] it cannot be too earnestly enforced on the minds of all who voluntarily seek work that lays them under the authority of others, that subordination to constituted authority is a *duty* from a high point of view and a *necessity* from a worldly point of view. Let no one accept a post without a settled resolution to believe that their superiors in official position *are* superiors, or they would not be so placed. The law of subordination runs through the whole course of social life. Why then, should women attempt to reverse that law by foolish jealousies, unjust fault-findings, or unworthy suspicions? If a girl will not submit in the home life, let her not imagine herself fitted for encountering the various little roughnesses which must inevitably crop up between subordinates and superiors, equally unknown to each other.
>
> (87)

This passage struggles to find the terms in which to define the particular kind of duty and public service demanded of the female Post Office clerk; it darts between the rhetorics of domestic, commercial, moral—and even divine—duty, as if searching for the right register. Unlike the *Gazette*-approved occupations of nursing, needlework, and teaching, Post Office work did not have direct access to the languages of philanthropy, maternalism, or virtue. Rather, Post Office work incorporated women into a non-familial structure. The *Gazette* passage emphasizes that Post Office work involved "roughnesses" because it demanded interpersonal communication between people who are strangers to each other. Women postal workers worked among and served a dispersed crowd of people whose connections to one another might be *anything*, as long as they were postal. It is this promiscuous quality of postal work for which the *Gazette* writer is anxious to compensate, and it is subordination for subordination's sake that will transform a girl employed by the Post Office from a loose woman whose fingers might touch anyone, anywhere, into a good and loyal wife. Just as Trollope's tale ultimately likens the qualities that make a good telegraph girl to the qualities that make a good wife, this passage relates the subordination required in the Post Office to the submission required in the home. The passage starts and ends with the woman's will; she "voluntarily" enters the employment in which she will, by definition, be a subordinate, and she must not try and "reverse" that hierarchy. Much as she is therefore a policed subject, she is also one who unhinges the relation of woman to kinship.

The article's author is intriguingly specific about the kind of behavior that would interfere with the hierarchy of the Post Office department. The female employee is minded not to harbor "foolish jealousies, unjust fault-findings, or unworthy suspicions." This language suggests the obligations and emotions of the personal relationship. The failings could even be imagined as the faults of a peevish wife. Employment by the Post Office, this author argues, may not train a woman in the specific, hands-on skills of household management and childrearing, like nursing or teaching would. Rather, its influence will be on her affective life; she will be trained to feel the pleasures of submission and the rewards of acting upon a sense of duty.

"Public duty" was itself a fractured notion. As civil servants, Post Office employees were the instruments and reflection of the State, but as individuals, they were not part of the State. It was a paradoxical position: public servants were not members of the public. A passage from *Post Haste*, an 1880 collection of postal tales written by the popular adventure-story author R. M. Ballantyne, demonstrates a fascination with the curious position of female postal workers who were the mediators of everyone else's intimate and commercial business, but not their own:

> May Maylands chanced, by a strange coincidence, to command the instrument in direct connection with Cork. The telegrams just laid beside her were those destined for that city, and the regions to which it was a centre of redistribution. Among others her own village was in connection with it, and many a time had she yearned to touch her keys with a message of love to her mother, but the rules of the office sternly forbade this. The communicative touch which she dispensed so freely to others was forbidden to herself. If she, or any other telegraphist in St. Martin's-le-Grand, wished to send a private message, it became necessary to step out of the office, go to the appointed place, pay her shilling, and become one of the public for the occasion. Every one can see the necessity for such a rule in the circumstances.
>
> (15)[22]

---

[22] This tale comes from chapter 2 of *Post Haste*, subheaded "Tells of woman's work and some of woman's ways."

Ballantyne presents this story as something more than a tale of a shop girl who is tempted to help herself to the goods. It is rather a story of a girl who finds that her employment simultaneously provokes and denies her most heartfelt expressions of love. The story derives sentimental appeal by inviting the reader to momentarily imagine the telegraph office as a cruel machine that legislates against that most "natural" of connections between mother and daughter. The irony works because, as Harriet Martineau had put it, the postal system had been reformed *in order* that a working girl could "ease her heart by pouring out her cares and difficulties to her mother before she slept" (2:426). Ballantyne's rhetorical feint thus highlights the strange civic position of the civil servant and resonates against the idea that the nation's communication networks were a way of maintaining the bonds between separated family members. The story resolves, however, into moralizing that May Maylands must exercise restraint only in order that "every one" can gain the benefit of the Post Office. The telegraph is able to connect up dispersed families, but only by enforcing its own household rules; May has to subjugate her filial duty to her duty to the State.

The rules of May's workplace test even her physiological discipline; her fingers tap out myriad messages, but one message is forbidden—her own. The crux of this story is that the telegraph or postal message must always be mediated. There is no such thing as a "private message"; you must be "one of the public" to send a message, and you must send it through a public servant. Your communication must always pass through the hands of an anonymous Post Office worker and even the Post Office worker herself must consign her message to anonymous hands. May Maylands is invoked to dramatize the moment the telegraph girl "steps out" of the office, showing how leaving the office transforms her into the citizen and the daughter she is prevented from being while at her post. The same moment is also highly dramatized in "The Telegraph Girl," when Abraham Hall has to request permission to break the office's rules, to get Lucy to leave the office during work hours, so that he might propose marriage to her. For Lucy, leaving and breaking the law of the office transforms her into a wife.

The civic status of the postal worker, and the reason that stepping out of the Post Office was so transformative an act, had recently been defined in law. Postal workers were the intermediaries through whom written intercourse passed from writer to reader, but, legally, the workers were regarded as impressionable and cognizant readers rather than mechanical processors. The Telegraph Act of 1868 legislated against workers revealing or tampering with the contents of telegrams. The main section of the law determines that "any person having official duties connected with the post-office [...] who shall, contrary to his duty disclose or in any way make known or intercept the contents or any part of the contents of any telegraphic messages or any message intrusted to the Postmaster-General for the purpose of transmission" (qtd. in Carmichael 77–78) could be imprisoned for up to twelve months. The law also contains a subsection, however, which reads:

> This provision does not prevent the "publication" of a libel to the telegraph clerks: *Williamson v. Freer* (L.R.9, C.P.393; 43 L.J.C.P. 161; 30 L.T. 332; 22 W.R. 878).

> When a communication libellous in itself, but such that the occasion of it would have rendered it privileged if made by letter to the person to whom it was addressed, was, in fact, made by means of a telegram, it is not privileged, though made *bona fide*, because the mode of conveying the information necessarily involved publication to the post-office clerks, and it is no less a publication because this section makes the disclosure of the contents of a telegraphic message by any official in the post-office a misdemeanour. Communications or messages transmitted through telegraph offices are not privileged, and the clerks transmitting the same must disclose their contents in a Court of Justice: *Waddell, In re* (8 Jur. [N.S.] 181, Part II.; *Ince, In re,* 20 L.T.421).
>
> (qtd. in Carmichael 77–78)

The telegraph workers do not, then, merely convey messages—they are the means of them becoming published. Not only are they public servants, but also their bodies are designated by law as a site of publication; private messages that pass through the sensory organs of telegraph workers are transformed into published texts; their contents have been made public and are therefore subject to the laws of libel. That the stories of Lucy Graham and May Maylands focus on the transformative nature of the moment they leave the office is therefore highly symbolically charged. Not only did employment as a civil servant change the nature of girls' citizenship, but also their telegraphic bodies transformed private texts into public texts.

Trollope wrote a companion to his short story—a factual article titled "The Young Women in the London Telegraph Office," also published in 1877. Despite the informative frame of this piece, Trollope's object is to unveil the telegraph girls' private loves, pleasures, and desires. Trollope invites the reader, whom he calls "the stranger" ("YW" 379), to survey the metropolis[23] and follow him from the streets into the interior of the Post Office:

> Those who pass from Cheapside into Newgate Street after the lamps have been lighted may observe, on looking up, that the whole top floor of this new building is illuminated. It is here that the eight hundred young women are at work, and their business consists in the receipt and dispatch of telegraph messages.
>
> ("YW" 378)

The article occupies the journalist-as-voyeur mode of urban investigative literatures; Trollope declares that the "condition of the girls" and not the telegraphy will be the focus of his article ("YW" 379). These girls, however, are not to be found in the dimly lit streets, which are the territory of the prostitute, the public woman usually focused on by the urban investigator.[24] These women have been rescued from this fate by the beneficent

---

[23] At the end of the article, Trollope also directly addresses the editor of *Good Words* as a fellow "investigator": "You, Mr. Editor, are much concerned with the conduct of a large population in a large city. What do you think of this representation as to the conduct of eight hundred young women in the middle of the metropolis?" ("YW" 384).

[24] For a description of the urban investigator's relationship to the figure of the woman in public, see Judith R. Walkowitz, *City of Dreadful Delight: Narratives of Sexual Danger in Late-Victorian London* 20–21.

Post Office and are safely housed in a large, elevated, illuminated room. Furthermore, social documenters such as Henry Mayhew reported on the "public woman" from the streets, exhorting the women to "tell their own tale" and "publish" their sentiments (20).[25] The kind of exchange in which a prostitute deals lends itself to confession to an author—they will have sex with a man for money and will also therefore have conversation with Mayhew. The telegraph girl, however, is differently participant in exchange between strangers. Throughout his article, Trollope's desire to hear the telegraph girls' own stories and thus "judge somewhat of their inward natures" ("YW" 379) is repeatedly frustrated. Instead, the girls are constantly talking between themselves, and their work is itself a "noise" of "multitudinous communications" that Trollope can only observe and write about from a distance. He *desires* to be privy to the girls' intercourse but never gets to hear them. Consequently, both Trollope's voyeurism and the girls' homosocial conversation take on a distinctly sexualized character: "Oh!—if I could only know what those two pretty girls in the distance were talking about!" he laments ("YW" 379). Despite his hammed-up frustration, Trollope recognizes that his distance and lack of interaction with the girls is an integral condition of their work:

> "May they talk?" I asked. Now I certainly had heard them talking—a low hum of cheery young female voices, very pleasant to the ear [...]. When messages are coming and going the operator may not speak or be spoken to [...]. Secrecy is essential. There seems to be no ground for fearing that any undue use is ever made of those multitudinous communications which are always passing under the eyes or through the ears of these young women. But the temptation might be great if any outside sinner were able to hold free communication with that room at any time.
> ("YW" 383–84)

Trollope's emphasis upon the ways in which messages pass through the young women's sensory organs—"under the eyes or through the ears"—is echoed by the "pleasant" effect the girls' conversation has on his own ears. These are communicative girls, but their communication is limited to the sending and receiving of anonymous messages or sending messages between themselves.

Talking and flirting are the twin focal points of the article; Trollope is, in his own words, "anxious" about these practices and he portrays them as linked.[26] He writes, "But I was very anxious to know whether they flirted for there are young men in the same room" ("YW" 380), and later he repeats himself, "But was there any flirting? I was very

---

[25] For original, see Henry Mayhew, "Second Test—Meeting of needlewomen forced to take to the streets" in *The Unknown Mayhew*, ed. Eileen Yeo and E. P. Thompson (New York: Schocken Books, 1972), 168. Conveniently available and qtd. in Walkowitz 20.

[26] In *John Caldigate*, Trollope also links talking and flirting. The "Mrs. Cromptons, Mrs. Callanders, and Miss Greens" are enraged at the prospect of Euphemia Smith seducing John, but they do not know what to do about it, for "talking is allowed on board ship, and even flirting, to a certain extent" (*JC* 65).

anxious on that head when I saw the young men" ("YW" 383). Anxious he may be, but not to banish all flirting—just that of his male competitors. Trollope's tone throughout the essay is itself highly flirtatious; he refers constantly to the girls' prettiness and repeatedly informs the reader that he is not about to enlighten anyone about telegraph technology as "I did not pay by any means as much attention as I ought to have done to the new system, so much was my attention taken up with those two pretty girls—and with others" ("YW" 380).

Vigilant against any messenger-boys flirting with the girls, Trollope dedicates the essay to his own sensory pleasures. When he discovers that late attendance is a punishable offence, he uses the opportunity to imagine a young lady languishing in bed: "And how would it be if some gentleman who wanted his horse at the covert-side punctually at eleven should lose his run with the foxhounds because some young lady found herself too comfortable in bed?" (Trollope, "YW" 383). Trollope's joke is a self-reflexive one. The gentleman that the slugabed telegraph girl should be serving is Trollope himself; the reference to hunting is a reference to his personal passion for the sport. Like the sleepy telegraph girl, he also knew how to be paid to play. In his autobiography he describes his duties as General Post Office Surveyor in Ireland and writes of how he managed to hunt on Post Office time and expenses.[27] Trollope's references to the transgressions and disciplining of the girls are titillated rather than fraught with panic. The only anxiety he expresses is a concern about who is co-respondent to the girls' attractiveness. The question of flirting and talking initially arises for Trollope because of the occasional presence of men in the telegraph room, but the question of the girls' influence on *each other* through conversation and physical proximity quickly becomes prominent. The entire article emphasizes that the women in the telegraph room operate as a mass—the opening words of the piece are "Eight hundred young women at work, all in one room," and Trollope repeatedly wonders at the fact that so many women all work together in one place. Later, he attributes the attention that the girls pay to their dress to the effect of having "a large number of girls […] come together" ("YW" 380), and when he inquires about

---

[27] Trollope's private joke about tardiness is even more pertinent, since he notes in this passage of his *Autobiography* that his habit of measuring and scheduling postmen's routes by riding them himself on horseback when they themselves would have to make them by foot meant that he "was sometimes a little unjust to them," and the unfeasibility of the routes thus adversely affected the punctuality demanded of the telegraph girls (*Autobiography* 1: 120). Trollope also confesses that he "very soon achieved a character for irregularity" himself as a postal clerk. He robustly defends his relaxed approach to civil service duties, however, declaring himself a better "public servant" than his colleagues who were critical of him (*Autobiography* 1: 59). He was a staunch anti-Hillite for the same reasons; he thought Hill despotic and attacked him for treating postal employees as "so many machines who could be counted on for their exact work without deviation," declaring that "I never came across any one who so little understood the ways of men" (*Autobiography* 1: 177–78). Thus it would seem to be Hill whom Trollope has in mind when he writes of the Secretary of the General Post Office in "The Young Women" as "an officer of majestic power outside the Telegraph Office, who may be supposed to be a sort of Jupiter up in the clouds" ("YW" 383). This ironically inflects his subsequent declaration that "it is always well that punishment should seem to come from some inscrutable and awful power at a distance" ("YW" 383).

talking, he again features a pair of girls in conversation with each other: "If two girls of twenty can be got to sit close to each other without talking, human nature must have been changed up in the Telegraph Office" ("YW" 383).²⁸ "Young Women" is prompted by and devoted to Trollope's own flirtatious, heterosexual pleasures: his flaneur-like persona pushes open the door to the telegraph room of eight hundred women as if it were a pastry shop. But his delectation of the women encompasses figuring them as stimulating each other as much as him. It becomes part girl-on-girl fantasy and part a portrait of desires more transitive than he had perhaps bargained for. That girls might be provided for him by the State is thrilling to him. The fact that their close-packed bodies are resonance machines, which make mail public and make each other communicative, legible, and closest to each other, means that when Trollope turns this vision into a short story, one girl consents to marry another.

THE SOCIALIST SPHERE: *THE REBEL OF THE FAMILY*

Eliza Lynn Linton's 1880 novel, *The Rebel of the Family*, follows the fortunes of an independence-seeking heroine, Perdita, who takes employment in the Savings Bank section of the General Post Office.²⁹ Born into a family that carries a double-yoke of impoverishment and good breeding, Perdita is an inky-fingered and plainly dressed socialist, frustrated by life with silly sisters and a "well-bred conventionalist" (1: 10) of a mother who all survive on watered-down soup and a fiction of gentility. While her mother takes refuge from their financial troubles in schemes and dreams of marrying her other daughters to men of fashion and station, it is Perdita who maintains financial and moral order in the family, first by working at the Post Office and eventually by marrying a tradesman.

Like Trollope's Lucy, who thinks of herself as a "young man" and determines that she "was not to depend upon feminine good looks, or any of the adventitious charms of dress for her advance in the world" ("TG" 356), Perdita lives in "frayed and fettering rags" (Linton, *RF* 1: 59) and wishes that she were a boy who could work, or that there were a civil war, so that she could "disguise [herself] as a man and enlist on the side of the people!" (Linton, *RF* 1: 31).³⁰ Her battle cry is "liberty and country" (Linton, *RF* 1: 29) and her avowed cause is socialism. Perdita's Shakespearian namesake in *A Winter's Tale* was a princess who was put in a vessel that floated to the seacoast of Bohemia; Lynn Linton's Perdita, who finds that her quest for social and financial independence washes her up at the doorsteps of unconventional households, determines upon being bohemian rather

---

²⁸ He also talks about the dangers of "contact," stressing that one "young woman of bad character" could be "fatally noxious" ("YW" 379).

²⁹ Women were first employed in this department in 1874 (Daunton 218).

³⁰ Perdita's surname is also a mark of her leveling tendencies. Gerard Winstanley was the leader of the seventeenth-century proto-socialist sect, the Diggers. Throughout the novel, the idea of establishing a just society, or socialist utopia, is paramount.

than bourgeois. Like Lucy Graham, Perdita's employment at the Post Office is part of a search to find an alternative household, one built upon completely different values from those of her blood family.

One of these households is the West Hill Society for Women's Rights, which offers female emancipation and a home in which the place of heterosexual marriage is usurped by lesbian love. Bell Blount, the president of the Society, lives with a "wife," Connie Tracy,[31] and her relationship with Perdita is described in sexually predatory terms. She woos Perdita, with kisses of "strange warmth" (Linton, *RF* 1: 74) and tries to force her to smoke, making Perdita scared that she "would take her by main force and initiate her against her will" (Linton, *RF* 1: 281). Bell Blount offers not only sexual love, but also a household. She tells Perdita, "You are not in your proper sphere. Your real place is with us" (Linton, *RF* 1: 62). At the opening of the novel, Bell's lesbianism is presented as a powerful and potentially viable element of a utopian existence:

> Again that indistinct glimpse into the vast Unknown! Perdita's imagination burst up into a sudden flame at the suggestive vagueness of her new friend's words. She felt as if about to be initiated into those hidden mysteries wherein the springs of human history are to be found—as if about to be admitted into a secret sect working beneath the surface of society, sapping the bases of wrong and preparing the ground for the glorious establishment of truth and justice.
>
> (Linton, *RF*1: 65–66)

Bell's words thrill Perdita; her dreams of "the sacred duty of insurrection against tyranny" (Linton, *RF* 1: 12) are momentarily fulfilled by the subversive nature of this "secret sect" and by the suggestiveness of Bell's language.

Blount is a compelling figure and her unorthodoxies are attractive to Perdita, but she is eventually rebuffed by Perdita and ridiculed by Lynn Linton's narratorial voice. Perdita comes to reject Blount's lesbian relationship as a false model of emancipation, essentially critiquing it for its butch-femme mimesis of heterosexuality, as she regards Blount's wife Connie as "as much Bell Blount's creature as if she had been a man's mistress to be discarded [...]. Bound to serve and obey" (Linton, *RF* 2: 49). As with Trollope, Lynn Linton is suspicious of those who "bind" subordinates to them, and Bell Blount's command over Connie is a symptom of her highly ambivalent position within the narrative. Having initially presented Bell Blount's household as an attractive alternative home for Perdita, Lynn Linton sets its feminist politics and lesbianism up in opposition to Perdita's politics of, and hopes for, class-based social equality. Perdita is described as "a woman

---

[31] Bell Blount is also referred to as "Mrs. Blount" in the novel, as she has an estranged husband. She may have been inspired by or modeled on Lady Monson, a friend of Lynn Linton's, who separated from her husband after only a few days of marriage. Lady Monson held literary evenings, was an enthusiastic supporter of the women's rights movement, and had female lovers. See Nancy Fix Anderson, *Woman Against Women in Victorian England: A Life of Eliza Lynn Linton* 63.

who sympathized with the 'hands' " (Linton, *RF* 1: 121), and Bell's hand is sensual and fine-skinned, rather than laboring and leveling: "Something in Mrs. Blount's face chilled and repelled her, she did not know why; she only felt that this was not the ideal for which she was looking, and that supreme good did not lie in the leading of that soft, milk-white, caressing hand" (Linton, *RF* 1: 66). Mandy Merck describes how "the lesbian hand has a cultural history in which it figures both as an instrument of sexual contact and as a marker of gender transitivity" (127). Lynn Linton certainly figures Bell Blount's hand as sexually seductive and transitive; both femme and butch in character, it is an insinuating *and* a "leading" limb. If Bell's hand is figured as a point of connection—between her and the "caressed" Perdita, or between genders—it is conversely figured as incapable of class transitivity, of reaching out to the "hands." Its determinedly aristocratic and racially reserved character is signaled by its Marie Antoinette shade of "milk-white." It loves, rather than labors. It touches, but is untouched by work. In contrast to Perdita's hands, which are stained with ink,[32] Bell's hands are peculiar in their whiteness and demonstrate a "delicacy of touch," to use Postmaster Scudamore's phrase, which is unnerving to Perdita.

Sustaining this figuration of hands as indicative of the suitability of the suitor, Lynn Linton pits Bell's unnatural advances against those of Leslie Crawford the chemist, who waits for Perdita outside her workplace at the Post Office and "with the most natural manner in the world, [...] went up to Perdita and held out his hand" (Linton, *RF* 3: 246). Crawford's hand is direct, egalitarian, and businesslike, offered to Perdita against the backdrop of her workplace. It thus trumps the manipulative and seductive hand of the lesbian salon. This novel quite literally points an accusing finger at sexual radicalism, but this narrative effort to demonize the lesbian unravels by means of its own tropes. If the hand does indeed feature, as Merck suggests, as a site of transitivity, it has the quality of a cursor, a symbol indicating the position at which one of any number of actions will take effect. Perdita's Post Office setting is a place that mediates and congregates any number of possible narratives, lives—and in her particular case—life savings and interest. Can we see the hand as a diacritical mark, a signal that at this point in the text we could pursue an "other" narrative, via a transitive mode of reading? Katherine Rowe's study *Dead Hands: Fictions of Agency, Renaissance to Modern* emphasizes the hand as a site of immanence and negotiation "between intention and act" (7). She proposes that "dead hands articulate what might be called the dispossessive conditions of identity, in which the body, its alienable parts, and even its voluntary motions fail to ratify the rights, authority or propriety of the self" (12). In Lynn Linton's novel, the hand appears

---

[32] Perdita's mother regards Perdita's hands with horror, regarding the signs of work as if they were those of treason: "'What is this?' her mother asked, pointing with the tip of her scissors to the thumb and first two fingers of the right hand. 'Ink,' answered Perdita, as guiltily as if she had said blood" (Linton, *RF* 1: 26). This passage neatly pokes fun at Perdita's mother's double standards. She gestures at Perdita's stained hands to denounce her for working, but does so with a pair of scissors—the tool of the needleworker. The difference, of course, lies in the domesticity of her needlework, as opposed to the public nature of the Post Office work that will lead Perdita away from marriage and into the dangerous waters of lesbian households and tradesmen's arms.

at the moments when Linton is struggling to steer us toward a particularly awkward narrative option. That the heroine's romantic crisis, her choice between Bell and Leslie, comes to rest on the figure of their hands literalizes the paradigmatic idiom of selection: "on the one hand … but on the other." The trope of the hand clearly functions to produce, or signpost, a site of divergence. It refers the reader to the idea of giving one's hand in marriage; Perdita's decision to spurn Bell's hand in favor of Leslie Crawford's is an exchange of hands, or if you like a handshake, that seals the novel's contract with the heterosexual marriage plot. It is a contract won, however, late in the game and by a low-cost bidder. It is possible to push past the flimsy walls of this plot structure by engaging a transitive reading practice that crosses the novel's own narrative boundaries, toward a different—but gestured toward—text.

That alternate text might well be Eliza Lynn Linton's *The Autobiography of Christopher Kirkland* (1885). This autobiography includes a powerful scene that I understand as a rewriting and recasting of Bell Blount's caressing hand. Christopher, Lynn Linton's thinly disguised, cross-gendered self-portrait, is describing his passion for Adeline Dalrymple, an older married woman who is refined, captivating, and possesses "an almost feverish activity of mind, an almost dangerous energy of thought" (1:174). He loses himself in his giddy passion for her, forgetting social convention and how "things look from the outside" (1: 177):

> "Time and space may divide us from each other, and circumstances may be stronger than our will; but thought overrides matter, our souls are ever one and inseparable, and the bond of the spirit once made is indissoluble. Love is in itself immortality. It cannot die; it cannot change; and no force in nature can kill it."
>
> She laid her white and scented hand on mine, so brown and large and bony—and bent her head till she looked full and straight in my eyes. I was sitting on a low stool by her side; she was on the window-seat made in the embrasure.
>
> "You, dear boy, will go into the world far away from all of us here," she said; and—was it my fancy? or did that sweet voice which always reminded me of pearls tremble, and something as tender as tears come into her glorious eyes?— "but, wherever you go, my spirit will go with you, surrounding you, guarding you, one with your very breath, your very life. Never forget that, my child. I am with you always—like God and with God—in the future always, as I have ever been in the past."
>
> Her hand closed on mine with an almost convulsive grasp. It burnt like fire, and the diamonds on her fingers and at her throat flashed as if by their own internal light. Her voice had sunk almost to a whisper, and something seemed to pass from her to me which thrilled me like electricity. I could not speak. My heart suddenly swelled so that it strangled my voice and cut short my breath. I only felt a dumb kind of desire to carry my life to her hands and worship her as I would have worshipped the Eternal Mother of men and things. She was beyond womanhood to me—she was the casket that embodied and enclosed the Divine.

As I looked at her, she still bending down her head and looking into my eyes, I felt a strange rapture and loss of myself in her personality.

(1: 199)

In this version of the handclasp, the "white and scented" hands are not demonic, but rather, divine. Christopher desires, even, to deliver his life into these hands. The sexual power of the hand is as evident here and it was with Bell, the difference being that here the sexual encounter is consummated. When Adeline's hand closes on Christopher's, it is with the shudder ("convulsive grasp") and heat ("like fire") of orgasm. What Perdita could not bring herself to consummate, Christopher, the heterosexual proxy of Eliza Lynn Linton, can. Upon this sexual consummation, Christopher feels "something pass from her to me which thrilled me like electricity" and leaves him wordless, breathless. Robbed of his powers of communication, he is able to be all feeling and all desire, and the rapture that comes to him comes, emphatically, through loss of himself and through having passed into the being of his beloved. This is the rapture that Perdita never finds. The concluding lines of *The Rebel of the Family* pay lip service to "that Love which alone makes our life divine" (397), but run decidedly short on any passion. It is only by *passing* over from *Rebel* to the *Autobiography* that we find erotic satisfaction. *Passing* is what Lynn Linton is doing, by donning the male, heterosexualizing guise of Christopher. Christopher is then, however, reabsorbed into the feminine when he "passes" into Adeline and loses himself in her. This loss is enabling, rebirthing, and it translates Christopher and the world around him:

Henceforth all things were transformed for me, and life meant a new existence as it had a new *message*. The sunrises and the sunsets, the song of the birds, the flowers in the fields, the shadows of the clouds on the mountains, the reflections in the lake and the ripple of the blue waves, the voice of the waters making music in cascades, the budding and the fall of the leaves of the trees—all were the circumstances of a more beautiful world than that in which I had hitherto lived. Nature had a *secret language* which was revealed to me, and I understood the *hidden meaning* of things which hitherto had had no meaning at all.

(203–4, my italics)

In the earlier passage, quoted above, Christopher loses one kind of communicative capacity—speech—but here, the self is made communicative again by the power of erotic exchange.[33] Significantly, Christopher is not now exchanging words with words, but

---

[33] The term "to make a pass" does not, according to the OED, definitively acquire amorous or sexual meaning until the 1920s. It is clear from this passage that this meaning is, however, nascent at this earlier date and, furthermore, it seems likely that the idiom accrues erotic meaning via the business of mesmerism. To "make a pass" during hypnotism refers to the practice of passing hands over a person without touching them, sending them into a mesmeric trance. This usage dates back to the 1840s, and Linton certainly describes Christopher entering something similar to a trance—"a strange rapture"—mesmerized by Adeline. For more on the relation of communication technologies to mesmerism, see Pamela Thurschwell, *Literature, Technology and Magical Thinking, 1880–1920* (Cambridge: Cambridge UP, 2001).

rather finds a correspondence between the natural world and language. Words get in the way when they bear the burden of meaning—Christopher describes the look in Adeline's eyes as "more eloquent than words," and he loses the sense of her actual words because they "filled my ears with too much music" (203). And so, finally, under the sign of discursive respite—of wordless exchanges and unintelligible polyphony—we are delivered a lesbian love scene.

This scene cannot happen in *The Rebel of the Family* because Lynn Linton immobilizes the possibility of communication or overlap between political causes. She disavows lesbianism by pitting sexual politics against social politics. Bell Blount vociferously and explicitly criticizes Perdita's socialist theories as "nothing in comparison to the franchise" (Linton, *RF* 1: 300–301) and later still in the novel, she explicitly desires to disassociate her cause from "Red Republicanism" (Linton, *RF* 3: 135). Invited to enter a lineup from which Perdita might find an equal companion, Bell is rejected and framed as a sexual menace to the socialist utopia for which Perdita is searching (Meem 550).[34] One of the ways in which Bell Blount is established as an enemy of socialism is through an epistolary metaphor that allies her letters with private, coded, or secret communication. The link between letters and spying was an incendiary matter for Lynn Linton. Her one-time husband, Chartist engraver William James Linton, helped uncover the government plot to intercept the mail of revolutionary exile Giuseppe Mazzini.[35] There is therefore peril in the air when, early in her relationship with Perdita, Bell assures her that she can freely

---

[34] In "Eliza Lynn Linton and the Rise of Lesbian Consciousness," Deborah T. Meem goes on to characterize Bell Blount as a "vampire lesbian on the prowl" (551). While Bell is undoubtedly portrayed as a woman who desires to overwhelm and dominate women, she is not the character whom Lynn Linton actually casts as vampirically threatening. Curiously, it is "pretty little Eva," the flirty, flighty, flagrantly heterosexual sister, who is repeatedly portrayed in vampiric—or cannibalistic—terms. When she laughs, she reveals "two full rows of the loveliest little sharp white teeth that can be imagined—very small, very even; but for all their beauty, teeth that somehow suggested the eating of flesh" (Linton, *RF* 1: 23), and, again, when flirting with Sir James Kearney, she "laughed and showed all those small white teeth so curiously suggestive of the double action—kissing and eating" (Linton, *RF* 1: 172–73). (The idea of kissing-biting teeth is reiterated by George Egerton in her 1893 story "A Cross Line," where the female protagonist demonstrates sexual power over her husband, when she "shuts his eyes with kisses, and bites his chin and shakes it like a terrier in her strong little teeth" [17]). As critics such as Meem and Nancy Fix Anderson have noted, Lynn Linton's work is riven with contradiction, especially when it comes to female sexuality, and Meem's misplacement of the vampiric sexual epithet is evidence of this. Lynn Linton also fantasized of herself as a "fiend-woman" or "vampire glutting itself on human blood" (N. F. Anderson 22). Compounding the confusion around Eva's sexuality, Lynn Linton not only connects vampiric sexual aggression with her, but also links her to the sins of Sodom: Sir James wonders whether Eva is "a real bit of luscious fruitage or only a Dead Sea apple with a rosy skin and ashes for pulp" (Linton, *RF* 1: 218). Apples with ashes for pulp are the apples of Sodom; this is a reference to the sins of Sodom and Gomorrah.

[35] In 1844 it was revealed in the *Times* that Home Secretary Sir James Graham had ordered the Post Office to intercept Mazzini's letters, which caused a large and very public scandal. William Linton helped Mazzini prove that the seals on his letters had been broken and resealed and that the time stamps on the envelopes had been tampered with to account for the delay in the handling of his letters. Lynn Linton was very proud of his role in this episode and she attacks Graham in her 1885 cross-gendered, semifictional autobiography *The Autobiography of Christopher Kirkland* as "the paid and authorized spy of that House of Hapsburg of which [...] no evil was too great to be believed" (*CK* 2: 250).

choose to come and live with her: "We are not," she reminds her, living "in days when you could be [...] sent to the Bastille by a *lettre de cachet*" (Linton *RF* 1: 67). The reference to lettres de cachet—the blank warrants for arrest used in the French ancien régime—signals Bell's sinister intent, particularly as the Winstanley family view Perdita as "an upsetting rebel [who] would be the focus of a local revolution, and the neighbouring gentry would cut her and hers as deliberate traitors to their order" (Linton *RF* 1: 121). While not exactly compelled to live with the Society by order of a sealed letter, Bell Blount herself courts Perdita by writing to her every day:

> There were letters which made Perdita's cheeks burn, she scarcely knew why [...] she was in a strange halting state of feeling altogether. Half attracted and half repelled—fascinated by the woman's mental power and revolted by something too vague to name yet too real to ignore.
> (Linton *RF* 2: 50–51)

Bell's letters to Perdita elicit a physical reaction from her: a blush. This is the same reaction that Perdita has when she is kissed and touched by Bell, and Bell, too, "flushed wildly" when Perdita agreed to stay with her. Throughout the novel, Perdita expresses a hatred of her blushes, as they communicate feelings that she wants to suppress or hide.[36] Bell rebukes her for this, saying that her blushes "show the passion and vitality of your nature—which are just the qualities that attracted me" (Linton *RF* 1: 65). Bell, in other words, reads or deciphers Perdita's "nature" through physiological signals. Bell's daily letters communicate desire in much the same way that their blushes do; the letters are passionate, recall her physical caresses, are a form of exchange, and appeal to what Bell views as their corresponding natures. They call on Perdita to enter a mode of feeling, to give in to her fascination, whereas when Leslie Crawford "read[s] the secret writing of [Perdita's] poor wayward soul," he does so to "command," "protect," and "guard her from herself" (Linton *RF* 1: 262–63). The "communicative touch," to use Ballantyne's phrase, that arises between Perdita and Bell is one that Lynn Linton develops only to condemn it as dangerous. But Bell fascinates because she literally embodies communication. When Perdita first meets her, she appears with a halo of whitened hair, dressed in "a kaleidoscopic arrangement of colours [...] a walking rainbow" (Linton, *RF* 49). Materializing like a goddess, Bell's rainbow attire likens her to Iris, who in Greek mythology is goddess of the rainbow and *messenger* of the Olympic gods (the name has a double meaning: "iris," meaning rainbow and "eiris," meaning messenger). Bell is "Bell," not "Belle"—an "odd-looking" (Linton, *RF* 49) woman whose role is that of, first, a sensorium, then, second,

---

[36] Perdita's blushes also betray Lynn Linton's covert autobiographizing. In an interview, Lynn Linton spoke of her hatred of her own tendency to blush: "Many and many a time I blushed till I cried; even when I was a woman of thirty or forty, the tears have started, from the simple physical process of rushing blood." Mrs. Alex Tweedie, "A Chat with Mrs. Lynn Linton," July 1894: 357 (qtd. in Fix Anderson 18).

an alarum. She does indeed bear a message for Perdita, namely that Perdita should "take [her] life in [her] own hands" (Linton *RF* 1: 67), but Bell's communicativeness exceeds the message. She loiters after its delivery and desires to deliver more than this communiqué of emancipation. Bell is media. And in Lynn Linton's hands, the communication network and the queer connections that it materializes are portrayed as sinister and in need of regulation.

Both Lucy Graham's and Perdita Winstanley's sexually ambiguous roles are resolved by marriage. Their work at the Post Office provides what Lady John Manners calls the "preliminary training" required to "rule a household intelligently." Lady Manners explains that

> young ladies do not devote themselves irrevocably to the public service as if they were entering a convent. In fact, the public life of many of them is concluded by the presentation, not of the red or blue riband and of one of those stars which, according to the author of "Endymion," are the "poetry of dress," as is occasionally the case with retiring male officials, but with the gift of a plain gold ring.
>
> (40)

The allusion to Benjamin Disraeli's *Endymion* is apposite. *Endymion* is a novel that addresses the influence of women over the public careers of the men they love, and Lady Manners uses the reference to bolster her suggestion that women can have a powerful influence over the public sphere, without assuming permanent public positions themselves. Lynn Linton was not wholly, or at least not consistently, adverse to women working outside of "their own natural portion of the field of labour," as she expresses it in her article "The Modern Revolt," but hated the thought that it would become the commonplace and urged acknowledgement of the importance of child-rearing and housekeeping to "the State and the race" ("MR" 148, 144). Lady Manners is similarly concerned about women's "natural" roles and assures the young women entering the civil service that their work there will doom them neither to celibacy nor manliness. They will wear neither the nun's veil nor the public man's medal but can fully and happily expect to end up wearing a wedding band.

Lady Manners' assurance that public work is not incommensurate with feminine garb and a marriage plot is an attempt to shut the gate after the horse has bolted. The civil service does, for Lynn Linton and Trollope, offer women a way to experience nonfemale roles. Both Lucy and Perdita enter homosocial or homosexual domestic orders and workplaces by way of rejecting the frivolities of femininity and imagining a masculine identity for themselves. Trollope describes Lucy's eventual marriage as a release from masculinity, as a rescue from the "hard, outside, unwomanly work" ("TG" 369) of the Post Office. Perdita, too, had to imagine herself as masculine in order to distance herself from what her eventual husband calls an emasculated age: "It is this false god of Caste [...] this absurd belief in rank [...] which is taking the true manhood out of our country" (Linton, *RF* 3: 284), he declares. In both stories the girls' aspirations toward masculinity are deemed admirable, since masculinity represents industry, duty, and patriotism.

In neither story, however, can the girls *successfully* adopt the heterosexual role of the male as provider, and in each story their valorized masculinity eventually gives way to a new femininity invigorated by the girls' tourism in the masculine realm. Employment at the Post Office does not actually give the women the financial or domestic independence that they imagine it will. Lucy cannot, after all, support her household on her Post Office income, nor can Perdita secure financial stability for hers. Both come to rely upon the money of their husbands-to-be. Perdita's fiancé's income even enables the marriages of Perdita's sisters. Neither does either girl find fellowship with the other workers; despite her socialist politics, Perdita is disappointed to find that most girls work in the office for "prosaic" rather than romantic or imperialist reasons:

> She had expected to find in them the same political principle and high-strung earnestness which she herself carried into her work—the same proud consciousness of participating in the conduct of the Imperial Government which made her routine business letters and dry rows of figures essentially poems—and she found instead the dullest indifference to the whole thing [...]. Neither heroines nor martyrs were they, but just a congregation of commonplace young women whose family finances were scanty, and who preferred employment that took them away from home and into society, to that which would have kept them within four walls and in the bosom of their family.
>
> (Linton, *RF* 2: 52)

Lynn Linton both applauds Perdita's commitment to Queen, country, and empire and also gently mocks her desire to find her patriotic enthusiasms reflected in a female workforce. The ideal of imperial duty is laudable, but the excessive ("high-strung") enthusiasm that Perdita attaches to it is represented as a dangerous capacity. After all, it was the same kind of overwrought politics, principles, and earnestness that nearly led Perdita into the arms of Bell Blount. This passage suggests that Lynn Linton has an appreciation for the very levelheaded prosaism of the Post Office girls that Perdita despises. This appreciation clarifies—if such a word can be applied to Lynn Linton's astoundingly conflicted brand of feminist antifeminism—into praise in *The Autobiography of Christopher Kirkland*: "The Post Office and the Telegraph Office put money into the pockets of some hundreds of industrious girls," she writes, and she sees this as a means by which "the running [between men and women] has been more equalised" Linton, *KC* 3: 10–11).

This equalization of relations between men and women through work is central to both *The Rebel of the Family* and "The Telegraph Girl." Lucy and Perdita find expression for their industriousness at the Post Office and then find equally industrious men to marry. I opened this chapter asking how and why this late-century fiction could figure female postal workers as lesbian. Another answer lies partly with the vexed "complex mechanisms," to use Foucault's phrase, linking marriage and work at this time. Both Trollope and Lynn Linton are concerned with the problem of the nonindustrious middle-class married woman. They both object to the way in which women can be "bound" to men, either through being lazy, frivolous, and dependent themselves, or through being unequal, exploited, and subjugated by men. In "The Modern Revolt," Lynn Linton makes this explicit, declaring that women's modern desire to work "has two meanings: the one, a noble protest against the frivolity and idleness into which they have suffered themselves to sink; the other, a mad rebellion against the natural duties of their sex, and those characteristics known in the mass as womanliness" ("MR" 142). Trollope's and Lynn Linton's fiction figures women learning to reconfigure the function and duties of marriage, forging partnerships in which the wife and the husband have distinct roles, but are similarly focused on work and duty. The interstitial spaces in which both young women do this learning are those of the Post Office and the lesbian household, two configurations of duty that, as I have shown, are constitutive of one another.

The lesbian partnership, in each story, is a cautionary tale—Bell Blount is held up as a terrifyingly masculine predator and Lucy Graham's flirtation with lesbianism masculinizes and exhausts her. But the lesbian partnerships are also valorized as a potentially useful developmental phase. The same-sex relationships are, in both stories, hypermimetic of traditional heterosexual marriage and as such are used to show up two different kinds of inequalities that can be produced within heterosexual marriage. Bell Blount's "wife" is exploited, "bound to serve and obey," and Sophy Wilson is frivolous, frittering away her "husband's" money. The same-sex relationships allow Lucy and Perdita to switch scripts—to take, or imaginatively inhabit the role of the husband—and thus see what makes a bad wife. In other words, Lucy and Perdita both experience husbanding, and are able to experience—from within same-sex relationships— the failures of the "bonds" of marriage not defined by mutual duty. Lesbianism is used as a pedagogical space, through which the girls can pass, emerging unfallen and still marriageable. The Post Office similarly keeps the girls sexually pure and marriageable, but is a place in which passion and devotion can be turned to Queen and country. Lucy and Perdita are passed through both lesbianism and the Post Office in order that they learn *civic* virtues that can be translated back into *domestic* marriages, founded now on a reinvigorated model of duty and industriousness.

DISSENT, DIVERSITY, AND MODERNITY: THOMAS HARDY'S *A LAODICEAN*

Trollope's and Lynn Linton's stories confront the complicated role of the Post Office woman worker within an institutionalized, civic structure, but are less direct in their exploration of the material "complex mechanisms" of the communication network and communication technologies themselves. In *A Laodicean*, however, Hardy explores a fascination with the queer effects of communication machines. The heroine of *A Laodicean*, Paula Power, is not a Post Office employee, but she and her "frank and communicative"(Hardy, *Laodicean* 32) companion, Charlotte De Stancy, are passionate telegraphers. Their passion attaches both to the communication technology and to each other; it is Paula and Charlotte who are described as "more like lovers than girl and girl"

(Hardy, *Laodicean* 50). An 1882 reviewer of *A Laodicean* picked up on the oddity of both the characters and their pastimes when he described it as a book in which "the author showed us very queer people doing very queer things" (Rev. of *A Laodicean* 674–75). The queerness of both the female characters and the communication technology of which they are so fond is signaled by the way that lesbianism and telegraphy together continually disrupt a heterosexual marriage plot. Paula is a "modern maiden" (Hardy, *Laodicean* 17) who inherits a new fortune that her father had made in railway construction, and she lives in a derelict medieval castle. Her competing suitors are George Somerset, who is an architect, and Captain De Stancy, who is an aristocrat, brother of Charlotte, and one-time owner of Paula's castle. While Paula repeatedly refuses to exchange either kisses or letters with her male suitors, she is constantly engaged in the exchange of telegrams, physical affection, and tokens of love with Charlotte. The "inscrutability" (Hardy, *Laodicean* 91, 96) that marks her relationship with her male suitors is inversely matched by the communicative nature of her relationship with Charlotte.

The novel opens with the architect Somerset using the "musical threads which the post-office authorities had erected all over the country" to find his way to the village in which he intends to spend the night. The "friendly" humming thread that Somerset uses to guide him across the country landscape is the telegraph wire, a "mark of civilisation" that he trusts more than the country road when the two fork off in different directions. The wire seems to have a vigor of its own; it "plunges," "sings," and "leaps" over hill, hedge, and hollow (Hardy, *Laodicean* 21). But its song is something of a siren song; it leads Somerset literally off the beaten track and instead of guiding him to the village, he finds himself at De Stancy castle, into which he is surprised to see the wire disappear. Inside the castle, the other end of the wire is attended by two unmarried women who live there together, Charlotte De Stancy and the current owner of the castle, Paula Power. Like Trollope's magazine pieces and Linton's novel, Hardy's "Story of To-day," as the novel is subtitled, associates unmarried women, their same-sex love, and their households, with communication networks.

The telegraph wire is the direct line to Paula Power that so eludes her male suitors. When Somerset first follows it, he observes how it sails over the obstacles—a moat and a girdling wall—designed to keep uninvited guests out of the castle. Somerset himself has to "withdraw" from the defended castle this night and spends the bulk of the novel puzzled and thwarted by Paula's distant ways. She and her castle are impenetrable to her male suitors, whereas the singing telegraph wire vanishes "through an arrow-slit into the interior" (Hardy, *Laodicean* 22). The arrow-slit—an aperture designed to allow projectiles exit but not entry—is an image of invagination that fits with Paula's role as a "maiden" and her sexual repudiations of Somerset and Captain De Stancy. The men may find barricades (like "girdle" walls) to Paula's affections, but the telegraph wire does not; the anthropomorphized wire and its messages "leap" freely into or out of the "loophole" (Hardy, *Laodicean* 35, 210) of the castle's keep. Telegraphy and Charlotte find the literal and metaphorical loophole to Paula's self-containment and they have access to the "interior" that Somerset and De Stancy seek.

The image of an aperture with a wire or line threaded through it is also found in a description of the acclaimed railway tunnel made by Paula's father. Somerset regards the scene:

> Somerset looked down on the mouth of the tunnel. The absurdity of the popular commonplace that science, steam and travel must always be unromantic and hideous, was proved on the spot. On either slope of the deep cutting, green with long grass, grew dropping young trees of ash, beech, and other flexible varieties, their foliage almost concealing the actual railway which ran along the bottom, its thin steel rails gleaming like silver threads in the depths. The vertical front of the tunnel, faced with brick that had once been red, was now weather-stained, lichened, and mossed over in harmonious hues of rusty-browns, pearly greys, and neutral greens, at the very base appearing a little blue-black spot like a mouse-hole—the tunnel's mouth.
>
> (Hardy, *Laodicean* 96)

This description of a man-made structure that has been obscured or incorporated into nature—"lichened," "mossed" and made harmonious with the landscape—matches the description of the castle. The castle is "muffled in creepers" (Hardy, *Laodicean* 22) and its driveway is "half overgrown with green" (Hardy, *Laodicean* 21). A castle, like a railway or a telegraph wire, is a part of a national infrastructure: it is merely the more antique form. A castle once functioned as a "post" in a nationwide network of fortified buildings that together formed a defense and communication system. Hardy shows us an England in which these infrastructures do not disrupt the landscape, but become an organic, almost invisible part of it. When Somerset gets access to the inside of the castle and climbs up to the battlements, he can see clearly the telegraph wire that before he had only seen at a distance, "vanishing" into the keep, and he uses an organic simile to describe it. Now "the arrow-slit and the electric wire that entered it, like a worm uneasy at being unearthed, were distinctly visible" (Hardy, *Laodicean* 25).

While this means that the railway and telegraphic technologies do not disrupt the landscape, they most certainly perturb Somerset and De Stancy. The vanishing point of both the wire and the tracks is descriptively invaginated: either as a slit that opens to an interior, or as rusty red, mossed over tunnel with a mouth. Paula Power has the power that her last name suggests over the technologies of intercourse, and it is a power that, at least temporarily, unmans her suitors. When Somerset first sees the castle's telegraph machinery in action, it is conveying a message between Charlotte and Paula, and it is a message about him. Somerset does not understand the machinery's language and is discomforted by the resultant secrecy: "There was something curious in watching this utterance about himself, under his very nose, in language unintelligible to him" (Hardy, *Laodicean* 42). There is something "curious," something queer,[37] about the communication passing across him and being about him, but not being understood by him; it takes place across his body, "under his nose," proving the faculties of this sensory organ useless and mocking his imperfect powers of comprehension and reaction. The women's confidential telegraphic communications thus disable Somerset's masculinity. This emasculation is not, however, represented in traumatic terms. Jay Clayton's excellent reading of *A Laodicean* points out that the unmanning of Somerset stimulates him. Rather than being castrated, something which implies merely a turn of the heterosexual table and the woman taking over the phallus, the scene instead queers Somerset. Clayton calls these the "queer effects" of the telegraphic machinery (220). This reading, focusing on effect rather than subjectivity, is wonderfully commensurate with Hardy's emphasis on the machinery's powers of flow and flux. The communication machinery's capability for exchange and interchange is not limited to the messages themselves. The network makes myriad interfaces possible, some of which will be queer—in this case, girl to girl—and it can allow the correspondents themselves to experience the exchange of subject position. The "curious" quality of the telegraph that Somerset senses is its capability to bring about imaginative exchanges of subject position, exchanges which can include transpositions of sex, gender, and sexual desire.

Postal communication's capacity to cross sexual wires is made apparent in an interview Hardy granted the author, critic, and translator, William Archer. In this interview, first published in the *Pall Mall Magazine* in April 1901, Archer asked Hardy if it was true that he used to write love-letters for the local girls of his boyhood village. Hardy's reply is defensive:

> MR. HARDY. (*reluctantly*). Well—yes, to their soldier sweethearts in India [...]
>
> W.A. That was part of Samuel Richardson's apprenticeship, too. He trained for Clarissa, you for Tess.
>
> MR. HARDY. But I think you will find that Richardson's case was different. He was employed to compose the letters; I was only the amanuensis. Indeed, I was chosen on account of my tender years—because I could write, and read the replies, yet couldn't understand. They looked upon me as a mere writing machine, or a sort of phonograph to be talked into. And as a matter of fact I understood very little, and took very little interest in what I wrote and read; though I remember to this day one lover's address, as given in his letter: "Calcutta, *or Elsewear.*"
>
> W.A. I fancy many of those letters remained written in your mind in sympathetic ink, only waiting for the heat of creation to bring them out.
>
> MR. HARDY. Possibly, in a sub-conscious way. The human mind is a sort of palimpsest, I suppose; and it's hard to say what records may not lurk in it.
>
> (qtd. in Gibson 67)

---

[37] A few pages later, a local uses the word "curious" to describe the relationship between Charlotte and Paula: "Now that's a curious thing again, these two girls being so fond of one another [...] they are more like lovers than girl and girl" (Hardy, *Laodicean* 50).

The "reluctance" that Archer parenthetically records is amusingly evident in the text of the interview.[38] Hardy's concern is to make it plain that—unlike Samuel Richardson—he did not *author* the words of love, and in fact did not even understand the discourse. To have done so, his anxious evasions make paradoxically plain, would imply that he himself desired the soldiers in India. Hardy takes refuge in the idea that he was a mere recording-writing machine in order to avoid being construed either as a girl or as part of a same-sex erotic epistolary exchange.[39] It is ironic, therefore, that what he finally admits to remembering is an "oddity"—the strange address "Calcutta, *or Elsewear*" [sic]. His defense against deviance breaks down, as indeed it does when Archer presses his point, rejecting Hardy's claim that the letter-writing left no impression upon him, insisting that the act of writing women's letters must have made him think *like a woman.* Moreover, Archer suggests that the "sympathetic ink" that had been suffused into Hardy's brain would get released in a moment of passion, through the "heat of creation." Archer makes fiction-writing sound like an erotic act, a kind of cross-gendered ejaculation. In order to generate the words of a woman, Hardy becomes, in that moment of writing, a woman writer. The communication network in which Hardy participated detached the epistle from the hand of the lover and inserted into the relationship a number of other variously gendered bodies—not only his own, but also those of the postal workers. The machine to which Hardy appeals as a standard of imperviousness is in fact a penetrating, penetrated network that creates and leaves traces of desire. As Marshall McLuhan might retort to Hardy, "the medium is the massage."[40] If the medium is, as Hardy insists, a machine, it is a desiring machine.

The postal medium's capacity for producing exchanges of gender and desire derives from its universal, organized character. A postal exchange means that it is not possible

---

[38] Hardy himself notes the trustworthiness of this interview text: he saw a transcript and wrote to Archer commending him for having been "wonderfully faithful in your reproduction." This letter testifies again to the anxiety that this particular interview had caused Hardy, both for what he revealed and for the intimacy of the encounter between the two men: Hardy requests omission of some of the more personal information that he had revealed under the pressure of Archer's interviewing techniques. In a letter to Florence Henniker, Hardy wrote that Archer "experimented on me in a new kind of interviewing: knowing him well I did not mind it at the time, but I have felt some misgivings since" (qtd. in Gibson 65–66).

[39] Hardy's concern to emphasize that writing, recording, and, by extension, dissemination machines are non-human is directly belied in *A Laodicean* when he writes, "The telegraph has almost the attributes of a human being at Stancy Castle. When its bell rang people rushed to the old tapestry chamber allotted to it, and waited its pleasure with all the deference due to such a novel inhabitant of that ancestral pile" (Hardy, *Laodicean* 52). Here, the telegraph is not only personified, but is also personified as a master or mistress of others, and it has "pleasures."

[40] Marshall McLuhan, *The Medium Is the Massage: An Inventory of Effects* (London: Penguin, 1967). McLuhan enjoyed the slip between "message" and "massage" for its association of communication with the accidental effects of desire, chaos, and the masses. His son Eric McLuhan explains: "The title was a mistake. When the book came back from the typesetter, it had on the cover 'Massage' as it still does. The title should have read The Medium Is the Message but the typesetter had made an error. When Marshall McLuhan saw the typo he exclaimed, 'Leave it alone! It's great, and right on target!' Now there are four possible readings for the last word of the title, all of them accurate: 'Message' and 'Mess Age,' 'Massage' and 'Mass Age.'" In Phil Baines, *Penguin by Design: A Cover Story 1935–2005* (London: Penguin, 2005), 144.

to imagine the trajectory—the single pathway—of a post-letter or telegraph without imagining the multiple pathways of the network. Just as the machine, despite Hardy's protestations, always mediates, the network always complicates the idea of a single line of connection between two correspondents. In *A Laodicean,* Hardy contrasts Paula, with her command of telegraph and railway networks, with her male suitors (and their supporters) who have merely one-track minds; they are each obsessed with blood-lineage. These men besiege Paula, plotting and contriving to win her hand and in the process, they make intriguingly similar interpretative mistakes. Captain De Stancy is urged to woo her by his illegitimate son, William Dare, in order that Paula's wealth and castle might once again become De Stancy property.[41] Somerset similarly has inheritance and genealogy on his mind. He interprets Paula's "preference" for the De Stancy line and her taste for the ancient as the desire for "family pedigree" (Hardy, *Laodicean* 212), and he goes in search of his own genealogical tree with which to press his suit. De Stancy's courtship of Paula is instigated and, quite literally, stage-managed by the illegitimate Dare and by Paula's uncle Abner Power. Abner Power similarly contrives to arrange the marriage for socially conservative reasons, believing that if Paula "finds the money, and this Stancy finds the name and blood, "'twould be a very neat match" (Hardy, *Laodicean* 237). Dare is the product of a mismanaged heterosexual union and seeks to compensate for the fragmentation of the kinship structure that he embodies, conspiring to patch together the semblance of a blood-descendancy. Both he and Abner Power seek to line up and conjoin the flows of blood, title, and money.

The relationship between Charlotte De Stancy and Paula Power bypasses the constructions of blood-lineage that the men try to reestablish. While Captain De Stancy and Somerset duel over who will become master of the castle, it is Charlotte who moves in as Paula's companion. Charlotte's residence at the castle confuses Somerset: "This is home to you, and not home?" he asks (Hardy, *Laodicean* 32), struggling and failing to understand and articulate the queer semantics of her domestic situation. Further—and particularly—confusing to him is Charlotte's lack of regard for her ancestral connections to the castle. Instead of searching for her history in the portraits of her blood ancestors, she thinks the pictures not "useful" and is "serenely conclusive" about the castle's current ownership: "It doesn't seem to me as if the place ever belonged to a relative of mine" (Hardy, *Laodicean* 32). Even her physiognomy reflects genetic *dissent* rather than *descent*; hers "was not the De Stancy face with all its original specialities; it was, so to speak, a defective reprint of that face: for the nose tried hard to turn up and deal utter confusion to the family shape" (Hardy, *Laodicean* 29). Charlotte's

---

[41] John Plotz argues that Hardy has an antipathy to "the legacy of cultural portability inherited from the Victorian novel," replacing it with attention to how "different individuals orient themselves in the world" (*Portable Property* 123). Hardy's characters are laden, he admits, but not with detachable cargo; instead they take with them their various ways of perceiving the world (*Portable Property* 124). Plotz's observation is highly applicable here: Somerset and De Stancy are too fixated on property and (social) portability, whereas the telegraphic girls regularly eschew ideas of belonging and belongings, and are animated rather by communication of various kinds.

relationship to the castle is also a confusion to the family shape; her presence there is a consequence of her love for Paula, rather than a consequence of her family line. Paula similarly deals out confusions to family shapes by conversely taking a "lively interest" in the castle's artifacts, demonstrating an " 'artistic' preference for Charlotte's ancestors instead of her own" (Hardy, *Laodicean* 212).[42] Her predilection for the De Stancy line is most certainly "artistic," as Oscar Wilde uses the term; it is a predilection not for any De Stancy but for *Charlotte*.

When the novel ends with Charlotte secluding herself in a nunnery and Paula marrying Somerset, it is not an unmitigated heterosexual resolution. Somerset encourages Paula to abandon hope of rebuilding the now burned and ruined castle and desires her to "recover, if you have not already, from the warp given to your mind [. . .] by the mediaevalism of that place." She asks if he would prefer her to be a modern spirit and he agrees, saying, "Yes; for since it is rather in your line you may as well keep straight on." Paula agrees: "Very well, I'll keep straight on; and we'll build a new house beside the ruin, and show the modern spirit for evermore [. . .] ." Her acceptance of the "line" Somerset assigns to her, and the "straight"—as opposed to "warped"—life they will make together is interrupted. The ellipsis marks a "repressed sigh" and an unfulfilled wish: "I wish my castle wasn't burnt; and I wish you were a De Stancy!" she bursts out. The alternative life that she grieves in this outburst is described earlier in the same paragraph in terms of another "line"; their decision to leave behind the castle was a bid to have a home "unencumbered with the ghosts of an unfortunate line" (Hardy, *Laodicean* 431). Paula's final words of the novel make it clear that she herself is haunted by desire and desires to be haunted. That this is a queer desire and that the yearned-for spectral presence is Charlotte is, as Terry Castle describes it, indicated through the trope of "the spectral lesbian [who] is ultimately expelled from the 'real' world of the fiction" (7) and through the epistemic mistake made by Somerset when he talks of Paula's medieval tastes.

Somerset's reference to Paula having been under the "warped" influence of "medievalism" flies in the face of a conversation he and Paula had shortly after meeting, when Paula informs him that she is "not a mediaevalist," but "Greek" (Hardy, *Laodicean* 82). Her declaration concurs with Charlotte's earlier representation of Paula's tastes in a conversation with Somerset. Upon hearing of Paula's interest in pottery, he declares that she must be a "practical" woman. Charlotte is quick to say that he misconstrues Paula: " 'Oh no! no!' replied Miss De Stancy in tones showing how supremely ignorant he must be of Miss Power's nature if he characterised her in those terms. 'It is *Greek* pottery she means—Hellenic pottery she tells me to call it' " (Hardy, *Laodicean* 36). Paula later gets

---

[42] This line is especially notable, as variants of it occur several times in the novel. We first read it as reported speech: "I have a *prédilection d'artiste* for ancestors of the other sort, like the De Stancys," she tells Somerset (Hardy, *Laodicean* 113). Somerset recalls it when watching Paula with Captain De Stancy and jealously wondering if this predilection will cause her to favor the Captain (Hardy, *Laodicean* 221). Hardy reiterates it, in free indirect discourse, when Captain De Stancy wonders if his ancestral connection to the castle will cause Paula to favor him (*Laodicean* 334).

Charlotte to explain to Somerset her ideas for building a Greek courtyard in the castle, which Somerset finds "rather startling" (Hardy, *Laodicean* 83). As they are considering the plan for this "anachronistic" architectural feature, the three of them spot the turret that Somerset had fallen into the day before (Hardy, *Laodicean* 82–83). They remember the story of a man who fell into the same turret, but could not get out and starved to death. Instead of imagining this fate for Somerset, Paula "arose and went across to Miss De Stancy. 'Don't *you* go falling down and becoming a skeleton,' she said [...] after which she clasped her fingers behind Charlotte's neck, and smiled tenderly in her face" (Hardy, *Laodicean* 84). As Charlotte is describing Paula's plans for the Greek colonnade that so startle Somerset, Paula pulls up a young sycamore tree that had sprung up between the joints of the paving (Hardy, *Laodicean* 84). Hardy's symbolism is blunt: Paula's presence in Stancy castle and her architectural plans for Greek features uproot some orthodoxies. Paula is most certainly not interested in the genealogical trees of either of her male suitors; instead, she desires the companionship (including, as the above passage implies, the body) of Charlotte and an architecture that echoes a culture in which such love finds its roots.

Paula's interest in Greek culture, her "modern" outlook and her queer relationship with Charlotte are interrrelated. Critics have hitherto largely ignored her interest in Greek culture, but it poses a significant complication to the notion that Paula is a woman torn between her love for the modern and her love for the medieval. Her declaration "I am Greek" (Hardy, *Laodicean* 82) also disrupts the critical commonplace that she is torn between wanting to marry Captain De Stancy and wanting to marry George Somerset. Linda Dowling's study *Hellenism and Homosexuality in Victorian Oxford* has established the cultural significance of scholarly interest in Hellenism that burgeoned from the 1860s onward.[43] Dowling points out that Hellenism offered a civic ethic that could respond to and supplant the "pinched" narrowing of Protestant religion, a narrowing which had been compounded by industrial modernity. For liberal thinkers such as John Stuart Mill, Matthew Arnold, and Benjamin Jowett, Hellenism promised to reinvigorate a stagnant culture and supplant the "older ideological structures of public life" (Dowling 35) through its emphasis on diversity and nonconformity. Dowling claims that this "diversity ideal" of Hellenism meshed with the "emphasis on diversity within both the English tradition of religious Dissent and the newer discourse of biological or Darwinistic evolution" (62). The rejection of "uniformity" and an embracing of "diversity," Dowling claims, paved the way for a late-Victorian "counterdiscourse of social identity and erotic liberation" (36).

---

[43] The account given by Richard Jenkyns in *The Victorians and Ancient Greece* of Victorian interest in Hellenism makes it quite clear that *A Laodicean* was in conversation with the debates surrounding it. He writes: "It is easy for us to think of the Victorian age, with its Gothic enthusiasm, as a period of reaction against the Hellenism of an earlier generation [...]. To some Englishmen Hellenism seemed alien to the time and place in which they found themselves; the Gothic spirit appeared to be their natural inheritance. Others took the opposite view" (Jenkyns 15–16). This tussle between the Hellenic and Gothic ideals is architecturally embodied in Stancy Castle.

The discourse of Hellenism, therefore, is a suggestive school of thought to pursue in relation to this novel that is so concerned with era and aesthetic, and intertwines these concerns with a story of same-sex love. The story opens with a scene set "on an ordinary plodding and bustling evening of the nineteenth century" in which Somerset witnesses Paula Power's last-minute refusal of baptismal immersion. The church is newly built, with "pseudo-classical" and "geometrically oppressive" ornamentation, in short, "ugly" (Hardy, *Laodicean* 13–14). It transpires that Paula had only agreed to the ceremony because it was her father's last dying request; this Nonconformist ceremony is consequently an act of personal conformity, which Paula cannot follow through. The ceremony and its building stand for "narrow religious character [...] self-effacement [and] assimilation," which Dowling identifies as the avowed enemies of Hellenism (57).

The two modern improvements Paula has added to the castle are the telegraph and a gymnasium modeled on those found in the new colleges for women.[44] Like the telegraph machinery that connects Charlotte and Paula, the gymnasium is also a site for same-sex desire; Paula's maid Milly Birch says that Paula is "bewitching" when she is in the gymnasium "Because when she is there she wears such a pretty boy's costume and is so charming in her movements, that you think she is a lovely youth and not a girl at all" (Hardy, *Laodicean* 169). The gymnasium, probably modeled on those at Girton and Newnham Colleges, Cambridge, which were founded in 1869 and 1871 respectively, is a marker of Paula's educated and independent nature, but is also a manifestation of her association with the Greek athletic, homoerotic aesthetic. Not only is the gymnasium a place where Paula's gender becomes mutable, and she can look like a boy rather than a girl, but the gym is a product of Paula's enthusiasm for "the physical training of the Greeks, whom she adores" (Hardy, *Laodicean* 170).

Before we learn of Paula's "predilection" for the Greek ideal, Somerset's first sightings of Paula connect her to the Greek aesthetic. When he spies her on the brink of descending into the baptismal pool, she is "clothed in an ample robe of flowing white, which descended to her feet," and instead of following the minister into the water, she "remained rigid as stone" (Hardy, *Laodicean* 16). She looks like one of the Greek statues that she later says she has admired in the British Museum (Hardy, *Laodicean* 84).[45] Paula is also described as a statue in a scene with Captain De Stancy, where her imperviousness to his romantic machinations and "double-entendre"[46] is signaled by her statue-like stillness: "At last

---

[44] Paula's gymnasium is a mark of her modernity. Walter Besant's *All Sorts and Conditions of Men* was published just one year later than *A Laodicean*, in 1882, and also features an heiress heroine who, inspired by the sporting facilities of her Cambridge college, builds her own gymnasium. In Besant's novel, the Newnham-educated brewery scion Angela Messenger disguises herself as a seamstress in order to establish a dressmaking business dedicated to improving the welfare of young female workers. When Angela declares her intention to set up a gymnasium on the shop premises, she is met with incredulous stares: "This was revolutionary, indeed" (Besant 105).

[45] Earlier in the novel Hardy directly compares Paula to Greek goddesses: "Not sensuous enough for an Aphrodite, and too subdued for a Hebe, she would, yet, with the adjunct of doves or nectar, have stood sufficiently well for either of those personages" (Hardy, *Laodicean* 59).

Paula spoke, so stilly that she seemed a statue, enunciating" (Hardy, *Laodicean* 190). Not only is Paula as still as a statue, but she is also as white as one, clothed in "flowing white." Richard Jenkyns has traced the homoerotic significance of whiteness through the work of Walter Pater, who, according to Jenkyns, "contrasts Greek whiteness with the spiritual unease of the modern world" (148). In *The Picture of Dorian Gray*, published ten years after *A Laodicean*, Oscar Wilde repeatedly portrayed Dorian as a Greek god: pallid, perfect, and posed, the embodiment of the Hellenism which Lord Henry espouses. Lord Henry believes that erotic liberation might lead the world to "forget all the maladies of medievalism, and return to the Hellenic ideal" (Wilde, *DG* 41). This conjunction of sexual frankness, rejection of medievalism, and embrace of Hellenism describes Paula Power perfectly, but did this discourse have homoerotic significance for women as well as men?

Eileen Gregory has analyzed the female homoerotics of the white and static forms of Greek sculpture through her study of the poetry of H.D. She shows how H.D. used references to whiteness and statues to encode a queer sexuality, embracing the "iconography of Dorian hellenism" as a discourse of "discipline, hardness and brilliance" (Gregory 102, 105).[47] We might also remember Robert Browning's description of Katherine Bradley and Edith Cooper, who wrote as Michael Field, as "two dear Greek women" (qtd. in Prins 77).[48] This homoerotic Hellenism was not a discourse exclusive to the male domain. Yopie Prins decides the matter in her essay "Greek Maenads, Victorian Spinsters," which directly addresses the question of whether women feature in the Greek homoerotic nineteenth-century tradition, noting, "The cultural prestige of Classical studies in nineteenth-century England and the fascination with Greek antiquity in particular created a desire among women to know the language of ancient Greece and, like their male counterparts, they discovered in ancient Greek a new language of

---

[46] The whole scene is a paradigm of "double meanings." Paula has been affected by noticing the same birthmark on De Stancy as on one of the ancestors in the castle's portraits, and "a new and romantic feeling that the De Stancys had stretched out a tentacle from their genealogical tree to seize her by the hand and draw her in to their mass took possession of Paula" (Hardy, *Laodicean* 187). De Stancy tries to cash in on her enchantment; he "ardently contrives" (Hardy, *Laodicean* 188) to focus her again on the portraits and leaps into a half-suit of armor in order to look "like a man of bygone times" (Hardy, *Laodicean* 189). This "Protean quality" of his impresses Paula, but his recitation of the poem, during which he "fixed his look upon her" to suggest "a present significance of the words" fails: "the idea of any such double-entendre had by no means commended itself to her soul" (Hardy, *Laodicean* 191). The past is capable of enchanting Paula out of her "natural unconcern" (Hardy, *Laodicean* 188), but she is impervious to verbal protestations of love—she fails to read between lines or detect hidden meanings in her suitor's words.

[47] The imagery is, for both H. D. and Hardy, filtered through the work of Walter Pater. Hardy both knew and read Pater. *The Literary Notebooks of Thomas Hardy* has a number of extensive entries meditating on Pater's work, particularly his theories of Greek culture. For discussions of Pater's "The Myth of Demeter and Persephone," see vol. 1, 305 and vol. 2, 268. For entries about Greek sculpture and the Greek spirit, see vol. 2, 43, 128.

[48] Prins's study, *Victorian Sappho*, further details the way that female homoerotics could attach to "thinking Greek" in the nineteenth century. Like Martha Vicinus, she sees Michael Field's Greek work as an adoption of the tropes of male homosexuality but points out that they also *adapt* this trope, "imply[ing] a lesbian eroticism distinct from the troping of homosexual desire" (Prins 77).

desire."[49] The connection of homoerotic Greek eros to women is made most explicit in *A Laodicean* in the passage where Paula compares her beloved Charlotte with a white statue; one of the most erotic scenes in the novel, it depicts the sensuousness so remarkably lacking from the relationship between Paula and Somerset or De Stancy. Coming across an "alabaster effigy of a recumbant lady" in a church, Paula sighs and says, "She is just like Charlotte." Then

> Paula drew her forefingers across the marble face of the effigy, and at length [she] took out her handkerchief, and began wiping the dust from the hollows of the features. [Somerset] looked on, wondering what her sigh had meant, but guessing that it had been somehow caused by the sight of these sculptures in connection with the newspaper writer's denunciation of her as an irresponsible outsider.
> (Hardy, *Laodicean* 111)

Once again Somerset finds Paula's nonverbal language illegible; just as he has proved himself unable to interpret both her blushes and her telegraphic signals, he cannot understand her sigh or her caresses of the statue. Later in the novel, frustrated by the nondemonstrative language of the telegram, he tries to force Paula to correspond by letter, hoping for explicit verbal expression of her sentiments. Throughout the novel Somerset is thoroughly disconcerted by Paula's "telegraphic" manner. Just as Somerset is frustrated by Paula's telegraphic, independent directness, there are indications that the type of womanhood embodied by these young, unmarried, independent girls was equally "startling" to the general public. A common complaint was that telegraph girls were too "brusque" and "impertinent" in manner. Even Lady John Manners, who commends the women workers for their satisfactory work, notes: "It may be hoped that in time the somewhat brusque manner in some of these damsels may become more like that of their foreign sisters, and that they will learn that gentle courtesy is not inconsistent with self-respect" (20). Lady Manners clearly thinks the girls are anything but old-fashioned "damsels"; she intimates that they are modern girls who put assertiveness before gentility.[50] In this *A Laodicean* scene, Paula's modernity and lack of reverence for antiquity is very much the issue. Somerset uncodes her "telegraphic" emotions by cross-referencing her sigh to a letter published in the newspaper that attacks Paula's plans to build her Greek courtyard, branding her an "iconoclast

---

[49] Yopie Prins, "Greek Maenads, Victorian Spinsters," in *Victorian Sexual Dissidence*, ed. Richard Dellamora, 43.

[50] A flirtatious moment in R. M. Ballantyne's May Maylands story suggests that such complaints were due to cultural frictions: "Although an artless and innocent young girl, fresh from the western shores of Erin, May had a peculiar, and, in one of her age and sex, almost pert way of putting questions, to which she often received quaint and curious replies [...]. In short May's conduct was such that we must hasten to free her from premature condemnation by explaining that she was a female telegraphist in what we may call the literary lungs of London—the General Post-Office at St. Martin's-le-Grand" (*Post Haste* 15). This passage flirts with the suggestion of sexual impropriety. The writer plays on the fact that, if it were not her *job* to interact in this way with people, "innocent" May would be open to "condemnation."

of blood [...] without respect for the tradition of the country" (Hardy, *Laodicean* 109). Paula's forms and impulses are wrong; as a modern, telegraphic girl with a taste for the Greek aesthetic she is a threat to the orders of race and nation.

The opening pages of the novel also present the telegraph as a machine that challenges ancestral and national orders. Somerset is disconcerted by the incongruity of the telegraph wire entering the castle and meditates on the nature of the telegraphic machinery. Instead of the insularity that the castle represents, the telegraph promotes "interchange" and universal "kinship" that is racial, intellectual, and moral:

> There was a certain unexpectedness in the fact that the hoary memorial of a stolid antagonism to the interchange of ideas, the monument of hard distinctions in blood and race [...] should be the goal of a machine which beyond everything may be said to symbolise cosmopolitan views and the intellectual and moral kinship of all mankind.
>
> (Hardy, *Laodicean* 22–23)

The crux of the matter is lineage; in this novel the network of telegraph wires runs counter to individuated lines of blood and title. The kinship of "all mankind" interferes with narratives of inheritance and genealogy. Hardy dramatizes the struggle between the two influences when William Dare recognizes that the telegraph's potential for engendering human contact threatens his plans for Paula's marriage to his father: "That wire is a nuisance, to my mind; such constant intercourse with the outer world is bad for our romance" (Hardy, *Laodicean* 207). The plural possessive pronoun—"our," instead of "your" romance—is highly ironic. Dare is complaining that the telegraph complicates matters by enabling communion with others at exactly the moment that he reveals how unnaturally commingled he and his father are. His point, however, remains; telegraph lines to the outside world allow an intercourse that is catholic rather than exclusive. The communication network as his enemy, he and Abner Power set about trying to manipulate its potential. Power intercepts telegrams between Paula and Somerset, and Dare forges a telegram that makes Somerset appear to be a gambler. They are not, however, part of the telegraphic network, merely criminals who break into its circuitry. It is Charlotte and Paula, however, who can actually operate the machinery, can work it "beautifully" and "delight" in it (Hardy, *Laodicean* 35). They find pleasure, not enmity, in its wires and use it to build friendship and connection rather than mischief.

The technology that stands for interchange and kinship therefore also stands for the love between the women. The telegraph signals the love between them: " 'Another message,' she said.—'*Paula to Charlotte.*' [...] Miss De Stancy blushed with pleasure when she raised her eyes from the machine" (Hardy, *Laodicean* 52). The telegraphic signals provoke a physiological sign of Paula's love for Charlotte—the blush. When Somerset suggests to Paula that she is Charlotte's "good friend," Paula "looked into the distant air with tacit admission of the impeachment. 'So would you be if you knew her,' she said; and a blush slowly rose to her cheek, as if the person spoken of had been a lover rather than a friend" (Hardy, *Laodicean* 35). As in *The Rebel of the Family*, in which the attraction between Bell Blount and Perdita was marked by the women's blushes, the blush functions here as a signifier of same-sex passion and correspondence between Paula and Charlotte. In *Telling Complexions: The Nineteenth-Century English Novel and the Blush*, Mary Ann O'Farrell has described how the blush can "partake of both body and language," and that in the nineteenth-century novel, the "ephemeral materiality" of the blush is a suggestive means of communication (3).[51] The blush is, as the title of O'Farrell's study implies, a means of telling, something that can make the body legible. In *A Laodicean*, the blush is the physiological manifestation of the telegraphic mode that binds the two women together.

While physiological and technological communication forge a bond between Charlotte and Paula, bodily disfiguration, distortion, and inscription characterize the men in the novel. Dare is tattooed with the name of his biological, but illegitimate father; Mr. Power's face is "pitted, puckered, and seamed like a dried water-course" (Hardy, *Laodicean* 236), and Dare contrives a photograph of Somerset, manipulating the image to show "distorted features and wild attitude of a man advanced in intoxication" (Hardy, *Laodicean* 319). The disfigured male bodies are manifest forms of the crises of representation upon which the plot of this novel turns and turns again. Hardy stages problems of reading and representation and a tug-of-war between information and misinformation throughout the novel.[52] The information and misinformation problems that beset the heterosexual relationships all concern the establishment of character, ancestry, and familial relation. Unlike the women who have functional and fluid communication between them, the men in the story get marked or scarred in their attempts to pursue kinship structures.

Hardy resolves the novel with Paula, in the lukewarm fashion indicated in the novel's title,[53] declaring that "somehow or other I have got to like George Somerset as desperately as a woman can care for any man" (Hardy, *Laodicean* 418) and marrying him. Charlotte subsequently writes to Paula to tell her that she has decided to withdraw from the "social

---

[51] Both O'Farrell and Kate Flint point out, however, that the blush was not necessarily seen as an involuntary response, which revealed an unmediated emotion or indicated a natural capacity for feeling. Rather, it signals the "subscription of the blushing body to the code of an extensive social network" (O'Farrell 7). See Kate Flint, *The Woman Reader 1837–1914* 89 and O'Farrell 111.

[52] Somerset's relationship with Paula is threatened by three material misinformations: a paragraph put in the local newspaper by Abner Power speculating that Paula and De Stancy were soon to be engaged, a telegram sent by Dare under Somerset's name that falsely suggested he had dissolute gambling habits, and the photograph doctored to portray Somerset as drunk. Hardy demonstrates a fascination with how material representations can take over the person they represent. Paula, Charlotte reports, was so taken with the telegraph technology that "she was sending messages from morning till night" (Hardy, *Laodicean* 35). Elsewhere, Hardy introduces the villains of the tale, each of whom are estranged blood-relatives, via their photograph or portrait. The novel questions the means by which we recognize and read people; at times material and technological representations are dangerous and manipulable, but at other times, they are only manifestations of human fictions.

[53] A Laodicean is someone who is indifferent to religion, like the Christians of the church of Laodicea mentioned in the *Book of Revelations* (3: 14–18).

world" and join a Protestant sisterhood. Calling Paula her "more than sister," she says her decision will mean that Paula will always be with her and "if an increase in what I already feel for you be possible, it will be furthered by the retirement and meditation I shall enjoy in my secluded home" (Hardy, *Laodicean* 427). The women's lives diverge, but it is clear that they have both chosen paths of duty. Duty is an affective commitment linked, as I have shown, to lesbianism. Repudiating a lesbian relationship for the sake of duty is therefore no repudiation of lesbianism at all. Just as there is a distinct whiff of resignation in Paula's declaration of her engagement to Somerset, which avoids the word "love" as determinedly as she avoided his kisses, Charlotte also presents her decision to join a convent as a compromise: "Whatever shortcomings may be found in such a community, I believe that I shall be happier there than in any other place" (Hardy, *Laodicean* 427). Just as Charlotte first loved Paula at a distance through the telegraph wires, she now must love her from behind convent walls. And Charlotte's own last name reminds of this. The "de Stancy" Paula Power yearns to be with can only, it seems, be loved at a "di-Stance."[54] As with Trollope's Lucy Graham, same-sex love is inextricably linked to discipline, devotion, and the erotics of distance.

Media and Measure

The opening scene of *A Laodicean* describes Somerset occupied with measuring and copying the architectural detail on a doorway on the village church. To ensure precision of his copy, he uses a curious instrument:

> He took his measurements carefully, and as if he reverenced the old workers whose trick he was endeavouring to acquire six hundred years after the original performance had ceased and the performers passed into the unseen. By means of a strip of lead called a leaden tape, which he pressed around and into the fillets and hollows with his finger and thumb, he transferred the exact contour of each moulding to his drawing.
> (*AL* 7)

What neither Hardy, nor any of his subsequent editors note, is the name of this leaden measure. It is called a "Lesbian rule." The phrase, and instrument, is cited by Aristotle in *Nichomachean Ethics*: "For when the thing is indefinite the rule also is indefinite, like the leaden rule used in making the Lesbian moulding; the rule adapts itself to the shape of the stone and is not rigid, and so too the decree is adapted to the facts" (5.10: 99). A Lesbian rule goes around corners and curves, and can be fitted to molding so that a precise

---

[54] On the contrary, Paula's other suitor—Somerset—has a name that implies tumbling circularity. "Somerset" is another word for "somersault." It means either to somersault oneself, or to cause a person to turn a somersault, and was still in use in the late nineteenth century. See the OED entry for "somerset." Somerset will make a "complete overturn" in Paula, as she turns away from her passion for Charlotte De Stancy, toward her lukewarm marriage with Somerset.

copy can be made, or exact measurements taken. It conforms, as Aristotle emphasizes, to the most nonconformist of shapes.

There are several ways in which this instrument is a fitting emblem for the novel's heroine, Paula Power, who answers the accusation that she's a medievalist with the retort "I am an eclectic" (92). She embodies nonconformism and irregularity in that she is a Dissenter, a castle-dwelling heiress to an industrial fortune, and she loves Charlotte better than any of her male suitors. But in this opening scene, the Lesbian rule is firmly in the hand of Somerset, and he, too, finds close, even erotic, affinity with its adaptive nature. Hardy presents Somerset as eccentric in his pleasures. Somerset is described finding sensual pleasure in the molded stonework, and the dramatic emphasis of this scene is that Somerset literally turns his back on the glorious sunset that Hardy tells us most others would consider the highlight of the setting. Somerset's tastes render the visual secondary to the tactile. Alerted to the sun's spectacular, glamorous leave-taking only by "the warmth of the moulded stonework under his touch," it is in the touch of the stonework that he finds satisfaction. This touch is animating because of the sense it brings him of connection to others, connection made across the ages. The technology he employs is reproductive, and it is also retrospective, enabling him to imitate the work of those who are long dead.

Bathed in the medium of the photographic, that is to say light, Somerset is indifferent to its "chromatic effect," preferring the tactile, sculptural "fillets and hollows" that he must feel with his fingers. The stonework takes on feminine and sexual associations—"fillets" usually adorn the heads of maidens (OED), and the fingering of sculptural "hollows" consequently appears as sexually penetrative and caressing. It is a scene that will later find its counterpart and consummation when Paula wipes the dust from the "hollows" of the sculpture that reminds her of Charlotte (111). The bendy Lesbian rule becomes too bendy for Somerset, almost something of a boomerang, when his beloved Paula turns out to be as invested in exploring feminine curves as he is. But the setbacks to Somerset's heterosexual courtship, and indeed the gender/sexuality organization of the characters, receive less descriptive attention than the technologies of tactility that they employ. Both Somerset and Paula use an intermediating instrument to feel: for Somerset this is the Lesbian rule and for Paula it is a handkerchief. In *Touching Feeling*, Eve Kosofsky Sedgwick remarks that "the sense of physical touch itself, at least so far, has been remarkably unsusceptible to being amplified by technology" (15). An exception, she notes, is breast examination in which women are taught to use "a film of liquid soap, a square of satiny cloth, or even a pad of thin plastic filled with a layer of water to make the contours of the breast more salient to their fingers" (15). Cutaneous contact involves friction that can confuse the hermeneutic capacities of touch: these intermediating materials reduce "noise" and instead amplify the signal features. Sedgwick's point, however, is that the diagnostics of touch are little more than third cousin twice removed to the "literally exponential enhancements of visual stimulus" (15) that she dates as having entered the cultural vernacular in the nineteenth century. She cites *Middlemarch*'s narrative ability to "zoom in a mere two sentences from telescope to microscope" to argue that once such ranges of visual perception became commonplace, ocular proof thoroughly overtook the "authority of the fingers" (15).

Telegraphy is, however, a technology that "zooms," vanquishing range in the form of distance *and* relies upon acuity of touch or ear. The signals it sends are not visual, and the body becomes the echo chamber to the message. Sedgwick's point, that modernity separates touch from sight, holds, however, when we remember that Hardy frames this story as a meeting of the ancient and the modern. Paula Power, and her telegraphy, produces a point of interference between the wavelengths of modernity and antiquity, and this interference produces some crossed wires, some queer effects. Feeling, in this novel, happens through and across intermediating surfaces and spaces. And because these media themselves signify, because they have histories and characters, they not only convey desire but also transfer it and transform it. The business of communicating across distance detaches the communication from bodies, animates it through the form of the media involved, and reconfigures the relationship of the correspondents through having rendered the message exchangeable and mobile. Telegraph wires are always crossed, their messages are—by definition—mixed. Indeed, the trope of crossed wires is exhibited through the transferred apparatuses involved in the "touching sculpture" scenes. Somerset, who desires and courts Paula, is equipped with the Lesbian instrument. Paula, whose primary affective and erotic attachments are to Charlotte, is furnished with the accessory preeminent in the flirtations and betrayals of heterosexual love plots: the handkerchief.

Amplification is the most apt term through which to analyze *A Laodicean*. The resonance *between* the two "feeling sculpture" scenes is produced in part because they are scenes *of* resonance: a "hollow" is an amplifying chamber; Somerset uses the Lesbian rule amidst such silence that "every trifling sound could be heard for miles" (11); and the "faintly clicking sound" (206) of Paula and Charlotte's telegraphic machinery reverberates throughout the novel. Such amplification is figured as more enabling than visualization. As I begin arguing above, Somerset's copying by means of the rule stands in implicit opposition to another reproductive technology of representation: photography—or what Hardy later calls "the heliographic science" (320). Although photography is not explicitly referenced, its lexicon suffuses the scene, and the novel unfolds to reveal a dastardly photographer who uses "ingenious device[s] in photography" (367) to misrepresent his rival. Hardy emphasizes that the results are most convincing to the uninitiated (319, 320), and thus falls in line with Roland Barthes's phenomenological assertion in *Camera Lucida* (1980) that "the photograph possesses an evidential force" but "its testimony bears not on the object, but on time." Barthes describes the totalizing effects of the medium and

---

[55] Barthes's commentary on photography becomes even more pertinent to the photographic blackmail of Hardy's novel, when Barthes notes that "the Photograph sometimes makes appear what we never see in a real face (or in a face reflected in a mirror): a genetic feature, the fragment of oneself or of a relative which comes from some ancestor" (103). Dare's use of the "photographic portrait of a peculiar nature" attempts to make Somerset appear peculiar in nature, specifically, degenerate. It attempts to type him as an inveterate drunk.

the way that it offers itself as the whole story, disavowing others: "in the Photograph, the power of authentication exceeds the power of representation" (88). Likening the *stasis* of photography to an "arrest" (91), he argues that it immobilizes time in such a way as to divorce one from the past (it "blocks memory," 91) and "it is *without future*" (90).[55] Sculpture, however, mobilizes. It frees us from the arrest of photography by allowing adoration and interactive ritual (90). In *S/Z* (1970), Barthes directly and forcefully celebrates this interactivity: "Free-standing, penetrable, in short *profound*, the statue invites visitation, exploration, penetration" (208). My comparison flattens out, mangles even, the rippling, reflective, and desiring texture of *Camera Lucida*, which describes a coming-to-love and a coming-to-love-the-losses of the medium of photography. Carolyn Dinshaw, among others, has described *Camera Lucida* as a queer historical project distinguished by its "emphasis on the cross-temporality" (50) of the connective somatic relations proffered by photography. But still, *Camera Lucida* is wary of the fixities of the form, fearing that, as Michel Foucault urged, "Visibility is a trap."[56] In *A Laodicean*, Somerset turns his back on the Kodak Moment[57] and the attempted entrapments of a photographer-villain, and Paula Power threads her telegraph wire through the medieval precursor to the panopticon: the arrow-slit. Her renovation disarms the unidirectional visual mechanics of the arrow-slit with the two-way communication of the telegraph. Paula and Somerset both initially favor the replacement of specularizing technologies with haptic technologies, that is to say with the media of touch. Somerset loses his attraction to pliancy as he progresses further into suitorship of Paula, and by the end of the novel, married to Paula, he urges her "to keep straight on" (431). No more Lesbian rule. Paula, however, remains allied with forms of intermediation that interrupt the heterosexual resolution of her life and the novel. When Charlotte writes to her from the convent, assuring her "you will *always* be with me" (427), she writes "with the fellow pen to yours, that you gave me when we went to Budmouth together" (427). The town of "Budmouth" and the exchange of phallic pens that occurred there, form Hardy's leering implication of the women's sexual intimacy with each other. The writing instruments in their hands, and the post-letters they exchange, will be Charlotte and Paula's somatic connection from here on out.

Thoroughly intermediated by convent walls, geographical distance, a postal system and—indeed—heterosexuality and marriage, can we say that Charlotte and Paula's love for each other survives this narrative? To answer in the affirmative, I turn to what is literally the last gasp of the novel. When Paula enunciates a postscript to her marriage, wishing her castle un-burned, and lamenting that Somerset is no De Stancy, she does so as she "repressed a sigh" (431). Not merely the affective symptom of regret, a sigh recalls us to the idea of media: a *media* is a linguistic term for a "voiced stop in ancient Greek; (more

---

[56] Michel Foucault, *Discipline and Punish*, trans. Alan Sheridan (Penguin, London, 1991), 200.

[57] I use the phrase only half-facetiously. The origins of the Kodak company date back to the same year that *A Laodicean* was published. It began as the Eastman Dry Plate Company in 1881 and registered the trademark Kodak in 1888.

widely) a (voiced) unaspirated stop" (OED). When Paula holds back, or unaspirates, her sigh and voices her reservations about her marriage, she is mediated and mediating. Although she does not return to physically living with Charlotte, the novel ends with this return to the "communicative" life they used to enjoy together. And it is as media, which in Latin means "middle," that we should understand the curious term that titles the novel, but appears nowhere in it. If Paula is "Laodicean," lukewarm or "middling" in her love for all of her male suitors, this is not mere apathy but rather an aesthetic, erotic affiliation: a lesbian passion for media.

But what might it mean to argue for a mediating lesbian ending to a novel by Thomas Hardy? Is such a reading merely a wishful overlaying, catachrestic even? This is certainly a reasonable objection when we remember that Hardy disavowed a lesbian interpretation of Sue Bridehead, asserting that there is "nothing perverted or depraved in Sue's nature. The abnormalism consists in disproportion; not in inversion."[58] Perhaps, however, overlaying a lesbian reading to *A Laodicean*, or even *Jude the Obscure*, is to take up the method of the architectural instrument that stirs Hardy imagination: the Lesbian rule. The Lesbian rule *overlays* in order to takes its impression, and its pliancy is as modifying as it is modified. Amy Villarejo's pertinent and brilliant study *Lesbian Rule: Cultural Criticism and the Value of Desire* finds in the leaden measure "an ethical principle, a principle of pliancy of judgment" (5). She argues that "*lesbian* is best understood as 'catachresis,' a metaphor without an adequate referent." (18). Villarejo uses "lesbian" not as a noun, but as a "modifier" (4). To protest that Hardy could not have produced a lesbian heroine is to value the authenticity of the lesbian heroine (or, on the other end of the political spectrum, to protest the lesbian heroine), but Villarejo's work suggests that authenticity is a ruse and that representation of the lesbian is always already catachrestic, "always the possibility of something else" (28). Along with Villarejo, I see little use in disciplining a metaphor to the exact contours of its referent, and I am more taken by the notion that a metaphor can produce possibility simultaneous to constraint. The leaden rule can passively comply, but it can also leave impressions, and the transferrals it enables—transporting medieval or Greek shapes into a modern age, for example—can have a protensive, disruptive existence. Such potential derives from the involvement of proxy surfaces and subjects: that is to say, utilizing the substitute of a telegram for physical contact, for example, renders the technology itself eroticized, and erotic charge more meandering. The erotics are not dependent upon, nor contained within, the particular subjects, or organization of the subjects, involved in the exchange. Rather they find a network of relations through the instruments of exchange. Seemingly compliant, the Lesbian rule is also defiant. In *A Laodicean*, the multidirectional instruments of the Lesbian rule and the telegraph insinuate into the heterosexual marriage plot. When we stop reading for the message, or reading for the plot, or the content, or the character, and allow ourselves to be distracted by the media—this is when queer relations emerge.

---

[58] Letter of November 20, 1895.

SIMILES AND CIRCUITS

In the interview entitled "Friendship as a Way of Life," Michel Foucault critiques the assumption that homosexuality is always about finding and unearthing the secret self. He says that instead of considering one's homosexuality in order to ask: "Who am I?" it would be better to ask, "What relations, through homosexuality, can be established, invented, multiplied, and modulated?" (Foucault, "Ethics: Subjectivity and Truth" 135). The narratives I have analyzed in this chapter investigate the various relations that can be invented and modulated through imagining queer desire and partnership. They are stories that portray female homosexuality through the filters of simile ("more *like* lovers") or hostility ("Mrs. Blount's face chilled and repelled her"), filters which are clearly distancing. This very distancing, however, reveals a complex network from within which all variety of human relationships are possible. That these women work for or communicate through postal networks fulfils the civic logic of the postal system: postal reform promised a "universal" lifting of the "tax on knowledge" and the barriers to human intercourse. The organization of communication through bureaucracy became rhetorically figured as democracy, and governmental and cultural dedication to bureau-democracy fostered fictions about the marvel of unlimited, indiscriminating interfaces. Some of these interfaces were indiscriminate in regard to gender and the sexual orientation of the resulting relationships: when the marriage plot goes postal, queer fictions ensue.

Foucault goes on to describe homosexuality as a technology that reveals the spectrum of connections open to all people and reorients those who fear "the formation of new alliances and the tying together of unforeseen lines of force" ("Ethics: Subjectivity and Truth" 136). Queer love, he concludes, "short-circuits" the rigid channels of law, rule, and habit (Foucault, "Ethics: Subjectivity and Truth" 137), and homosexuality that is untrammeled by a fear of polysexuality is part of achieving a "great community fusion" (Foucault, "Ethics: Subjectivity and Truth" 138). His metaphor is one of lines and junctions and circuitry. Through this metaphorics, he invokes the notion of the network as an instrument that can reorganize society without limiting it. His model mirrors the idealized vision that Thomas Hardy has of the potential of Paula and Charlotte's love. "That the two [women] should be such intimate friends," Hardy writes, "was an engaging instance of that human progress on which [Somerset] had expended many charming dreams in the years when poetry, theology and the reorganization of society had seemed matters of more importance to him than [...] a big house and income" (*Laodicean* 40). Somerset drinks to the health of and salutes the two women who "had found sweet communion a necessity of life, and by pure and instinctive good sense had broken down a barrier which men thrice their age and repute would probably have felt it imperative to maintain" (Hardy, *Laodicean* 40).

Women's new modes of entry to public—civic—life, enabled these three writers to imagine the ways in which they broke down barriers that had previously restrained not only women, but men too. Somerset's tribute to the women's relationship points out the limitations to which men of "age and repute" often feel beholden. He recognizes that their lives are performances, but, given the regulation props of property and propriety, they are only allowed to rehearse the same, singular, limited role. Through his articulation of the passionate relationship between the telegraphing women, Hardy briefly imagines how roles could be switched or modified and conventions broken past. The telegraph wire does not ask the gender or wealth or reputation of the lovers that it serves: it is a connection, rather than a "barrier." The "Sweet communion" of love and telegraphy stems from and flows back into a fleeting vision of a reorganized society in which the logic of a communication network engenders intercourse between a diversity of people and configurations of gender.

4

All Red Routes

BLOOD BROTHERHOOD AND THE POST IN DOYLE, KIPLING, AND STOKER

ANGLO-AMERICAN BROTHERHOOD

Thomas Jefferson's first draft of what came to be known as the *Declaration of Independence* is openly concerned with the kinship between Americans and English. In sections ultimately edited out or condensed by Congress, Jefferson calls the English "brethren" and remembers that the settlers' adoption of one common king laid "a foundation for our perpetual league and amity" (Jefferson 963). He describes the importance of "our connection and correspondence" but notes that as he is drawing up the Declaration, the English are sending over "not only soldiers of our common blood, but Scotch and foreign mercenaries to invade and destroy us. These facts have given the last stab to agonizing affection, and manly spirit bids us to renounce forever these unfeeling brethren" (Jefferson 963). Jefferson makes it clear that kinship is not a metaphor, that Americans are blood relations of the English and no one else. Jefferson is insulted by the "foreign" mercenaries because they show England's disregard for the "connection and correspondence" between the English and Americans. "Amity" gives way to "Agonizing Affection" as England violently turns against a loving younger brother, who suffers the stabbing torments of betrayed love. This experience is, for the young nation, the end of innocence: England's "unfeeling" violence enacted by proxy rouses America's "manly spirit." Now mature, America renounces the brother that aroused passion through "connection and correspondence" and extinguished it through severing that tie. Thus Jefferson narrates the birth of the United States as no birth at all, but as a breakup. "We might have a free and a great people together," he writes, "but a *communication* of grandeur and freedom, it seems, is below [Britain's] dignity" (my italics 963). The love between the two countries was lost through Britain's stubborn refusal to correspond. "Deaf to the voice of justice and consanguinity" (Jefferson 963), Britain broke lines of communication, and in severing conversation, lost its special place in the United States' affections: "We must endeavor to forget our former love for them," Jefferson concludes, "and hold them as we hold the rest of mankind, enemies in war, in peace friends!" (963).

A few generations later, "correspondence" and "communication"—the postal kind— resurfaced as instruments that might revive feelings of brotherhood between England and America. The development of twinned imperial discourses and the rise of the communication network fueled the desire of many in Britain and America to recall that earlier notion of Anglo-American blood brotherhood. As it was most popularly manifested, Anglo-American reunionism had a sentimental goal; restoration of the "connection and correspondence" about which Jefferson wrote, achieved through postal correspondence. Reunionists petitioned for an Atlantic penny postage to swell the flow of letters, telegrams, and postcards that they thought could bind together the nations again. Just as Harriet Martineau had earlier in the century argued that the Penny Post could overcome the ruptures in family life caused by industrial migration, others now asked if communication networks could bind together the imagined racial rupture caused by the loss of Britain's first empire, America. The British postal routes and telegraph lines that increasingly spanned the globe were known as "All Red Routes"[1]—the epithet made steamer routes and ocean cables seem like veins, and the promise of this rhetoric was that once again the two countries could share a heartbeat. Toward the end of the century, pressure grew in Britain for the refederation of the two, with more extreme advocates arguing that an ocean was no longer any barrier to the two countries becoming one, ruled by one government. They urged union at any cost, even that of renouncing Queen and country.[2] By the late 1890s, reunion fever reached its highest pitch and for late-century writers of imperial narratives, nervous about the scramble for Africa or the possible loss of India, coalition with the United States featured large as an apotheosis of imperial logics. Reunion sentiment was so popular by 1898, and its racist ideologies were so mainstream, that Pears' Soap ran an advertisement in *Harper's Weekly* that showed conjoined American and British flags with the caption "Pears' Soap and an Anglo-American Alliance would Improve the Complexion of the Universe"[3] (see figure 4.1).

---

[1] For accounts of the exponential growth of Victorian communication networks, see Christopher Browne, *Getting the Message: The Story of the British Post Office* (1993); M. J. Daunton, *Royal Mail: The Post Office Since 1840* (1985), and Daniel Headrick, *The Invisible Weapon: Telecommunications and International Politics, 1851–1954* (1991).

[2] W. T. Stead claimed that "in his later years" Rhodes "expressed to me his unhesitating readiness to accept the reunion of the race under the Stars and Stripes if it could not be obtained in any other way" (*Last Will and Testament* 62–63).

[3] This advertisement stands out from the other regularly placed Pears' advertisements in that year of *Harper's Weekly*. None of the other advertisements are illustrated: this one is also much larger than the text-only ads and much pithier. All the other ads explicitly address a desire for white skin: "Whoever wants soft hands, smooth hands, white hands," for example. It is worth noting that their discourse around whiteness and whether it can

FIGURE 4.1 Pears' Soap advertisement from *Harper's Weekly* (1898).

This imperial hubris was the late-century climax of reunionist thinking, but its roots extended back to the midcentury, to a movement spearheaded by an eccentric but vocal figure. In 1847 an autodidact philanthropist from Connecticut named Elihu Burritt, who

---

be bought, is "natural," or is occupational is highly confused. The advertisement claims on the one hand that you can get the benefit of Pears' "if the skin is naturally transparent; unless occupation prevents" and on the other that "the colour you want to avoid comes probably neither of nature or work, but of habit" (*Harper's Weekly* 30 July 1898)." For an extensive reading of the "commodity racism" of Pears' soap advertisements, see Anne McClintock, *Imperial Leather: Race, Gender and Sexuality in the Colonial Contest* 207–31.

was known as the "Learned Blacksmith," founded a Christian pacifist organization that he called the League of Universal Brotherhood. Burritt and his sympathizers believed there was a racial correspondence between the United States and Britain, a correspondence that they hoped could be mobilized to obliterate what they saw as the false divisions of nationality. Burritt founded his league in response to the 1845–46 British-American conflict over ownership of Oregon. The spat nearly resulted in war, and both countries scrambled to find reasons to like one another again.[4] An appeal to racial brotherhood as stronger than the ties of nation proved attractive on both sides of the Atlantic. On 3 January 1846, for instance, the *London Times* published an editorial that urged the two countries to find a peaceful solution to the conflict, appealing to "ties of blood and interest" between the two nations. "We are," it concluded "two people, but we are of one family" (Editorial 4).

Elihu Burritt regarded the Post Office as the most powerful engine of reunion. His Anglo-American society printed envelopes that proclaimed their aim "To Make Home Everywhere And All Nations Neighbours" (see figures 4.2 and 4.3). The League's use of envelopes for promotional purposes was fitting; Burritt believed that Universal Brotherhood could be realized through a Penny Postage scheme extending beyond the shores of England. For Burritt and his followers, "Ocean Penny Postage" was both the metaphor and the instrument that could build a global, universal community. League members had to sign a pledge never to fight under any military banner; instead, they pledged to march behind the emblem of the penny stamp and to campaign for "the abolition of all restrictions upon international correspondence and friendly intercourse" (Burritt, *Peace Papers* 141). Unimpeded epistolary intercourse was the primary, concrete, political task for this League that espoused the benefits of a global unity comprised of religious, commercial, social, and ethnic fellowship.

In his campaign against Anglo-American national division, Elihu Burritt nonetheless saw Britain as having an imperial centrality. In Burritt's second "Olive Leaf for the English People" of March 1847,[5] he explains why he believed that "of all nations upon earth, England alone [was] able to establish an OCEAN PENNY POSTAGE." The news-sheet, designed to be distributed among the general population,[6] both advocates and illustrates the benefits of what Homi Bhabha has pithily called "dissemiNation."

---

[4] For a concise history of the Oregon territory, see Anders Stephanson, *Manifest Destiny: American Expansion and the Empire of Right* 35–36, 42–44.

[5] The League's Olive Leaves were newsletters and press releases, publicizing the reunion manifesto. The name reflects the Christian and pacifist ambitions of the organization.

[6] Burritt was supremely adept at fitting his media to his message and his promotional methods illustrate the degree to which his imagination was fired by the possibilities of a continuous, free-flow of information and affection. Burritt set up a complex Anglo-American pen-pal system, which was designed to forge literal and sustained postal bonds between peoples and nations. He also used to send boys into railway carriages to distribute his pamphlets; he realized that people in transit were actually immobilized and were therefore more likely to read and be receptive to promotional material. Distributing literature on a train meant that his ideas were quite literally put in motion and circulated across land as well as among people.

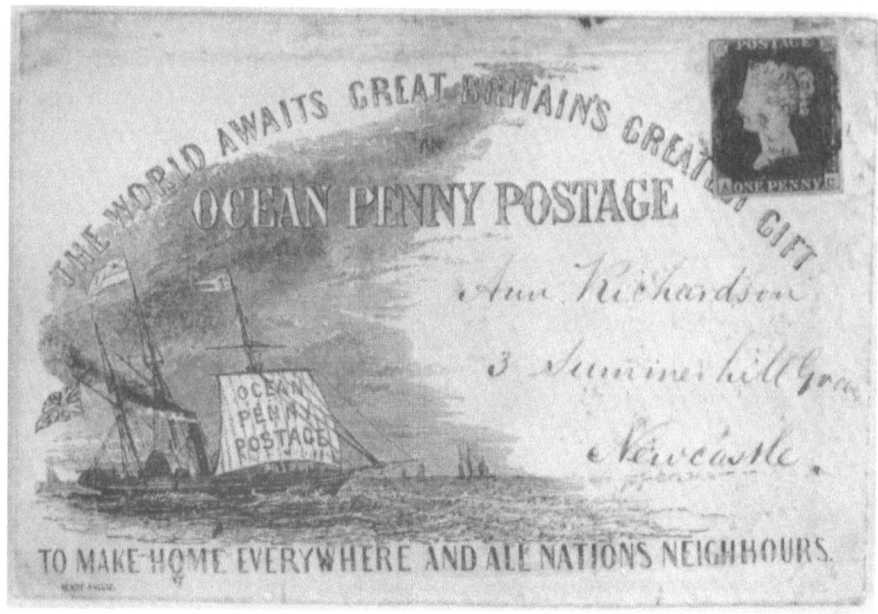

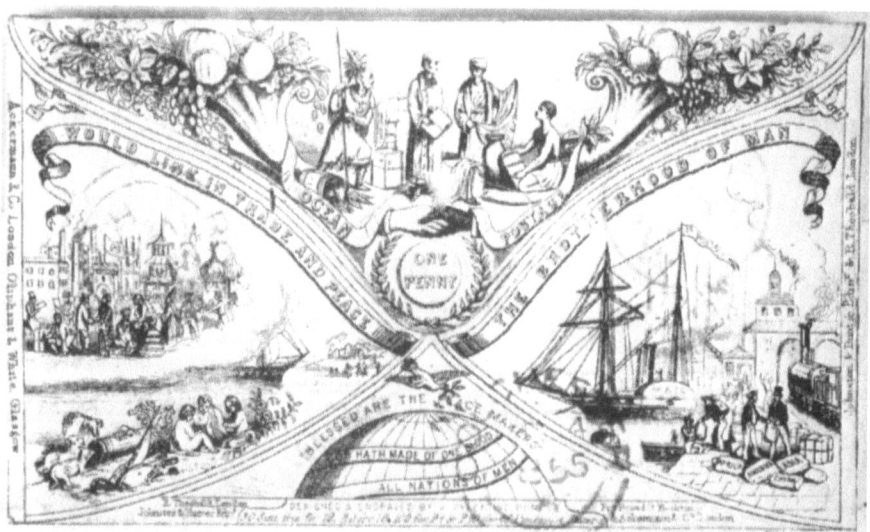

FIGURES 4.2 and 4.3 Envelopes from Elihu Burritt's League of Universal Brotherhood.

Bhabha links processes of splitting and dissemination to fictions of national unification, pointing out that the emergence of the "later phase of the modern nation," in the mid-nineteenth century, coincided with "one of the most sustained periods of mass migration within the west, and colonial expansion in the east" (291). In a seeming paradox, narratives of nation aggregated around the dispersal of its people. Burritt's plans for Ocean Penny Postage latched on to the consequences of the dispersal of British people, characterizing it as a racial diaspora. In this way, although the League of Universal Brotherhood loudly renounced nationalism, they actually reinscribed it in the fashion of Bhabha's paradox, signing it up to the cause of internationalism and retaining the idea of imperial governance. Burritt's pamphlets circulated a glowing description of England to Englanders, suggesting that because they themselves were so perfectly unified, they alone could unify the world:

> To meet this world's want must be the work of *one* nation, in order to give an energetic integrity to the enterprise: and that nation must be distinguished from all others by its relative position, its physical constitution, the character and condition of its population, the genius of its language, its industrial and commercial economy, the constitution of its government, its material wealth and pecuniary resources, its present and prospective relations with the rest of the world [...]. If America or China possessed [these distinctive qualities] but one; without that one, neither of them could do this work for the world. If the steam and other mercantile navy of America were ten times its present tonnage, it could not send ocean postmen to England, or take England's letters to Alexandria, Bombay, Calcutta, or to any seaport of India or China. If China had a steam navy of more tonnage than all the navies of the rest of the world put together, she could not carry the letters of England and France to America. Both those nations, and all others similarly situated, must for ever lack the faculties of local position, which England alone possesses, to establish an Ocean Penny Postage.
>
> (Burritt, *Olive Leaf*)

England's destiny as a unifying power derives from the boon of "relative position" and "the faculties of local position" that Burritt believes "England alone possesses." Burritt naturalizes this imagined centrality—he says that it would not be possible for America or China "ever" to acquire it—but he cannot follow through with specifics about how a country can hold a central position on a spherical planet. On the one hand, Burritt's terms suggest geographical specificity—England enjoys a "particular location of residence," he says; apparently England simply occupies the best place on the globe to organize and power the international postal machine. It is "naturally" at the nexus of a ready-made global network. On the other hand, these same phrases are pointedly nonspecific; England's position is not "particular" but simply "relative" or "local"; England has "faculties of local position" and is always capable of being close to somewhere else. Burritt's philanthropic Anglocentric reasoning produces a geographic conundrum worthy of the most robust Anglo-Imperialist; England is always local, England can make everywhere a home.

The impulse "to make home everywhere" was recognized as an essential element of the colonial enterprise.[7] The expansion of England produced a white diaspora; a population of English citizens who were dislocated from England and engaged in processes of relocating and reproducing England on foreign soil. Under the terms of so complex a procedure, epithets of nationality or geography were problematic, as we see in Burritt's confused descriptions of England's global position. Racial identity, however, offered a solution to the problem that geographic or national identity posed for imperialism; Burritt ends up celebrating a race community that crossed national borders and geographical boundaries. This race patriotism needed a communications machine that could similarly cross borders and boundaries. A passage in a book on colonial postage published in 1854, seven years after Burritt founded the League, imagines post-letters as the bearers of sweet English breezes,[8] elaborating the theme thus:

> What father, driven by the demands of business or benevolence, or in the public service, to be absent from his home, would not feel the frequent letters of his sons, his daughters, the childish first scrawls of his little ones, coming by every mail,

---

[7] The terms "colonialism" and "imperialism" are not identical, but are often interchangeable. Edward Said explains why, giving the following working definitions: " 'imperialism' means the practice, the theory and the attitudes of a dominating metropolitan centre ruling a distant territory; 'colonialism,' which is almost always a consequence of imperialism, is the implanting of settlements on distant territory" (9). My use of the term "imperial" in application to years pre-1870 draws from Patrick Brantlinger's precept that although many scholars of Victorian imperialism focus on the "high" or "formal" imperialism of the years 1870–1918, imperialist discourse is to be found alive and kicking in literature of the 1830s onward. See Patrick Brantlinger, *Rule of Darkness: British Literature and Imperialism, 1830–1914* ix–x, 3–16. Debates that seek to define imperialism and stages of imperialism through markers such as land or economy falter because the discursive power of imperialism dismantles such borders and boundaries. The imperialist steps lightly over national borders, and as often as not carries communication technologies with him. Elleke Boehmer outlines how many scholars have defined the high imperialism of those years as "more officially expansionist, assertive, and self-conscious" (vx). Brantlinger, however, questions whether "self-consciousness" is the primary characteristic of imperialism. He points out that it is precisely the *lack* of self-consciousness and "easy confidence about British world domination" in literature from the early and mid-nineteenth century that marks it as imperialist (Brantlinger x). Imperiousness, in other words, is a guise of imperialism, and if these early texts do not exhibit the aggressive militarism and militant racism associated with the later century, they nonetheless assume a powerful and commanding Anglocentric influence to which High Imperialism would later refer. Early Victorians imagined themselves at an imperial center, and this very imagining lay at the center of empire. Edward Said describes the importance of "will, self-confidence, even arrogance" needed to maintain an empire which the British ruled by minimal presence. "The enterprise of empire," he writes, "depends upon the *idea* of having an empire" (11). Thomas Richards posits continuities between Romanticism and Victorian Imperialism: "The impulse towards the universal in Shelley, the project of a complete knowledge of the world in Coleridge, the ability of Blake's visions to span the globe," he writes, "contributed a great deal to imagining the Empire as a concordant whole" (*Imperial Archive* 7).

[8] The breezes parallel lines of communication and colonization. This metaphor recalls *Cranford* and Elizabeth Gaskell's description of Peter's letters carrying sweet English breezes that I discussed in the introduction. For a fascinating account of how this trope is played out in Charlotte Brontë's *Jane Eyre*, and how Jane is figured as a "sweet wind from Europe," a sweet English breeze that contrasts with colonial contagion, see Alan Bewell, "Jane Eyre and Victorian Medical Geography."

to be like guardian angels hovering around him, to keep off every contaminating breath, and fanning with their wings the pure flame of domestic love in his heart? Children, too, absent at school, boys put to trade, young persons pushing their fortunes in any of the thousand forms of enterprise created by our own Anglo-Saxon race, would find that the frequent "letters from home"—the kind greetings of father and mother, of sister and brother, would surround them as with a continual presence of home, with all its blessed restraints and genial influences. It would so strengthen the stakes of the paternal tent that the heart could never be torn from its hold; and it would so lengthen its cords that it would cover every member of the household, however far removed. The old roof-tree would send its fibres, and spread out its shadow, to embrace and shelter every wanderer who had been born at its root.

(Derecourt 7)

The formulation is clear: Anglo-Saxonism helped by postal networks can overcome geographical boundaries and distance. But what we also begin to sense is how this formulation strains the family structure, and is shadowed by the possibilities of other forms of love and connection. The passage opens by promoting the postal system as a means of surrounding peripatetic members of the Anglo-Saxon race with "a continual presence of home." This writer tropes the idea of webs or lines of connection, envisioning the postal network as expansive familial tent cords and the spreading roots and fibers of a family tree that can overcome geographical divides.⁹ It is clear that these stretched cords, roots, and fibers are ties that bind: the wanderer is "surrounded," "restrained," and "influenced" via imagery decidedly Old Testament in flavor. The references to "paternal tents," "old roof-trees" and "wanderers" invoke a notion of the English as a seminomadic founding tribe and serve to assert the importance of behaving like founders even when abroad. You may wander, but with the help of letters from home, you will not stray from the fold. The nineteenth-century family was dispersed by colonial enterprises, civic service, and industrial labor. The writer suspects that these endeavors afield structurally threaten familial cohesion and the sanctity of "domestic love." Being away from home exposes you to "contaminating breaths" that imperil "domestic love." These exhalations are figured as impure, contagious, excessive, and monstrous—hence the need for the flapping cherubim/post-letters who form fortifications for the blood family.

It was common to characterize the postmen who carried Britain's letters as seraphim and cherubim. The 1840 Mulready envelope—the illustrated envelope that had been designed to function as the first prepaid stamp but was soon abandoned for the Penny Black adhesive

---

[9] Andrew Carnegie repeatedly uses the trope of the "tree" of race that binds us together. In *The Reunion of Britain and America*, he writes that race is the tree upon which "grow the one language, one religion, one literature, and one law which bind men together and make them brothers in time of need as against men of other races" (2).

FIGURE 4.4 Mulready Envelope, portraying Britannia sitting at the center of an imperial scene, dispatching "winged messengers" in the form of angelic post-boys to all corners of the globe.

stamp—portrays Britannia sitting in the center of an imperial scene, dispatching "winged messengers,"[10] in the form of angelic post-boys, to all corners of the globe (see figure 4.4). As in the Derecourt passage, the imagery is highly sentimental about the dispersed family,

---

[10] So called in a contemporary description of the envelope design, quoted in T. Martin Wears, *The History of the Mulready Envelope* (17). That postal metaphors were found to turn so readily to spiritual metaphors could be the subject of another study. Wears characterized Rowland Hill as the "apostle" of Post Office reform (10)

and how the post can virtually reunite far-off fathers with children and wives, eager for news. But postletters being embodied—as "winged messengers"—creates some interesting problems. Like the "contaminating breaths," they are (airborne) intermediaries to the family. The sentiment of the illustration and the Derecourt rhetoric attempt to compensate for the fact that the bureaucratized communication system formed a network that was actually much more impersonal and extensive than the family tree, and its functionaries were intermediaries in mailed communications of love and affection that as often as not went against normative heterosexual reproduction. Most viewers of the Mulready envelope focused their attentions not on the vignettes of family feeling, or international trade, but on the flock of naked messenger-boys.

Distance and intermediation create a discursive and affective gap, in which relations can become inverted. Go-between "winged messengers" might be benevolent, or they might be shadowy and—as I shall explore via Bram Stoker's work—even vampiric. As Judith Halberstam says of *Dracula*, "Technologies of monstrosity are always also technologies of sex" (Halberstam 88) and together postal technology, monstrosity, and sex breathe down the neck of heterosexual domestic love. This chapter will show how the figures and function of the bureaucratic administrators of imperial networks—vampiric and otherwise—often overshadowed the very family ties that they were purported to facilitate. The homosocial and often homoerotic structures of imperial bureaucracy and postal networks came, across the course of the century, to uphold and further the project of Anglo-Saxonism even more effectively than strained languages of heterosexual family structures.

In the introduction, I claimed that reform of the British Post Office both drove and was driven by colonialist and expansionist ideology. I also outlined the way in which the new communication and transportation networks were represented as annihilating time and space. Colonialist enterprise and the expansion of communication networks both radically reconfigured the relationship of the national to the international. What, then, were the fissures and problematics in this reconfiguration? In the first place, literary and political constructions of "universal brotherhood" were constructions not of universalism, but of a brand of Anglo-Saxon imperialism aided and abetted by the growth of the communication network. In the second, the fraternal bonds between men signified by the phrase "universal brotherhood" had a homoerotic inflection and this homoeroticism served to bolster the racial continence and correspondence—prefigured

---

and a vast number of Christian publications used the idea of the boundlessness of Victorian communication networks to help readers imagine the correspondence between God and man. Examples of these publications include Ethel Ruth Boddy, *Two Girls or Seed Sown Through the Post* (1893); *Story of a Little Boy Who Put a Letter in the Post Office* (1860); and *Links with the Absent; or, Chapters on Correspondence by a Member of the Ursuline Community, Thurles* (1882). There was also an evangelical publication titled *The Postman* (1880–84), the subtitle of which explained the postal metaphor—it was "A Paper for the People and a House to House Evangel." The paper included a column called "Post Cards," comprised of short guiding messages, and in the October 1880 issue they advertised an almanac featuring Rowland Hill "which will be presented to Tea Purchasers during November and December" (16).

by Jefferson—that Anglo-Saxonism connoted. The bridge between the imperial fiction of Anglo-Saxonism and the discourse of homoerotics was buttressed by the notion of comrade-love.

The first part of this chapter explores the work of three writers—Arthur Conan Doyle, Rudyard Kipling, and Bram Stoker—that demonstrates how blood brotherhood was best sustained not through heterosexual procreation, but through the postal kind of intercourse: bureaucratic, networked, homosocial, and homoerotic. These are all "straight," white writers, hell-bent on pursuing colonial themes through postal plots. Each has strong homoerotic currents running through his homosocial postal stories, and I trace how each attempted to harness and control those queer effects. But the queer possibilities of imperial postal plots were not universally reviled, and to conclude the chapter, I ask what happens when white gay men turn, excitedly, to the Post Office for visions of racial unity. To do this, I explore the postal reflections of three "homosexual" writers: Walt Whitman, Edward Carpenter, and … Bram Stoker.

FROM UNIVERSAL BROTHERHOOD TO RACIAL CONSOLIDATION: ANGLO-AMERICAN REUNIONISM

In his 1898 essay "The Reunion of Britain and America," Andrew Carnegie references William Cowper's metaphor of shared blood to claim that the Atlantic is no longer a barrier between the two countries and their populations:

> The difference of land and water lying between people has hitherto been great, and, in the words of the poet, […] we can say that
> "Oceans interposed
> Make enemies of nations, who else,
> Like kindred drops, been mingled into one."[11]
>
> This is quite true of the past; but oceans no longer constitute barriers between nations. These already furnish the cheapest of all modes of communications between men.
> (Carnegie, *Reunion* 10–11)

Both Cowper and Carnegie fantasize that blood brotherhood could transcend nation. For Cowper, nations are strangely liquid, and the ocean solid: a barrier that keeps the blood of nations from naturally amalgamating. But, Carnegie triumphantly declares, the development of communication technologies means that the nineteenth-century ocean

---

[11] Carnegie misquotes lines 17–19 from the original William Cowper poem called "The Timepiece," which run as follows: "Mountains interposed, / Make enemies of nations who had else / Like kindred drops been mingled into one" (Cowper 139).

has become a channel—a web of channels—that will actually facilitate the transnational mingling of kindred drops. The Atlantic is now "the very agency which brings them so close and will ultimately bind them together" (Carnegie, *Reunion* 13). In other words, "kindred drops"—which, as I will show, must always be Anglo-Saxon—can now correspond with each other through the vein-like "All Red Routes."

Postal networks not only materially enabled cross-national communication, but they also symbolized it. Writing in the periodical *The Nineteenth Century* in 1898, Conservative MP J. Henniker Heaton declares that under Britain's newly implemented Imperial Penny Postage scheme, "the postage-stamp would become the symbol of Imperial unity, nay, more, the symbol of universal Anglo-Saxon brotherhood" ("Postal Utopia" 764). It was widely acknowledged across the course of the nineteenth century that the Victorian "revolution in communications [...] brought the colonies much nearer" to the mother country and that the unity engendered by and through the "All Red Routes" had great imperial utility (Kendle 1). Heaton suggests, however, that "universal Anglo-Saxon brotherhood" was different from and "more" desirable than "Imperial unity." In his vision of a community bound by postal communication, racial fraternity trumps colonial collectivity.[12] His insistence on "Anglo-Saxon" racial fraternity thereby fastidiously—possibly genocidally—steps over the implicitly undesirable racial amalgamations risked by emphasizing colonial or imperial unity. For Arthur Conan Doyle, America provided the resolution to this contradiction, perhaps because America seemed already to have solved the problem of the racial other, through enslavement, economic subjugation, and genocide. America, ascendant as a white nation, is imagined as the home of Britons' white blood-relatives, and as such it held a special place in this trope of "universal brotherhood."

In "The Noble Bachelor," published in the *Strand Magazine* in 1892, Sherlock Holmes gave voice to Doyle's own hope that Americans and Britons would one day be "citizens of the same world-wide country under a flag which shall be a quartering of the Union Jack with the Stars and Stripes."[13] This was by no means an eccentricity on Doyle-via-Holmes's part: Doyle was one of many avid supporters of a movement that clamored for Anglo-American reunion and the fantasy that such a reunion would result in a federation of the Anglo-Saxon race.[14] "The tendency of the age," Carnegie summed it up, "is towards consolidation" (*Reunion* 32). "Recovering" America at the end of the nineteenth century was an essential part of the project of imagining a white Anglo-Saxon diaspora that was

---

[12] The idea that the empire was a gaggle of colonies that had no real relationship to each other or, for that matter, to the supposed mother country, was a staple of midcentury Liberal opposition to colonization. But it also is apparent in the pro-colonial historian Sir John Seeley's famous conclusion that Britain's apathy to the colonies made it seem as if it had "conquered and peopled half the world in a fit of absence of mind [...]. We constantly betray by our modes of speech that we do not reckon our colonies as really belonging to us" (Seeley 10).

[13] Arthur Conan Doyle, *The Penguin Complete Sherlock Holmes* 299-300.

[14] For full accounts of Anglo-American reunion sentiment or "rapprochement" at the turn of the century, see Stuart Anderson, *Race and Rapprochement: Anglo-Saxonism and Anglo-American Relations, 1895–1904* (1981); Charles S. Campbell, *Anglo-American Understanding, 1898–1903* (1957); and Alexander E. Campbell, *Great Britain and the United States, 1895–1903* (1960).

so fluid and perpetual that it no longer needed a home turf. For many, it was the ultimate and most perfect form of imperialism: in an empire, racism is a more pliant form of patriotism than nationalism. The most notorious imperialist of them all, Cecil Rhodes, even asserted that in the name of Anglo-Saxon unity he would advocate renouncing Queen and country and become American. The journalist W. T. Stead, himself an avid campaigner for Anglo-American reunion, claimed that "in his later years" Rhodes "expressed to me his unhesitating readiness to accept the reunion of the race under the Stars and Stripes if it could not be obtained in any other way" (*Last Will* 62–63).

Cecil Rhodes ensured there would be a living legacy of reunion sentiment through his scholarships funding American students' study in England.[15] W. T. Stead describes in his book-length edition of Cecil Rhodes's last will and testament how Rhodes possessed the most "sublime conception of the essential unity of the race" (Stead, *Last Will* 52). Stead emphasizes that this unity was based not on land and its dominion, but on the alliance of blood:

> Mr. Rhodes's last Will and Testament reveals him to the world as the first distinguished British statesman whose Imperialism was that of Race and not that of Empire. The one specific object defined in the Will as that to which his wealth is to be applied proclaims with the simple eloquence of a deed that Mr. Rhodes was colour-blind between the British Empire and the American Republic. [...] He did this [founded the Rhodes scholarship] of set purpose, and in providing the funds necessary for the achievement of this great idea he specifically prescribed that every American State and Territory shall share with the British Colonies in his patriotic benefaction.
>
> (Stead, *Last Will* 52)

This passage is insistent on the particularity of Anglo-American racial unity (a "specific object," "specifically prescribed") to Rhodes's vision; his will sought to bind together the empire and the republic and bolster a belief in their indivisibility.[16] Rhodes understood the role that telecommunications could play in fostering colonial cohesion: he sought to extend a telegraph line across Africa, and the iconic "Rhodes Colossus" cartoon of Rhodes published in *Punch* depicts him hoisting telegraph wires from Cape Town to Cairo. The crux of the cartoon's joke is Rhodes's straddling pose, which makes his crotch loftily central to the continent. To stand beneath Rhodes's telegraph wires is to be between the legs of this cocksure bureaucrat. But though Rhodes's stance is mythic, the accompanying satirical verse hails him as a "Brobdingnagian Bagman" (see figure 4.5), ridiculing him

---

[15] The "Colonial Scholarships" were set up to service students from each colony, but an especially large number were allocated to the United States. See Robert I. Rotberg, *The Founder: Cecil Rhodes and the Pursuit of Power*. With the collaboration of Miles F. Shore (New York and Oxford: Oxford UP, 1988), 667.

[16] For many pro-reunion writers, the American War of Independence was actually proof positive of the strength of the blood-ties between Americans and Britons. Andrew Carnegie claimed: "There is no British statesman who does not feel that if the Britons in America had not resisted taxation without representation, and fought out the issue to the end, they would have been false to the blood in their veins" (*Reunion* 4).

All Red Routes   161

FIGURE 4.5 The Rhodes Colossus from *Punch* (1892).

as an overgrown Boy Messenger, his head in the clouds of puerile fantasy. The parabolic droop of the telegraph wires inverts Rhodes's wide stance, suggesting that his grand plans are impotent, and the shining, greatly magnified centrality of Lake Victoria, just where said delivery boy might have urinated or even masturbated, undermines Rhodes's bid for telecommunicative mastery of the continent, figuring it as puddling incontinence.

Skeptical as some were of Rhodes's drive to catch up the falterings of empire with the filaments of a communication network, Rhodes's prestigious scholarships are a lasting remnant of similar drives: they assert the power of intra-colonial communication, and the desirability of a white Anglo-American imperial fraternity. For the homosexual Rhodes, this fraternal indivisibility of England and America structurally and literally took the place of his own homosexual relationship. The "Last Will and Testament" that set up the Rhodes scholarship replaced an earlier will that Rhodes had drawn up in October 1882, in which he left everything he owned to his secretary and lover, Neville Pickering. This earlier will became null when Pickering died in 1886. Rhodes scholars thus owe their stipends to the imperialist exchangeability of homosexual love for race chauvinism.[17] Parenthetically, the pathos of Rhodes's bereaved love owes something to the mail: unable to secure a seat on a coach home, he was able to be with his dying lover in his last days because he made the fifteen-hour, three-hundred-mile journey home riding on postbags on top of the vehicle.[18]

"A STUDY IN SCARLET:" CONAN DOYLE'S WHITE BROTHERHOOD

In Arthur Conan Doyle's first Sherlock Holmes story "A Study in Scarlet" (1881), we are introduced to our narrator, Dr. John H. Watson, before we meet the great Holmes himself. Watson opens the tale by detailing his record of service in the colonial Afghan campaigns and then memorably describes that because he had "neither kith nor kin in England [...] I naturally gravitated to London, that great cesspool into which all the loungers and idlers of the Empire are irresistibly drained" (Doyle 15). Laura Otis has noted that Doyle thus establishes both London and Watson as imperial bodies "under siege" (99).[19] Watson's metaphor is certainly one of invasion: the capital is a "pool," into which contaminated colonial waterways flow and introduce sepsis.[20] And Watson's own body has also been invaded: a Jezail bullet has pierced the soldier-surgeon's shoulder, leaving him with a shattered bone, a grazed artery and, most damagingly, "shaken nerves" (Doyle 19).

---

[17] The Pickering will was Rhodes's third will. The famous scholarships emerged in will number eight. See Rotberg, *The Founder* 663–67. Rotberg points out that Rhodes derived the idea of the scholarships in large part from another homosexual, J. Astley Cooper, editor of the London weekly *Greater Britain* (Rotberg, *The Founder* 664).

[18] See Rotberg, *The Founder* 194.

[19] See Laura Otis, *Membranes: Metaphors of Invasion in Nineteenth-Century Literature, Science and Politics* 99, 104. In "Revaluating Identity in the 1890s: The Rise of the New Imperialism and the Eyes of the New Detective," Ronald R. Thomas also writes of the wounded Watson "representing the British imperial policy in need of rehabilitation" (194).

[20] Doyle's "cesspool" reframes a racialized waterways metaphor employed by the literary critic who is recognized as introducing race as a critical category into literary study in the nineteenth century. Hippolyte Taine in *Histoire de la littérature anglaise* (1863) tells us that race "is no simple spring but a kind of lake, a deep reservoir wherein other springs have, for a multitude of centuries, discharged their several streams." See Henry Louis Gates, "Writing 'Race' and the Difference It Makes.", 3-4.

Bones, arteries, nerves: these are the body's infrastructures, its support and network systems. Watson comes to London—its drains and sewers figuring the Thames as part of an empire-wide network of waterways—because his physiological networks are damaged and his familial networks, of "kith and kin," have disintegrated. Both Watson and London look like imperial nerve centers suffering from the degenerating and exhausting effects of serving the colonies. "A Study in Scarlet" is not, however, a story of thieving Sikhs, Tongan murderers, "coolie diseases," or Indian swamp adders. These come later in the Holmes canon. Rather, the very first Sherlock Holmes story is a tale about America and Americans. The United States underwrites the later fictions about blowpipes, diseases, and adders and thus adds a twist to critical readings that suggest that late-century writers like Doyle wrote against the fear that Britain's colonial children could strike back, violate, and infect them.[21] The United States, figured as the first colony and as a white colony, provides a possible antidote to the degradations of the second, predominantly nonwhite empire. Doyle turned to the crown jewel of Britain's First Empire, America, in order to reclaim a white confederacy and restabilize Britain's imperial position. As we examine themes of empire in the Holmes canon, we must recognize that Doyle appeals to an imperial bond between the United States and Britain in order to consolidate a white brotherhood that can resist attack and the degenerating effects of the Second Empire.[22]

Both in his Holmes stories and other writings, Doyle consistently applied a language of kinship to relations between America and England. In an interview with the *Cincinnati Commercial Gazette* (1894), Doyle asserted that "there is no subject on which I take so keen an interest" as "warmer friendship between the two great nations of the English-speaking race [...]. Neither nation recognizes as it ought the kinship of the other" (qtd. in Orel 73).[23] Doyle saw America as a country that had come of age and was on the point of forming international alliances. He publicly and repeatedly exhorted America to remember that Great Britain was its "own kin" and that the British would be America's only "natural friend" in war. He likewise went on record in Britain attacking journalists' hostility toward the United States and reminding Britons of America's accomplishments. It had worked hard, he said, to expand—"peopling" itself and "opening out" (qtd.

---

[21] See, for example, Otis 101 and Stephen D. Arata, "The Occidental Tourist: *Dracula* and the Anxiety of Reverse Colonization" 623.

[22] Doyle's biographer John Dickson Carr suggests that in 1900 Doyle wrote an essay entitled "An Anglo-American Reunion" in which he made a plea for closer understanding between the two nations and warned that "unless this essential relationship was brought about by good will, then it might be forced into existence in some future time as a measure of self preservation against an eventual threat from Russia" (144). I have been unable to locate this essay, but the emphasis upon reunion as a strategic defense is echoed in much of Doyle's journalism and interviews.

[23] For original, see "Conan Doyle in His Study: Theory of Sherlock Holmes Concerning the Whitechapel Murder," *Cincinnati Commercial Gazette* (10 June 1894): 17, conveniently available and qtd. in Orel 73.

in Orel 162)[24] and he thought America should be praised especially for "the filling up of the great West" (qtd. in Orel 73). Such work is, of course, the work of genocidal erasure of Native peoples, and the whitening of the population. In this and other interviews, Doyle explicitly likens American westward expansion with Britain's acquisition of colonies and the way in which Britain "has pegged out claims for the English-speaking race all over the globe, how she brought civilization to so many dark places, and how she has stood for freedom all through the history of Europe" (qtd. in Orel 73). The English language, civilization, freedom, and—crucially—the dissemination of these boons are, for Doyle, values common to both countries. He believed that

> the only natural and permanent alliance upon earth is that between these two countries, having a common language, common blood, common moral and religious ideas, and up to the last century a common history […]. I believe the English-speaking races must either coalesce, in which case the future of the world is theirs, or else they will eternally neutralize each other and be overshadowed by some more compact people, as the Russians or the Chinese. They should pool their fleets and their interests […]. It would be the first great step towards the abolition of war and the federation of mankind.
>
> (qtd. in Orel 73)

In this passage we can see that Doyle's plans for Anglo-American reunion were fueled by a rhetorical imperative of racial unity. If the two countries allow national difference to stand in the way of racial brotherhood, he claims, then a more unified people could dominate. Historian and reunionist Goldwin Smith had used that same strange word, "compact," to define a nation: "When there is a solid mass of people of one race inhabiting a compact territory, with a language, religion, character, laws, tendencies, aspirations and sentiments of its own, there is *de facto* a nation" (qtd. in Stead, *The Americanization of the World* 105–6).[25] Smith's definition makes it quite clear that a "compact" people is one that is, as the Oxford English Dictionary glosses the word, "not sprawling, scattered or diffuse." They are rather racially and geographically bound together; their race and geography correspond to each other. And this is how Doyle uses the word too: the Russian population is compact because it inhabits Russia, the Chinese because they occupy China. Doyle implies that it is time for the imperialist call to "disseminate," which has resulted in exhaustion and decay, to now morph into a call to "consolidate." In this interview, as in the opening to "A Study in Scarlet," he uses an image about the collection of fluid: he writes that it is time for Britain and the United States to "pool" their fleets and their interest. This time, however, the image implies conservation and preservation

---

[24] For original, see Bram Stoker, "Sir Arthur Conan Doyle Tells of His Career and Work, His Sentiments Towards America, and His Approaching Marriage," *New York World* (28 July 1907): E1, conveniently available and qtd. in Orel 162.

[25] For a complete description of Goldwin Smith's passion for Anglo-American reunion, see Elisabeth Wallace, "Goldwin Smith on England and America" 884–94.

of health rather than stagnancy and disease. In turning attention from Britain's Second Empire to its first, Doyle's network metaphor shifts from being one of "cesspools" and "drains" to one of arteries and veins. An Anglo-American "pooling" of blood and interest can revitalize that contaminated "pool" of which Watson speaks in "A Study in Scarlet."

The case at the center of "A Study in Scarlet" involves the mysterious deaths of two Americans in London. It transpires that the two dead men are Mormons and that their murderer, a man called Jefferson Hope, killed them in vengeance for having carried away his betrothed. Halfway through the narrative, when Holmes has handcuffed his suspect, Doyle breaks off Watson's first-person narrative of Holmes and London to hand the story over to an omniscient narrator. This narrator traces the roots of the mystery, tracking the American characters' involvement in westward Mormon migration across America and the battle between the Mormons and the non-Mormon Jefferson over his beloved. This narrative split shuttles the reader from 1878 London to the American West of 1847. It is a striking, midstory shift of time, narration, and nation, and it is this trans-Atlantic, split-screen quality to the story that has been off-putting to many twentieth-century critics. Jacqueline Jaffe identifies the geographical with generic discontinuity:

> Doyle did not yet know how to [avoid breaking the "thread of the detective interest"], therefore the interest in the detective in this story *is* broken. The two parts of "A Study in Scarlet" are completely different from each other. The American adventure story, set in the arid, sunbaked plains of Utah, is juxtaposed to the English detective story, set in gaslit, foggy London, without any viable transition. By using two such different locations, Doyle had to write two separate stories, a position that left him with a badly split narrative.
>
> (36)

Jaffe makes clear differentiations between geographies and genres, and she sees each as having a distinctly national stamp. Her vivid descriptions identify each contrasting landscape with what she sees as contrasting genres: the exposed American landscape is built for the "adventure" story, while the shadowy English streets breed the "detective" story. What is lacking, Jaffe concludes, is passage or "transition" between both lands and genres.

Doyle, however, had a distinctly opposite view about essentializing relationships between regions and literary form. In an interview printed in *Ladies Home Journal* in 1895,[26] Doyle warned readers of the tendency in England toward "local fiction" and laments the way in which the United Kingdom was becoming "divided up" through new, regional fiction writing. "It looks as if," he complained, "the map of literature were being broken up into counties. [...] It should be borne in mind that the emphasis must be laid not on the local, but on the universal elements, and it will be a great mistake to emphasize the sectional tendency as opposed to the national tendency" (qtd. in Orel 130). Although

---

[26] For original, see "Literary Aspects of America: An After Luncheon Talk Between Dr. A. Conan Doyle and Hamilton W. Mabie," *Ladies' Home Journal* 12 (March 1895): 6, conveniently available and rpt. Orel 128–

his map metaphor is geographical, the "tendencies" of which he speaks are racial: though he speaks of "nation" here, later in the interview he talks of needing to "forget the old-time hostilities" between England and America. The spectre of a divided, "sectional" England raises for Doyle the ghost of the severance between the British and the Americans. He exhorts both countries to reject discreet nationalism and embrace universal brotherhood, and he sees shared literature and culture as a way toward this destiny: "The community of interest and of art which literature is constantly fostering must tend insensibly [...] to bring the two races together" (qtd. in Orel 132).[27]

As a child Doyle had voraciously consumed American fiction and although he did not visit the States until late in life, he felt boyishly fused to an American landscape: he "knew the Rockies like my own back garden. [...] It was an everyday emergency to have to set the prairie on fire in front of me in order to escape from the fire behind" (qtd. in Orel 92).[28] As an adult, Doyle looked back to a pre-Revolution America, when an American wilderness *was* Britain's colonial back garden, and he looked back in order to champion a future reunification. For Doyle, the arid, sunbaked plains of Utah *were* contiguous with gaslit, foggy London. The transition between Great Britain and America that Jaffe dismisses as unviable was a very real possibility to Doyle and others. "I believe," Doyle concludes in the *Ladies Home Journal* interview, "in the future supremacy of the English-speaking races" (qtd. in Orel 132). Under this logic of white imperialism, national borders—like the Atlantic for Carnegie—dissolve into an irrelevance.

The blood referenced in the title "A Study in Scarlet" thus takes on significance beyond that of murder. The very first time that Dr. Watson and his readers ever meet Sherlock Holmes, Holmes is making what he calls "the most practical medico-legal discovery for years [...] an infallible test for blood stains" (Doyle 18). He demonstrates it for Watson, by adding a drop of his own blood to a liter of water: "You perceive," he says, "that the resulting mixture has the appearance of pure water. The proportion of blood cannot be more than one in a million" (Doyle 18). The chemicals he throws into the seemingly pure water, however, stain the liquid, precipitate "a brownish dust," and disclose the presence of the blood corpuscles. A delighted Holmes explains that unlike other tests for blood, his new test is reliable "whether the blood is old or new"

---

[27] The phrase "community of interest" was something of a refrain in debate about expansion, refederation, and the promise of postal communication. General Booth, for example, uses it in *In Darkest England and the Way Out* (1890) to describe how communication technology has brought about a global sense of Anglo-Saxon cohesion: "The world has grown much smaller since the electric telegraph was discovered and side by side with the shrinkage of this planet under the influence of steam and electricity there has come a sense of brotherhood and a consciousness of community of interest and nationality on the part of the English-speaking people throughout the world" (143). Earl Grey also uses it in his article "How Shall We Retain the Colonies?" 946, and, in *The Reunion of Britain and America*, Andrew Carnegie quotes American statesman Richard Olney (who drafted a famously threatening declaration to Great Britain in the Venezuela dispute that I discuss later in this chapter) using the phrase to describe the "natural" friendship between Great Britain and the United States (2).

[28] For original, see Arthur Conan Doyle, "My First Book," *McClure's Magazine* 3, no. 3 (August 1894): 225–28, conveniently available and qtd. in Orel 92.

(Doyle 18). In fact, as the story progresses, we see that the "old blood" of Britain and the "new blood" of America are, on both a rhetorical and chemical level, indistinguishable.[29] The murderer, Jefferson Hope, trusts that because he and his two victims are Americans, his deeds and motives will be invisible in the metropolis of the "old country." Hope believes that he can "vanish in an instant among the four million inhabitants of this great city" just like the single drop of blood in the million particles of water.[30] He has not bargained, however, for Holmes, whom Watson dubs a "bloodhound" (Doyle 36) and who specializes in reading that which seems invisible. It is immaterial if the blood is old or new: Holmes distills Hope out of the streets of London just as swiftly as he revealed the hemoglobin in the water.

If a combination of Holmes and London defeat Jefferson Hope, is this not Doyle asserting British supremacy, rather than urging unity? Isn't Jefferson Hope, as Philip Shreffler succinctly puts it, "the very image of the American frontier" (137)? He seems to be stamped through and through with nationality: his first name invokes Thomas Jefferson, and his last is suggestive of the promise and vitality that Doyle believed this new nation held. He has spent his life in America as a hunter, scout, trapper, prospector, and ranchman; his lexicon is that of wild animals and land formations, and he is repeatedly described as "savage," "wild," and "fierce." Does this not fundamentally set him apart from Holmes and the civilization of London? Holmes is, however, notoriously uncouth; he lives (untidily) at the halfway address "221B," and the first thing Watson learns of him is that he has been known to beat his dissection subjects with a stick (Doyle 17). And rather than representing an establishment, he is an "eccentric" who has "amassed a lot of out-of-the-way knowledge" (Doyle 16). Like Hope, Holmes is a hunter and tracker who can deduce events from prints in the earth or a pile of ashes.[31] The edge that Holmes has over Hope is his command of communication systems; he goes straight from the scene of the crime to "the nearest telegraph office" (Doyle 32). It is a telegram that confirms Hope's name and identity and that allows Holmes to send his Baker Street Irregulars in search of him. Hope is too unworldly, too New Worldly, to understand how the network systems of civilization can be used to track him down.

---

[29] In "A Study in Scarlet," all drops of blood or water seem to lead back to America. Earlier in the story, Holmes's newspaper article on deduction is quoted: " 'From a drop of water,' said the writer, 'a logician could infer the possibility of an Atlantic or a Niagara without having seen or heard of one or the other' " (Doyle 23).

[30] Hope's murder weapon is also a transparent, soluble one: he uses poison pills that "readily dissolve" in water.

[31] Not only is Holmes a tracker, but Doyle also repeatedly likens him to the figure of the "red Indian." Holmes's beating of his dissection subjects apes the Plains Indians practice of "counting coup," which entailed striking or touching the enemy and escaping unharmed. In "The Crooked Man" he refers to Holmes's "red-Indian composure that has made so many regard him as a machine rather than a man" (412). In "The Naval Treaty," he describes Holmes as having "the utter immobility of countenance of a red Indian" (460). In an interview he described the real-life model for Holmes, his Edinburgh medical school professor, Mr. Joseph Bell, "who would sit in the patient's waiting-room with a face like a Red Indian and diagnose the people as they came in, before they had even opened their mouths" (qtd. in Orel 57). Read in light of his Anglo-Saxon reunionist convictions, Doyles's portrayal of Holmes as a "red Indian" is way of imagining a white indigene for America.

His assumption that he could not be traced between the United States and Britain is a fatal mistake. For Holmes, who "has never been known to write where a telegram would serve," the Atlantic was not such a leap (Doyle 955).[32] All it takes from Holmes is a single telegram to America to determine Hope's identity. Holmes's ascendancy over Hope is not narrated as a nationalized triumph, but as an assertion of his superior knowledge of the connection between America and Britain. Hope's belief that the city and the transatlantic divide will conceal him shows that he misunderstands the reach of both local and international information networks, and the indissoluble connection between Britain and America.

Lines of narrative, blood, and communication technologies converge. Holmes deduces a single "chain of logical sequences." Doyle looks to an Anglo-Saxon bloodline that traversed the Atlantic. Holmes wraps up this case by corresponding across trans-Atlantic ocean telegraph cables. "A Study in Scarlet" was originally titled "A Tangled Skein," an echo of Holmes's reference in the story to "the scarlet thread of murder running through the colourless skein of life" (Doyle 36). A skein is a network, and Holmes pursues the scarlet thread through the channels of communication, the "All Red Routes" of transatlantic postal communication that Elihu Burritt's League of Universal Brotherhood had campaigned vigorously to expand. From the Imperial Conference of 1887 onward, those who believed that improved communication lines were critical to England maintaining an imperial world profile stepped up the pressure to expand the imperial postal service. Conservative MP J. Henniker Heaton was one of many who used the telegraph line as a metaphor for the bloodlines that fretted a white diaspora. In February 1896, Heaton pled his case for Imperial Penny Postage before the Colonial Secretary, Joseph Chamberlain, with these words:

> What we want is some cheap and ready means of bridging over the chasm of distance between our people and the millions of their colonial kindred, of restoring the broken arch in their communications and the severed link in their sympathies, of weaving the innumerable delicate threads of private and family affection into a mighty strand that shall bind the Empire together, and resist any strain from our foes or the Fates.
>
> (Potter 177)

Once again the imagery suggests the shoring up of defenses:

> It is often gloomily predicted that such a tremendous agglomeration as the British Empire will inevitably fall to pieces and dissolve like its predecessors. […] I venture to reply that, in the postal and telegraphic services the empire of our Queen possesses a cohesive force that was utterly lacking in former cases. Stronger than death-dealing

---

[32] This is from Doyle's "The Adventure of the Devil's Foot."

warships, than devoted legions, than natural wealth, or wise administration, are the scraps of paper that are borne in myriads over the waves, and the two or three slender wires that lie hidden beneath the fathomless depths below. Not a misfortune, or cause of rejoicing, of hope, astonishment, or apprehension can occur in any portion of the empire without a thrill of sympathy vibrating through the mass. The telegraph and mail lines are the nerves and arteries of the whole.

(*Postal Reform* 42)

Heaton vividly conflates the slender, vibrating wires buried beneath the Atlantic with the Anglo-Saxon nerves and arteries that join the people of two nations, and make them in sympathy with each other. Both, he asserts, are the red routes to brotherhood. And this transnational white brotherhood, he claims, soothes fears about loss of imperial power and dominion. Through having telegraph-wire nerves and postal route arteries, empire ensures its own vibrancy and is its own self-defense system: the body of empire is virtual and responsive. And that body has woven into its core "private and family affections."

Proponents of an imperial communications system believed that a networked body self-regulates, and Doyle's story exploits this idea. Holmes tracked Jefferson Hope's identity down via the red route of a telegraph cable, but it is the other form of red route that ultimately delivers punishment to the American murderer. Jefferson Hope does not die at the end of the rope of British justice, but dies "naturally" as the result of an aortic aneurysm. An aneurysm, as Doyle the doctor would well have known, is the blockage and rupture of an artery: a failure of the blood circulation. If blood "will out" across national borders, it also metes out justice without the help of a juridical structure. Doyle offers white brotherhood, anchored by postal ties, as an invigorating alternative to the networks of nation, law, and an imperialism made precarious by the potential of invasion and degeneration through its own structures.

"A Study in Scarlet" is a study in brotherhood, good and bad. The Mormons are the villainous kind of brotherhood, and Holmes and his domestics are the good. What demonizes the Mormons is their sexual culture (their "accursed and shameless harems"), which produce murder and vengeance, and Holmes counters their polygamous relations with his own strange alliances. The murder resulting from "two men alone in a house" who had walked in "together as friendly as possible—arm-in-arm," is met by Holmes's domestic relations with Watson, with his gang of street boys, and with his intimacy with the communications network. Of the Baker Street Irregulars, Holmes says: "There's more work to be got out of one of those little beggars than out of a dozen of the force [...]. The mere sight of an official-looking person seals men's lips. These youngsters, however, go everywhere and hear everything. They are as sharp as needles, too; all they want is organisation." This street fraternity of urchins ("the dirtiest and most ragged street Arabs") who open men's lips and are connected to everything, stays with Holmes throughout his career. Just as Holmes is not himself a member of the police force, and forms an unofficial counterpart to Inspector Lestrade, Holmes's ragamuffin crew are a nonuniformed version of the telegraph and post-boys. They are the *irregulars*, the queer counterparts to the already queer telegraph boys; unkempt and illegitimate doubles for those in The Service. They freely navigate the highways and byways of London, picking up information and also helping to "fill up the gap of loneliness and isolation which surrounded the saturnine figure of the great detective."[33] They are equally at home in the underworld and the main streets, and they courier information between these worlds. "A Study in Scarlet" is the first Holmes story. At the other end of his career, in a story published in 1901, *The Hound of the Baskervilles*, Holmes's alliance and reliance on the queer Boy Messenger is fully expressed. Holmes engages a fourteen-year-old telegraph boy to serve as his valet while he is living in hiding on the "queer" and "uncanny" Devon moors. The Cleveland Street affair had broken just a little over ten years before this story was published, and the sexual connotations of live-in telegraph boys still had currency. Holmes remembers a boy named Cartwright who "showed some ability" during an investigation which "saved [the] good name, and perhaps [the] life" of a manager at a district telegraph office. Cartwright is summoned: "A lad of fourteen, with a bright, keen face, had obeyed the summons of the manager. He stood now gazing with great reverence at the famous detective." The awed and eager Cartwright (whose telegraphic profession overwhelms the antique business of cart-making—still the business of carrying—that gives him his family name) is the agent by which Watson experiences the reverse gaze. Watson is sent to the moors by Holmes, who is supposedly back in London absorbed in a blackmailing case. Watson sends letters home to Holmes and spies on the urchin he sees running around the moors. When Watson stumbles on the dilapidated hut, he finds a note that reports on his own movements and consequently realizes that the urchin he'd spied through the telescope has in fact been spying on him. He reflects: "Always there was this feeling of an unseen force, a fine net drawn round us with infinite skill and delicacy, holding us so lightly that it was only at some supreme moment that one realized that one was indeed—entangled in its meshes." The net is a fully realized metaphor in this story: the villain is an entomologist who runs around with a butterfly net, and when Holmes realizes his guilt, in a chapter called "Fixing the Nets," he declares that he will soon have him "fluttering in our net as helpless as one of his own butterflies." As usual, Holmes utilizes the same routes as his villains, triumphing by turning their own kinds of methods and weapons against them: in this story the villain and his sinister butterfly net are trapped by means of a postal network. The case is solved by a crisscrossing of mail, misdelivered telegrams, letters that are delayed, reports that are post-forwarded, and postscripts that are half-burned: "But sometimes a letter may be legible even when burned." From the plains of Utah, to the rugged moors of Devon, Doyle dramatizes how the queer connections of postal functionaries, regular and irregular, a web of boys and telegraphs, can decipher even our most obliterated postscripts.

---

[33] This is Doyle's description of the role of the "fresh and smiling face of Billy, the young but very wise and tactful page" whom we find tending to Holmes at the opening of "The Adventure of the Mazarin Stone."

BROTHERS IN ARMS: KIPLING'S HOMOPHILIC FANTASIES

The notion of the American adopting and revitalizing the duty of the wearied British colonist finds full expression in Rudyard Kipling's infamous poem "The White Man's Burden" published in *McClure's Magazine* in February 1899. This poem is regularly cited as a manifesto of British imperial enterprise and illustrative of Kipling's role as the bard of the British Empire. It was not, however, written about Britain, but about American imperialism in the Philippines, and the poem reads as a message of exhortation and instruction from the experienced European imperialist to the newly fledged American. The opening stanza uses the language of heterosexual procreation to urge America to disseminate the seeds of empire:

> Take up the White Man's burden—
>   Send forth the best ye breed—
> Go, bind your sons to exile
>   To serve your captive's need;
> To wait, in heavy harness,
>   On fluttered folk and wild—
> Your new-caught sullen peoples,
>   Half devil and half child. (Kipling, "White Man's Burden" 290)

The offspring of the American nation—the best-bred sons—are to serve and raise the wild devil children of the empire. But the last stanza also figures America and Americans as children, in a different way:

> Take up the White Man's burden!
>   Have done with childish days—
> The lightly-proffered laurel,
>   The easy ungrudged praise:
> Comes now, to search your manhood
>   Through all the thankless years,
> Cold, edged with dear-bought wisdom,
>   The judgement of your peers.
>   (Kipling, "White Man's Burden" 291)

The poem might seem to assume the form of a letter from parent to child: a transatlantic, transgenerational message from the parent country, addressing America as its once-child to grow up, become a man, and raise its own children.[34] The metaphor of the colony as

---

[34] The message was delivered at what looked like a turning point: the American-Philippine war had begun 4 February and two days later The Treaty of Paris ceded Puerto Rico, Guam, and the Philippines to the United States and placed Cuba under U.S. control.

a child of Britain was, after all, very common.³⁵ But Kipling's poem does not fulfil this parent-child paradigm: it sounds more like Jefferson's fraternal metaphorics of 1776. First, the genders of both countries are wrong: America was most commonly figured as Britain's *daughter* and Britain was almost always the *mother* country.³⁶ Second, the connotations of the final image, the "lightly-proffered laurels," suggest a pedagogical, rather than a parental bond. The laurels are the accolades of the schoolroom and the youthful athlete. They are of Greek genesis, having originally been worn by the victor at the Pythian games held in honor of Apollo. Apollo was the god who represented the perfection of youthful manhood, and, in his 1895 biography, author, critic, and homosexual activist John Addington Symonds describes youthful "peripatetic rhapsodies" in which he made up poems about the beautiful boy-loving god: "The kernel of my inspiration," he writes, "was that radiant figure of the young Apollo, doomed to pass his time with shepherds, serving them and loving them" (Symonds, *Biography* 1: 49–50). His contemplation of Apollo leads him to realize what he had obscurely known—that "Man loves man" (Symonds, *Biography* 1: 49–50).

In Greek love, or masculine love, as he sometimes calls it, Symonds describes how "the elder, in these unions of friends, received the name of 'inspirer' or 'lover,' the younger that of 'hearer' or 'admired'" (*Key of Blue* 63). The structure of address in Kipling's poem echoes this social-sexual exchange between experience and youth. "White Man's Burden" is both an epistle and an exemplum, and it stands between two corresponding, correspondent nations, urging the younger to emulate or be inspired by the older imperial nation. Furthermore, Kipling's exhortation to the youthful America to go to war with the Philippines matches Symonds's emphasis on the fact that Greek homosexual comradeship had a military role: "When the youth grew up and went to battle with his comrade, he assumed the title of bystander in the ranks" (*Key of Blue* 63). The love was, Symonds emphasized, disciplined, governed by strict laws and customs, and therefore served to promote "a martial spirit in the population, […] binding the male members of the nation together by bonds of mutual affection" (*Key of Blue* 63). In a similar mode, Kipling's last stanza casts America not as a son emulating the father, but as a youth coming of age under the tutelage of an older man, finally taking his place as a "peer" through imperial, military conquest. His exhortation of the United States to comradeship and manhood through an invocation of the Greek ideal matches Symonds's portrayal of homosexual passions as "educational and military agents" (qtd. in White, *Nineteenth-Century Writings* 170).³⁷

---

[35] George Eliot, for example, characterized American poetry as a teenager, writing in an 1856 review of R. W. Griswold's *The Poets and Poetry of America*, that American "poetic literature […] may be said, figuratively speaking, to be in its teens" (210).

[36] For an account of this relationship and its changes across the American Revolution and first decades of the nineteenth century, see Shirley Samuels, *Romances of the Republic, Women, the Family and Violence in the Literature of the Early American Nation* 3–14.

[37] For original, see Symonds's *A Problem in Greek Ethics*, conveniently available and qtd. in White, *Nineteenth-Century Writings* 170. Symonds corresponded with Kipling about Kipling's novel *Soldiers Three*. In 1889 Symonds wrote praising the work and Kipling responded in the language of homoerotics. He wrote that if his book was

Kipling's model of is one of homoerotically fueled imperial development and regeneration. Kipling's jingoism grew from and danced around the "breaking strain" of patriot duty, which he recognized had exhausted many of his characters (qtd. in Wurgaft 169, 145).[38] For Kipling, therefore, and for late-century Victorians in general, the revitalization of imperial and racial cohesion was a key concern. A discourse of brotherhood and comradeship could provide that cohesion, because of, not in spite of, its transgenerational homoerotic structure, in which the adult generation tutors and invigorates the youth.

From the early 1890s onward, Symonds's historical contextualizations of homosexual love stressed its capacities for national or racial uplift, a view opposed to the scientific discourses that sought to pathologize male-male love, defining it as a form of degeneracy. Symonds claimed that homogenic love "was in its origin and essence masculine, military, chivalrous [...] and flourished in the highest-gifted of all races" (*Key of Blue* 66). W. T. Stead made a similar connection between the health of a race and free expression of male-male love when he complained that homosexual scandals would give a bad name to masculine comradeship and that, in turn, would harm the race. Stead wrote to Edward Carpenter: "A few more cases like Oscar Wilde's and we should find the freedom of comradeship now possible to men seriously impaired to the permanent detriment of the race" (qtd. in Weeks, *Sex, Politics and Society* 109).[39] Racial strength and purity, in other words, *needs* homosociality and homosexuality—it needs them not to be criminalized. Stead's and Symonds's claims about racial strength match Kipling's portrayal of homosexual bonds of racial brotherhood as an alternative to lines of procreative descent. A nation suffering from imperial fatigue did not need to reproduce itself and its weakness heterosexually; it needed to refederate, homosexually.

VAMPIRIC THREATS, ANGLO-AMERICAN SOLUTIONS

The late-nineteenth-century high priest of fatigue theories, Max Nordau, chooses a postal illustration for his insistent thesis that "humanity can point to no century in which the inventions which penetrate so deeply, so tyrannically, into the life of every individual are crowded so thick as in ours" (37). Nordau chooses to compare life in the 1890s with life in 1840, a date which he vaguely describes as marking "the irruption of new discoveries in

---

successful, it was because he loved his characters "as you loved a man called Benvenuto Cellini and in your translation showed that love." Kipling then said that he had "come to London to start that queer experience known as a literary career" and offered to send his work to Symonds, who was twenty-five years older and an established man of letters, so that Symonds might mentor him and warn him when he "slid from decent work" (*Letters* 348).

[38] For further discussion of how Kipling's fiction is dominated by characters suffering from physical or mental decay, disfigurement or degeneration, see Zoreh T. Sullivan, *Narratives of Empire: The Fictions of Rudyard Kipling*. Sullivan identifies what she calls the "fear of boundary loss" that these characters experience in the face of the boundless spaces of empire (18).

[39] For original, see "Stead to Edward Carpenter," *Edward Carpenter collection, Sheffield City Library*, Ms. 386-54 (1–2), (June 1895), conveniently available and qtd. in Weeks, *Sex, Politics and Society* 109.

every relation of life" (38). Why choose this seemingly random date as marking the birth of modernity? Eighteen-forty was the year in which the Penny Post scheme was introduced and Nordau's description of the "wear and tear" caused to the nervous system, brain, and body by the strain of modern life has a postal focus. He dwells particularly on the "little shocks" of travel and what he calls the "constant expectation of the newspaper, of the postman" (Nordau 39). He then emphasizes that "the collective postal intercourse between all countries [...] amounted, in 1840, to 92 millions; in 1889, to 2,759 millions" (Nordau 38) and that "a cook receives and sends more letters than a university professor did formerly" (Nordau 39). The Penny Post is the symptom; Nordau's diagnosis is excess of (democratized) civilization. The postal metaphor works for Nordau's description of the perpetuation of social degeneration because it is itself a circulation system, and the modernity that he surveys from the vantage point of the 1890s has, according to him, brought nervous exhaustion and hysteria (Nordau 40).[40] He has a particular horror of daily, speedily mass-circulated texts and the constant flows of knowledge for which he says the Anglo-Saxon people have a particular craving.[41] The Penny Post scheme that was promoted as a way of opening up the world to the working classes and as a relief to the "tax on knowledge" that high postage costs were considered to constitute, is criticized by Nordau for *overtaxing* the nerves of the general public. The "collective postal intercourse" engulfs them. The early-century metaphorics of postal routes as the arteries of the nation and empire and the Post Office as a heart that pumps lifeblood to all citizens turns against itself in Nordau's account. The knock of the postman implicates the cook in a constant exchange of text and information for which Nordau implies she is not equipped; unlike the professor, she is no man of letters. But the civilizing engine of the Penny Post nonetheless entangles the cook in its network, and thus her own bodily network, her nervous system, is exhausted. At the fin de siècle, the heart has become weak, the veins are varicose, and if we remember that Nordau describes technology's incursions into the "life of every individual" as "tyrannical penetrations," we realize that a vampiric threat lurks at the nexus of the bloody networks of modernity.

Vamped and varicose veins are also the metaphor of choice for Jack London in his description of Britannia's broken-down reproductive health in the 1903 urban exposé *The People of the Abyss*. This book is an American cousin of the late-nineteenth-century urban exploration texts of George Sims, Andrew Mearns, or General Booth that expose the "barbarism" of the impoverished city-dwelling Briton.[42] In this following passage, Jack

---

[40] Although Nordau is himself something of a hysterical commentator, other fin de siècle writers such as H. G. Wells developed this theme of an excess of civilization that led to degeneration. This is what Wells's Time Traveler in *The Time Machine* (1895) discovers, for example, in the Eloi; the refined, but fragile and enervated children of futurity.

[41] Nordau writes: "The Anglo-Saxon race [...] has [...] in high degree, that strong desire for knowledge [...]. This fine and high-minded craving for knowledge has proved at once the strength and the weakness of the English" (75–76).

[42] London opens the book with the conceit of author-as-traveler: "I went down into the under-world of London with an attitude of mind which I may best liken to that of the explorer" (*PA* vii). Like George Sims who,

London claims that England's imperialism is exhausted, the work of Britannia's childbearing done, and her stock run out. He opens with a quote from Kipling's "The White Man's Burden":

> England has sent forth "the best she breeds" for so long, and has destroyed those that remained so fiercely, that little remains for her to do but to sit down through the long nights and gaze at royalty on the wall. [...] In South Africa the colonial teaches the Islander how to shoot, and the officers muddle and blunder; while at home the street people play hysterically at mafficking, and the War Office lowers the stature for enlistment. It could not be otherwise. The most complacent Britisher cannot hope to draw off the life blood, and underfeed, and keep it up forever. The average Mrs. Thomas Mugridge has been driven into the city, and she is not breeding very much of anything save an anaemic and sickly progeny which cannot find enough to eat. The strength of the English-speaking race to-day is not in the tight little island, but in the New World overseas, where are the sons and daughters of Mrs. Thomas Mugridge. The Sea Wife by the Northern Gate has just about done her work in the world, though she does not realize it. She must sit down and rest her tired loins for a space; and if the casual ward and the workhouse do not await her, it is because of the sons and daughters she has reared up against the day of her feebleness and decay.
> (London, *PA* 184–85)[43]

Like Kipling's poem, this passage portrays the New Worlders as standing in the imperial wings, waiting to replace and support the exhausted Briton. Britannia—and her representative on earth, Mrs. Thomas Mugridge—has overextended herself. She has scattered her strongest seed abroad, throughout an empire, and this dissemination has sapped her strength as a mother. Mrs. Thomas Mugridge, and by extension Mr. Thomas Mugridge, are portrayed as so worn down that they are themselves a hybrid race who can only produce hereditary feebleness. The structure behind Jack London's thinking is that of the blood network (familial and racial), and he, too, comes to rest with a vampiric metaphor. England's loins now only produce "anaemic" children because Britons' pursuit of empire has involved "drawing off the life-blood" from the mother country. Jack London returns

---

as I shall later discuss, mocks readers' ignorance of the "continent" at their doorsteps, London pokes fun at the famous and still extant travel company of Thomas Cook: he writes "But O Cook, O Thomas Cook & Son, pathfinders and trail-clearers, living sign-posts to all the world and bestowers of first aid to bewildered travellers—unhesitatingly and instantly, with ease and celerity, could you send me to Darkest Africa or Innermost Thibet, but to the East End of London, barely a stone's throw distant from Ludgate Circus, you know not the way!" (*PA* 3). William Booth similarly asks, "As there is a darkest Africa is there not also a darkest England?" (11). In the same passage, Booth declares that "Civilisation [...] can breed its own barbarians" (11) and Jack London's idea of the "abyss" of East London very much matches Booth's notion of "the submerged tenth," the impoverished East End dwellers.

[43] The phrase "the sea wife" is a reference to Rudyard Kipling's 1893 poem "The Sea-Wife."

to this vampirism at the end of the book, when he concludes that it is the wasteful and inefficient "MISMANAGEMENT" (314) of the country that has "drained the United Kingdom of its life-blood" (316).

There are two vampires in Jack London's picture: the empire and "gentlemen of no occupation" (315), both of whom have turned vampiric under bad management. Under the mantra "Things profitable must be continued," Jack London explains that neither the empire nor the gentleman work and turn a profit for England, thus making the country and its folk "worn-out" and "pasty-faced" (316). Jack London's formulation follows that of Karl Marx who writes of capital as "dead labour, which vampire-like, lives only by sucking living labour" (Marx 1: 342). The empire, gentlemen, and capital are all models of bad circulation. The gentlemen that Jack London despises are overbred idlers who, he writes, do not "plough" or "plant." Their seed—both reproductive and vegetable—is stored, not circulated. The empire draws off resources, but does not pump them back to England, and capital, too, preys on its own producers. There is a fine line, it seems, between health-giving circulation and self-destructive circularity.

Jack London waves aside the worn out, heterosexual Mugridge procreators and turns instead to the reproductive potential of homosocial bureaucratized management systems. To reinvigorate the nation and its empire, he explains, Mr. and Mrs. Thomas Mugridge must be wheeled out and a bureaucrat wheeled in. In *The People of the Abyss*, the ever-spreading family tree of heterosexual reproduction needs to be replaced by a state network of administrators that can facilitate the reinvigoration of British blood through Anglo-American brotherhood. David Greenberg and Maria Bystryn make the claim in their article "Capitalism, Bureaucracy and Male Homosexuality" that administration, or civil management, helps to displace the heterosexual nexus.[44] Homosexuality, they write, is made possible under the "principles of bureaucratic administration" because these homosocial, merit-based principles "contrast sharply with those of a society" based on biological heterosexual descendancy (Greenberg and Bystryn 42). Under the twinned logics of empire and capitalism, instead of being condemned as "unproductive" sexual expression, homosexuality gained in potential as a model of sexual continence, discipline, and civic virtue.

Christopher Lane has objected to this kind of coupling of sexuality to "hydraulic definitions of desire, in which sexual repression appears amenable to political service," arguing that we should be more dubious about rhetoric that asserts the efficiency of empire, and pay more attention to allegory and "the failure of self-mastery" (2). For Lane, "sexual desire between men frequently ruptured Britain's imperial allegory by shattering national unity"

---

[44] Greenberg and Bystryn's argument has fellowship with the work of John D'Emilio's Marxist theorization of homosexuality and capitalism. D'Emilio argues "Only when individuals began to make their living through wage labor, instead of as parts of an interdependent family unit, was it possible for homosexual desire to coalesce into a personal identity" (8). Jeffrey Weeks similarly points out that we need to see "the emergence of new definitions of homosexuality and the homosexual" as part of "the restructuring of the family and sexual relations consequent upon the triumph of urbanisation and industrial capitalism" (*Coming Out* 2).

(4). Lane's account usefully brushes aside instrumentalizations of homosexuality in favor of depicting the turbulence of same-sex masculine desire. What happens, however, if turbulence and bureaucracy are theorized together? What happens when that national unity, or that imperial body, is configured as a "ganglion" of telegraphic nerves and postal arteries? Imperialism itself, as "Little Englanders" recognized, involved the shattering of national unity that had to be negated en route to national and imperial chauvinism. And the figure of the network amplified this dialectical process: the communication network could be engaged to stand for national and imperial unity only through producing the shattering effect of dissemination. As concern turned away from the "power of reproduction" itself to the notion that we must pay sole "regard to vitality of produce" (Pouchet 97),[45] and the racial makeup of that produce, a space opened up for the homosexual to be seen as a loyal placeholder. Loss of emphasis upon a single familial line of descent coincided with the rise of the network and combined to allow the administrator to take the place of the procreator. Under the desire to render all English-governed lands "homogenous"[46] we see an imaginative turn toward those who were, to use Symonds's term, "homogenic."

In "The White Man's Burden," Kipling exhorts America to grow up and construct a white imperial bureaucracy based on homosocial bonds with peers, rather than the parental bonds of descent referenced in the first stanza. And for both Jack London and Kipling, the administration that needs to be formed is refederation between Britain and the United States. As opposed to the Mugridgian coupling available on the "tight island," which is so debased that it is racially impure, Anglo-American reunion is transatlantic, but occurs neither across the sexes nor across races. Instead of producing degenerative variance, "sickly progeny" that function as a degenerated race, Anglo-American reunion consolidates what Jack London calls "Blood empire" (316). Bad imperialism results from circulation systems so overextended that they are susceptible to sluggish, sapped, or reverse flows like vampirism. Good imperialism means sending letters, via a homosocial bureaucratic network, to America, letters that call for Anglo-Saxon confederation.

THE SECOND EMPIRE: BLOOD AND WIRE

Writers whose focus was Britain's "Second Empire" were similarly worried about dissemination and enervation, and the necessity to adjudicate colonial contact zones through

---

[45] This is how Georges Pouchet, a polygenist, discussed racial hybridity in *The Plurality of the Human Race* (1864). In *The Races of Man*, Robert Knox invokes Pouchet to argue that hybrid races are never self-supporting and can only survive on the "infusion of [...] fresh blood from the parent race or species" (495). Both qtd. in Robert J. C. Young, *Colonial Desire: Hybridity in Theory, Culture and Race* (1995) 15.

[46] I borrow the term from Matthew Arnold who uses it to describe a vision of a nation that unifies and is unified through communication. In his *Reports on Elementary Schools 1852–1882*, he wrote: "It must always be the desire of a Government to render its dominions, as far as possible, homogenous, and to break down barriers to the freest intercourse between the different parts of them" (11).

homosocial bureaucracies. Colonialist enterprise and the expansion of communication networks both radically reorganized relations of proximity and adjacency. Annihilations of compass, nation, class, and race are what Kipling is describing in his famous ballad about the meeting point of the unmeetable: "East is East and West is West, and never the twain shall meet [...]/But there is neither East nor West, Border, nor Breed, nor Birth,/When two strong men stand face to face, though they come from the ends of the earth." The refrain fixates on the terminal: the dissolution of differentiating boundaries that occurs with the meeting of men who come from the *ends* of the earth. The "never/but/when/tho'" frame of his refrain mimics the polarizing motions of attraction and repulsion in a metaphysics of racism. But the correct metaphor here is perhaps not magnetism (the poles are wrong, for a start: East and West exert no magnetic force), but rather electricity. G. W. F. Hegel describes the agency of electricity as a uniting of differentials:

> Electricity is infinite form differentiated within itself, and is the unity of these differentials; consequently the two bodies are inseparably bound together [...]. Negative electricity is attracted by positive electricity, but repulsed by negative. In that the differentials unite themselves, they communicate themselves to each other; as soon as they have posited a unity, they fly apart again, and vice versa.
>
> (174)

The kind of uniting Hegel describes is thoroughly provisional: it is not only a uniting of "differentials" but it is also unity "posited," unity in passing. It happens in a moment of communication that is simultaneously the moment of parting. The literalization of electrical communication is the telegraph, and it is a technology in which Kipling repeatedly sees metaphysical possibilities of union. In his poem "The Deep-Sea Cables," the narrator joins with, perhaps even is, the telegraph cables on "the great grey level plains of ooze." Kipling sees a double-matrix in these subaqua telegraph lines, figuring them as both an interconnecting network and a breeding ground:

> Here in the womb of the world—here on the tie-ribs of earth
>   Words, and the words of men, flicker and flutter and beat—
> Warning, sorrow, and gain, salutation and mirth—
>   For a Power troubles the Still that has neither voice nor feet.

The poem works as a kind of re-Creation story, using evolutionary language to describe the possibilities of machine culture with the eerie romance reminiscent of the fiction of H. G. Wells. Kipling imagines a soundless deep-sea desert, a "waste of the ultimate slime" from which new life—new social or political life—can be reborn. The power of the cables animates "timeless Things" and "the words of men" animate "a new Word." This Word "whispers" a kind of benediction: "'Let us be one!'" Mark C. Taylor describes the matrix as the technological womb, theorizing that communication systems communicate us back to ourselves, to our maternal origins. Taylor makes this argument through Sigmund Freud's *The Future of an Illusion* (1928) in which Freud figures the telephone as an instrument that can return us to the womb, a means of circuiting us back to our original "dwelling-house" (52). Taylor reads this alongside a nineteenth-century source depicting telephone devices, arguing that telephonic communication was always figured "from man to woman" (51) and that "teledildonics is more than a century old" (51). The very concept of teledildonics, however, signals detachability. A dildo is not a penis for the very reason that it is detachable, prosthetic, and in this case, can be used at a distance. We should not, therefore, seek to suture the technology to one gender/sex formation, but rather should recognize that the extensions of the self that can be practiced through the technology assume mobility. The child's game of Telephone is all about the transformations that occur over the line; its pleasures derive from misheard whispers morphing into new meaning. The teledildo/telecommunication device is a mobile figure, available for the production of mobile, exchangeable relations of gender and sexuality. And indeed the matrix of Kipling's whispering deep-sea cables is, contrary to the dictionary definition of a matrix, nonmaternal and nonfeminine; this "womb" is man-made, rendered generative only by the "words of men" and "men talk" and the death of "father Time." When Virginia Woolf complains about Kipling's writing as a "purely masculine orgy," observing "Kipling has [no] spark of the woman in him," she lands on the appropriate metaphor.[47] Kipling's bodies are atomized, electrical. The "sparks" he finds are between men, and men's greatest connective moments are not with women, nor with men, but with the extensions and prostheses of men, with systems of filiation. As Christopher Lane describes it, all sexual desire appears to Kipling as "ungovernable" and to be repudiated (Lane 35). Racial fraternity must be preserved, but both heterosexual and homosexual desire threatens to debilitate this fraternity and colonial masculinity more generally (Lane 25).

In Kipling's short story "His Chance in Life," a telegraph operator named Michele D'Cruze seizes the opportunities afforded by a village riot, his official position and the one-eighth of white blood in his veins. The operator has a brief moment of glory, shooting at the crowd and asserting that "until the Assistant Collector came, he, the Telegraph Signaller, was the Government of India in Tibasu" (63). This moment, in which his heart "was big and white in his breast" (63) is produced from his taste of responsibility and his long-distance love for Miss Vezzis. But the "White drop" (63) dies out when he comes face to face with an Englishman, and when D'Cruze's bravery is rewarded and he gets to marry and have "sprawling" children (63), the honor fades and he cannot recount his tale. D'Cruze sinks back into the blackness through which Kipling damns him and Miss Vezzis: D'Cruze is "a poor, sickly weed and very black" (60) and Miss Vezzis "was as black

---

[47] Virginia Woolf, *A Room of One's Own* 102.

as a boot." He simultaneously descends into the quagmire of heterosexual, mixed-race procreation. The chance, or the spark, that cannot be recovered is both the "White drop" and the sense of himself as the Telegraph Signaller. His whiteness is animated, for a flickering moment, not through the possibility of biological reproduction, but through the electrifying power and authority of the telegraph wires.

Kipling, who proposed to his wife by telegram, was entranced by the notion that communication at a distance could produce peace and unity. For Kipling, the mail is the agent of Pax Brittanica par excellence. It is even free from the imperium of the never-setting sun: the telegraph cables lie "a league from the last of the sun" and in "The Overland Mail," Kipling posits that "the great Sun himself must attend to the hail"/"In the Name of the Empress, the Overland Mail!" The facility of the communication network in bringing about a universalism before which even the sun and the tides bow down is, he proposes, unassailable. Such disingenuousness about the neutrality of media, especially that crisscrossing occupied land, was made short shrift of by Mahatma Gandhi in *Hind Swaraj* (1909). English infrastructures "had sucked our life-blood," he writes (15). Gandhi repeatedly figures communication and transport networks as draining India of its vitality and resources, making it vulnerable to infections—literal and metaphorical. Railways, he proposes, "have spread the bubonic plague" (47) and this same "facility of means of locomotion" has "also increased the frequency of famines" because people can take advantage of more lucrative markets and send their produce far off in search of profit (47). The British don't have to rule, he declares— their civilization does it for them: "It is not the British people who are ruling India, but it is modern civilisation, through its railways, telegraphs, telephones" (130). Gandhi's critique of media reminds his readers that British rule was always intermediated, and that intermediation itself is a tool of empire. Frantz Fanon would later drive home the same point. In *The Wretched of the Earth* he writes: "The intermediary does not lighten the oppression, nor seek to hide the domination; he shows them up and puts them into practice with the clear conscience of an upholder of the peace; yet he is the bringer of violence into the home and into the mind of the native" (29). Gandhi argues that the systems enabling government by proxy, and government at a distance, must be rooted out to avoid reproducing in the independent India the likeness of Britain: Gandhi contests that media merely enables and has itself no shaping force. And when he claims "machinery is like a snake-hole which may contain from one to a hundred snakes" (110), he is turning vehicles back into the metaphors they have always been. Colonial telepresence is, as Gandhi describes it, bloodsucking, plague-bringing, snake-multiplying. Media matters.

POSTAL DRACULA

The late-nineteenth-century congruence of vampirism, imperialism, vigorous Americans, homosocial bureaucracies, and postal routes, finds its apotheosis in Bram Stoker's 1897 novel *Dracula*. It is not commonly observed that *Dracula* is an epistolary novel.[48] But it is a novel in which veins and arteries are tangled up with postal "All Red Routes." Indeed, Stoker gets much mileage from the figure of the dead—undelivered, written by the undead—letter. The book is textually chaotic, reflecting what David Wellbery calls "the noisy reservoir of all possible written constellations, paths and media of transmission, or mechanisms of memory" (xii), and the story, as a multimedia, polyglot archive, testifies to the ability of an alien to infiltrate the nation or the civic body through communication and transport systems. Count Dracula is a correspondent: he reads, writes, sends mail, intercepts mail, sends telegrams, and when his London lair is found, his table is strewn with the tools of an avid letter-writer: "notepaper, envelopes, and pens and ink" (Stoker, *Dracula* 262). He even uses parcel post, delivering great boxes of mold from his homeland to his various London addresses. If we recall Elihu Burritt's mandate of "making home everywhere," and the writer who saw the post as providing "a continual presence of home," Dracula most certainly achieves this through mailing and distributing sustaining crates of Transylvanian soil around London. Dracula not only sends, but also summons by mail. It is his demanding letters that bring Jonathan Harker to Transylvania in the first place, and Harker's first task is to hand over to Dracula a sealed letter "entrusted" to him by his employer. Soon enough the telegrams of the vampire-hunters and of the vampire they hunt pass through the same Post Offices, the same cables, the same postal workers, a media machinery which does not distinguish between pursuer and pursued, but instead sends and receives with two-way equanimity. Interpenetration is the topos here: Dracula is, as he himself describes it, a colonized, if resistant, subject of a repeatedly invaded land, a victim of much spilt blood.[49] He designs his own invasion of England by which he wires himself into the nation's communication and transport systems: he wishes to perfect both his written and spoken English and he studies the London directory, the timetables and maps and imperial indexes. In other words, he wants to pass into both the discourse and the discourse networks of the country so that he can attack from within. And Jonathan Harker, the clerk Dracula employs to help in his "transfer to London" (Stoker, *Dracula* 53), follows postal coordinates.[50] He carries letters to Dracula, can find Castle Dracula only through locating the nearest "post town" (Stoker, *Dracula* 10), and has his way to the castle paved by the Count's carefully planted letters. It is a route that will lead him into the desiring arms of the Count, and Harker's epistolary obedience feminizes

---

[48] An exception is Alison Case who perceives a lineage between Samuel Richardson and *Dracula*, noting particularly that both Lovelace and Harker employ shorthand, and have trouble smuggling letters (226–27 and 236). She argues: "Shorthand refers as much *back* to Richardson and the epistolary novel as *forward* to modern business practices" (note 10, 241). "Tasting the Original Apple: Gender and the Struggle for Narrative Authority in 'Dracula,'" *Narrative* 1, no. 3 (1993): 223–43.

[49] For Dracula's description of Transylvania's history of invasion and colonization, notably the rule of the Turks, see Stoker, *Dracula* 33–35.

[50] Harker, our first narrator, is a clerk, and the novel's author was too: Stoker took a job as a civil service clerk in 1870, following in the footsteps of his father who was a clerk at Dublin Castle.

him. When Harker sits down in the castle to write his diary, he imagines himself as a love-struck lady in a courtly fiction: "Here I am, sitting at a little oak table where in old times possibly some fair lady sat to pen, with much thought and many blushes, her ill-spelt love-letter" (40). When Harker writes, reads, or carries mail, he makes himself palimpsest with an antique, feminine, epistolary self. This "little oak table" scene recalls the youthful Stoker who wrote his own love-letter to Walt Whitman, a letter in which he reflects on how writing a letter allows him to "speak" a love that crosses and recrosses gender and generation until each man is heterogeneously passionate, sturdy but vulnerable, and relationally composite—father and wife: "How sweet it is," Stoker tells Whitman, "for a strong healthy man with a woman's eyes and a child's wishes to feel that he can speak so to a man who can be if he wishes father, and brother and wife to his soul" (Traubel 4: 185).

Stoker invokes the epistolary mode as a way of fashioning gender and sexual style for his protagonist. He also turns to postal means for the mechanics of a plot that might eliminate this protagonist. Dramatically, Dracula plans to obscure Jonathan's death through a plot involving dictated, postdated letters.[51] Jonathan is all-too aware that his life might be obliterated by a postmark: "Last night one of my post-dated letters went to post, the first of that fatal series which is to blot out the very traces of my existence from the earth," (49) he writes. When Jonathan tries to circumvent this terrible coordination of posting and vamping, by paying gypsies (themselves racially peripatetic in a way that is both appealing and useful to a vampire) to convey nonmanipulated letters, Dracula intercepts and destroys them. The Count thus attempts to command control over both the lifeblood in Jonathan's veins and the "red routes" of postal communication, en route to his infiltration of England.

> Franco Moretti remarks that in this network of letters, diaries, notes, telegrams, notices, phonograph recordings and articles, the narrative function proper, namely the description and ordering of events, is reserved for the British alone. We never have access to [Abraham] Van Helsing's point of view, or to [Quincey] Morris's, and still less to Dracula's.
>
> (77)

Moretti's point is that the form of the novel allows British cultural codings, forms, and values to reign supreme. While I agree that these codings triumph in the novel, they only do so after having ingested many aliens, bloodsucking and otherwise. Moretti suggests that the discursive thoroughfares in *Dracula* are blocked off to foreigners—"reserved for the British"—but in fact Van Helsing and Quincey Morris *are* allowed textual expression. The novel contains seven letters, telegrams, and memoranda from Van Helsing (Stoker,

---

[51] Arthur Conan Doyle's story "The Five Orange Pips" involves a similar series of time-delayed letters that schedule a murder. In this plot, the correspondence of postmarks to the murderers' dates of transportation registered with Lloyd's leads Sherlock Holmes to solve the case. For an excellent analysis of this story in relationship to postal marginalia and international media, see Siegert 143–44.

Dracula 106–7, 130, 161–62, 167, 181, 313–18, 318–20), some of which are very lengthy and expressive. The "laconic" Morris has one self-authored letter (Stoker, *Dracula* 62), and although the novel does not contain anything directly authored by Dracula, the effects of his textual interventions, interceptions, and correspondence litter the novel. In this novel, authoring and having narrative function can take the form of recording, remembering, delivering, or disseminating. And by this point in the century, the novel is now fully concerned with postal marks and envelopes rather than the contents of the letters they carry. Novels and networks are not as stable and impermeable as Moretti seems to suggest. In the late nineteenth century, the fear that the colonized subject could utilize the discourse networks and the imperial transport systems to their own ends was accompanied by a renewed excitement in the potential of the mail and government-run communication technologies to galvanize social, political, and racial bonds.

Dracula's attempt to take command of networks and use them to invade England finds its parallel and match in an international team of comrades who pool their media, knowledge, and skills to thwart the vampire. I want to focus on one of these international characters in particular. When Jonathan finally triumphs in the novel-long struggle against the Count, the friend who joins him in this triumph is his *American* friend, Quincey Morris. In a scene involving synchronized hand-to-hand combat, Count Dracula is vanquished and killed by the Anglo-American pairing of Jonathan Harker and Quincey Morris. Their transatlantic alliance defeats the Eastern European vampire-Count who has managed to make his way to British soil, to begin vampirically infecting British women, and to assume his intended dominion of the land. In the final scenes of the novel, Jonathan and Quincey function as the military alliance that can destroy this threat. Dracula's death scene, witnessed and recorded by Mina who stands in a "strategic point" (Stoker, *Dracula* 321) equipped with field glasses, is militaristically choreographed around Jonathan's and Quincey's conjoined but separate roles. Dracula is at rest in one of his boxes of earth and mold from his homeland, which is set upon a cart, surrounded by gypsies. They are racing toward the sunset and the Count's castle. Quincey rides up to intercept them from the south and Jonathan from the north. The two men stop the party in unified, but distinct voices: Mina notes that "all at once two voices shouted out to: 'Halt!' One was my Jonathan's, raised in a high key of passion; the other Mr. Morris's strong resolute tone of quiet command" (Stoker, *Dracula* 323). They both charge at the cart, but Quincey and Jonathan have very different effects upon the "undisciplined [...] shouldering [...] pushing" (Stoker, *Dracula* 324) gaggle of gypsies defending Dracula's crate. Mina writes:

> Jonathan's impetuosity, and the manifest singleness of his purpose, seemed to overawe those in front of him; instinctively they cowered aside and let him pass. In an instant he had jumped upon the cart, and with a strength which seemed incredible, raised the great box, and flung it over the wheel to the ground. In the meantime, Mr. Morris had had to use force to pass through his side of the ring of Szgany.
>
> (Stoker, *Dracula* 324)

Jonathan speaks with "passion" and acts with similar "impetuous" energy; this inspires such awe and submission in the gypsies that he does not have to physically fight them. Instead, they quite literally bow down to him. He manages to commandeer the cart by being evidently commandeering, by looking the part. In true imperial form, Jonathan represents a force that suppresses resistance and commands compliance from a native rabble. The sword-work is left to another, the American Quincey, who does not have the same imperious power over the rabble and "had to use force" against the gypsies and their knives, getting mortally wounded in the process. All along he is the one who has supplied the (American-made) arms and is admired for his prowess as a hunter, and here, too, he seems to represent physical struggle. Despite his wound, he finds enough frenzied strength to join Jonathan in ripping off the lid of the crate and the two of them stab the vampire, reducing him to dust. The duo's triumph glistens with the blood and sweat of imperial- and homo-erotics.

When the two men fall upon Dracula's prone body and plunge their kukri and bowie knives into him, their weapons signal imperial triumph over the vampire. A kukri knife is a curved knife used by Ghurkas in India and, as Stephan Arata notes, thus symbolizes British imperial rule (621–45). The bowie knife, named after James Bowie, a famous Texan adventurer said to have fought with the knife at the battle of the Alamo, is emblematic of American westward expansion. The Oxford English Dictionary's entry for "kukri" gives an example that describes the two knives as cousins: "The Ghoorka Kukri, the American bowie knife, or any other kindred instrument."[52] The kinship between these weapons mirrors the kinship between Jonathan and Quincey. It is the *confederation* of these two men, their weapons and their expansionist agendas, that drives this scene. To begin with, Jonathan and Quincey's double-act is a change of script; the killing of Dracula had originally been planned as an exploit in which all the male vampire-hunters would participate.[53] In place of this, the coalition between Jonathan and Quincey, Quincey's death in Jonathan's embrace and his consequent regeneration in little Quincey, Jonathan's son, all draw attention to Quincey's role as a brother-in-arms to the British heroes that he has played throughout the novel.[54]

The brotherhood is so pronounced, we learn that Quincey's comradeship with Seward and Holmwood extends to *before* the time in which the novel opens, when they were hunter-soldier-adventurers together. This is a rare point of retrospection in the narrative. Dracula's ancient tales of his progenitors aside, Quincey's reminiscences about his adventures with Seward and Holmwood are the only real histories in the novel. The novel's

---

[52] The OED example is cited from A. Forbes, *Pall Mall Gazette* (19 March 1884).
[53] In his journal, Jonathan describes how the vampire-hunters had "arranged what to do in case we get the box open. [...]. Van Helsing and Seward will cut off his head at once and drive a stake through his heart. Morris, Godalming and I shall prevent interference" (290).
[54] Stoker's other engagements of American characters and settings, including violently racist depictions of Native Americans, can be found in "The Squaw" in *Dracula's Guest* (1914), *The Shoulder of Shasta* (1895), *Lady Athlyne* (1908).

multimedia, fragmented form is so shaped by that which is "modern" and the narrative is so comprised of that which the preface calls "exactly contemporary" (Stoker, *Dracula* 5), that these glimpses into Quincey's past are most striking. This sense of historicity that attaches to him narratively also attaches to him nationally. Quincey Morris is not merely American, he is a Texan and the importance of this is underscored by the insect-munching, vampirically enslaved Renfield in a surprisingly lucid speech about civic roles and progress. Renfield addresses Arthur, Quincey, and Van Helsing as gentlemen "who by nationality, by heredity, or by the possession of natural gifts, are fitted to hold your respective places in the moving world" (Stoker, *Dracula* 215).[55] Quincey, in Renfield's mind, is the one fitted through nationality; he tells Quincey that he should be proud of his state of Texas, for

> its reception into the Union was a precedent which may have far-reaching effects hereafter, when the Pole and the Tropics may hold allegiance to the Stars and Stripes. The power of Treaty may yet prove a vast engine of enlargement, when the Monroe doctrine takes its true place as a political fable. (Stoker, *Dracula* 215)

Quincey Morris's alliance to the expansionist implications of the 1823 Monroe Doctrine invoked by Renfield is heightened through his name-kinship with the Secretary of State who was the primary author of the doctrine: John Quincy Adams.[56] Renfield's political analysis takes the form of projection making; he looks to the "hereafter," and he predicts a future in which the Monroe Doctrine will be read as a founding document.

Looking to the future in moments of cogency is a specialty of Renfield's; we learn that when he "spoke coherent words for the first time," it was to say "I shall be patient, Master. It is coming—coming—coming!" (Stoker, *Dracula* 98). Renfield's first intelligible words, then, are about the arrival of a vampiric empire. The second speech, similarly made when he is, according to Dr. Seward, "more rational in his speech and manner that

---

[55] This passage has resonance with the novel's insistent, ambivalent juxtapositioning of the ancient and the modern. Renfield's expression "holding your respective places in the moving world" could be read two ways—are they men of the future, who move with a moving world, or men of the past, men who can maintain, keep "hold" of their places, despite the whirl of modernity?

[56] Quincey Morris is not the only character in the novel whose name ties him to the Monroe Doctrine. The doctrine was invoked in 1861 during the Lincoln administration by the Secretary of State who proposed to divert attention from the impending crisis of civil war by launching an effort to liberate Cuba as a part of a campaign to stamp out all traces of European colonialism in the Americas. This Secretary of State was William H. Seward. *Dracula*'s Dr. John Seward is not American, but, as I shall explore later in the chapter, constantly admires Quincey Morris's American characteristics. That Bram Stoker would have infused his novel with specific references to American politics and history is not so surprising considering how diligently he researched the country before touring there with Henry Irving. Jonathan Harker researches Transylvania using the resources of the British Museum (Stoker, *Dracula* 9–10), and before traveling to the United States, Stoker did the same thing. He was disappointed not to find a comprehensive source "from which an absolutely ignorant stranger could draw information," but found copies of an Act of Congress and the Sessional Orders of Congress, and from there built a reference library of works that ranged from school books to histories to books of etiquette (Stoker, *Personal Reminiscences* 1: 368).

I have ever seen him" (Stoker, *Dracula* 214) is about the coming of an American empire. Both of these empires threaten, or threaten to overshadow, Britain. Renfield's specific reference to Texas and the Monroe Doctrine raises the spectre of conflict between the two powers and begins to make clear how Stoker relates United States expansionism to British imperialism. The Monroe Doctrine was an anti-European manifesto: it asserted United States sovereignty on the American continents over and above colonizing claims from European powers. Furthermore, the 1845 announcement of the joint congressional resolution inviting Texas to enter the American Union was followed by the paragraph in which President James K. Polk had asserted United States' title over Oregon. Under the weight of these implications, Renfield's commentary associates the United States with a future dominance that usurps the place of the British as an imperial world power. If the two nations are brothers, there is competition between them.

This is not surprising if we consider that during the eighteen months before *Dracula* was published in June 1897, political hostility between Britain and the United States was running so high that many, especially the British, believed that the two countries would have to go to war. Moreover, the skirmish stemmed from the United States' belief that Britain was spitting in the face of the Monroe Doctrine. The source of conflict was the Venezuela boundary dispute of 1895–96 in which Britain and Venezuela found themselves in an altercation over the boundaries of British Guiana. The conflict centered on the right to control the mouth to the Orinoco River, and the trade artery that the river constituted. It was a conflict, in other words, over a network rather than an actual landmass, and President Grover Cleveland's administration regarded Britain's claim as signaling expansionist intention. On 17 December 17 1895, President Cleveland addressed Congress, asserting that Britain's claim violated the Monroe Doctrine and reaffirmed American intentions to remain dominant in the Western Hemisphere.[57] To many, war appeared to be imminent and soon after President Cleveland's message, there was widespread British—and fairly extensive American—outcry. Overwhelmingly, the protest was based on the notion that an Anglo-American war would be a violent rupture to the Anglo-Saxon race and that a war between the two countries would be a civil war, unnatural and fratricidal. Eight hundred British workers signed a petition declaring that a conflict between Britain and the United States would be "a crime against the laws of God and Man" (Langley 159). In a gesture asserting that the medium was the message, a number of British literary figures *telegraphed* a joint public plea to their American counterparts whom they addressed as "kith and kin," to help end "the crisis in the history of the Anglo-Saxon race" (qtd. in Stead, *Always Arbitrate* 40–41). Thomas Hardy, George Meredith, Alfred Austin, John Ruskin, and Rider Haggard among others, signed their names to the

---

[57] In his account of the conflict, *Struggle for the American Mediterranean: United States-European Rivalry in the Gulf-Caribbean, 1776–1904*, Lester D. Langley points out that this assertion "formally invoked the Monroe Doctrine for the first time by transforming it from a policy statement into a doctrine of hemispheric public law" (153).

claim that for the united Anglo-Saxon race "there is, we trust, such a future as no other race has yet had in the history of the world [...]. We ask you to join us in helping to protect that future" (qtd. in Stead, *Always Arbitrate* 40–41).[58]

Despite initial fears of war, the Venezuelan dispute galvanized the notion of the special racial relationship between America and Britain that would grow to predominate in the twentieth century, and the discourse of Anglo-Saxonism and race-patriotism rose to new heights. Andrew Carnegie explained the "noise" over Venezuela as a product of each country's shared "land hunger," shared because of the shared blood in their veins ("Venezuelan Question" 129). "The English-speaking race," Carnegie states, "is the 'boss' race of the world" ("Venezuelan Question" 130), and "it is a root passion, some of us think a prerogative, of our race to acquire territory" ("Venezuelan Question" 131). He saw the simultaneous grasping for territory as a "race trait," a consequence of both nations being possessed of the same "dominating spirit" ("Venezuelan Question" 134). Stoker's references to Quincey's "dominant spirit" and his portrayal of American-British relations must be read in the light of the Venezuelan dispute. Stoker was in the United States, touring with actor Henry Irving, at the time of the dispute, and had personally met President Cleveland in December 1887 (Stoker, *Personal Reminiscences* 2: 230). The debate completely engulfed Britain in the year immediately prior to the publication of *Dracula*, and it roused enormous public energy around the subject of Anglo-American relations. Stuart Anderson describes how, under the initiative of W. T. Stead, a conference promoting the peaceful solution of arbitration was organized.[59] Once again, the sending of messages, which themselves begged for better communication between the nations, was a dominant feature of the political action. Thousands and thousands of letters, petitions, and memorials arrived at Parliament seeking arbitration and, on 3 March 1896, a huge demonstration was held at Queen's Hall, London, where "those in attendance were entertained by a chorus wearing sashes representing the Union Jack and the Stars and Stripes" (Anderson 106–7).

The Venezuela dispute was a political flash point in which the United States had tested its imperial strength against Britain. The rhetoric of blood-brotherhood that became the popular British antidote to the hostility was thus an enthusiasm tinged with fear about United States' ambition for supremacy. This ambivalence is precisely what we see in *Dracula*. Quincey Morris is cast as both a brother and a rival. He stands with his Anglo-Saxon comrades, valiant against the threat of a vampiric empire from Eastern Europe but he also represents an American imperial power that threatens to overshadow the Britons. The novel, therefore, uses his strengths and then safely kills him off, and the vitality and vigor that have distinguished him throughout the novel pass into his namesake, Jonathan and Mina's child. Quincey Morris plays the role of a reinvigorator; his strong American spirit filters back into British veins through the production of a British child. Although

---

[58] I also draw much of my account from the excellent chapter on the Venezuelan dispute in Stuart Anderson, *Race and Rapprochement: Anglo-Saxonism and Anglo-American Relations, 1895–1904* 95–111.
[59] This was held at Sion College, London, on 4 January 1896.

Morris is himself removed as an active participant, his association with futurity results in him being transfused into it; he promotes the British race with his healthy blood and thus assures its future.

Revisiting the scene of Dracula's death reveals it to be as concerned with the future of American expansionism as it is with the vanquishing of the Count's own imperialist ambitions. The scene is shot through with urgency, as the men race to kill Dracula, and Dracula races to reach the castle, "before the sun should set" (Stoker, *Dracula* 324).[60] The visual focus of this highly topographical scene is always toward the horizon. Earlier in the novel, Quincey gets associated with the horizon in a broken idiom from Van Helsing. The Professor commends Quincey's initiative, saying "Friend Quincey is right! [...]. His head is what you call in plane with the horizon" (Stoker, *Dracula* 257). Van Helsing is perhaps trying to say that Quincey is level headed, but his version of the expression draws together suggestions that Quincey is the man of the future. A Texan, and an American empire, in other words, is over the horizon. It may eventually be an American, rather than a British, empire upon which the sun will not set. In Stoker's own published reflections on the United States, *A Glimpse of America: A Lecture Given at the London Institution*, he refers to America as the "Sunset Land," a land in which the children of Britons can seek their fortune and build a future.[61] The passage is worth quoting at length, as it expounds on Lucy's characterization of Quincey Morris as "so young and so fresh" (Stoker, *Dracula* 58) and expressively characterizes the United States as new and virile:

> We have not, all the world through, so strong an ally, so close a friend. America has got over her childhood. The day of petty jealousy has gone by. Columbia is strong enough in her knowledge of her own power and beauty to sail, unruffled and unawed, into the salon of old Time amidst the queens of the world. There is every reason we can think of why the English on both sides of the Atlantic should hold together as one. Our history is their history—our fame is their pride—their progress is our glory. They are bound to us, and we to them, by every tie of love and sympathy; on our side, by the bright hopes of parents who send their children to seek fortune in the Sunset Land; on theirs, by the old remembrances of home and common kin, and by the memories of their buried dead. We are bound each to each by the instinct of a common race, which makes brotherhood and the love of brothers a

---

[60] "At sunset," Mina explains, "the Thing [...] would take new freedom and could in any of many forms elude all pursuit" (Stoker, *Dracula* 322).

[61] The phrase "Sunset Land" was often applied to the American West. In 1871, for example, Rev. John Todd published a book called *The Sunset Land; or, The Great Pacific Slope* (Boston: Lee and Shepard) about California. Stoker's first published story collection, a book of children's fairy stories called *Under the Sunset*, published in 1882, imagines "a fair land Under The Sunset" that is "like our own Country in many ways." Although a highly fantastical land, Stoker's interest in cross-national racial brotherhood shines through: "If a child from that Country was beside a child here you could not tell the difference between them [...]. They talk the same language as we do ourselves. [...] When they come to us in their dreams we do not know they are strangers; and when we go to their Country in our dreams we seem to be at home" (Stoker, *Under the Sunset* 2).

natural law; a law which existed at the first, and which, after the lapse of a century, still exists—whose tenets were never broken, even by the shocks of war, and whose keen perception was never dimmed in the wilderness of stormy sea between.
(Stoker, *Glimpse of America* 47–48)[62]

This passage resolves the relationship of the United States to England through the language of functional, healthy networks of blood-ties. The United States features as a friend, ally, fellow ruler of the seas, child and descendant. But Stoker wraps all of these roles up in the mantle of racial brotherhood and the "instinct of a common race."

This sense of Anglo-American brotherhood is most certainly underscored in the ending of *Dracula*, an emphasis that alleviates British anxiety about United States imperial competition. As Jonathan supports the dying Quincey, and the sun finally falls, Quincey points and calls out for the men to look at Mina: " 'Now God be thanked,' he cries, 'that all has not been in vain! See! The snow is not more stainless than her forehead! The curse has passed away!'" (Stoker, *Dracula* 326). The mark that fades from Mina's forehead is, as Talia Schaffer points out, like the mark of Cain.[63] What Schaffer does not point out, is that the mark of Cain is the sign of murderous dissent between brothers, commonly interpreted as a stain of race difference. When Quincey so joyfully declares, "The curse has passed away!" it reminds us of Stoker's declaration in *A Glimpse of America* that "the day of petty jealousy has gone by" between the United States and Britain. This scene thus references and reiterates the importance of the bonds of white brotherhood: the mark of shame that signaled the "unnatural" slaying of one brother by another is dissolved and simultaneously invokes Stoker's literary and personal friendship. The embrace between Jonathan and Quincey also marks them as blood brothers. Throughout the novel, the exchange of blood has resulted in kinship, and as Quincey's blood gushes over Jonathan, their brotherhood is sealed.

After collapsing with "blood [...] spurting through his fingers" (Stoker, *Dracula* 324), Quincey dies in Jonathan's lap with his head on Jonathan's shoulder (Stoker, *Dracula* 326). Several scholars have shown how the intimacy of this scene, the consequent birth of little Quincey and the flowing of Morris's "spirit" into the child, signals that this is a homosexually procreative union.[64] I would like to go one step further with the critical readings that

---

[62] Stoker later wrote that when he met H. M. Stanley, Stanley said of the book that it "had in it more information about America than any other book that had ever been written" (Irving 1: 369).

[63] More precisely, Schaffer reads the scar on Mina's forehead as the mark of *Caine*. Hall Caine was one of Stoker's closest friends, a fellow novelist and the person to whom the novel is dedicated. Schaffer correlates Mina's mark with the "foul stain" that Hall Caine felt Oscar Wilde's crimes, or criminalization, brought upon the literary craft (Schaffer 418).

[64] See Schaffer 419–20 for an excellent reading of how Quincey's spurting blood functions as semen, and how little Quincey is the result of procreative homosexual sex. In " 'Kiss Me with Those Red Lips': Gender and Inversion in Bram Stoker's *Dracula*" (1984), Christopher Craft similarly notes the curious fluidity of bodily fluids in *Dracula*—how blood, semen and milk morph into each other—and goes on to explore the homoerotic and homosexual implications of this fluidity (107–33).

see little Quincey as homosexually sired to ask what follows his birth? The novel's answer is clear: little Quincey himself begets homosocial reunion. Stoker tells us that the child *brings about* union between men: a confederacy, a brotherhood. His "bundle of names"—which calls to mind the bundle of papers that Jonathan tells us comprise the novel—"links all our little band of men together" (Stoker, *Dracula* 326) and unifies the narrative.[65] Little Quincey literally embodies the links or "bonds" of brotherhood that Stoker describes in *A Glimpse of America* and carries them into the future. The child is the manifestation of the healthy homosocial network and the living proof of an ultimate triumph over the unhealthy, undead homosexual union that Dracula attempted with Jonathan Harker.[66] Just as Jack London seeks to build the bonds of imperial brotherhood by avoiding the procreative female body, this brotherhood also forms across the body of a woman, which disappears into an ellipsis in the narrative. The reader is present throughout Quincey Morris's death scene, and then the novel cuts to seven years later and the news of little Quincey and his bundle of names. Mina's carriage of the child and her birthing of him is elided. The correspondence between son and namesake takes place "between men," to invoke Eve Kosofsky Sedgwick's term. Rather than producing, Mina remembers, organizes, and archives. This function lies at the root of her name: "min" means "remembrance, memory, mention" (Oxford English Dictionary), and it was clearly something Stoker liked to see in a woman. In *The Jewel of the Seven Stars*, Stoker has another female character notable for her memory: Margaret, who is described as "remarkably clever and acute-minded [...] with a prodigious memory; so that her store of knowledge, gathered unthinkingly bit by bit, had grown to proportions that many a scholar might have envied" (78–79). Mina functions as an index to the material that she gathers and transcribes. She provides men with access to the archives that they cannot read because it is in shorthand or on a wax cylinder. Regenia Gagnier explains this mnemonic trope in *Dracula*, through identifying two models of generation: "the evolutionary or genealogical mode [...] represented as 'memory,' and the non-rooted, non-unique operations of modern science, technology and bureaucracy, or information [...] represented as 'fact' and 'records' " (147). *Dracula* rejects the genealogical, heterosexual mode of production for little Quincey, preferring instead a bureaucratic, organizational production that makes a list of men's names. This homosexually procreative posse and Quincey's birth-mother Mina together collate the two models of generation differentiated by Gagnier. The posse and Mina are both agents of memory and all things secretarial, neither allied with evolution nor linear genealogy. Both Mina and Jonathan are themselves orphans. Little Quincey is therefore severed from a conglomeration of grandparents and forebears, and is birthed instead out of a contemporaneous concurrency of friends and lovers, who band together under the name of a dead

---

[65] Jonathan refers to the birth of little Quincey, then describes retrieving the "papers from the safe" and reviewing "the mass of material" from which the novel will be organized (Stoker, *Dracula* 326).

[66] For an excellent analysis of Dracula's failed attempt to seduce Harker, and the homoerotics between Dracula and Harker more generally, see Craft 107–33.

friend and lover. Stoker ends his novel with a conservative capstone of marriage and babies and futures: they can look backward, Harker notes, "without despair, for Godalming and Seward are both happily married" (326) and Van Helsing dandles Little Quincey on his knee (327). On the one hand, little Quincey is an expression of the cult of the child-as-future that Lee Edelman critiques in *No Future* for its phobic relation to queerness. He is the palliative to the vision of near apocalypse that forms the bulk of the novel. On the other hand, little Quincey is a fractured product of reproductive futurism: his (elided) birth is antigenealogical, and the mandate for him to remember this adventure will have to be made through a mass of typewriting, a plurality of men, and his mother.

Mina thus functions as a secretary for the joint authoring of little Quincey by the male vampire-hunters.[67] Just as the concluding homosexual union of the male characters occurs over the elided body of a woman, a woman formed the pretext for homosocial bonding at the beginning of the novel too. The woman in this instance is Lucy Westenra, and her body and her love disappear behind the only text authored by Quincey Morris—a letter to his friend and British aristocrat, Arthur Holmwood (who becomes Lord Godalming across the course of the novel). This correspondence "between men" is mailed, or maled, across the affections of Lucy Westenra. On proposing marriage to Lucy, Quincey learned from her that his bid to win her hand would not succeed because she loved Arthur. The very next day, Quincey wrote to Arthur, setting aside his feeling for Lucy and instead rousing and reiterating their own bonds of friend- and comradeship:

> My dear Art,—
> We've told yarns by the camp-fire in the prairies; and dressed one another's wounds after trying a landing at the Marquesas; and drunk healths on the shore of Titicaca. There are more yarns to be told and other wounds to be healed, and another health to be drunk. Won't you let this be at my camp-fire tomorrow night? I have no hesitation in asking you, as I know a certain lady is engaged to a certain dinner-party and that you are free [...].
>
> (Stoker, *Dracula* 62)

Quincey not only invokes memories of their campfire days, but also flirtatiously extends the language to the present, inviting Arthur to revisit the "camp-fire" in his home, the rugged rendezvous standing in opposition to the civilized "dinner-party" that the "lady" will be attending. The letter seeks to paper over a potential schism between the men, one

---

[67] As Jennifer Fleissner argues, the secretarial woman was a force to be reckoned with in the late nineteenth century, and Fleissner shows that feminist readings of *Dracula*, even those as groundbreaking as Jennifer Wicke's "Vampiric Typewriting: *Dracula* and Its Media," have tended to anachronistically underestimate the agency of the stenographic woman. As I contended in chapter 3, women's clerical work was not necessarily alarming to a late-century reader, and Fleissner's article takes care to distinguish between Mina's valuable contributions to vampire-hunting and the vamped and vamping threats of other female characters in the novel. Jennifer Fleissner, "Dictation Anxiety: The Stenographer's Stake in *Dracula*," *Nineteenth-Century Contexts* 22 (2000): 417–55.

that a woman creates. Quincey seeks to revive a friendship where he fears resentment might fester. The two men could be rivals, jealous of each other's relationship to Lucy, but instead Quincey appeals for comradeship. Once again, this matches the language in which Stoker describes relations between America and England: "days of petty jealousy are gone."[68] Quincey's reference to dressing wounds calls to mind the homoerotic intimacy written of by Bram Stoker's idol and ardent pen pal, Walt Whitman, in his poetry drawn from his experiences as a wound-dresser in civil war hospitals.[69] Stoker wrote of Whitman's nursing in *Personal Reminiscences of Henry Irving*, emphasizing that Whitman's role was heroic and comradely: "A man amongst men! With a herculean physical strength and stamina; with courage and hope and belief that never seemed to tire or stale he moved amongst those legions of the wounded and sick like a very angel of comfort materialised to an understanding man" (Irving 2: 101). Stoker's portrait of Whitman as a muscular "angel of comfort" recalls how Trollope flattered himself that his postal work, achieved riding manfully on horseback across Ireland, made him a "beneficent angel" (see chapter 2, 81). Both portraits invoke angels as messengers and agents of affective cohesion. Comradeship is the result. Quincey tells Arthur they will be joined by another comrade-in-arms, John Seward, with whom they had spent time in Korea. Quincey and John, Quincey writes, "both want to mingle our weeps over the wine-cup, and to drink a health" (Stoker, *Dracula* 62) to Arthur and Lucy. This desire to blend their tears together over wine prefigures the blending of their bloods in both Lucy and little Quincey's veins and enacts the metamorphosis of fluids—water into wine into blood—that dominates the novel. Arthur's reply by telegram is immediate, unreservedly enthusiastic —"Count me in every time"—and tantalizing: "I bear messages," he writes, "which will make both your ears tingle" (Stoker, *Dracula* 62).

Arthur clearly continues to make Quincey's ears tingle, as the two men proceed to spend the bulk of the novel joined at the hip. Quincey functions as a kind of erotic hub for the Holmwood, Seward, and Harker brotherhood, one that mirrors both Lucy Westenra's wish that she could marry three men and the way she functions as the erotic meeting point for the love and blood of Arthur, Quincey, and John Seward. Quincey ends his life in an embrace with Jonathan, is admired passionately by John, and spends most of the novel as the constant companion of Arthur. This companionship begins when Arthur returns to his family home after the death of Lucy, and Quincey accompanies him. Quincey literally replaces Lucy and fulfills the homoerotic model of being

---

[68] This portrayal of America and Britain as competitive lovers or siblings was prevalent in the late 1890s. For example, in a political paper issued by the *Review of Reviews* called "Always Arbitrate Before You Fight: An Appeal to All English-Speaking Folk" (1896), editor W. T. Stead cites a Professor Van Holst of Chicago University who notes that the two countries are "rivals" who are "jealous" of each other (6).

[69] Edward Carpenter refers to Whitman as a poet of homogenic love, "the enthusiasm of whose poems on Comradeship is only paralleled by the devotedness of his labours for his wounded brothers in the American Civil War" (qtd. in White, *Nineteenth-Century Writings* 127). For original, see Edward Carpenter, *Homogenic Love and Its Place in a Free Society* (1894).

comrades-in-arms that John Addington Symonds describes: "Fraternity in arms played for the Greek race the same part as the idealisation of women for the knighthood of feudal Europe. [...] these comrades [were] staunch to each other in their love and elevated by their friendship to the pitch of noblest enthusiasm" (*Greek Poets* 220–22). In fighting vampiric forces from feudal Europe, Quincey and Arthur put aside the idealization of women and become a dynamic duo. From the point of Lucy's death onward, their undifferentiated coupling is almost comical in its insistence: they travel, knock on doors, shrink back, take care of horses, and "follow up clues" (Stoker, *Dracula* 236) together, and they appear simultaneously, clad in pajamas and slippers, when Renfield is near death.

It is only in the tracking of Dracula that variance emerges between the two men. The crew is planning how to track down and sanitize the Count's earth boxes that he has scattered across London. Lord Godalming says that he may "be of some use here," having servants, horses, and carriages, who can be posted across London. Morris objects that carriages with "heraldic adornments in a byeway of Walworth or Mile End would attract too much attention [...]. It seems to me that we ought to take cabs" (Stoker, *Dracula* 257). Like Doyle's Jefferson Hope, who becomes a cab driver in order to effectively and anonymously track his victims round London, Quincey understands how to enter the city's transport networks. Like the postal system, the cabs are accessible to all and anonymous—an organized miscellany. As an English blue blood, Lord Godalming does not know how to blend with the city. He and his carriages are too marked, too notable. Quincey is the one who thinks along the right lines: it is at this point that Van Helsing commends Quincey for having his head "in plane with the horizon" (Stoker, *Dracula* 257). The Professor repeats his praise later when Quincey proposes they hunt Dracula armed with the American-made Winchester rifles, saying "Quincey's head is level at all times, but most so when there is to hunt" (Stoker, *Dracula* 282). The aristocratic Godalming is by no means defunct; he demonstrates strength and resilience throughout the novel and his old boy networks play an important role in the information-collection central to tracking down the Count,[70] but he works best in partnership with his American friend who has the survival skills supposedly typical of his nation.

These skills are described and praised by John Seward, who also casts and praises Quincey for his role as a hunter. Like the American Jefferson Hope in "A Study in Scarlet," who is described by Doyle as a passionate "man of action," Quincey Morris is consistently portrayed as a rugged type,[71] who takes command in combat scenarios. While the crew is waiting anxiously for the return of Dracula in the Green Park house, John Seward appreciates Quincey Morris's leadership:

---

[70] For an incisive reading of how imperial control over information is what defeats Dracula the "colonial creature," summarized as "The dead travel fast but data travels faster," see Thomas Richards, *The Imperial Archive* (London: Verso, 1993), 62.

[71] In *The Shoulder of Shasta*, a Western that Stoker published in 1895 after touring California with the Lyceum, there is a rough prototype of Quincey Morris, called Grizzly Dick, a frontiersman who similarly carries a Winchester rifle and a bowie knife.

> I could not but admire, even at such a moment, the way in which a dominant spirit asserted itself. In all our hunting parties and adventures in different parts of the world, Quincey Morris had always been the one to arrange the plan of action, and Arthur and I had been accustomed to obey him implicitly. Now, the old habit seemed to be renewed instinctively. With a swift glance round the room, he at once laid out our plan of attack, and, without speaking a word, with a gesture, placed us each in position.
>
> <div align="right">(Stoker, <i>Dracula</i> 266)</div>

Seward's reference to Quincey's "spirit" is echoed in Mina's thoughts that close the novel about how some of Quincey's "spirit" lives on in her son. As in "A Study in Scarlet," it is the American who adopts the role of the up-and-coming Anglo-Saxon imperialist. To understand this, it is worth reviewing a list of the "different parts of the world" that we learn Quincey has hunted in. In his letter to Arthur, Quincey mentions the Marquesas, Titicaca, and Korea. We also learn that he has been in the Pampas (Stoker, *Dracula* 138). These hunting grounds are all places in South America or the South Pacific, places in which America was flexing its expansionist muscles either alongside, or in place of, European interests in the late nineteenth century. In the 1890s, Britain and America both had military presence in Korea, for example, united in resistance to Japan's growing commercial control. The references to South America link Quincey to Renfield's praise of the Monroe Doctrine and its declaration of the American continent as out-of-bounds to European colonizers. Through these geographical references, Quincey is clearly delineated as a neoimperialist.

Stoker celebrated the United States' imperialist mood and ventures. In his 1906 description of Henry Irving's 1888 performance at the United States Military Academy at West Point, Stoker recalled his pride at seeing "over the proscenium of the little stage the flags of Britain and America draped together and united by a branch of palm," and he admires the bright, youthful cadets—"splendid young fellows"—who expressed their comradeship by flouting regulations and together throwing their caps into the air (Irving 1: 293). Stoker remarks that "every one" of the cadets "justified himself later on the deadly heights of Santiago or amid the jungles of the Philippines" (Irving 1: 295).[72] These victories marked the acquisition of America's first overseas empire, and Stoker's "thrill" and "pride" over the entwined, united American and British flags is the pride of a reunionist and a race-patriot. Like Kipling, Stoker looked to the Spanish-American war as proof that America had accepted the white man's burden and had come of age as an imperial power; he wrote of his "joy that England's first-born child has arrived at so noble a stature" (*Glimpse* 47). But as a *grown* child of England, the refederation of the nations

---

[72] Stoker is referring here to the Spanish-American war of 1898, famous for the Santiago battle fought on the slopes of San Juan Hill, following which America annexed the Philippines and Puerto Rico through the Treaty of Paris ratified in 1899.

that he desired had to be figured not as the prodigal son's return to the fold, but as a fraternal alliance formed through healthy, homosocial networks of blood and nation.

Throughout his descriptions of both Quincey and the West Point cadets, Stoker emphasizes their youth and vitality. In *Dracula*, Americans are the answer to the vampiric imperial decay that threatens Britain. When John Seward admires Quincey's fortitude and moral fiber, he admires him for his racial strength, his generative potential:

> What a fine fellow is Quincey! I believe in my heart of hearts that he suffered as much about Lucy's death as any of us; but he bore himself through it like a moral Viking. If America can go on breeding men like that, she will be a power in the world indeed.
>
> (Stoker, *Dracula* 156)

Seward makes it clear that Quincey has withstood the strain better than the "sad" and "broken" (Stoker, *Dracula* 152) Holmwood and also better than Van Helsing who has what Seward describes as a "fit of hysterics" (Stoker, *Dracula* 157). Holmwood's and Van Helsing's afflictions are signs of degenerative decay, the consequence of which is defined as loss of imperial future: Holmwood cries out that "the whole of life seems gone from me all at once, and there is nothing in the wide world for me to live for" (Stoker, *Dracula* 152). Nothing in the "wide world" indeed: this *loss of interest* in the global is the perspective of the exhausted imperialist. So Stoker turns to the nation that he considers to be of the same racial stock as England, bound to them by ties of blood and interest, in order to end the narrative with a reinvigorated child. The regenerative act— the final embrace between Jonathan and Quincey—is at once same-sexed and, as Stoker conceived it, same-raced. American brotherhood thus functions here to anchor Britain against the stormy imperial waters of racial difference and degeneration.

Is, however, the American proto-imperialist in league with the Transylvanian proto-imperialist, instead of the British? Quincey Morris's death-day may coincide with little Quincey's birthday some time later, but it is also the same date as Count Dracula's death, and several critics have asked if there are links between Quincey and Dracula. Stephen Arata wonders if Quincey has more alliance to Dracula than the "Crew of Light" in the novel. Franco Moretti similarly links them by characterizing them both as traveling salesmen for monopoly capitalism,[73] and David Glover, too, pairs the two characters when he calls them both "frontiersmen" (74). There are certainly intriguing parallels drawn between the vampire and the American. One of these occurs when Morris prepares to confront Dracula and tells Harker:

---

[73] Although Moretti's Marxist reading of capitalist economies in the novel is an important one, his repeated characterization of Quincey as a "financier" has no basis in the text. We need rather to see him as a neoimperialist, and acknowledge that in this novel capitalism and expansionism go hand in hand.

"I shall not wait for any opportunity," said Morris. "When I see the box I shall open it and destroy the monster, though there were a thousand men looking on, and if I am to be wiped out for a moment!" I grasped his hand instinctively and found it as firm as a piece of steel. I think he understood my look; I hope he did.

(Stoker, *Dracula* 285)

The phrase Harker uses to describe the strength of Quincey's handshake recalls Harker's encounters with Dracula. Harker "meets" Dracula twice—once when the vampire is disguised as a coach driver, then as the Count—and on each occasion Harker remarks on the "prodigious strength" (Stoker, *Dracula* 17) of Dracula's hands. In fact, he uses the same image that he uses for Quincey, saying that Dracula has a "grip of steel" (Stoker, *Dracula* 17). I am not persuaded, however, by readings that stabilize these connections and argue that Quincey is in literal, conspiratorial league with the Count. The parallels between them serve rather to show different models of imperialism. Their likeness is also symptomatic of a general fluidity that exists between the novel's male characters. We could, for example, also draw strong links between Jonathan Harker and Dracula. In many ways Dracula is not so different from an English nobleman.[74] And when Harker subdues the gypsies, it exactly mirrors a scene early on in the novel when Dracula, disguised as a coachman, drives Harker to his castle. As wolves attack the vehicle, Jonathan hears Dracula's voice "raised in a tone of imperious command, and [...] as he swept his long arms, as though brushing aside some impalpable obstacle, the wolves fell back" (Stoker, *Dracula* 20). The men, including Dracula, are radically fluid. Their blood mixes together, they look like each other, they shadow each other's actions. They are capable of being aroused, inflamed, and influenced by those close to them—which leads us to understand that the alliances they form, rather than their individual characteristics, are paramount. In this story of good and evil, men must ally themselves with the forces of good, but it is *alliance* itself, rather than the polarities, that emerges as the primary term. It is alliance that will determine whether the resultant network of men, blood, and empire will be a good or a bad one, a vampiric or a regenerative one. In this way, Dracula and Quincey *are* paired, but not as coconspirators, rather as opposite examples of what kind of blood network could be valued and should be embraced by Britain.

When Harker subdues the natives, he overawes them with his "manifest singleness of purpose" (Stoker, *Dracula* 324). The word "manifest" attaches particularly to Jonathan and Mina throughout the novel. In his journal, Jonathan notes that through the labor of going "over all the diaries again and again" they learn to resist the pain and fear inflicted by Dracula and find instead "something of a guiding purpose manifest throughout" (Stoker, *Dracula* 274) which leads Mina—still wearing Dracula's scar on her forehead—to suppose

---

[74] In "Dracula's Legacy," Friedrich Kittler remarks how Dracula is like the English gentleman: he "forgets not to speak English when he is not even speaking to his guest [...] dislikes garlic as otherwise Anglo-Saxons dislike it [... and his] words are simultaneously commands" (153).

that "we are the instruments of ultimate good" (Stoker, *Dracula* 275). Mina then helps the team track Dracula down by rewiring her vampiric connection with him under hypnosis so that the team gains information about his whereabouts; "some new guiding power [was] in her manifest" (Stoker, *Dracula* 314). This rewiring is another form of the postal interception that the Count had earlier exercised on Jonathan and reveals much about how networks function in the book. Dracula's telepathic correspondence with Mina gets co-opted to good ends: if, as Stephen Arata describes, *Dracula* plays out a fear of "reverse colonization" and of the vampire-imperialist traveling from East to West to overcome him in his own land, the vampire-hunters merely reverse the lines of communication. That they do this through a version of manifest destiny—a manifest "guiding purpose" whereby Jonathan slays the Count with "manifest singleness of purpose"—returns us to the question of American influence and the geographical imperative to Anglo-American reunion that Elihu Burritt had endorsed.

John L. O'Sullivan, the American who coined (or in some accounts, merely popularized) the phrase *manifest destiny*, first used it in an article on the annexation of Texas.[75] He had written earlier on the same theme, if not using that phrase, when he wrote of how America was "destined for better deeds" than the "monarchies and aristocracies of antiquity" (O'Sullivan, "Great Nation" 427). "Our annals," he writes, "describe no scenes of horrid carnage, where men were led on by hundreds of thousands to slay one another, dupes and victims to emperors, kings, nobles, demons in the human form called heroes" (O'Sullivan, "Great Nation" 427). O'Sullivan's account is grimly fantastical, ignoring the devastation and removal of Native nations and flying in the face of the internecine struggle over slavery that was on the horizon. His words, however, resonate with Dracula's equally romanticized lecture on Transylvanian history, when the Count tells Harker that "there is hardly a foot of soil in all this region that has not been enriched by the blood of men, patriots or invaders" (Stoker, *Dracula* 27). Dracula boasts to Harker of the very things O'Sullivan deplores, addressing him as a fellow imperialist, being bred from the loins of a similarly blood-soaked nation. These comparisons are made in order that Stoker's novel can adjudicate between good and bad blood empires. The United States emerges from this comparison as a virtuous, white version of Transylvania, a nation that has chosen the correct form of network.

At the end of the nineteenth century, concern about the future of the British Empire manifested itself in debate about good and bad forms of empire. In the opening pages of Joseph Conrad's 1899 novel *Heart of Darkness*, Marlowe travels down the Thames thinking of the Roman Empire. He concludes that the Romans stood for a degenerate, power-hungry imperialism different from that of nineteenth-century Briton: "What saves us is efficiency—the devotion to efficiency," he claims (Conrad 10).[76] The Romans "were no

---

[75] This article, "Annexation," was published in the July-August 1845 edition of the *United States Magazine and Democratic Review*, which O'Sullivan also edited.

[76] For a discussion of the "national efficiency movement" of the late nineteenth century, see Daniel Bivona, *British Imperial Literature, 1870–1940: Writing and the Administration of Empire*, particularly chapter 1 and conclusion.

colonists, their administration was merely a squeeze [...]. They were conquerors, and for that you want only brute force" (Conrad 10). Under Marlowe's terms, the British are bureaucrats rather than brutes, administrators rather than conquerors. John Addington Symonds used a similar condemnation of the Romans to bolster his vision of Greek love as civilized: "The nobler type of masculine love developed by the Greeks is [...] that which more than anything else distinguishes the Greeks from the barbarians of their own time, from the Romans" (qtd. in White, *Nineteenth-Century Writings* 167). Just as the Romans' imperial incontinence was the wrong kind of expansionism, Jonathan imagines Dracula seeking to "satiate his lust for blood, and create a new and ever-widening circle" of vampires (Stoker, *Dracula* 53). Vampiric blood-exchange wastes and decays. Homosocial Anglo-American unity, on the other hand, is portrayed as a good form of blood-exchange, regenerative and procreative.

Transylvania and London are portrayed by Stoker as disconcertingly similar. Dracula describes Transylvania as a "whirlpool of European races" (Stoker, *Dracula* 33), and London is similarly described by him as containing "whirl and rush of humanity" (Stoker, *Dracula* 26). Harker also thinks of London as a crowded, "teeming" (Stoker, *Dracula* 53) metropolis. Stoker's metaphors of waterways and organisms are reminiscent of Conan Doyle's/Watson's description of London as a cesspool. It could be said of Count Dracula that he, like Watson, seeks "kith and kin in England," and thus "naturally gravitated to London, that great cesspool into which all the loungers and idlers of the Empire are irresistibly drained" (Doyle 15). Thus, if we see the United States and Transylvania as two imperial options for Britain and its metropole, what hangs in the balance is the British Empire's destiny as an imperial network. That Transylvania and the United States are opposed, if comparable, is clear even from their names. "Transylvania" means "across the woods"—the prefix "trans-" is a designation of travel and flux. The *United* States, on the other hand, is a designation of confederation. This is why Stoker so pointedly emphasizes the Monroe Doctrine as a fable of future unity. A "united" brotherhood is what he would desire imperial networks to bring about for Britain, over and against the dangerous flows and refluxes of Transylvania. In *Dracula*, Stoker portrays an age and a culture in which networks and the annihilation of time and space had helped build an empire, but an empire that is then susceptible from both within and without. In the face of internal exhaustion and external infiltration, Britain needs to shore up its destiny; Stoker turns to the United States to consolidate a Blood Empire that can transfuse fresh, vital Anglo-Saxon blood back into Britain in order that the mother country might regenerate.

Dracula depicts a fin de siècle Britain tussling with the problems of imperial and textual reflux. Just as the postal service opened up a world for the British imperialist, by the end of the nineteenth century, fiction begins to emerge in which the colonized subject uses these same lines of communication to bite back. George Sims described the goal of his 1883 exposé of London slum housing, *How the Poor Live*, as "to awaken in the general mind" an interest in "a dark continent that is within easy walking distance of the General Post Office" (103, 1). Using a conceit common to late-century "urban explorer" writing, Sims racializes class and maintains that the London slums contain a "colony"(10) of "wild races" and "savage tribes" (1) like those found in "far-off" (3) lands.[77] Sims references the Post Office as a standard of universality, proximity, and civilization, hailing it as an institution to which every reader can relate, one that stands for state-sponsored enlightenment over the contrastingly "dark" barbarism of the poor. The primary goal of the passage, though, is to shock, to "awaken," the reader. And the shock derives from a simple threat: while we should clearly be ashamed that London is home to the kind of deprivation seen on "other" continents, we should also be afraid or at least thrilled that this barbarism is "within easy walking distance" of the General Post Office. If the Post Office is a dissemination engine, then the possibility that this barbarism can be spread by the P.O. is very real. This contaminatory threat prefaces Sims's recurrent theme that the dissemination of civilization can de-civilize Britain. Britons can be so concerned with extending themselves to the "Zenanas, the Aborigines, and the South Sea Islanders," (Sims 3) that they ignore the white poor at their door. Sims thus presents a variation on the old theme of the postal network "annihilating time and space." Sims invokes the Post Office to remind readers of *both* the glory and the excesses of dissemination and Britain's imperial overextension. Organized information networks do not keep that which is nonwhite, heathen, and undesirable at a distance; it rather brings these regions and inhabitants into proximity with the upright citizen. Sims sites darkness in the national bosom, revealing the possibility that through the G.P.O., "the empire writes back."

GAY MEN AT THE POST OFFICE

In pursuit of the conceit of "writing back," I am going to turn to three gay writers, who found that the Post Office could accommodate the kinds of diversity they delighted in: Walt Whitman, Edward Carpenter … and Bram Stoker. In this section, I turn from the later Stoker as a straight writer of paranoid fantasy fiction and travel back to his younger, passionate self; a man who loved men. Walt Whitman had several transatlantic correspondents, whom he valued for their long-distance fervor. In his introduction to the Everyman edition of *Leaves of Grass* in 1912, biographer Horace Traubel recalled: "He would tell me about his supporters. 'They are very few,' he would say: 'but they are devoted.' He one day gave me a bunch of letters to take to the post-office. They were all to Englishmen." Two of these fervent Englishmen were Edward Carpenter and Bram Stoker. Stoker visited Whitman in Camden three times, and then almost two years after Whitman's death, he returned to Philadelphia to receive a bequest made in Whitman's will. Thomas Donaldson, who looked after Whitman's affairs, handed Stoker a "large envelope" saying,

---

[77] Jack London, for example, also equivalencing of the dark races with the benighted classes, scoffs at the churchgoing Londoners who ignore the poverty and suffering of East Enders and instead make money from their suffering, taking profits which "come to them from the East End stained with the blood of children" and sending them to "educate the black boys of the Soudan" (282). Elsewhere, London's comparisons are more direct: "A woman of the lower Ghetto classes is as much the slave of her husband as is the Indian squaw" (London 222).

"That is for you from Walt Whitman. I have been keeping it till I should see you." The envelope contained original lecture notes and a letter to Donaldson in which Whitman said, "Enclosed I send a full report of my Lincoln Lecture for our friend Bram Stoker" (Stoker, *Personal Reminiscences* 2: 111). Stoker closes his narration of this exchange with one dramatic, vampiric line: "This was my Message from the Dead" (*Personal Reminiscences* 2: 111). This was not a Dead Letter, gone astray between addressees, but rather an undead, or immortal letter. It was a "message" of the power of one man's love for another to overcome death, and for this love to be intensified through spatial and temporal delay, across oceans and national borders and kept alive in the hands of an intermediary.[78] Whitman's "Death of Lincoln" lecture was written about a man who "gets almost nearer me than anybody else" (Traubel, *With Walt Whitman* 1: 38). Whitman too remains beloved and alive to Stoker, after his death. Stoker regarded *Dracula* as a study of immortality[79] and in both that novel and other writings, he displays keen interest in the passions that can be animated by both fast and delayed mail.

In *Personal Reminiscences of Henry Irving* (1906), Stoker recalls first writing to Whitman in 1876, and is still—thirty years on—irrepressibly chuffed that Whitman replied so fast. Stoker sounds like an infatuated youth when he backs up his boast with a calculation about the post: "Mails were fewer and slower thirty years ago than they are to-day. My letter was written in the early morning of February 15. Walt Whitman wrote in answer on March 6, and I received it exactly two weeks later; so that he must have written very soon after receipt of my letter" (*Personal Reminiscences* 2: 97). Stoker, who Whitman called "a broth of a boy,"[80] got into quite a lather setting up his postal relation with Whitman. The letter that Stoker recalls writing on the morning of 15 February 1876, was in fact dated 14 February : written, in other words, on Valentine's Day.[81] This Valentine letter is itself merely a cover letter for another, which Stoker enclosed. The enclosure is a passionate

---

[78] The intermediary in this case is Donaldson, a biographer and clerk-manager of Whitman's affairs. Stoker occupied the same set of relations to his beloved Henry Irving. And according to biographer Daniel Farson, Irving was unable to requite the love—except once, postally. Farson describes Irving addressing Stoker as "You, above all men whom I hold dear …" as an afterthought, written literally on the posterior exterior of a letter: it was "scribbled on the back of an envelope […] written in indelible pencil in Irving's seismograph hand" (Farson 198). For more on love-notes written on the rear of envelopes, see chapter 5.

[79] On 24 May 1897, Stoker sent a copy of *Dracula* to his friend and four-time prime minister W. E. Gladstone. In the accompanying letter, Stoker proposes that a vampire tale may "interest you who have made so bold a guess at 'immortalililty' [sic]." Add. 44525 f. 221–22, 222.

[80] Thomas Donaldson, *Walt Whitman the Man.* (New York: Francis P. Harper, 1896), 82.

[81] I am reading Stoker's letter as a Valentine's card. By this time, Valentine's Day was a postally celebrated holiday in both England and America. The long-established practice of exchanging Valentine's gifts and verse had turned into the sending of romantic and racy mail on 14 February. Elizabeth Gaskell, for example, features the tradition in her novels *Mary Barton* (1848) and *Mr. Harrison's Confessions* (1851). In his study of the American "Post Age," David M. Henkin observes "Valentine's Day foregrounded the anonymity of postal exchange and also presented a rather promiscuous social picture" (151). For a history of the Valentine, see Frank Staff, *The Valentine and Its Origins* (London: Lutterworth Press, 1969). For an account of how cheap postage enabled "Valentine mania," see also Leigh Eric Schmidt, "The Fashioning of a Modern Holiday: St. Valentine's Day, 1840–1870," *Winterthur Portfolio* 28 no. 4 (Winter 1993): 209–45.

epistle written four years earlier, in 1872, which Stoker had been too shy to send and had kept in a drawer for all those years. Rather than diminishing his passion, however, the delay of delivery has intensified it: "The four years which have elapsed have made me love your work fourfold" (Traubel 4: 180). The original letter is structured by a series of invitations for Whitman to burn it (Traubel 4: 181), invitations that are both anxious and arousing: if Whitman does go ahead and burn the letter, he will, Stoker coyly observes, "miss the pleasure of this next sentence" (Traubel 4: 182). In the paradoxical syntax of the closet, Stoker veers between timidity and bravura, disclosure and concealment:

> If you are going to read this letter any further I should tell you that I am not prepared to "give up all else" so far as words go. The only thing I am prepared to give up is prejudice, and before I knew you I had begun to throw overboard my cargo, but it is not all gone yet. I do not know how you will take this letter.
> (Traubel 4: 182).

Whitman took the letter well and embraced Stoker as a friend. But like Dracula clinging to his boxes of mold, Stoker would indeed prove incapable of throwing overboard the kind of "cargo" against which Whitman's life and poetry stood. It was a cargo of sexual shame, fear of disgrace, and a taste for censorship. In the first letter Stoker strains against the leash of his "conservative country" and toward the "truths" he finds "sung" by Whitman, but it is only in postal intervals that Stoker can touch those truths: both the delay of posting this original letter and later its passage to another (kind of) country allow Stoker to express homosexual comradeship as a blessing. He closes the epistle "but at all events I thank you for all the love and sympathy you have given me in common with my kind" (Traubel 4: 185).[82]

As critics such as Talia Schaffer have ably shown, Stoker was to abandon hopes for sympathy for his kind, and, indeed, to abandon his kind altogether in their times of need. Stoker deserted his friend Oscar Wilde when he was beset by sexual scandal and effectively erased all trace of that friendship. As a result of Wilde's trial and his own subsequent gay panic, Stoker also turned to a very public and vehement approval of censorship, publishing an essay on the subject in 1908 called "The Censorship of Fiction." Michael Moon reminds us that when we talk of Whitman and censorship, we cannot neglect the thoroughly integrated question of Whitman's self-censorship, and thus the creative effects of censorship.[83] A related point might be made about Stoker. There are (seedy) erotic possibilities to be found in Stoker's loud denouncements of vice and his muscular defenses of the censor. In his novel *Lady Athlyne* (1908), Stoker writes of the prisoner Lord Athlyne that "at this time they were occasionally getting letters. These had of course gone through the hands of the censor and their virginity thus destroyed."[84] Since Stoker published this novel in

---

[82] Horace Traubel, *With Walt Whitman in Camden*, vol. 4, ed. Sculley Bradley (Carbondale: Southern Illinois UP, 1959).
[83] See Michael Moon, *Disseminating Whitman* 26–58.
[84] Bram Stoker, *Lady Athlyne* (London: William Heinemann, 1908), 47.

the same year as "The Censorship of Fiction," the antivice essay's virulent endorsement of censorship might therefore be read as a fantasy of textual deflowering.[85]

Stoker's endorsement of censorship might have satisfied his own kink, but it also brought him into conflict with his friend Whitman. Stoker couldn't understand why Whitman didn't cut out the bits of his poetry that people found offensive: a conservative view that stood completely counter to Whitman's.[86] Whitman himself repeatedly decried the infamous American censor Anthony Comstock, and everything he represented, for exercising "a sort of censorship over the mails [...] I hate all censorships, big and little" (*Walt Whitman in Camden* 4: 193). Whitman had suffered his own poetry being sifted through the postal maw of Comstock. On 28 June 1882, Whitman wrote to William D. O'Connor, by the 3 P.M. post: "I think the enemy (in Boston) have formally appealed to the Post Master General to order L of G. excluded from the mails under the Comstock statutes."[87] Then that same day, by the 6 P.M. post, he wrote again to O'Connor asking him to look into "whether there has been any consideration of the question of sending *Leaves of Grass* through the mails, and the decision thereon, at the P O Department—& send me word at once" (*Correspondence* 3: 295–96). On 7 July, Whitman described himself cheered by the news that the Boston Postmaster had officially ordered for his book to "*pass unmolested through the mails*" (*Correspondence* 3: 296). His politics are the inverse of Stoker's, but the metaphor is the same: censorship = sexual molestation. Whitman urgently requests "an authentic copy of the P. O. letter." The next year Whitman was yet more jubilant when Comstock was defeated in a case prosecuting free-love leader Ezra H. Heywood for circulating two of Whitman's "Children of Adam" poems. Whitman crowed: "A[nthony] C[omstock] retires with his tail intensely curved inwards" (*Correspondence* 3: 338–39). Whitman wins the point: he "retires" Comstock by caricaturing him in a compromised, self-sodomizing position.

Whitman also mocked Comstock by dubbing him "Saint Anthony,"[88] a joke that mocks the supposed purity of the antivice campaigners who (like most antivice campaigners) had to view or partake in the pleasures in order to forbid them to others. But such hypocrisy aside, Comstock's fears were quite precisely Whitman's pleasures. Comstock campaigned under the principle "We assimilate what we read. The pages of printed matter become our companions."[89] Whitman and, most important, his followers, followed a visionary—rather than punitive—version of that same belief. Edward Carpenter, one of Whitman's other English disciples, pen pals, and visitors, had exactly

---

[85] Bram Stoker, "The Censorship of Fiction" in *The Nineteenth Century and After* (London: Spottiswoode, 1908), 64: 479–87.
[86] For a description of Whitman and Stoker clashing over the issue, see Bram Stoker, *Personal Reminiscences of Henry Irving* 2: 107.
[87] *The Collected Writings of Walt Whitman: The Correspondence,* vol. 3, ed. Edwin Haviland Miller (New York: New York UP, 1664), 295.
[88] *With Walt Whitman in Camden* 4: 92.
[89] Preface to Anthony Comstock's *Traps for the Young* ix.

the political courage Stoker lacked and was firmly opposed to censorship. Biographer Sheila Rowbotham notes that in a diary entry, Carpenter describes celebrating the 1915 death of Anthony Comstock—by attending a lecture on the diversity of women's sexual desires.[90] Carpenter wrote a book-length memoir and appreciation of Walt Whitman's life and work called *Days with Walt Whitman* (1906) that opens with Carpenter visiting Whitman in Camden, enjoying the pleasures of their conversation. In a section of the text that addresses the question of Whitman's "intimate relations," Carpenter moves past questions of children and marriage and comes to rest on Whitman's "urge to closest contact [...]. He is not satisfied with communication through words and printed pages" (*Specimen Days* 139). Carpenter illustrates his point by quoting Section 42 of "Song of Myself" that abjures "words of routine" and "leap[s] beyond yet nearer bring: / This printed and bound book—but the printer and the printing-office boy?" Not only had Whitman's printed word brought Carpenter across the sea to meet the poet in person, but also Carpenter well knew that Whitman's "communication" reached through his printed pages, across the printing machines to embrace not only the reader, but also all the men involved in the dissemination of his text, including the printer and the office boy.

The erotics of touch enabled through networks of communication and travel was not merely a metaphor for either Whitman or Carpenter. When Carpenter visited Whitman, he met Whitman's young lover, or "convoy" as Whitman described Harry Stafford.[91] "Convoy" was an apt epithet, since Stafford was an errand boy for a Camden printer when he met Whitman in 1876. In his correspondence with Whitman, Carpenter regularly inquired about the well-being of Stafford and his family. At some point during his relationship with Whitman, the restless Stafford turned from the business of print to that of telegraphs and Whitman replies to Carpenter assuring him of the health of Stafford who is "still telegraphing."[92] As for Carpenter, he met his lover George Merrill on a train in a group of men "chatting and chafing" (Rowbotham 179) among themselves. The train was an engine of transit, jostling social and sexual relations, allowing the upper-class Carpenter to rub shoulders with his working-class future lover. As biographer Rowbotham describes it: "Trains, like Whitman's trams, promised an arousing random anonymity—an in-between, dynamic space where conventions rooted in fixed places and specific times might be suspended" (Rowbotham 179).

Both men found their lovers in the connections produced by telegraph and train, and these erotics were also and immediately a politics of connection that proposed brotherhoods beyond national borders. In *Days with Walt Whitman*, Carpenter drew out Whitman's rapturous investments in universal communication:

---

[90] Sheila Rowbotham, *Edward Carpenter: A Life of Liberty and Love* (London: Verso, 2008), 382–83.
[91] On 13 March 1877, Whitman writes to his friend John Burroughs that he would be glad to visit him in Riverby, bringing along Stafford "as he is my convoy like—We occupy the same room and bed." *Correspondence* 3: 79.
[92] *Correspondence* 3: 253 and also 227.

Whitman realized from the first that this universality was the very key and centre of his utterance, and set himself deliberately to emphasise it. Many things conspired, with him, to this result—the girdling of the earth in his time, and the extraordinary developments of locomotion and intercommunication which were bringing together East and West, and all races and classes, creeds and customs, into close touch and acknowledgment of each other.

(*Days with Walt Whitman* 82).

Whitman, who in his older age described taking the ferry between Camden and Philadelphia as his greatest pleasure, relished the erotics of transport and communication, the fluidities of both. His technology poems of the 1860s and 1870s envision the communications network as a sexual lattice that will unify the old world with the new. In "Passage to India" (1869) he writes:

In the Old World the east the Suez canal,
The New by its mighty railroad spann'd,
The seas inlaid with eloquent gentle wires;
[............................]
The earth to be spann'd, connected by network,
The races, neighbors, to marry and be given in marriage,
The oceans to be cross'd, the distant brought near,
The Lands to be welded together

(411-12)

In this vision, the social relations are made indissoluble, "welded," via a technology that is humanly fibrous: the telegraph wires are "eloquent gentle wires." In "Song of the Exposition," written two years later, Whitman would repeat himself: "the Atlantic's delicate cable,/[...] This earth all spann'd with iron rails." It is a vision in which the engineer becomes the poet and vice versa, as it is in the "circumnavigation of the globe" that "all these separations and gaps shall be taken up and hook'd and link'd together" ("Passage to India"). Whitman revels in the promise of modern technology and communication networks to produce sensual connection between people and a cultural and world unity. His all-unifying "I" (akin to the "our" I discuss in chapter 1), which had previously strained to unite a divided America finds new postbellum expression in these industries of communication and transportation—and this time the scale is global. In "Years of the Modern" (1865) his vision is of kings and tyrants fading in the glow of energetic, "average" man who has access to "the steamship, the electric telegraph, the newspaper," and he asks, "Are all nations communing? Is there going to be but one heart to the globe?" and in "On the Beach at Night Alone" he asserts, "A vast similitude interlocks all." This interlocking similitude looks like both sexual and racial union. In "Starting from Paumanok" (1860), his vision is of a telegraphic, corresponding heartbeat through which America and Europe can feel each other: "See, through Atlantica's depths, pulses American, Europe reaching—pulses of Europe, / duly return'd." This is vision of union: of America and Europe fusing through a pulse. The lines are embedded in others in which a locomotive is "panting" like a strapping field laborer, and the steam cylinders of the printing press are pistons throbbing with sex. For Whitman, these industries seem inexhaustibly lusty and he crowns his vista on "ceaseless vehicles" with the summation "commerce." As Paul Gilmore elaborates, such sexualization was common parlance:

> […] telegraphic "commerce" was imagined to all but eliminate bodily boundaries through a nearly sexual union of individual American bodies into one national body. "Commerce," the term most often used to describe the telegraph's province, referred not simply to business transactions, but, as the *Webster's Dictionary* of the era euphemistically phrased it, "Familiar intercourse between the sexes." This sexual aspect of the telegraphic union, its ability to unify the nation in "closest and most intimate relations" through a "subtle fluid," is underlined by the frequency and popularity of anecdotes about couples who married over the telegraph.
>
> (810)

Turning his attention to Whitman specifically, Gilroy further asserts that for the poet "the telegraph became a vehicle for imagining not simply a cultural and spiritual exchange between races that would unite them in brotherhood, but also a bodily, sexual exchange which would link the nation and the world in one blood" (824). Gilmore distinguishes Whitman from other contemporary commentators on the telegraph, who routinely "imagined a global telegraphic body racially divided into the brain and the hands" (824), but even though Whitman reaches to racial communion, it is a strictly limited communion. The racial brotherhood Whitman imagined conjured by the telegraph was distinctly articulated as that familiar white fantasy ethnicity, articulated through its daydreamer's version of miscegenation: Anglo-Saxon. Whitman's vision of union was of *reunion* and his late-century reunionist sentiment could or least did not avoid "oneness" signaling "whiteness." Whitman made these racial hopes patently clear in a prose piece he published in the *Brooklyn Daily Times* titled "The Moral Effect of the Cable" (1858). Whitman writes:

> It is the sentiment of *union* that makes the popular heart beat and quiver. It is the union of the great Anglo-Saxon race, henceforth forever to be a unit, that makes the States throb with tumultuous emotion and thrills every breast with admiration and triumph. The popular instinct now-a-days says that England and the United States are no longer to keep each other at arms-length […]. They feel that England and America alone stand faithful and true to the great cause of freedom. They both

feel that this Telegraph Cable […] will link together nations that in heart and feeling are hereafter to be one.[93]

Yearning for what Whitman had called "one common orbic language" ("Song of the Exposition," 203), and for engineers to help produce a new, unified body, the dream turned easily to a racial cohesion that threatens homogenization and imperial refederation.

EPISTOLARY AMANUENSIS

Grand and passionate gestures toward cohesions of peace and harmony brought Whitman to this race-bias. But paradoxically it was from within the divisive horror of war that Whitman found a less vaunting erotics, and a model of writing letters for, to, with, and *as* another. He embodied the union he desired between correspondents through his work as a letter-writer for wounded soldiers during the American Civil War. "Several wanted word sent home to parents, brothers, wives, & c., which I did for them, (by mail the next day from Washington)" (*Specimen Days* 27). Whitman describes writing a letter to a soldier's mother, then "envelop'd and directed his letter, & c." (*Specimen Days* 27). He also distributed letter-writing supplies: he "supplied the men throughout with writing paper and stamp'd envelope each" (*Specimen Days* 28), quickly running out because "the men were much in need" (*Specimen Days* 28).[94] As Trollope, Hardy, and Jonathan Harker discover, being an amanuensis requires writing in all sorts of voices, and all sorts of relation—"all sorts" that make them ventriloquize love in all its forms. Whitman writes: "I encourage the men to write, and myself, when called upon, write all sorts of letters for them, (including love-letters, very tender ones.)" (*Specimen Days* 29). Tender letters, gentle telegraph wires: for Whitman the epistolary relation enfolds a poignant sexuality of intimacy and distance. He will help bury many of these soldiers whose letters he helped write, and he will bury them with a postal metaphor: "My comrade I wrapt in his blanket, envelop'd well his form" ("Vigil Strange I Keep on the Field One Night"). Sometimes the post runs ahead of the envelop'd death, posthumous, postdated, postponing only the bad news that the son was dead by the time they read it. In "Come Up from the Fields Father," parents in Ohio receive a letter from their soldier-son, bearing news of the perilous condition that has already killed him in the interval between writing and receiving. But the mother's dismay at the intermediating hand:

---

[93] Walt Whitman, "The Moral Effect of the Cable," *Brooklyn Daily Times* (20 August 1858) in Holloway and Schwarz, eds., *I Sit and Look Out* 159–60, 160.

[94] Whitman also wrote letters for the prisoners at Sing Sing prison. He told Edward Carpenter: "It was a whim" (*Days with Walt Whitman* 25).

Open the envelope quickly,
O this is not our son's writing, yet his name is sign'd,
O a strange hand writes for our dear son, O stricken mother's soul!

returns us, the reader, to the "strange" and loving hand—the hand of the poet—that lives on, loves on.[95] In another poem, which stages the poet himself taking his dying leave, Whitman makes it plainer yet that these posthumous messages are like Derrida's "sperm post card" (*The Post Card* 24) —they are "Curious envelop'd messages delivering,/ Sparkles hot, seed ethereal down in the dirt dropping" ("So Long!"). The poet's messages may have fallen, seemingly lost, on the dirt of battlefields and somber Ohio plots, but his poetic, postal hand is not estranging and deathly: rather, troops of young men will generate and grow from this seeded place. Whitman reportedly asserted to Carpenter: "I think there are truths which it is necessary to envelop or wrap up" (*Days with Walt Whitman* 43). But these are "divine things well envelop'd" ("Song of the Open Road"), made more pleasurable in the delivering.

---

[95] I part ways from critic Elizabeth Hewitt on this poem. She writes: "The essential problem with epistolarity, as Whitman describes it, is that delivery occurs over time: because the delivery of the letter is not instantaneous, it cannot repair the distance between (in this particular example) a loving mother and her dear dead son" (175). A queer reading, however, that looks beyond the parental dismay, can bring into view the erotics of distance, the exquisite agony of loss, and the erotics of the hand that wrote prosthetically for Pete.

5

Postscript

HENRY JAMES'S PUBLIC SERVANT

"CONSCIOUS OF ONE'S POSSIBILITIES"

Henry James's 1898 novella *In the Cage* is the apotheosis of the postal literature this study has described and explored. With anthropological attention to detail, James observes the operations at a Post Office, while paying scant attention to, evacuating even, the content of the messages that pass through it. Myriad telegram texts pass between three main characters: Lady Bradeen and Captain Everard send each other numerous telegrams that are all processed (read, written, sent and remembered) by the unnamed postal functionary heroine. The content of these many telegrams, however, is meaningless: often "nothing passed between them but the fulness of their silence" (278). Although there is zero content in these exchanges, there is plenty of relation. The relation comes not from what is said between the woman and the man in the course of their affair, but from the fact that their communication passes through the hands of a third figure. The unnamed telegraphist, who spends her time filling in the literal blanks on telegraph forms and the corresponding blanks in narrative —"the gaps and blanks and absent answers" (287), as she calls them—generates relation from her position as an intermediary.

Critics have noted, "Consciousness in late James seems to exist between people, in relations, rather than 'inside' them" (Thurschwell 96), "disseminated" between characters (Cameron 77). Letter- and message-sending therefore provides James with peculiar possibilities: it is a metaphor and instrument of consciousness that manifests between people and across distance, difference, misunderstanding—across, in short, "gaps and blanks." While we see these postal possibilities most fully and directly engaged in *In the Cage*, James had seeded the idea in comic form in his 1878 short story "A Bundle of Letters." In this story, James satirizes the correspondence of visitors to a Parisian boarding house who prefer to see the continent from hotel rooms, affect either sophistication or naïveté, or pursue experience in the form of "things that happen to people in novels." Louis Leverett, guilty of the latter, lectures his correspondent: "The great thing is to live, you know—to feel, to be conscious of one's possibilities; not to pass through life mechanically and insensibly, like a letter through the post-office." Leverett, whose last name perhaps suggests he is as twitchy as a rabbit and who is commonly taken to be a self-satirizing portrait of James himself, is a pompous and failed aesthete. A letter from an English boarder, Evelyn Vane, suggests that although Louis is always talking about the color of the sky, he likely has only ever seen it through a windowpane.[1] All the story's correspondents lack consciousness: of their own faults, of the intentions of their tutors, and none is aware that others might be—and indeed are—writing about them. Narrative, in other words, is legible only to the author and the reader of "A Bundle," never to the characters. Plot, consciousness, relation—anything other than chatter—lies only *between* the letters, and from what can be gleaned reading *between* the lines. When Leverett sermonizes about the importance of living life conscious of its possibilities, it is clear that his simile for an *un*conscious life—the post-letter—is heavily ironized by James. Not only does Leverett denounce the only medium through which he himself lives, but also the post-letter is anything but "mechanical and insensible" in "A Bundle." It is instead the only thing that is telling and aggregating. It collects stories as it passes between writers and readers, and it materializes the relations that the individual writers ignore or cannot perceive. In *In the Cage*, the telegraphist tells Everard that his "set" expose their worst attributes to her "with as good a conscience as if I had no more feeling than a letter box." Like Leverett, this set does not realize that a "letter box," or the discourse functionary that attends it, witnesses and even feels all feelings. In the era of the communication network, and for the class who "wired everything, even their expensive feelings" (237), this discourse functionary who feels all feelings and aggregates all stories is the public servant.

"THE IMMENSITY OF THEIR INTERCOURSE"

In *In the Cage*, consciousness and relation are formed not only from interchange between people, but also from *multiple* interchanges between *multiple* people. The story's postal setting and its protagonist's telegraphic occupation were inspired, James explains in the novella's preface, by visits to his own favorite Post Office where he says he had "come to enjoy the fruits of frequentation" and the "amenities of intercourse" (414). Like James, the telegraphist finds "stories and meanings" (241) in Post Office traffic, the customers she served, and "the

---

[1] This mockery of Leverett matches a friendly critique leveled against James himself, by the lesbian novelist Violet Paget, who wrote under the name Vernon Lee. In her short story "Lady Tal" (1892), Lee casts a "dainty but frugal bachelor" whom she describes as a "Henry James, of a lesser magnitude." This bachelor channels his sexual passion into a "passion for investigating" the lives of others.

immensity of their intercourse" (241).² As James portrays it, frequenting—or working at your local Post Office brings you into contact with myriad intersections and interchanges, and it is this "immensity" which is so "fruitful" for both author and author-like protagonist.

A working-class heroine is a rare thing in the James canon. But James affords his humble telegraphist, whom he calls "our obscure little public servant" (234), the credit of being an author. Through the telegraphist, the novella allegorizes the production of fiction; this is made clear from echoes between the description of the telegraphist and a description of writing in "The Art of Fiction." James writes:

> Experience is never limited, and it is never complete; it is an immense sensibility, a kind of huge spider web of the finest silken threads suspended in the chamber of consciousness and catching every air-borne particle in its tissue. It is the very atmosphere of the mind; and when the mind is imaginative—much more when it happens to be that of a man of genius—it takes to itself the faintest hints of life, it converts the very pulses of the air into revelations.³

The telegraphist's "eye for types amounted [...] to genius" (239). She sits behind a cage/web, sometimes further trapped in the sounder chamber, an "innermost cell of captivity, a cage within the cage, fenced off from the rest by a frame of ground glass." And she fits perfectly James's requirement that an author have an imaginative mind—the powers of her imagination prompt and structure the story, and our intimacy with the telegraphist is intimacy with her imaginative capacity (indeed the word "imagine" and its cognates are used more than a dozen times across the course of the tale).

James—who had so loftily rebuked Trollope for being a postman—finds his avatar in the postal worker. In the preface, James describes the Post Office as a kind of story depot, a terminus of human relation. Waiting for service at the PO is, James observes, "one of the commonest and most taken-for-granted" experiences in London, and he contends that the idea for his story "must again and again have flowered (granted the grain of observation) in generous minds" (414). This description emphasizes frequency and plurality: every intelligent person must have thought of this story, repeatedly. James was certainly alert to the idea that the Post Office was a place that could transform and transport you. In *Notes of a Son and Brother* (1914), he transcribes part of a letter from his brother William to himself, in which William describes becoming overwhelmed by emotion in a Post Office. "Sweet was your letter and grateful to my eyes. I had gone in a mechanical way to the P.O. not hoping for anything [...] but the graphic account I read in the letter he gave me of the sorrow of *my* mother almost made me shed tears on the floor of the

---

² Tony Tanner also likens the story-spinning telegraphist to James himself, noting that as she weaves tales from "whiffs and glimpses" (239), James's own writing grew best out of fragments. He would often stop a raconteur at the beginning of her story if that beginning had stimulated his imagination: knowing more would stymie his own narrative production. *The Reign of Wonder* 310–19.
³ Henry James, "The Art of Fiction" in Gard, *The Critical Muse* 194.

P.O." (*Henry James Autobiography* 309). In another account, William attaches similar passion to the receiving of family letters, illustrating this vivid description with a cartoon of himself in lettered and unlettered states (see figure 5.1):

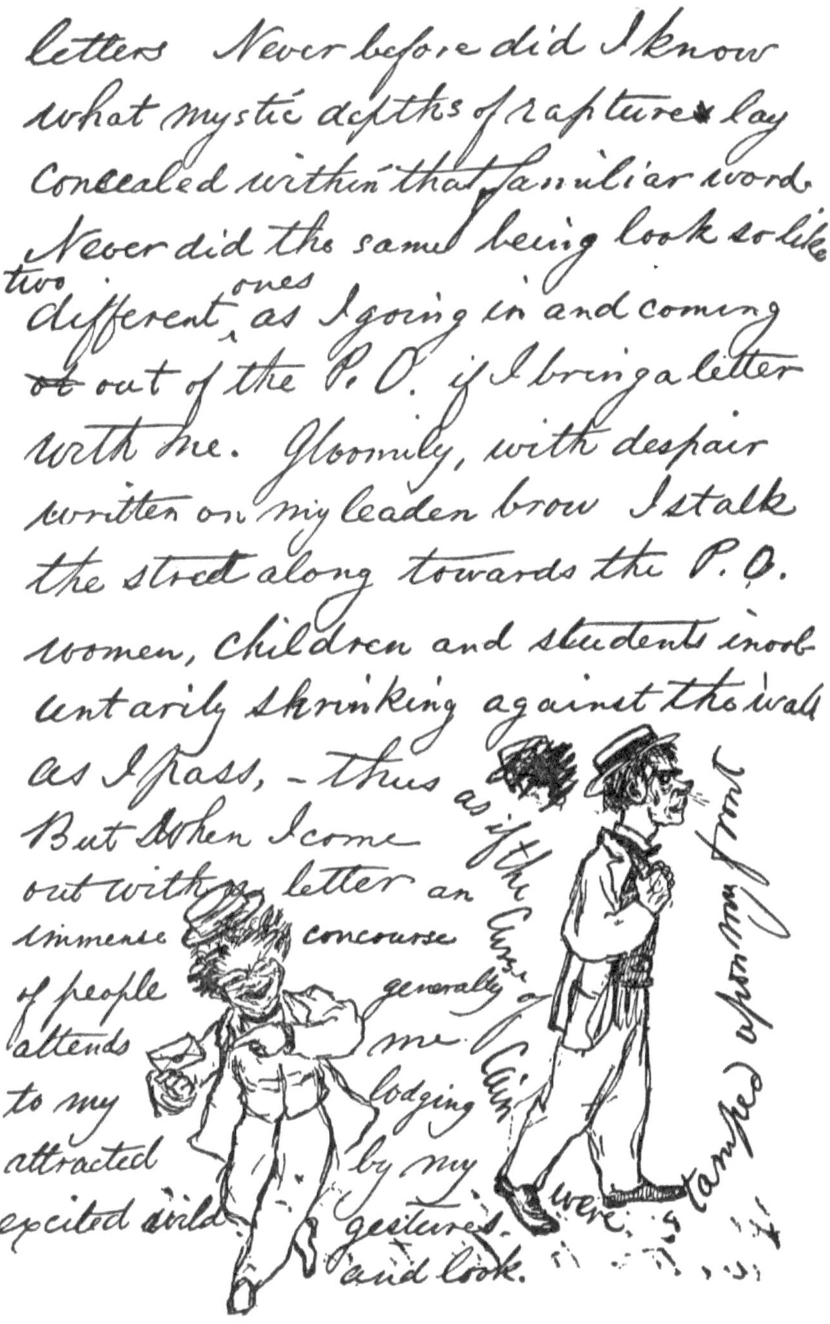
letters Never before did I know
what mystic depths of rapture* lay
concealed within that familiar word.
Never did the same being look so like
two different ones as I going in and coming
~~ot~~ out of the P. O. if I bring a letter
with me. Gloomily, with despair
written on my leaden brow I stalk
the street along towards the P. O.
women, children and students involuntarily shrinking against the wall
as I pass, – thus as if the Curse of Cain were stamped upon my front
But when I come
out with a letter an
immense concourse
of people generally
attends me
to my lodging
attracted by my
excited wild gestures
and look.

FIGURE 5.1 Letter from William James to Henry James.

The first few days, the first week here, I really didn't know what to do with myself or how to fill my time. I felt as if turned out of doors. I then received H.'s and Mother's letters. Never before did I know what mystic depths of rapture lay concealed within that familiar word. Never did the same being look so like two different ones as I going in and out of the P.O. if I bring a letter with me. Gloomily, with despair written on my leaden brow I stalk the street along towards the P.O., women, children and students involuntarily shrinking against the wall as I pass—thus, as if the curse of Cain were stamped on my front. But when I come out with a letter an immense concourse of people generally attends me to my lodging, attracted by my excited wild gestures and look.

(*Henry James Autobiography* 312–13)

William's path to the Post Office is lonely and atomizing, but on his return he is accompanied by a crowd. The receipt of a letter multiplies the self, ebulliently. The Post Office seems to be a backdrop for William's stigmatized self, both coming ("curse of Cain") and going ("wild gestures and looks"). But it is the stigmatized self that is full of life, just as his sketch interrupts the lines of William's letter, producing a blot, and forcing his sentences to curve around his cartoon.

And the Post Office is so capacious that it provides a setting for all manner of existence, from the quotidian to the existential:

[This] scene of the transaction of so much of one's daily business, haunt of one's needs and one's duties, of one's labours and one's patiences, almost of one's rewards and one's disappointments, one's joys and one's sorrows, had ever had, to my sense, so much of London to give out, so much of its huge, perpetual story to tell, that any momentary wait there seemed to take place in a strong social draught.

(414)

Like the capacious "our" I describe in chapter 1, James's impersonal, possessive pronoun "one's" gives way to "many"—its discrete, formal self crowded out by a barrage of postal business. "One" becomes caught up in *serial* fiction (the "perpetual story") and *crosswinds* ("social draught") that are without bounds or segregation. Stories and sociality are not, however, the same as people; James and the telegraphist are stirred by situations, not people. Any core sample taken from the notebooks in which James planned his writing, reveals sketches comprised of plot, scenes, circumstance, and relation, rather than personalities or character studies. The telegraphist is similarly unmoved by the brute demands of personage; in fact, her imaginative faculty is actively threatened by the "abundance of her contact with the human herd" (232). When the crowd is fleshly, importuning, or plotting, the telegraphist has to withstand it and wait for the "flashes, the quick revivals, absolute accidents all" that revive her intensity of being, and her story-making facility. She loathes the "cunning hostility of Mr. Buckton and the importunate sympathy of the counter-clerk" and most of all "the daily, deadly, flourishy letter from Mr. Mudge" (232), the telegraphist's fiancé. These interactions are sodden with other people's content and intent, and are generic, predictable, and banally literary. In common with other nineteenth-century postal literature, the interior of the romantic letter from her male suitor fails to interest either the telegraphist or the narrator—its message is missing and clearly doesn't bear repeating. But where the epistolary fails, the postal animates: "Some one had only sometimes to put in a penny for a stamp, and the whole thing was upon her" (232). Mudge's letter is killingly decipherable, but the impersonal, bureaucratic exchanges with strangers who hand over their pennies for stamps, whose obscure business and passions pass through the cage and through the fingers of the telegraphist, can conjure something complete and animate. As I described in the introduction, the iconic penny stamp, bearing the Queen's head and "1d" had reconfigured the way that "one" could represent "many." Any post-letter could passage anywhere to anyone, thus engaging what James elsewhere called "every kind of contradiction of common experience,"[4] these infinite disseminations facilitated by the integer "1/one." The telegraphist is supremely capable of apprehending this exact equation, since all the words she reads are measured in pennies. For her work she charges telegram customers a penny a word (244), for her leisure she reads "ha'penny novels" (255), and from both trifling texts she can construe worlds otherwise lost to her. These are worlds of social status, finery, and romance, and she can transport herself from her public cage into the most intimate setting: "She had never seen a boudoir, but there had been lots of boudoirs in the telegrams" (268).

If her work affords her "immensity" from which she gains information and interest, the telegraphist's own romantic and domestic life is defined by limitation and lack. She is hemmed in at work by the pressing smells of the shop's comestibles, and the home life to which she has resigned herself is emphatically "little." Her fiancé "Mudge" proffers only acoustic insult: a sludgy, middling name that surely Matthew Arnold would have denounced as disgustedly as he did "Wragg." Marriage to Mudge will clearly suffocate her: she wonders "how she could bear any man so smugly unconscious of the immensity of her difference" (248). Mudge is indifferent, and the echoing word "immensity" counterpoints this dull betrothal to her stimulating telegraphic work. Of course this telegraphic work can also be stifling; she counts words "as numberless as the sands of the sea" (229), an expression that casts her as a Cinderella swamped by her labors. The social and economic fall that has landed her in this office has in this way sentenced her to a life of drudgery; drudgery that at present seems only to give way to postmarital Mudgery. But because of both the curious nature of the postal work and her own capacities for observation and imagination, she is fired with flashing thoughts that this endless labor might give way to a new, sparkling life. But will this new life be marriage to a prince? Or a captain? On the one hand, the telegraphist might seem to desire this, given her diet of romances—perhaps she hopes only for a more glamorous marriage than the one she seems headed for. She certainly fixes on Everard with hopes that look similar to those of a shop-girl or

---

[4] In *A Small Boy and Others*, James recalls traveling from Lyons to Geneva in two carriages "in which we were to 'post'" (283). The carriage "bristled with every kind of contradiction of common experience" (283).

servant who might, by virtue of the proximities to quality that their job affords them, marry up. But when she gets her evening on a park bench with her would-be lover, the interchange is less about marriage and futures and more about the pleasures, harmless and otherwise, of knowledge:

> "All I get out of it is the harmless pleasure of knowing. I know, I know, I know!"— she breathed it ever so gently. "Yes; that's what has been between us," he answered much more simply.

This is a novella all about how misunderstanding can be understanding, and how knowing might not entail recognizing. It grows out of the creative germ planted in its first line—the idea that a telegraphist might *know* "a great many persons without recognizing the acquaintance" (229). The telegraphist is intimate with strangers. It is her (unnamed) impersonality that allows her to be so interior to the sexual transgression of others. The novella relishes this quirky, rich, literary feature of everyday living, and the regrettable inverse of the telegraphist's situation is seen in the characters who recognize acquaintance, but know nothing. Her suitor Mudge and her friend Mrs. Jordan may share some of the young woman's more superficial ambitions for social betterment, and their acquaintance is built of perceived similarities of taste and status, but ultimately theirs is a world of "bland firm thrift" (241) and shilling tulips. Mrs. Jordan has imagination—indeed has "invented a new career for women" (231)—but the girl can outwit her because Mrs. Jordan uses her imagination to one end only: exaggeration of her intimacy with grandeur. The girl is haughty about the superiority of her own job to Mrs. Jordan's: "Combinations of flowers and green-stuff, forsooth! What she could handle freely, she said to herself, was combinations of men and women" (232). Neither Mudge nor Mrs. Jordan has anything like her "play of mind" (232). In the vein of "A Bundle of Letters," James's narrative offers the reader a mocking perspective on the telegraphist's hauteur. We see that in some ways she is a version of the people she despises. But the story also sinks us too deep into her empathizing, energized world for us to see her as a hypocrite—she is not guilty of double standards, instead she is living a double life: the connections she makes through her cage were "neither more nor less than the queer extension of her experience, the double life that, in the cage, she grew at last to lead" (239).

Eric Savoy has drawn critical attention to the importance of this phrase "queer extension of her experience," brilliantly describing the story as a complex investigation into the "knowledge effect" ("Queer Effects" 286). Savoy emphasizes that this story operates under the shadow of the Criminal Law Amendment Act, the Cleveland Street Affair and Oscar Wilde's trials: "spectacular scandals of the 1890s which turned largely on the testimony of working-class servants" (287). Resituating the story historically, Savoy asks us to pay more attention to the "telegraphist's function as 'spy' and her consequent threat to upper-class privacy" (290). Savoy's reading is foundational, and has been joined by several other accounts, but in order to tell the story of gay male anxiety these readings unsex the girl and cast her as the working-class threat to upper-class homosexual scandal, without asking about her own desires.[5] These readings presume her to be heterosexual: she becomes the straight man to the queer reading. I would instead propose that the doubleness of the telegraphist, and the more-than-doubleness of her clients produces queer effects that entangle her; her life is queer because it is postal. We need to take the Lesbian rule (see chapter 3) to the telegraphist: her bending of the bars of the telegraphic cage, her entanglements in telegraphic wires, and the way gaps and blanks make her "flash" throughout the story must be seen as themselves queer and queering.

In his later novel *The Ambassadors* (1903), James would write of how Lambert Strether had a "queer quantity" of past experience that leaves him "changed and queer" (110, 209). Multiplicity, in this formulation ("quantity") engenders queerness. We see this most dramatically not in the telegraphist's interactions with Everard, but in her interactions with Everard's lover. A woman—who we later learn is Lady Bradeen—hands over three telegrams, two of which are signed with different names—Mary and Cissy. The telegraphist has, we are told, a "peculiar affinity" for this kind of entertainment, and her "hand was quick to appropriate" these intriguing correspondences. The telegraphist admires the woman's looks: "Mary was very handsome, the handsomest woman, she felt in a moment, she had ever seen—or perhaps it was only Cissy." Not knowing with whom, exactly, she is dealing, the telegraphist gets the feeling she gets when she's called out of the stupor of labor; "there almost always suddenly would come a sharp taste of something; it was in her mouth before she knew it; it was in her mouth now." This physiological mnemonic, a sensation that might augur a seizure of some kind, is both startling and sensuous in its orality.[6] The telegraphist then extends herself to the woman, an extension that is queer both because it is a same-sex fascination and also because it involves one subject getting utterly lost in another.[7] The telegraphist is swept away by the vision of this woman:

> To Cissy, to Mary, whichever it was, she found her curiosity going out with a rush, a mute effusion that floated back to her, like a returning tide, the living colour and splendour of the beautiful head, the light of eyes that seemed to reflect such utterly other things than the mean things actually before them; and, above all, the high

---

[5] See also Nicola Nixon, "The Reading Gaol of Henry James's 'In the Cage' " for an account of how Wilde's trials may have influenced *In the Cage*.

[6] For a wonderful discussion of food in *In the Cage* specifically, and James's work more generally, see "Henry James' Art of Eating" by Jennifer L. Fleissner. Of this line in the story, Fleissner notes that the telegraphist's imagination is repeatedly figured as feeding her and stimulating her olfactory and gustatory systems. Fleissner argues that although most critics have erected an impermeable divide between the material world of "hams and the cheeses" and the life of the mind, this is a story in which the body ultimately is not despised. Just as James's own aestheticism didn't make him wave aside hefty helpings of roast beef or plum pudding, the telegraphist is someone who can "savor" (51), even when she has to make do with scraps and small tastes, and indeed she relishes the "particular combination of pleasure and deprivation" (50).

[7] In "The Author of 'Beltraffio': The Exquisite Boy and Henry James's Equivocal Aestheticism," Kevin Ohi points out, "One curious meaning for queer [. . .] is an oversusceptibility to interest or obsession: 'absorbed or interested,' says Webster's, 'to an extreme or unreasonable degree' " (755).

curt consideration of a manner that even at bad moments was a magnificent habit and of the very essence of the innumerable things—her beauty, her birth, her father and mother, her cousins and all her ancestors—that its possessor couldn't have got rid of even had she wished.

(234)

Cissy/Mary is a thoroughly multiple subject. Overtaken, or "rushed" by the telegraphist, she not only bears two names, but also is made of "innumerable things," and bears the traces of innumerable people. She is the antithesis of the monogamous subject: engaged in an extramarital affair, she is also the consummate product of planned exogamies, a reflection of her other relatives—so much so that she has a kind of double vision—looking at things in front of her, she sees "utterly other things" (234). With the ocular equivalent of a Midas touch, Lady Bradeen can turn meanness into magnificence, and of course one of the beneficiaries of this gaze will be the humble telegraphist herself. Part of the telegraphist's thrall is due to her fascination with Lady Bradeen's class. She is both desiring of its habits and horrified by its profligacy: telegraphing "extravagant chatter" costs "an amount of money that would have held the stricken household of her frightened childhood, her poor pinched mother and tormented father and lost brother and starved sister, together for a lifetime" (239).[8] Her critique is peevish rather than revolutionary; she is convinced that she could do better with their advantages, and she cherishes a "triumphant vicious feeling" that she carries "their silly guilty secrets in her pocket." But these feelings—otherwise those of the servant listening at the keyhole—are refurbished and elevated by the media with which she works. As an intermediary, she is a participant in and necessary to the correspondences she processes. She theorizes that Cissy/Mary might use different names because she is "wiring by deputy" for others ... and this is what our unnamed telegraphist does too: wires by deputy. If the telegraphist imagines, then, taking the place of someone in the upper classes, she gets to take that place when she sends their telegraphs. She becomes their proxy. And since "there were times when all the wires in the country seemed to start from the little hole-and-corner where she plied for a livelihood," she is as "well-connected" as her customers.

She is also in correspondence with both the Captain and her Ladyship, and in correspondence with each of them through the other. When she again admires the handsomeness of her ladyship, looking at her eyes and lips "with a strange passion,"

---

[8] This passage links telegraphic expenses with social costs. In a very different mood, James played with the same connection in a telegram of his own. Declining a social invitation, James telegraphed: "Impossible impossible impossible if you knew what it costs me to say so you can count however at the regular rates ask Miss Robbins to share your regret I mean mine" (H. J. to Mrs. Hugh Bell, *The Legend of the Master* 21). The joke is that the author (infamous for his compound clauses) here finds the declarative "economy" of telegraphic writing delightfully stimulating ... prompting him to be not at all economical. Of most interest to me is that he ends by "confusing" to whom the regrets belong. This backs up my thesis that telegraphic communication could switch subject positions, detaching subjects from their intimate feelings. For more on the "social cost" of telegraphic exchange, see Jennifer Wicke, "Henry James's Second Wave" 151.

she both understands more about Captain Everard *and* is referred back to the thrill of looking at Lady Bradeen: "She was with the absent through her ladyship and with her ladyship through the absent." Being able to feel through and beyond absence, being able to perceive who isn't there, grows out of and produces a polygamous relation. This polygamy makes the telegraphist socially and sexually hybrid. When the telegraphist finally meets with Everard outside of the office on a park bench, that park bench becomes, as Everard relaxes into the contradictions of the situation, like a "satin sofa in a boudoir." The sofa/bench sets the telegraphist amidst similarly mixed narrative signs: occupying the role of servant, she is also playing out her romance plot, but finds herself surrounded by intimations of prostitution—the park is scattered with red lamps, and "there were other couples on other benches whom it was impossible not to see, yet at whom it was impossible to look." When she exclaims that she would "do anything" for him, she is perfectly aware that "the place, the associations and circumstances, perfectly make it sound what it wasn't." Knowledgeable as ever, the climax of this recognition comes when she concludes "and wasn't that exactly the beauty?" The scene becomes pleasurable to her for *not* being what it seems. For being something *other*.

This moment in the story defies various generic possibilities. Like Trollope's telegraph girl Lucy, whom I discuss in chapter 3, James's telegraphist is not a silly romantic heroine. She is not a prostitute. Nor is she a blackmailer. She is, emphatically, an *agent*. She has brought them here, to this unlikely bench. She has reached through the bars of the cage and produced social and sexual rupture. This rupture will most likely be temporary—this is, after all, no fairy story. But it still produces reverberations. By the end of the tale Everard himself will be revealed to be something other than what he seems: the telegraphist learns belatedly that he is not wealthy, but rather beset by debts and that when he marries Lady Bradeen, he will own nothing in the house: he stands closer to the position of servitude and even prostitution than she realized. Indeed, when the telegraphist and Mrs. Jordan declare that Lady Bradeen "nailed him," it is clear that he is left without much agency. He experiences the confinements and dangers that might be thought to attend the telegraphist: despite the supposed protection of his sex and his class, Everard is now "in the cage."

Who, then, ends up with whom? This marriage plot ends without any marriages, and I would argue that the foggy ending of the tale maintains the blurring of persons and relations that has made up the bulk of the novella.[9] Just as the telegraphic and

---

[9] David Kurnick's work on *The Awkward Age*—a novel that was published in the same year as *In the Cage*—makes a similar point about James's blurring of subjects and subject positions, in addition elegantly connecting this blurring with James's genre blending. Kurnick writes: "*The Awkward Age* is distinctive not only for its formal strangeness but for its refusal to identify sexual perversions with discrete individuals, for its demurral from the idea of interiority in favor of a model of group consciousness, for its attack on the power of the marriage plot to assign significance to certain parts of a life story, and for its mapping of a less punishing scene of sexual publicity than those current in fin-de-siècle culture" (110). Kurnick's point is that *The Awkward Age*

postal machineries produced some queer effects (alias identities, codings, inappropriate enthrallments), the fog, too, is a queer special effect, making things "vague" and "sightless" and "half-lost" and allowing acoustic disjunction: when " 'Good-bye!' Came out of the fog" and " 'Good-bye!' went into it," these utterances are untagged—we don't know which words are Mrs. Jordan's and which are the telegraphist's, and cannot tell whose voice goes "in" and whose came "out."[10] These voices are thrown. And thrown voices are ones detached from their origin, they are anatopic and can scramble our perceptions of proximity and our faith in the congruence of persons and voices.[11] This is what *In the Cage* achieves: the story of the intermediary makes us admit that there are third persons in any intimate exchange, and that to touch one is to touch an*other*. At the end of the tale, the telegraphist realizes that from now on she will hear of Everard "only through Mrs. Jordan, who touched him through Mr. Drake, who reached him through Lady Bradeen" (330). Despite being on her way to a "little home," the telegraphist remains in a circuit, caught up in serial touching that extends her beyond (and through and between) the marital and beyond (and through and between) the heterosexual.

IN THE CAGE, OUT OF THE CLOSET

James "enjoy[ed] the fruits of frequentation" and the "amenities of intercourse" at his local Post Office with great regularity. Steven H. Jobe estimates that 10,500 to 12,000 letters by Henry James still survive and there are something in the region of 25,000 letters by the James family.[12] Henry was hugely fond of postal and telegraphic correspondence, and he displayed particular pleasure in availing himself of postscripts, marginalia, cryptics, palimpsest, and emendation. The playfulness evident in these post- and superscriptions is decidedly camp and not infrequently daring. In 1884 Edmund Gosse complimented "the Author of

---

gets away with portraying an impressive array of sexual oddity and transgression without wheeling in the spectre of punitive measures. James similarly swerves from punitive sexual publicity in *In the Cage*—though Everard fears blackmail, the telegraphist does not use her knowledge to such ends, the mistake in the intercepted telegraph prevents widespread scandal and Everard is saved from the kind of publicity that destroyed Oscar Wilde. Describing a turn in the legal proceedings against Wilde, James wrote to his friend Gosse in horror at the vision of the courtroom housing "a nest of almost infant blackmailers!" (letter dated April 28, 1895. See Moore 127).

[10] This scene's ingredients of fog, detached voices, and wandering, half-lost selves recalls an anecdote about Henry James collected by Simon Nowell-Smith in *The Legend of the Master*. One of Walt Whitman's first biographers, Bliss Perry, remembers (or claims to remember) James's account of becoming lost in the wilds of New Hampshire when visiting his brother: "I shall never forget Henry James the novelist explaining to John Morley how he strayed off the road [. . .] 'I had been *lost* had not a peasant emerged from the wood with a bundle of faggots upon his shoulder and directed me to the Post'" (*The Legend of the Master* 48). The anecdote's humor derives from its cocktail of straying, strange men, stigma (faggots are a sign of heresy) and the (b)anality of the post.

'Beltraffio,' " evidently praising James for "divining" something about J. A. Symonds.[13] In a return letter to Gosse, James used a postscript to make an elaborate demurral:

> P.S. Perhaps I *have* divined the innermost cause of J. A. S.'s discomfort—but I don't think I seize [. . .] exactly the allusion you refer to. I am therefore devoured with curiosity as to this further revelation. Even a post-card (in covert words) would relieve the suspense of the perhaps-already-too-indiscreet—H. J.[14]

"The Author of Beltraffio" was inspired by Gosse's account to James of Symonds's marriage. This letter therefore sits in the midst of a chain of flirtatious exchange: Gosse narrated it, James wrote it, Gosse praised its perspicacity ... and then James requests explication of how perspicacious he's been exactly. Interpretation—divination of homosexuality—travels back and forth between James and Gosse, with one relinquishing the theory no sooner than the other takes it up. They pass the revelation of Symonds's homosexuality between them, a demonstration of serial theorizing of the kind that would be fictionalized a few years later by Oscar Wilde in "The Portrait of Mr. W. H." (1889). The climax of this exchange is James's request for a *postcard* spelling out the "allusion." That a discussion all about "discomfort" and "discretion" should be concluded by the sending of that most open of communications—the postcard—is a grand joke. In fact, that very year the 1884 Post Office Protection Act had decreed that a postcard was the only kind of mail that the P.O. could prosecute as indecent.[15] That the open postcard would have to be written in conversely non-open, "covert words" is a jest James clearly felt worth repeating: he places it within parenthesis "(. . .)"—a textual device that mimics the whispered aside, but since a page can't whisper, the brackets merely draw extra attention to their contents. James takes great pleasure in repeatedly opening and closing the secret of the homosexuality shared between Gosse, Symonds, and himself, via a medium that is itself both public and private.

Symonds features in another postscript from James to Gosse, one inscribed on the envelope of the letter containing James's famous reaction to the Wilde trials. In the actual letter, James decries the "squalid gratuitousness" of the "mere exposure" suffered

---

[11] In *A Small Boy and Others*, Michael Moon helpfully introduces this term "anatopic" in relation to James. He points out that James doesn't seek male-male eros "in the here and now," but is rather deploys "strategic anachronism and anatopism" (31).

[12] See Pierre A. Walker and Greg W. Zacharias, "James's Hand and Gosse's Tail: Henry James's Letters and the Status of Evidence" 74.

[13] Gosse's letter is missing, possibly destroyed when James held a great bonfire of letters toward the end of his life. Many critics, including Fred Kaplan, interpret "Gosse's identification of a particular allusion in the story to Symond's [*sic*] homosexuality" (*Henry James* 303).

[14] Letter dated 9 June 1884. See Moore, *Selected Letters* 32.

[15] This act was designed not for "the suppression of vice but the protection of the Post Office and its servants," so only openly obscene communications would be prosecuted. Anything that was securely wrapped would not. This interpretation came under scrutiny on several occasions, including during a case in 1891 when indecent photographs

by Wilde, though admits that a fall from " 'brilliant' conspicuity" to the enclosure of a "sordid prison-cell" (Moore 126) makes Wilde more interesting. The letter thereby displays fascination with the space (what James calls the "gulf") between conspicuity and incarceration. This fascination becomes amplified by what James writes on the outside of the envelope. On the flap (namely, the backside) of the envelope James wrote "Quel Dommage—mais quel Bonheur—que J. A. S. ne soit plus de ce monde!"[16] The seesaw of emotion expressed in the message—shame and happiness—matches the open secret postal antics in which James once again indulges. For readers of James who "mumble the bone"[17] of his homoerotic subtexts, this is no subtext, but rather supertext. A postscript so "post" that it is not afforded the privacy of being interior, but instead sits on the envelope alongside the Post Office stamps and markings. It also, of course, becomes a pretext in the sense that Gosse would have seen and read this first, before viewing the contents of James's letter. Being in French, the most flimsy, affected even, form of code, further extends the play (Eric Savoy calls James's francophilia "campy").[18] It should also be borne in mind that "French Letter" was already slang for a condom, for protection, by mid-century. Through this "PS" James simultaneously flirts with Gosse, the postal workers who deliver the letter, and with disaster of the kind visited on Wilde.[19] James's postal dalliance with humiliation, exposure, and even prosecution delineates a relationship between the post and the closet: both are capacious and both have a swinging door between public and private. James relishes that swing and wants little to do with efforts to pin the door either open or shut.

In the Cage faintly damns anyone who imagines that they can break into closed-off worlds. Mrs. Jordan wants "in" to a world of high society, a desire that the telegraphist despises as excessively literal. Mrs. Jordan's job allows her into—specifically, "all the rooms"—and she "dilat[es] on the initiations thus opened up to her" (231). Mrs. Jordan *opens* out ("dilates") all the *ins* ("initiations") that are "*open*ed up" to her. In short, Mrs. Jordan gapes. She takes the door off its hinges, or at least she *thinks* she does. Indeed, this is exactly the metaphor to which James turns: "a *door* more than half open to the

---

became unwrapped during carriage. But there was unwillingness on the part of the Postmaster-General to prosecute anything other than postcards or letters "having similar indications on the outside of the covers thereof." In 1895 the same question arose, in relation to the prosecution of Walter McIntosh, a dealer in indecent photos. Once again the P.O. hesitated to prosecute and the Postmaster-General agreed, endorsing the minute as follows: "Approved. I concur with the Solicitor that the Post Office should take action only in those cases in which it is necessary for the protection of its own servants." Packet 371 S/1892 Files 1-9 Post 29/549.

[16] This letter is postmarked 8 April 1895. See Moore, *Selected Letters* 126.

[17] For James's fondness for this phrase, see Fleissner 49.

[18] Eric Savoy, "Subjunctive Biography" 252. It should also be borne in mind that "French letter" was already slang for a condom by the mid-nineteenth century.

[19] The OED records examples from 1856 onward. See entry for "French." For another example of James using a postscript to get playful about shame, see his letter to Gosse of 11 April 1892, with a PS that reads "Excuse this blot on my character." Editor Rayburn S. Moore clarifies that "James here refers to an ink blot on the stationery" (Moore 87).

higher life couldn't be called anything but a thin *partition*. Mrs. Jordan's imagination quite did away with the thickness" (my italics).[20] Mrs. Jordan might fantasize about eliminating the division between her and the upper class, but the partition of the telegraphist's cage, and of the postal system more generally, is granted much more subtlety and interest by the narrative. The telegraphist's "barrier" is "a frail structure of wood and wire," a "transparent screen" that "fenced out or fenced in" (229), depending on which side of the counter you stand. It is emphatically permeable, "pervaded" by smell, and it mediates somatic experience: the telegraphist transacts business through the "gap" in the barrier, reaching across the impediment of a shelf "that her forearm ached with rubbing" (229).[21] The structure of the cage is so mediating of feeling that the syntax of this sentence confuses whether the shelf or the arm is doing the aching. Unlike Mrs. Jordan, who desires to inhabit a simple prepositional state — "in"— the telegraphist is allied with the more complicated prepositions "in-between" and "across."[22] This sounds like, of course, the classic definition of "queer," as articulated by Eve Kosofsky Sedgwick. Sedgwick looks to the root word "quer," meaning "slantwise" or "across," to describe the contrary tendencies of queer narratives and subjectivities.

The telegraphist and the new communication network of which she is a part, use wires that crisscross the nation and can themselves get crossed. Communication in this story is full of accident, interception, misinterpretation, and crossed purposes. This is relished by James; the story ends with the fog traversed by the voices of Mrs. Jordan and the telegraphist, and fogs of misunderstanding that produce "crossing" seem pleasurable to him. In another short story, "Flickerbridge," James writes: "They were perfectly at *cross*-purposes, and it was the better, and they wandered together in the silver haze with all communication blurred" [my italics].[23] Cross-purposes may well be more pleasurable, since they allow space for queer interpretations. When Mrs. Jordan and the telegraphist disappear into the communication-fog, they pass into marital futures that are more discursive than anything else: "so much talk" (302).

It is oftentimes a crossing-out that produces queer effects in James's letters. Pierre A. Walker and Greg W. Zacharias have studied a manuscript of yet another letter James wrote to his friend Edmund Gosse, revealing a queer cross-text that has been erased by

---

[20] This line is taken from James's revision of the story published in 1908. The 1898 original simply read "the social door might at any moment open so wide" (231).

[21] Further indication that James confers authorial, or proto-authorial status on his telegraphist can be found in James's account of his own susceptibility to the vibrations ("pulse") of a social group. In his autobiography *A Small Boy and Others*, James describes being more interested in spectators than a drama on the stage "have become thus aware of our collective attitude . . . I am not sure I wasn't thus more interested in the pulse of our small party, under my tiny recording thumb, than in the beat of the drama" (*A Small Boy* 163). James's "recording thumb" matches the telegraphist's recording and aching "forearm" and they share powers of subject reversal: James turns spectators into watched subjects, just as the telegraphist "reads" the senders of messages.

[22] The word "between" is notably allied with the telegraphist: it is used on seventeen occasions in relation to her.

[23] "Flickerbridge" *Novels and Stories* 23: 409.

the letter's rendering into print, and/or by editorial decision. Rayburn Moore's clear-text edition of James's letters to Gosse transcribes the letter: "The blaze of summer is upon us and I shall presently edge away from the fire. I leave this place July 1st & return to England by the 25th. I hope this will be in time to put a little salt on your tail before you fly away" (72). Walker and Zacharias describe how the manuscript

> shows that in the third sentence of this passage James began to write: "I hope this will be in time to put my hand." The manuscript also shows that he crossed out the word "hand," but not "my," wrote "a little" above the canceled "hand," and then completed the sentence. In the manuscript, then, the sentence reads: "I hope this will be in time to put my hand "a little" salt on your tail."
>
> (72)

James hopes to put his hand on Gosse's tail? Since the words "my hand" are still legible, Walker and Zacharias hypothesize that "James might have wanted Gosse to read his joke" (73). I would add that James might also have wanted to *post* his joke to Gosse. To put salt on the tail of a bird is to be so close as to be able to catch it. The expression is employed to echo the conventional valediction about catching the post—echo it and queer it. When Fred Kaplan observes that James's erotically playful moments are contained mostly in his correspondence and are "characteristic of the mystery of James's sexual self-consciousness; [they] seem either impossibly innocent or embarrassingly explicit" (406).[24] Eric Savoy emends Kaplan's either/or formulation to one of both/and, arguing that this revision "accommodate[s] the distinctive convolutions of the Jamesian closet" ("Embarrassments" 231). Such "circumlocutory discourse," Savoy argues, derives from self-contestatory homosexual subjectivities that gesture toward "the 'something' they will not name" (406). In his fiction, James produces the circumlocutory sentences, and in his correspondence the mail does the circumlocuting for him. When James extends his hand to Gosse through the mail, it allows palimpsestical double-meanings and doubled selves that are neither fully exposed nor entirely concealed. James's correspondence makes a queer extension of himself much like his telegraphist's postal work affords her a "queer extension of her experience" (239).

It is the diverse and "queer extensions" of the nineteenth-century communication network that I have sought to explore across the course of this book. The reform of the nineteenth-century British Post Office recast communication by post as an organized, universal civic practice. The discursive invitation of "all people" into a communications

---

[24] For another example of a passionate postscript, one that has not fully survived erasure, see James's letter to Frederic W. H. Myers of 13 November 1894. The postscript reads "Let me add that I regretted more than I could express at the time the mutilation of that meeting of ours at Torquay. I should have been exceedingly glad of another day or two and more talk beneath the hawthorn shade. And. . ." Editor Leon Edel writes: "Here eight lines—about forty words—have been erased, clearly not by HJ and probably by the recipient." *Henry James Letters* 3: 489.

network simultaneously invited Victorians to understand the communications network played an essential role in discursively materializing "all people," by making them geographically connected, and giving them literal and figurative addresses or coordinates. Letter exchange was increasingly imagined not as a direct, limited interchange between two parties, but as traffic or a journey through a national or imperial web that mediates all correspondence from all Britons. This, I argue, is why we find a number of nineteenth-century fictions in which narrative emphasis falls upon that which is ancillary to the letter: postmarks, addresses, or postal workers. Through the model of the network, the rise of a postal culture was constitutively—figuratively and literally—related to both the emergence of a discourse of sexual difference and the constant "formation of new alliances" that imperial expansion entailed. If the nineteenth-century network served to disclose and materialize social, geopolitical, racial, and sexual webs of interchange that were inherently plural, it similarly did not command a single ideological inflection; it was neither consistently liberationist nor was it resolutely repressive. It was of as much interest to emerging homosexual rights campaigners as it was to those dedicated to Anglo-Saxon racial continence; indeed, there was considerable overlap between these ideological positions. The reformed postal system had the capability to enable and engender connections between people, and also to police them; it could be a focus of both desire and fear. Promoted as a civilizing machine, it functioned as a discursive engine through which relations could be established, invented, multiplied, and modulated.

WORKS CITED

Abelove, Henry. *Deep Gossip*. Minneapolis and London: U of Minnesota P, 2003.
Ablow, Rachel. *The Marriage of Minds: Reading Sympathy in the Victorian Marriage Plot*. Stanford: Stanford UP, 2007.
Achebe, Chinua. "Today, the Balance of Stories." *Home and Exile*. New York: Oxford UP, 2000. 73–105.
Adams, James Eli. *Dandies and Desert Saints: Styles of Victorian Masculinity*. Ithaca, NY: Cornell UP, 1995.
Adamson, James. *Sketches of Our Information to Rail-Roads*. Newcastle: Edward Walker, 1826.
Alldridge, Peter. "'Attempted Murder of the Soul': Blackmail, Privacy and Secrets." *Oxford Journal of Legal Studies* 13.3 (1993): 368–87.
Anderson, Nancy Fix. *Woman Against Women in Victorian England: A Life of Eliza Lynn Linton*. Bloomington: Indiana UP, 1987.
Anderson, Stuart. *Race and Rapprochement: Anglo-Saxonism and Anglo-American Relations, 1895–1904*. London: Associated UP, 1981.
Arata, Stephen D. "The Occidental Tourist: *Dracula* and the Anxiety of Reverse Colonization." *Victorian Studies* 33 (1990): 621–45.
Aristotle, *The Nicomachean Ethics*. Trans. David Ross. Oxford: Oxford UP, 2009.
Armstrong, Isobel. *Victorian Scrutinies: Reviews of Poetry, 1830–1870*. London: Athlone Press, 1972.
Arnold, Matthew. *Reports on Elementary Schools 1852–1882*. 1889. London: Printed for His Majesty's Stationery Office, 1910.
Austin, Alfred. "The Poetry of the Period." *Temple Bar* 26 (July 1869): 464.
Austin, J. L. *How to Do Things with Words: The William James Lectures Delivered at Harvard University in 1955*. New York: Oxford UP, 1962.

Baines, Phil. *Penguin by Design: A Cover Story 1935–2005*. London: Penguin, 2005.
Ballantyne, R. M. *Post Haste: A Tale of Her Majesty's Mails*. London: James Nisbet, 1880.
Barthes, Roland. *Camera Lucida*. Trans. Richard Howard. New York: Hill and Wang, 1981.
———. *S/Z*. Trans. Richard Miller. New York: Hill and Wang, 1974.
Baudrillard, Jean, "The Ecstasy of Communication." Trans. John Johnston. *The Anti-Aesthetic: Essays on Postmodern Culture*. Ed. Hal Foster. Seattle, WA: Bay Press, 1983. 126-134.
Bhabha, Homi K. "DissemiNation: Time, Narrative and the Margins of the Modern Nation." *Nation and Narration*. Ed. Homi K. Bhabha. London: Routledge, 1990. 291–322.
Bech, Henning. *When Men Meet: Homosexuality and Modernity*. Trans. Teresa Mesquit and Time Davies. 1987. Cambridge: Polity Press, 1997.
Beckson, Karl, ed. *Oscar Wilde: The Critical Heritage*. New York: Barnes and Noble, 1970.
Beer, Gillian. *Darwin's plots: Evolutionary Narrative in Darwin, George Eliot, and Nineteenth-Century Fiction*. London: Routledge and Kegan Paul, 1983.
Bell, David F. *Real Time: Accelerating Narrative From Balzac to Zola*. Urbana and Chicago: University of Illinois Press, 2004.
Bentley, Nancy. "Marriage as Treason: Polygamy, Nation, and the Novel." *The Futures of American Studies*. Eds. Donald E. Pease and Robyn Wiegman. Durham, NC : Duke U P, 2002. 341-370
Besant, Walter. *All Sorts and Conditions of Men*. 1882. Oxford: Oxford UP, 1997.
Bewell, Alan. "Jane Eyre and Victorian Medical Geography." *ELH* 63 (1996): 773–808.
Bivona, Daniel. *British Imperial Literature, 1870–1940: Writing and the Administration of Empire*. Cambridge: Cambridge UP, 1998.
Boddy, Ethel Ruth. *Two Girls or Seed Sown Through the Post*. London: S. W. Partridge, 1893.
Boehmer, Elleke. *Empire Writing: An Anthology of Colonial Literature 1870–1918*. Oxford: Oxford UP, 1998.
Booth, General William. *In Darkest England and the Way Out*. London: International Headquarters of the Salvation Army, 1890.
Bowie, Archibald Granger. *The Romance of the Post Office: Its Inception and Wondrous Development*. London: S. W. Partridge, 1897.
Brady, Sean. *Masculinity and Male Homosexuality in Britain, 1861-1913*. Houndmills, Basinstoke, Hampshire: Palgrave Macmillan, 2010.
Bradshaw, David J., and Suzanne Ozment, eds. *The Voice of Toil: 19th-Century British Writings About Work*. Athens: Ohio UP, 2000.
Brantlinger, Patrick. *Rule of Darkness: British Literature and Imperialism, 1830–1914*. Ithaca, NY: Cornell UP, 1988.
Browne, Christopher. *Getting the Message: The Story of the British Post Office*. Stroud and Dover, NH: Alan Sutton, 1993.
Browning, Elizabeth Barrett. *Letters*. 2 vols. London: Bogue, 1897.
Burritt, Elihu. *Olive Leaf for the English People*. March 1847.
———. *Peace Papers for the People*. London: Charles Gilpin, [1851, 184?].
Campbell, Alexander E. *Great Britain and the United States, 1895–1903*. London: Longmans, Green, 1960.
Campbell, Charles S. *Anglo-American Understanding, 1898–1903*. Baltimore, MD: Johns Hopkins UP, 1957.
Carmichael, Evelyn G. M. *The Law Relating to The Telegraph, The Telephone, and The Submarine Cable*. London: Knight, 1904.

Carnegie, Andrew. *Autobiography of Andrew Carnegie*. London: Constable, 1920.

———. *The Reunion of Britain and America: A Look Ahead*. Edinburgh: Darien Press, 1898.

———. "The Venezuelan Question." *North American Review* 162 (February 1896): 129–44.

Carpenter, Edward. *Days with Walt Whitman: With Some Notes on His Life and Work*. London: George Allen, 1906.

———. "Homogenic Love, and Its Place in a Free Society. Printed for Private Circulation Only." Manchester, UK: The Labour Press Society Limited, 1894.

———. *The Intermediate Sex: A Study of Some Transitional Types of Men and Women*. 1908. New York and London: Mitchell Kennerley, 1912.

Carr, John Dickson. *The Life of Sir Arthur Conan Doyle*. New York: Harper and Brothers, 1948.

Case, Alison. "Tasting the Original Apple: Gender and the Struggle for Narrative Authority in 'Dracula.'" *Narrative* 1.3 (1993): 223–43.

Castle, Terry. *The Apparitional Lesbian: Female Homosexuality and Modern Culture*. New York: Columbia UP, 1993.

"Civil Service Examinations." *The Woman's Gazette, or News About Work* (March 1877): 87.

Clayton, Jay. "The Voice in the Machine: Hazlitt, Hardy, James." *Language Machines: Technologies of Literature and Cultural Production*. Ed. Jeffrey Maston, Peter Stallybrass, and Nancy J. Vickers. New York: Routledge, 1997. 209–32.

Cocks, H. G. *Nameless Offences: Homosexual Desire in the Nineteenth Century*. London and New York: I. B. Tauris, 2003.

Cohen, Ed. *Talk on the Wilde Side: Toward a Genealogy of a Discourse on Male Sexualities*. New York and London: Routledge, 1993.

Cohen, William A. *Sex Scandal: The Private Parts of Victorian Fiction*. Durham, NC: Duke UP, 1996.

Comstock, Anthony. *Traps for the Young*. New York: Funk and Wagnalls, 1883.

Conrad, Joseph. *Heart of Darkness*. 1899. New York: W. W. Norton, 1988.

Cowper, William. "The Timepiece." *The Poems of William Cowper*. Vol. 2: 1782–85. Ed. John D. Baird and Charles Ryskamp. Oxford: Clarendon Press, 1995. 139.

Craft, Christopher. "'Kiss Me with Those Red Lips': Gender and Inversion in Bram Stoker's *Dracula*." *Representations* 8 (Fall 1984): 107–33.

Croker, J. W. *London Quarterly Review*. 64.127 (October 1839): 282–317.

Dames, Nicholas. "Trollope and the Career: Vocational Trajectories and the Management of Ambition." *Victorian Studies* 45.2 (2003): 247–78.

Daunton, M. J. *Royal Mail: The Post Office Since 1840*. London: Athlone, 1985.

Dellamora, Richard. "Stupid Trollope." *Victorian Newsletter* 100 (Fall 2001): 22–26.

D'Emilio, John. *Making Trouble: Essays on Gay History, Politics and the University*. London: Routledge, 1992.

De Quincey, Thomas. *Confessions of an English Opium-Eater and Other Writings*. Ed. Grevel Lindop. Oxford: Oxford UP, 1985.

———. *De Quincey Memorials: Being Letters and Other Records, Here First Published*. 2 vols. Ed. Alexander Hay Japp. London: William Heinemann, 1891.

———. "The English Mail-Coach, or the Glory of Motion." 1849. *Confessions of an English Opium-Eater and Other Writings*. Ed. Grevel Lindop. Oxford: Oxford UP, 1985. 183–233.

Derecourt, Henry, comp. *Colonial and International Postage. A Collection of Extracts, Ideas, and Information on Postal Affairs, and Post Office Anomalies*. London: Charles Cawley, 1854.

Dickens, Charles. *Sketches by Boz [pseud.] Illustrative of Every-Day Life And Every-Day People: With 55 illus. by George Cruikshank and "Phiz" [pseud.] and an Introd. by Then Holme.* 1836. London and New York: Oxford UP, 1966.

———. *The Pickwick Papers.* 1836-7. London: Penguin, 1986.

Dinshaw, Carolyn. *Getting Medieval: Sexualities and Communities, Pre- and Postmodern.* Durham, NC and London: Duke UP, 1999.

Disraeli, Benjamin. *Tancred or the New Crusade.* 1847. Bradenham ed. Vol. 10. London: Peter Davis, 1927.

Donald, A. K. *Why There Is Discontent in the Post Office.* London: Labour Press, 1890.

Donaldson, Thomas. *Walt Whitman the Man.* New York: Francis P. Harper, 1896.

Donoghue, Emma. *We Are Michael Field.* Bath, UK: Absolute Press, 1998.

Dowling, Linda. *Hellenism and Homosexuality in Victorian Oxford.* Ithaca, NY and London: Cornell UP, 1994.

Doré, Gustave, and Blanchard Jerrold. *London a Pilgrimage.* 1872. New York: Dover, 1970.

Doyle, Arthur Conan. *The Penguin Complete Sherlock Holmes.* Harmondsworth, UK: Penguin, 1982.

DPP1/95/1. *Transcripts of the Cleveland Street Trials.* Kew, London: Public Record Office, 1889.

DPP1/95/2. *Transcripts of the Cleveland Street Trials.* Kew, London: Public Record Office, 1889.

DPP1/95/3. *Transcripts of the Recorder, Sir Thomas Chambers Q.C., of the Cleveland Street Trials.* Kew, London: Public Record Office, 1889.

DPP1/95/4. *Transcripts of the Recorder, Sir Thomas Chambers Q.C., of the Cleveland Street Trials.* Kew, London: Public Record Office, 1889.

Duggan, Lisa. *The Incredible Shrinking Public: Sexual Politics and the Decline of Democracy.* Boston: Beacon Press, 2002.

Edel, Leon, ed. *Henry James Letters Volume 1 1843–1875.* London: Macmillan, 1974.

———. *Henry James Letters Volume 3 1883–1895.* Cambridge, MA: Harvard UP, 1980.

Edelman, Lee. *Homographesis: Essays in Gay Literary and Cultural History.* New York and London: Routledge, 1994.

———. *No Future: Queer Theory and the Death Drive.* Durham, NC: Duke UP, 2004.

———. "Tearooms and Sympathy, or, The Epistemology of the Water Closet." *The Lesbian and Gay Studies Reader.* Ed. Henry Abelove, Michele Aina Barale, and David M. Halperin. New York: Routledge, 1993. 553–74.

Editorial. *London Times* Saturday, 3 January 1846: 4.

Eliot, George. Rev. of *The Poets and Poetry of America*, by R. W. Griswold. *Leader* 310 (Saturday, 1 March 1856): 210.

Ellmann, Richard. *Oscar Wilde.* New York: Vintage Books, 1988.

———. *The Origin of the Family, Private Property and the State.* 1884. New York: International Publishers, 1972.

Faderman, Lillian. *Surpassing the Love of Men: Romantic Friendship and Love Between Women from the Renaissance to the Present.* New York: Morrow, 1981.

Fanon, Frantz. *The Wretched of the Earth.* 1961. Trans. Constance Farrington. London: Penguin Books, 1967.

Farson, Daniel. *The Man Who Wrote Dracula: A Biography of Bram Stoker.* London: M. Joseph, 1975.

Favret, Mary. *Romantic Correspondence: Women, Politics and the Fiction of Letters.* Cambridge: Cambridge UP, 1993.

Field, Michael. [Katherine Bradley and Edith Cooper]. *Underneath the Bough: A Book of Verses*. London and New York, NY: G.Bell, 1893.
———. *Works and Days*. British Library Add. Ms 46777.
Fleissner, Jennifer L. "Dictation Anxiety: The Stenographer's Stake in *Dracula*." *Nineteenth-Century Contexts* 22.3 (2000): 417–55.
———. "Henry James' Art of Eating." *ELH* 75.1 (2008): 27–62.
Flint, Kate. *The Woman Reader 1837–1914*. Oxford: Oxford UP, 1993.
Foucault, Michel. *Discipline and Punish*. Trans. Alan Sheridan. London: Penguin, 1991.
———. "Ethics: Subjectivity and Truth." *Essential Works of Foucault 1954–1984*. Vol. 1. Ed. Paul Rabinow. Trans. Robert Hurley. New York: New Press, 1997.
———. *Histoire de la sexualité*. Paris: Gallimard, 1976.
———. *The History of Sexuality: An Introduction*. Vol. 1. London: Penguin, 1990.
———. *Power/Knowledge: Selected Interviews and Other Writings 1972–1977*. Ed. Colin Gordon. Trans. Colin Gordon, Leo Marshall, John Mepham, and Kate Soper. New York: Pantheon, 1980. 222–24.
———. "What Is an Author?" in "Aesthetics, Method, and Epistemology." *Essential Works of Foucault 1954–1984*. Vol. 2. Ed. James Faubion. Series Ed. Paul Rabinow. Trans. Robert Hurley and Others. London: Penguin Books, 1994. Essay based on a lecture first given on 22 February 1969. 205-222.
Freeman, Elizabeth. *The Wedding Complex: Forms of Belonging in Modern American Culture*. Durham, NC: Duke UP, 2002.
"Further Reports of Assistant Commissioners on Popular Education." *Postal Papers*. Vol. 21. Pt. 3. [2794] (1861): 116. London: Post Office Archive Library.
Fuss, Diana. "Inside/Out." *Inside/Out: Lesbian Theories, Gay Theories*. New York: Routledge, 1991. 1–10.
Gagnier, Regenia. "Evolution and Information, or Eroticism and Everyday Life, in *Dracula* and Late Victorian Aestheticism." *Sex and Death in Victorian Literature*. Ed. Regina Barreca. Bloomington: Indiana UP, 1990. 140–57.
Gardner, Simon. "Trashing with Trollope: A Deconstruction of the Postal Rules in Contract." *Oxford Journal of Legal Studies* 122 (1992): 170–94.
Gaskell, Elizabeth. *Cranford/Cousin Phillis*. Ed. Peter Keating. London: Penguin, 1976.
Gates, Henry Louis. "Writing 'Race' and the Difference It Makes." *"Race," Writing and Difference*. Ed. Henry Louis Gates, Jr. Chicago, IL: U of Chicago P, 1986.
Gibson, James, ed. *Thomas Hardy: Interviews and Recollections*. Houndmills, UK: Macmillan, 1999.
Gilmore, Paul. "The Telegraph in Black and White." *English Literary History* 69.3 (2002): 805–33.
Glendinning, Victoria. *Anthony Trollope*. New York: Knopf, 1993.
Glover, David. *Vampires, Mummies and Liberals: Bram Stoker and the Politics of Popular Fiction*. Durham, NC: Duke UP, 1996.
Goldberg, Jonathan. *Shakespeare's Hand*. Minneapolis: U of Minnesota P, 2003.
Greenberg, David, and Maria Bystryn. "Capitalism, Bureaucracy and Male Homosexuality." *Contemporary Crises* 8 (1984): 33–56.
Greenwood, James. "A Tale of a Breach of Promise." *A Queer Showman and Other Stories*. London and New York: Ward, Lock, 1885.

Greg, W. R. "Why Are Women Redundant?" *National Review* 14 (1862): 434–60.

Gregory, Eileen. *H. D. and Hellenism*. Cambridge: Cambridge UP, 1997.

Grey, Earl. "How Shall We Retain the Colonies?" *The Nineteenth Century* 28 (June 1879): 935–95.

Guattari, Félix. "Machinic Heterogenesis." 1993. Trans. James Creech. Reprinted in David Trend, ed. *Reading Digital Culture*. Malden, MA: Blackwell, 2001.

Halberstam, Judith. *Skin Shows: Gothic Horror and the Technology of Monsters*. Durham, NC and London: Duke UP, 1995.

Hall, N. John. Introduction. *John Caldigate*. 1879. By Anthony Trollope. Oxford: Oxford UP, 1993. vii–xix.

———. ed. *The Letters of Anthony Trollope*. 2 vols. Stanford, CA: Stanford UP, 1983.

———. ed. *The Trollope Critics*. Totowa, NJ: Barnes and Noble Books, 1981.

———. *Trollope: A Biography*. Oxford and New York: Oxford UP, 1991.

Halperin, David M. *How to Do the History of Homosexuality*. Chicago and London: U of Chicago P, 2002.

Hardt, Michael, and Antonio Negri. *Empire*. Cambridge, MA: Harvard UP, 2000.

Hardy, Thomas. *A Laodicean*. 1881. World's Classics Edition. Oxford and New York: Oxford UP, 1991.

Headrick, Daniel R. *The Invisible Weapon: Telecommunications and International Politics 1851–1945*. New York and Oxford: Oxford UP, 1991.

Heaton, J. Henniker. *Postal Reform: Ocean Penny Postage and Cheap Imperial Telegraphs*. London: Harrison, 1890.

———. "A Postal Utopia." *The Nineteenth Century* 43.255 (May 1898): 764–79.

Hegel, G. W. F. *Philosophy of Nature*. Vol. 2. Trans. Michael Petry. New York: Humanities Press, 1970.

Helsinger, Elizabeth K., Robin Lauterbach Sheets, and William Veeder, eds. *The Woman Question: Defining Voices, 1837–1883*. 3 vols. New York: Garland Publishing, 1983.

Henkin, David M. *The Postal Age: The Emergence of Modern Communications in Nineteenth-Century America*. Chicago and London: U of Chicago P, 2006.

Hewitt, Elizabeth. *Correspondence and American Literature, 1770–1865*. Cambridge: Cambridge UP, 2005.

Hey, Colin G. *Rowland Hill Genius and Benefactor 1795–1879*. London: Quiller Press, 1989.

Hill, Georgiana. *Women in English Life: From Medieval to Modern Times*. 2 vols. London: Richard Bentley, 1896.

Hill, Sir Rowland. *Post Office Reform; Its Importance and Practicability*. London: W. Clowes and Sons, 1837.

Hill, Sir Rowland, and George Birkbeck Hill. *The Life of Sir Rowland Hill and the History of Penny Postage*. 2 vols. London: Thomas de La Rue, 1880.

HO 144/238/A52539. London: Home Office Papers.

HO 144/477/X24427. London: Home Office Papers.

Holcombe, Lee. *Victorian Ladies at Work: Middle-Class Working Women in England and Wales*. Hamden, CT: Archon Books, 1973.

Holland, Merlin. *Irish Peacock & Scarlet Marquess: The Real Trial of Oscar Wilde*. London and New York: Fourth Estate, 2003.

Houlbrook, Matt. *Queer London: Perils and Pleasures in the Sexual Metropolis, 1918–1957*. Chicago and London: U of Chicago P, 2005.

Hyde, H. Montgomery. *The Cleveland Street Scandal*. New York: Coward, McCann and Geoghegan, 1976.

———. *The Other Love*. London: Mayflower, 1972.

Hyde, James Wilson. *The Royal Mail: Its Curiosities and Romance*. Edinburgh: W. Blackwood and Sons, 1885.

Jaffe, Jacqueline A. *Arthur Conan Doyle*. Boston: Twayne, 1987.

James, Henry. *The Ambassadors*. Ed. S. P. Rosenbaum. New York: W. W. Norton, 1964.

———. "The Art of Fiction." *The Critical Muse: Selected Literary Criticism*. London: Penguin Classics, 1987. Ed. Roger Gard. 186–206.

———. *The Critical Muse: Selected Literary Criticism*. Ed. Roger Gard. London: Penguin Classics, 1988.

———. *Henry James Autobiography*. Ed. Frederick W. Dupee. London: W. H. Allen, 1956.

——— *In the Cage. London Stories and Other Writings*. Padstow, Cornwall, UK: Tabb House, 1989.

———. *Novels and Stories*. London: Macmillan, 1921.

———. *Partial Portraits*. London: Macmillan, 1888.

———. *A Small Boy and Others*. New York: Charles Scribner's Sons, 1913.

Jefferson, Thomas. "Autobiography of Thomas Jefferson." *The Heath Anthology of American Literature*. Ed. Paul Lauter et al. 2nd ed. Vol. 1. Lexington, MA: Heath, 1994. 960–64.

Jenkyns, Richard. *The Victorians and Ancient Greece*. Cambridge, MA: Harvard UP, 1980.

Kaplan, Fred. *Henry James: The Imagination of Genius*. New York: Morrow, 1992.

Kaplan, Morris B. *Sodom on the Thames: Sex, Love, and Scandal in Wilde Times*. Ithaca, NY and London: Cornell UP, 2005.

Kaye, Richard A. *The Flirt's Tragedy: Desire Without End in Victorian and Edwardian Fiction*. Charlottesville: U of Virginia P, 2002.

Kearns, Katherine. *Nineteenth-Century Literary Realism: Through the Looking-Glass*. Cambridge: Cambridge UP, 1996.

Kendle, John Edward. *The Colonial and Imperial Conferences 1887–1911: A Study in Imperial Organization*. London: Longmans, 1967.

Kendrick, Walter. *The Secret Museum: Pornography in Modern Culture*. 1987. Berkeley: U of California P, 1996.

Kermode, Anita and Frank. *The Oxford Book of Letters*. Oxford: Oxford UP, 1995.

Kipling, Rudyard. "His Chance in Life." *Plain Tales from the Hills*. Oxford: Oxford UP, 1987.

———. *The Letters of Rudyard Kipling*. 2 vols. Ed. Thomas Pinney. Iowa City: U of Iowa P, 1990.

——— "The White Man's Burden." *McClure's Magazine* 4 (February 1899): 290–91.

Kittler, Friedrich. *Discourse Networks 1800/1900*. Trans. Michael Metteer with Chris Cullens. Stanford, CA: Stanford UP, 1990.

———. "Dracula's Legacy." *Stanford Humanities Review*. 1.1 (1982): 143–73.

Knox, Robert. *The Races of Men: A Philosophical Enquiry into the Influence of Race over the Destinies of Nations*. 2nd ed. London: Henry Renshaw, 1850.

Kurnick, David. " 'Horrible Impossible': Henry James's Awkward Stage." *Henry James Review* 26.2 (2005): 109–29.

Lane, Christopher. *The Ruling Passion: British Colonial Allegory and the Paradox of Homosexual Desire*. Durham, NC: Duke UP, 1995.

Langley, Lester D. *Struggle for the American Mediterranean: United States-European Rivalry in the Gulf-Caribbean, 1776–1904*. Athens: U of Georgia P, 1976.

Lansbury, Coral. *Elizabeth Gaskell: The Novel of Social Crisis*. New York: Barnes and Noble, 1975.

———. *The Reasonable Man: Trollope's Legal Fiction*. Princeton, NJ: Princeton UP, 1981.

Latour, Bruno. *Aramis or the Love of Technology*. Trans. Catherine Porter. Cambridge, MA: Harvard UP, 1996.

Lewins, William. *Her Majesty's Mails: A History of the Post-Office, and an Industrial Account of its Present Condition*. London: Sampson Low, Son and Marston, 1865.

Linton, Eliza Lynn. *Autobiography of Christopher Kirkland*. 3 Vols. London: Richard Bentley and Son, 1885.

———. "The Modern Revolt." *Macmillan's Magazine* 23 (December 1870): 142–49.

———. "Queen Bees or Working Bees." *Saturday Review* (12 November 1859): 576.

———. *The Rebel of the Family*. 3 vols. London: Chatto and Windus, 1880.

Lohrli, Anne, comp. *Household Words; a Weekly Journal 1850–1859, Conducted by Charles Dickens. Table of Contents, List of Contributors and Their Contributions Based on the Household Words Office Book in the Morris L. Parrish Collection of Victorian Novelists, Princeton University Library*. Toronto: U of Toronto P, 1973.

London, Jack. *The People of the Abyss*. London: Macmillan, 1903.

Macaulay, Thomas Babington. *The History of England from the Accession of James the Second*. 1848. Vol. 1. New York: Harper and Brothers, 1879.

MacColla, Charles J. *Breach of Promise: Its History and Social Considerations*. London: Pickering, 1879.

Manners, Lady John. *Employment of Women in the Public Service*. Edinburgh and London: William Blackwood and Sons, 1882.

Marcus, Sharon. *Between Women: Friendship, Desire, and Marriage in Victorian England*, Princeton, NJ and Oxford: Princeton UP, 2007.

Marcuse, Herbert. *Technology, War and Fascism: Collected Papers of Herbert Marcuse*. Vol.1. Ed. Douglas Kellner. London and New York: Routledge, 1998.

Martindale, Hilda. *Women Servants of the State 1870–1938: A History of Women in the Civil Service*. London: George Allen and Unwin, 1938.

Martineau, Harriet. *The History of England During the Thirty Years' Peace*. 2 vols. London: Charles Knight, 1849.

———. *The Pictorial History of England:Being a History of the People as Well as a History of the Kingdom*. Vol. 7. London: W. and R. Chambers, 1858.

Marvin, Carolyn. *When Old Technologies Were New: Thinking About Electric Communication in the Late Nineteenth Century*. New York and Oxford: Oxford UP, 1988.

Marx, Karl. *Capital*. 1867. Vol. 1. New York: International Publishers, 1967.

Masten, Jeffrey, Peter Stallybrass, and Nancy J. Vickers, eds. *Language Machines: Technologies of Literature and Cultural Production*. London: Routledge, 1997.

McClintock, Anne. *Imperial Leather: Race, Gender and Sexuality in the Colonial Contest*. New York and London: Routledge, 1995.

McLuhan, Marshall. *The Medium Is the Massage: An Inventory of Effects*. London: Penguin, 1967.

Meem, Deborah T. "Eliza Lynn Linton and the Rise of Lesbian Consciousness." *Journal of the History of Sexuality* 7.4 (1997): 537–60.
Member of the Ursuline Community, Thurles. *Links with the Absent; or, Chapters on Correspondence*. London: R. Washbourne, 1882.
Menke, Richard. *Telegraphic Realism: Victorian Realism and Other Information Systems*. Stanford, CA: Stanford UP, 2007.
Merck, Mandy. *In Your Face: 9 Sexual Studies*. New York: New York UP, 2000.
Michie, Elsie. "The Odd Couple: Anthony Trollope and Henry James." *Henry James Review* 27.1 (2006): 10–23.
Miller, D. A. "Secret Subjects, Open Secrets." *The Novel and the Police*. Berkeley: U of California P, 1988.
Miller, J. Hillis. *The Ethics of Reading: Kant, de Man, Eliot, Trollope, James, and Benjamin*. New York: Columbia UP, 1987.
"Minutes Before Select Committee on Postage." *Postal Papers*. Vol. 20. Pt. 2. [658]. Items 9149, 9175-76 (1837–38): 213–16. London: Post Office Archive Library, 1837–38.
Mitch, David F. *The Rise of Popular Literacy in Victorian England: The Influence of Private Choice and Public Policy*. Philadelphia: U of Pennsylvania P, 1992.
Mitchell, Sally. "Good Words." *British Literary Magazines: The Victorian and Edwardian Age, 1837–1913*. Ed. Alvin Sullivan. London: Greenwood Press, 1984. 145–49.
Moon, Michael. *Disseminating Whitman: Revision and Corporeality in Leaves of Grass*. Cambridge, MA: Harvard UP, 1991.
———. *A Small Boy and Others: Imitation and Initiation in American Culture from Henry James to Andy Warhol*. Durham, NC and London: Duke UP, 1998.
Moore, Rayburn S., ed. *Selected Letters of Henry James to Edmund Gosse, 1882–1915: A Literary Friendship*. Baton Rouge: Louisiana State UP, 1988.
Moran, Leslie J. *The Homosexual(ity) of Law*. New York: Routledge, 1996.
Moretti, Franco. "A Capital Dracula." *Signs Taken for Wonders: Essays in the Sociology of Literary Forms*. Trans. Susan Fischer, David Forgacs, and David Miller. New York: Verso, 1988. 90–104.
Muller, John P. and William J. Richardson, eds. *The Purloined Poe: Lacan, Derrida, and Psychoanalytic Reading*. Baltimore, MD: Johns Hopkins UP, 1988.
Nicholson, John Gambril. "Your City Cousins." 1892. *A Garland of Ladslove*. London: Privately Printed, 1911. 27.
Nixon, Nicola. "The Reading Gaol of Henry James's *In the Cage*." *ELH* 66 (1999): 179–201.
Nordau, Max. *Degeneration*. 1895. Lincoln: U of Nebraska P, 1968.
Nowell-Smith, Simon, comp. *The Legend of the Master*. London: Constable, 1947.
Nunokawa, Jeff. " 'All the Sad Young Men': AIDS and the Work of Mourning." *Inside/Out: Lesbian Theories, Gay Theories*. Ed. Diana Fuss. New York: Routledge, 1991. 311–23.
O'Farrell, Mary Ann. *Telling Complexions: The Nineteenth-Century English Novel and the Blush*. Durham, NC and London: Duke UP, 1997.
Ohi, Kevin. "The Author of 'Beltraffio': The Exquisite Boy and Henry James's Equivocal Aestheticism." *ELH* 72.3 (2005): 747–67.
"On the Appreciation of Trifles." *Chameleon* 1894: 58.
Orel, Harold, ed. *Sir Arthur Conan Doyle: Interviews and Recollections*. Houndmills, Basingstoke, Hampshire, UK: Macmillan, 1991.

———. "The Great Nation of Futurity." *The United States Magazine, and Democratic Review* 6.23: (November 1839): 426–30.
Otis, Laura. *Membranes: Metaphors of Invasion in Nineteenth-Century Literature, Science and Politics*. Baltimore, MD: Johns Hopkins UP, 1999.
"Our Old Nobility." *North London Press* 28 September 1889: 3.
Pall Mall Gazette 12 September 1889: 35.
Parr, Harriet. "The Post-Mistress." *Household Words* 12.292 (27 October 1855): 305–9.
Paterson, Mark. *The Senses of Touch: Haptics, Affects and Technologies*. Oxford and New York: Berg, 2007.
"Pears' Soap Advertisement." *Harper's Weekly* 30 July 1898.
Phillips, Charles J. *Fifty Years of Philately: The History of Stanley Gibbons, Ltd*. London: Stanley Gibbons, 1906.
Plotz, John. *The Crowd: British Literature and Public Politics*. Berkeley: U of California P, 2000.
———. *Portable Property: Victorian Culture on the Move*. Princeton, NJ and Oxford: Princeton UP, 2008.
Pope, Alexander. "Eloisa to Abelard." *Poetical Works*. Ed. Herbert Davis. Oxford: Oxford UP, 1978. 110–19.
Post 30/468, 46391/88. *Post Office Circular*. London: Post Office Archives and Records Office.
Post 30/468, E15611/1884. *Post Office Circular*. London: Post Office Archives and Records Office.
Post 30/1052, E22956/1903, file I. *Post Office Circular*. London: Post Office Archives and Records Office.
Post 30/1924, E 1976/1911. *Post Office Circular*. London: Post Office Archives and Records Office, 1908.
Post 33/3213, M1756/1931, file I, bottom A. London: Post Office Archives and Records Office.
The Postman: A Paper for the People and A House to House Evangel. London: Burnley, 1880–84.
Potter, Mrs. Adrian. *The Life and Letters of Sir John Henniker Heaton*. London: John Lane, Bodley Head, 1916.
Pouchet, Georges. *The Plurality of the Human Race*. Trans. H. J. C. Beavan. London: Anthropological Society, 1864.
Prins, Yopie. *Victorian Sappho*. Princeton, NJ: Princeton UP, 1999.
———. "Greek Maenads, Victorian Spinsters." *Victorian Sexual Dissidence*. Ed. Richard Dellamora. Chicago IL and London: Chicago UP, 1999. 43–81.
Redford, Bruce. *The Converse of the Pen: Acts of Intimacy in the Eighteenth-Century Familiar Letter*. Chicago: U of Chicago P, 1986.
Rev. of "First Report of the Postmaster-General, on the Post-Office. Presented to Both Houses of Parliament by Command of Her Majesty." *London Quarterly Review* 5 (October 1855): 158–79. Rpt. of *First Report of the Postmaster-General, on the Post-Office. Presented to Both Houses of Parliament by Command of Her Majesty*. London: Printed for Her Majesty's Stationery Office, 1855. Rpt. as rev. of "Ninth Report of the Postmaster General, on the Post Office" in *London Quarterly Review* 21 (October 1863): 209–38.
Rev. of *A Laodicean*, by Thomas Hardy. *Saturday Review* 54 (18 November 1882): 674–75.
Rev. of *The Picture of Dorian Gray*, by Oscar Wilde. *Scots Observer* 5 July 1890: 4. 181.
Reynolds's Gazette 29 September 1889: 3.
Richards, Thomas. *The Imperial Archive: Knowledge and the Fantasy of Empire*. London: Verso, 1993.

Robbins, Hollis. "Fugitive Mail: The Deliverance of Henry 'Box' Brown." *American Studies* 50:1-2, 2009. 5-25.

Robson, John. "Crime in *Our Mutual Friend*." *Rough Justice*. Ed. Martin Friedland. Toronto: U of Toronto P, 1991. 114–40.

Roscoe's Digest of the Law of Evidence in Criminal Cases. 8th ed. London: Horace Smith, 1874.

Rosenheim, Shawn. *The Cryptographic Imagination: Secret Writing from Edgar Poe to the Internet*. Ithaca, NY: Cornell U P, 1984.

Rotberg, Robert I. *The Founder: Cecil Rhodes and the Pursuit of Power*. With the Collaboration of Miles F. Shore. New York and Oxford: Oxford UP, 1988.

Rowbotham, Sheila. *Edward Carpenter: A Life of Liberty and Love*. London: Verso, 2008.

Rowe, Katherine. *Dead Hands: Fictions of Agency, Renaissance to Modern*. Stanford, CA: Stanford UP, 1999.

Royle, Nicholas. *Telepathy and Literature: Essays on the Reading Mind*. Oxford: Basil Blackwell, 1990.

Said, Edward. *Culture and Imperialism*. New York: Vintage, 1994.

Samuels, Shirley. *Romances of the Republic, Women, the Family and Violence in the Literature of the Early American Nation*. Oxford: Oxford UP, 1996.

Savoy, Eric. "Embarrassments: Figure in the Closet." *Henry James Review* 20.3 (1999): 227–36.

———. " 'In the Cage' and the Queer Effects of Gay History." *Novel: A Forum on Fiction* 28.3 (1995): 284–307.

———. "Subjunctive Biography." *Henry James Review* 27.3 (2006): 248–55.

Schaffer, Talia. " 'A Wilde Desire Took Me': The Homoerotic History of *Dracula*." *ELH* 61 (1994): 381–425.

Schivelbusch, Wolfgang. *The Railway Journey: The Industrialisation of Time and Space in the Nineteenth Century*. Leamington Spa, UK: Berg, 1986.

Schmidt, Leigh Eric. "The Fashioning of a Modern Holiday: St. Valentine's Day, 1840–1870," *Winterthur Portfolio* 28: 4 (Winter 1993): 209–45.

Schnapp, Jeffrey T. "Crash (Speed as Engine of Individuation)." *Modernism/Modernity* 6.1 (1999): 1–49.

Schor, Hilary M. "Affairs of the Alphabet: Reading, Writing and Narrating in Cranford." *Novel: A Forum on Fiction* 22.3 (1989): 288–304.

———. *Scheherezade in the Marketplace*. New York and Oxford: Oxford UP, 1992.

Section 11. Criminal Law Amendment Act. Written by Henry Labouchère. 1 January 1886.

Sedgwick, Eve Kosofsky. *Epistemology of the Closet*. Berkeley: U of California P, 1990.

———. *Tendencies*. Durham, NC: Duke UP, 1993.

Seeley, John. *The Expansion of England: Two Courses of Lectures*. 1883. London: Macmillan, 1909.

Select Series of Christian Tracts and Books. *Story of a Little Boy Who Put a Letter in the Post Office*. Dublin and London, 1860.

Seltzer, Mark. *Serial Killers: Death and Life in America's Wound Culture*. London: Routledge, 1998.

Showalter, Elaine. *Sexual Anarchy: Gender and Culture at the Fin De Siecle*. New York: Virago, 1990.

Shreffler, Philip A. "Let Me Introduce You to Mr. Jefferson Hope." *Studies in Scarlet*. Ed. F. Starr. Dubuque, IA: Gasogene Press, 1989. 122–41.

Siegert, Bernhard. *Relays: Literature as an Epoch of the Postal System*. Trans. Kevin Repp. Stanford: Stanford UP, 1999.

Simmel, Georg. *Georg Simmel: On Women, Sexuality, and Love*. Trans. and Intro. Guy Oakes. New Haven, CT and London: Yale UP, 1984.

———. *The Sociology of Georg Simmel*. Trans., Ed., and Intro. Kurt H. Wolff. Glencoe, IL: Free Press, 1950.

Simpson, Colin, Lewis Chester, and David Leitch. *The Cleveland Street Affair*. Boston and Toronto: Little, Brown, 1976.

Sims, George R. *How the Poor Live and Horrible London*. London: Chatto and Windus, 1889.

Singer, Godfrey Frank. *The Epistolary Novel: Its Origin, Development, Decline, and Residuary Influence*. Philadelphia: U of Pennsylvania P, 1933.

Smalley, Donald Arthur. *Anthony Trollope: The Critical Heritage*. New York, NY: Barnes and Noble, 1969.

Smiles, Samuel. *Duty: With Illustrations of Courage, Patience, & Endurance*. London: John Murray, 1880.

Smith, H. G. *A History of Postal Agitation: From 50 Years Ago Till the Present Day*. London: C. Arthur Pearson, 1900.

Smyth, Eleanor C. *Sir Rowland Hill: The Story of a Great Reform*. London: T. Fisher Unwin, 1907.

Staff, Frank. *The Penny Post 1680–1918*. London: Lutterworth Press, 1964.

———. *The Valentine and Its Origins*. London: Lutterworth Press, 1969.

Stead, W. T., ed. *Always Arbitrate Before You Fight*. London: "Review of Reviews" Office, 1896.

———. *The Americanization of the World*. New York, NY and London: Horace Markley, 1902.

———. *The Last Will and Testament of Cecil John Rhodes*. London: "Review of Reviews" Office, 1902.

Stephanson, Anders. *Manifest Destiny: American Expansion and the Empire of Right*. New York: Hill and Wang, 1995.

Stevenson, Robert Louis and Fanny Van De Grift Stevenson. *The Dynamiter*, subtitled *More New Arabian Nights*. London: Longmans, Green, and Co., 1885.

Stoker, Bram. "The Censorship of Fiction." *The Nineteenth Century and After*. London: Spottiswoode, 1908. 64: 479–87.

———. *Dracula*. 1897. New York: W. W. Norton, 1997.

———. *A Glimpse of America: A Lecture Given at the London Institution, 29th December 1885*. London: Sampson Low, Marston, 1886.

———. *The Jewel of the Seven Stars*. 1903. Oxford: Oxford UP, 1996.

———. *Lady Athlyne*. London: William Heinemann, 1908.

———. Letter to W. E. Gladstone. British Library Add. 44525 f. 221-2, 1897.

———. *Personal Reminiscences of Henry Irving*. 2 vols. New York: Macmillan, 1906.

———. *Under the Sunset*. 1882. North Hollywood, CA: Newcastle Publishing, 1978.

St. Stephen's Review 9 November 1889: 4.

Stubbs, Katherine. "Telegraphy's Corporeal Fictions." *New Media, 1740–1915*. Ed. Lisa Gitelman and Geoffrey B. Pingree. Cambridge, MA: MIT Press, 2003: 91–111.

Sturgeon, Mary. *Michael Field*. London: Harrap, 1922.

Sullivan, Zoreh T. *Narratives of Empire: The Fictions of Rudyard Kipling*. Cambridge: Cambridge UP, 1993.

Super, R. H. *Trollope in the Post Office*. Ann Arbor: U of Michigan P, 1981.

Swift, H. G. *A History of Postal Agitation: From 50 Years Ago Till the Present Day*. London: C. Arthur Pearson, 1900.

Symonds, John Addington. *In the Key of Blue and Other Prose Essays*. London: E. Mathews and J. Lane, 1893.

———. *John Addington Symonds A Biography: Compiled from his Papers and Correspondence by Horatio F. Brown*. 2 vols. London: John C. Nimmo, 1895.

———. *Studies of the Greek Poets I*. London: Smith, Elder, 1873.

Tanner, Tony. *The Reign of Wonder: Naivety and Reality in American Literature*. Cambridge: Cambridge UP, 1965.

Taylor, Mark C. "Terminal Faith." *Religion, Modernity and Postmodernity*. Ed. Paul Heelas with the assistance of David Martin and Paul Morris. Oxford and Malden, MA: Blackwell, 1998. 36–54.

Terry, R.C., ed. *Trollope: Interviews and Recollections*. New York: St. Martin's Press, 1987.

Thomas, Ronald. R. "Revaluating Identity in the 1890s: The Rise of the New Imperialism and the Eyes of the New Detective." *Transforming Genres: New approaches to British Fiction of the 1890s*. Ed. Nikki Lee Manos and Meri-Jane Rochelson. New York: St. Martin's Press, 1994. 193–214.

Thompson, Flora. *Lark Rise to Candleford: A Trilogy*. 1939, 1941, 1943. London: Penguin Books, 1996.

Thompson, Nicola. "Gender and the Literary Reception of Anthony Trollope." *Victorian Literature and Culture* 22 (1994): 151–71.

Thorburn, David, and Henry Jenkins, eds. *Rethinking Media Change: The Aesthetics of Transition*. Cambridge, MA and London: MIT Press, 2003.

Thurschwell, Pamela, *Literature, Technology and Magical Thinking, 1880–1920*. Cambridge: Cambridge UP, 2001.

Traubel, Horace. *With Walt Whitman in Camden*. 7 vols. Ed. Sculley Bradley. Carbondale: Southern Illinois UP, 1959.

Trollope, Anthony. *An Autobiography*. 2 vols. Edinburgh and London: William Blackwood and Sons, 1883.

———. *The Eustace Diamonds*. 1873. World's Classics Edition. Oxford: Oxford UP, 1973.

———. *Four Lectures*. London: Constable, 1938.

———. *He Knew He Was Right*. 1869. Ed. David Skilton. London: Everyman, 1993.

———. *John Caldigate*. Ed. N. John Hall. Oxford and New York: Oxford UP, 1993.

———. *Later Short Stories*. Ed. John Sutherland. Oxford and New York: Oxford UP, 1995.

———. *The Letters of Anthony Trollope*. 2 vols. Ed. N. John Hall. Stanford, CA: Stanford UP, 1983.

———. "The Telegraph Girl." 1877. *Late Short Stories*. Oxford and New York: Oxford UP, 1995.

———. "The Young Women at The London Telegraph Office." *Good Words* (1877): 377–84.

Trotter, David. *Circulation: Defoe, Dickens, and the Economies of the Novel*. Houndmills, Basingstoke, Hampshire, UK: Macmillan, 1988.

Turner, Mark. *Trollope and the Magazines: Gendered Issues in Mid-Victorian Britain*. Houndmills, UK: Macmillan, 2000.

Vicinus, Martha. *Independent Women: Work and Community for Single Women 1850–1920*. London: Virago, 1985.

Villarejo, Amy. *Lesbian Rule: Cultural Criticism and the Value of Desire*. Durham, NC and London: Duke UP, 2003.

Wagner, Richard. *Richard Wagner's Prose Works*. Vol. 1 "The Art-Work of the Future." 1892. Trans. William Ashton Ellis. New York: Broude Brothers, 1966.

Waldstein, Charles. "The English-Speaking Brotherhood." *The North American Review*. Vol. 167 (1898): 223–38.

Walker, Pierre A., and Greg W. Zacharias. "James's Hand and Gosse's Tail: Henry James's Letters and the Status of Evidence." *Henry James Review* 19.1 (1998): 72–79.

Walkowitz, Judith R. *City of Dreadful Delight: Narratives of Sexual Danger in Late-Victorian London*. Chicago: U of Chicago P, 1992.

Wallace, Elisabeth. "Goldwin Smith on England and America." *American Historical Review*. 59.4 (July 1954): 884–94.

Ward, Kathleen. "Dear Sir or Madam: The Epistolary Novel in Britain in the Nineteenth-Century." PhD Dissertation, University of Wisconsin-Madison, 1989.

"The Penny Post Act!" Comic Song Sung by Mr. Buckingham at the Royal Gardens Vauxhall. Written by James Bruton, Music Composed by J. Blewitt. Published by T. E. Purday, Cover Design and Lithograph by G. E. Madeley, 3 Wellington Street, Strand. John Johnson Collection, Bodleian Library, Oxford. Postal Folder 1. Music is housed in Post History Folder 2.

Ware, J. Redding. *Passing English of the Victorian Era*. London: Routledge, 1909.

Warner, Michael. *The Trouble with Normal: Sex, Politics, and the Ethics of Queer Life*. Cambridge, MA: Harvard UP, 1999.

Watson, Nicola J. *Revolution and the Form of the British Novel, 1790–1825: Intercepted Letters, Interrupted Seductions*. Oxford: Clarendon Press, 1994.

Wears, T. Martin. *The History of the Mulready Envelope*. Bury St. Edmund's: C. H. Nunn, "Stamps Collectors' Journal" Office, 1886.

Weeks, Jeffrey. *Coming Out: Homosexual Politics in Britain from the Nineteenth Century to the Present*. London: Quartet Books, 1977.

———. *Sex, Politics and Society: The Regulation of Sexuality Since 1800*. 1982. 2nd ed. London and New York: Longman, 1989.

Wellbery, David. Foreword. *Discourse Networks 1800/1900*. By Friedrich Kittler. Trans. Michael Metteer with Chris Cullens. Stanford, CA: Stanford UP, 1900. vii–xxxiii.

Welsh, Alexander. *George Eliot and Blackmail*. Cambridge, MA: Harvard UP, 1985.

Whistler, James McNeill. Letter to Waldo Story, 20/25 May 1884? Manuscript Division, Pennell-Whistler Collection, PWC 2/61/8. Library of Congress.

White, Chris, ed. *Nineteenth-Century Writings on Homosexuality: A Sourcebook*. London: Routledge, 1999.

———. " 'Poets and Lovers Evermore': Interpreting Female Love in the Poetry and Journals of Michael Field." *Textual Practice* 4.2 (1990): 202–3.

Whitman, Walt. *The Correspondence. The Collected Writings of Walt Whitman Vol. 3:1876–1885*. Ed. Edwin Haviland Miller. New York: New York UP, 1964.

———. "Passage to India." *Leaves of Grass*. Eds. Sculley Bradley and Harold W. Blodgett. New York: W.W. Norton and Company, 1973. 411-421.

———. "Song of the Exposition." *Leaves of Grass*. Eds. Sculley Bradley and Harold W. Blodgett. New York: W.W. Norton and Company, 1973. 195-205.

———. *I Sit and Look Out: Editorials from the Brooklyn Daily Times*. Ed. Emory Holloway and Vernolian Schwarz. New York: Columbia UP, 1932.

———. *Specimen Days & Collect*. Philadelphia: Rees Welsh, 1882.
Wicke, Jennifer. "Henry James's Second Wave." *Henry James Review* 10.2 (1989): 146–51.
———. "Vampiric Typewriting: Dracula and Its Media." *ELH* 39 (1992): 467–93.
Wilde, Oscar. *The Complete Letters of Oscar Wilde*. Ed. Merlin Holland and Rupert Hart-Davis. New York: Henry Holt, 2000.
———. *The Importance of Being Earnest and Related Writings*. Ed. Joseph Bristow. London: Routledge, 1991.
———. *The Picture of Dorian Gray*. London: Penguin, 1985.
Williams, Raymond. *Contact: Human Communication and Its History*. London: Thames and Hudson, 1981.
———. *Keywords*. New York: Oxford UP, 1976.
Woolf, Virginia. *A Room of One's Own*. 1929. San Diego, CA: Harcourt Brace Jovanovich, 1989.
Wordsworth, William. "Composed Upon Westminster Bridge, September 3, 1802." *Poems, in Two Volumes, and Other Poems, 1800-1807 by William Wordsworth*. Ed. Jared Curtis. Ithaca, NY: Cornell UP, 1983. 147.
Wurgaft, Lewis D. *The Imperial Imagination: Magic and Myth in Kipling's India*. Middletown, CT: Wesleyan UP, 1983.
Young, Robert J. C. *Colonial Desire: Hybridity in Theory, Culture and Race*. London: Routledge, 1995.

INDEX

Abelove, Henry, 57
abjection, 45
Adams, John Quincy, 185
Achebe, Chinua, 24
address, 29, 37, 42, 45, 64, 79n.18, 93, 96, 167
   invention of, 19–20
affect, 18, 37–38, 81, 99, 114, 141, 143–144, 157, 192
Africa, 149, 160, 175
alias, 62–64, 218
alien, 181–182
alienation, 42n.7, 79–80, 100, 121
alliance, 9, 37–38, 146, 223
   in *Dracula* (Stoker), 196
   fraternal, 195
   international, 163
   queer structures of, 82–83
   in "A Study in Scarlet" (Doyle), 169
   transatlantic, 149, 160, 164, 183
   See also race
amanuensis, 18, 131, 206
American Civil War, 185n.56, 192, 206
American-Philippine war, 171n.34, 172
American Revolution, 148–149, 158, 160n.16, 167, 172

amplification, 9, 22, 29, 63, 65, 86, 96, 220
   in *A Laodicean* (Hardy), 142–143
   in Foucault, 110
   via networks, 100, 177
Atlantic Ocean, 149, 158–159, 166, 167n.29, 168–169, 188, 204–205
America, *See* United States
angels, *See* messengers
Anglocentricism, 153, 154n.7
Anglo-Saxonism, 166n.27, 167n.31, 168–169, 174, 177, 186–187, 205, 223
   homoerotic, 157–158
   vs. imperialism, 159
   reunionism, 23–24, 37, 149–164, 167n.31, 177, 194, 197
   vs. familial structure, 155
anonymity, 2n.2, 5, 8, 46, 58n.37, 62–63, 79, 86, 115, 117, 193, 200, 203
Apollo, Greek God, 172
Arata, Stephen, 163n.21, 184, 195, 197
Archer, William, 131–132
archive, 29, 32, 71, 181, 190
aristocracy, 10, 14, 40, 47, 49, 51–52
Aristotle: *Nichomachean Ethics*, 141–142
Armstrong, Isobel, 22
Arnold, Matthew, 135, 177n.46, 213

arteries, 149, 159, 160n.16, 162–163, 165, 169, 174, 177, 181–182
Austen, Jane, 75, 77
Austin, J.L., 101, 107

Baker Street Irregulars, 167, 169–170
Ballantyne, R.M.: *Post Haste*, 114–115, 125, 138n.50
Barthes, Roland, 143–144
Baudrillard, Jean, 100
Beardsley, Aubrey, 65–66
Beer, Gillian, 34
Bhabha, Homi, 151–153
bigamy, 36, 83–84, 86, 88, 92, 94, 96
blackmail, 7–8, 36–37, 66, 68, 83, 94, 96, 143n.55, 170, 217
Blind Office, 19
blood, 23–24, 54, 174–6, 180, 197
  brotherhood (England and the U.S.), 148–149, 151, 158–160, 164–165, 167–168, 176–177, 187, 189, 198, 205
  circulation of, 18, 43, 169
  in *Cranford* (Gaskell), 28, 30,
  in *Dracula* (Stoker), 181–182, 184, 188–189, 192, 195–198
  and familial ties, 37–38, 107, 110, 120, 133, 155, 175, 189
  in *A Laodicean* (Hardy), 133, 139
  in *The Rebel of the Family* (Linton), 121n.32, 124n.34
  in "A Study in Scarlet" (Doyle), 165–169
  in "The Telegraph Girl" (Trollope), 107
  See also arteries *entries*; vampires *entries*
Bloxam, Jack, "The Priest and the Acolyte," 62–63
  See also *The Chameleon*
blush, 65, 76, 125, 138–140, 182
body, 8, 22, 95n.45, 140, 143, 169, 174, 177, 179, 215n.6
  atopic, 63–4
  in *the Autobiography* (Trollope), 78, 81
  backside, 77–78, 84, 96
  circulation system, 18, 43, 45
  civic, 103, 181
  female, 102, 119, 190–191
  in *A Laodicean* (Hardy), 131, 135
  as machine, 119
  procreative, 174–6, 190–1
  sensory organs, 117, 131

  in "A Study in Scarlet" (Doyle), 162–163
  of telegraph workers, 52, 55–58, 116, 119, 132
  telegraphic, 119, 205–206
  as text, 40, 42n.7, 55, 58, 102, 116
  See also nervous system
Booth, General, 166n.27, 174–175
Bowie, James, 184
Boy Messengers, 35, 39–40, 43–44, 53–58, 61, 156, 161, 170,
  and homosexual prostitution, 40, 43–44, 46–47 51, 54, 60–61, 65, 107, 113
  in *The Hound of the Baskervilles* (Doyle), 170
  immortality of, 53, 109n.17
  as intermediary, 36, 40, 45
  and Oscar Wilde, 39–40, 57, 69
  in "A Study in Scarlet" (Doyle), 170
  standardization of, 53–54, 56
  Trollope's reaction to, 59–61
  See also Cleveland Street Affair
Bradley, Katherine, *See* Michael Field
breach of promise, 88–90
Brontë, Charlotte: *Jane Eyre*, 154n.8
Browning, Elizabeth Barrett, 33, 111
Browning, Robert, 111, 137
Burritt, Elihu, 150–151, 152 fig. 4.2 and 4.3, 153–154, 168, 181, 197
  "Olive Leaf for the English People," 151
butch-femme, 120–121
Butler, Josephine: *The Education and Employment of Women*, 112n.21

capital, 14n.20, 100, 162, 176, 195
Carnegie, Andrew, 24, 155n.9, 158–159, 160n.16, 166, 187
  "The Reunion of Britain and America," 158
Carpenter, Edward, 8, 27, 31–32, 37, 158, 173, 192n.69, 199
  Days with Walt Whitman, 203–204, 206n.94, 207
  "Homogenic Love, and Its Place in a Free Society," 5, 7, 69, 192n.69
  The Intermediate Sex, 4
  Walt Whitman, friendship with, 202–204, 207
Carson, Edward, 67–68
  See also Oscar Wilde's trials
Castle, Terry, 134
censorship, 7, 201–3

See also Anthony Comstock
Chamberlain, Joseph, 23, 168
  See also Imperial Penny Postage
The Chameleon, 57–58, 61–62, 64
Charles I (king of England), 10
circulation, 10, 16, 19–22, 25, 30–32, 35–36, 38, 42–43, 75, 92–93, 100, 174
  in *the Autobiography* (Trollope), 77–78, 81–82, 98
  and intercourse, 4, 88
  and intermediation, 2, 4
  overextended, 176–177
  and queerness, 8, 98
  See also blood
citizenship, 12, 14, 17, 19–20, 22, 24, 25n.32, 103–104, 115–116, 159
civil servant, *See* public servant
Clarke, Sir Edward, 66–67
  See also Oscar Wilde's trials
class, 18, 23, 31, 33, 39, 51,105–106, 112, 120–121, 178, 199, 204
  equality, 3, 5–6, 9, 11, 13–14, 17, 19, 21, 45, 91, 106n.13, 120, 204
  and homosexuality, 5–6
  and gender, 96, 99, 102–106, 108, 112
  in *In the Cage* (James), 33, 217, 220
  middle-, 36, 99, 102–103, 105–108, 127
  poverty, 11n.16, 199n.77
  shame, 39
  telegraph workers, 55, 56n.32, 107
  transitivity, 39, 51–52, 58n.36, 60, 68–69, 119, 121, 203
  upper-, 203, 214–216, 220
  working-, 13, 17–19, 51, 103, 174, 203, 210, 214–215
Clayton, Jay, 9, 131
Cleveland, Grover, 186–187
Cleveland Street Affair, 35, 40–56, 60, 64–65, 69, 170, 214
  national ramifications of, 46
  Post Office as brothel, 35, 53
  publicness and publicity of, 41, 45, 47
  redefinition of public facility, 43–44, 46
  See also Criminal Law Amendment Act
Cleveland Street Scandal, *See* Cleveland Street Affair
closet, the, 88–89, 97, 220, 222
codes, 59, 67, 220
  in *A Laodicean* (Hardy), 131, 137–8, 140

Post-Office, 7, 26–7, 84–6
  in *The Rebel of the Family*, 124
  See also secrecy
Cole, Henry, 14
Coleridge, Samuel Taylor, 11n.16, 21, 154n.7
colonialism, 83n.24, 152, 154, 157, 160, 168, 178
  in *Dracula* (Stoker), 181, 183, 185n.56, 186, 193n.70, 194, 197–198, 199
  and homosexuality, 177–179
  vs. imperialism, 154n.7, 159
  and postal/communication reform, 17, 32–33, 97, 154–159, 178, 180, 183, 198–199
  in "A Study in Scarlet" (Doyle), 162–164, 166,
  and racial fraternity, 159, 179
  in "The White Man's Burden" (Kipling), 171, 175
  See also "All Red Routes" *entries;* post-colonialism *entries*
Comstock, Anthony, 7n.8, 202–203
Comstock Law, *See* Antony Comstock
Conrad, Joseph, 197–198
Cooper, Edith, *See* Michael Field
Cowper, William: "The Timepiece," 158
Criminal Law Amendment Act of 1885, Section 11, 35, 40–41, 47–54, 214
Croker, J.W., 14
cross-dressing, *See* dress
currency, 20, 28, 43, 56

Darwin, Charles, 34, 135
Dead Letters, 19, 27, 34, 181, 200
delay, 2, 27, 87, 170, 182n.51, 200–201
delivery, 28–9, 34, 64–5, 78, 206
Dellamora, Richard, 78–79, 80n.19
De Quincey, Thomas, 25–27, 86, 100n.2
  "The English Mail-Coach, or the Glory of Motion," 25–26
Derrida, Jacques, 10n.13, 207
Dickens, Charles, 27n.34, 30n.37, 85n.30
  Nicholas Nickleby, 15
  The Pickwick Papers, 53n.30
Dinshaw, Carolyn, 144
dispatch tube, 2–3
Disraeli, Benjamin: *Endymion*, 126
dissemination, 20, 22–23, 31–32, 38, 40, 42, 92, 132n.39, 151–152, 171, 208

in *the Autobiography* (Trollope), 81
vs. consolidation, 164, 177
in *Dracula* (Stoker), 183
in *John Caldigate* (Trollope), 92
and empire, 171, 175
and enervation, 175, 177, 199
and Henry James, 208, 213
and women workers, 102
distance, 2, 8, 14, 64, 84, 97, 110, 117, 146, 155, 180, 208
erotics of, 141, 206, 207n.95
and inverted relations, 157
in *John Caldigate* (Trollope), 84, 97
in *A Laodicean*, 129–130, 141, 144
and Penny Post, 10–11, 13, 14
in "The Telegraph Girl" (Trollope), 141
and telegraphy, 64, 143, 206
"The Young Women in the London Telegraph Office" (Trollope), 117
domesticity, 36, 113–114, 121n.32, 155,
for Boy Messengers, 44, 55
heterosexual, 128, 157, 213
lesbian, 12, 99, 103, 107–108, 111, 113, 126–128, 133
Donaldson, Thomas, 199–200
Doolittle, Hilda, 137
Douglas, Lord Alfred, 33, 61, 65–66, 68
"On the Appreciation of Trifles," 61–62
"Two Loves," 61
Dowling, Linda, 135–136
Doyle, Arthur Conan, 25, 158–159, 198
"The Five Orange Pips," 182n.51
The Hound of the Baskervilles, 170
"The Navel Treaty," 167n.31
"The Noble Bachelor," 159
"A Study in Scarlet," 37, 162–170, 193–194
dress,
cross-, 28–30, 96
in *John Caldigate* (Trollope), 96
in *The Rebel of the Family* (Linton), 119, 125–126
in "The Telegraph Girl" (Trollope), 111
in "The Young Women in the London Telegraph Office" (Trollope), 118
See also tailoring *entries*; uniforms *entries*
duty, 50, 52, 65, 127–128, 173
of Boy Messengers, 55, 57
civic, 46, 50–52, 102
and homosexuality, 110, 141

in *John Caldigate* (Trollope), 85–86, 93
in *A Laodicean* (Hardy), 141
in *The Rebel of the Family* (Linton), 126–127
in "The Telegraph Girl" (Trollope), 109–112, 128
of women postal workers 102, 109–111, 113–115, 126–128
See also lesbianism *entries*; "The Telegraph Girl" *entries*

Edelman, Lee, 45, 191
education, 18, 20–21, 102–103, 110
See also literacy
Edwards, Amelia, 72n.9
effeminacy, 36, 58n.36, 75, 78, 104, 126, 131, 181
See also Anthony Trollope
electricity, 33, 122–123, 178–179
Eliot, George, 73n.11, 77, 172n.35
Middlemarch, 142
Ellmann, Richard, 57n.35, 68
See also Oscar Wilde
e-mail, 32
empire, 32, 180
"Blood Empire," 177
and colonialism, 16n.22, 159n.12
and circulation, 175–176
in *Dracula* (Stoker), 185–188, 194, 196–198
as "empire writes back," 24–25, 199
the First Empire, 162, 165
in Holmes stories (Doyle), 163, 165
homosocial bonds of, 27, 37, 110n.10, 176
and imperialism, 12, 37, 154n.7, 127, 160, 177, 198
and telegraph and mail lines, 169, 174
and the Second Empire, 163, 165, 177
unification of, 23, 160, 168
in "The White Man's Burden" (Kipling), 171, 173n.38
See also colonialism *entries*; imperialism *entries*; vampirism *entries*
Engels, Friedrich, 83n.24
envelope, 1–2, 67–68, 83, 124n.35, 183, 199–200, 219–220
for Anglo-American society, 151, 152 fig. 4.2 and 4.3
backside of, 11n.16, 26, 200n.78, 220
in *Dracula* (Stoker), 181, 183
in *John Caldigate* (Trollope), 83–87, 93–94

inscriptions on, 65
and Oscar Wilde, 36, 67–68, 219–220
royal, 10, 14, 26
See also Mulready Envelope
epistolary fiction 1–2, 28, 181
Euston, Earl of, 46
See also Cleveland Street Affair
exchange, 43, 64, 222
blood, 189, 198, 205
postal, 2, 4, 5, 7, 22, 25, 65, 73, 104, 132
erotic, 4, 5, 12, 25, 37, 88, 123–125, 131, 132, 145, 177, 205, 218–219
queer, 38, 162,
telegraphic, 63–64, 177

family, 37, 155–157, 176
blood, 30, 38, 107, 155, 120
Britain and America, 151, 157, 168–169, 176
in *Cranford* (Gaskell), 28, 30
in *John Caldigate* (Trollope), 83–86, 88, 91–93, 95n.44
and inheritance, 88, 93, 129, 133, 139
in *A Laodicean* (Hardy), 133–134
in *Post Haste* (Ballantyne), 115
as Post Office, 44, 81–82
postal effects on, 17, 38, 55, 149, 155, 157, 169
in *The Rebel of the Family* (Linton), 119–120, 127
in "The Telegraph Girl" (Trollope), 107–108
-tree, 36, 155, 157, 176
and women, 103, 1113
Fanon, Frantz, 180
Field, Kate, 91–92
Field, Michael, 111, 137
flirting, 58–60, 65, 91–92, 97n.48, 117–119, 219–20
Forty Thieves, 26–27
Foucault, Michel, 31, 38, 47–49, 79, 110, 127, 146
on censorship, 7n.8,
on racial degeneracy, 51n.25
on sexual repression, 31
on visibility, 144
franking, 10, 11n.16, 14,
Freeling, Sir Frances, 10, 90n.34
Freeman, Elizabeth, 108
"French letter," 220

Freud, Sigmund, 95n.45
The Future of an Illusion, 179

Gardner, Simon, 90
Gaskell, Elizabeth, 25, 28n.36
Cranford, 27–31, 154n.8
Mary Barton, 200n.81
Mr. Harrison's Confessions, 200n.81
Gandhi, Mahatma: *Hind Swaraj*, 180
gender, 18, 127,
and civic service, 102, 104, 106, 132, 146–147
in *Cranford* (Gaskell), 29–31
cross-identifications of, 8, 30, 36, 74, 96, 106–108, 136, 182, 199, 122, 124n.35, 132, 172; *See also* Anthony Trollope *entries*; Thomas Hardy *entries*
deviation and detachment, 25, 37, 45, 71, 73, 91, 95n.45,
transitivity, 29, 31, 75, 83n.25, 96, 112, 121, 131, 136, 179
genealogy, 137n.46, 139, 190–191
in *A Laodicean* (Hardy), 133, 135
"General Post," game, 4, 29, 31
Ginsberg, Allen, 57
"going postal," 42, 146
Good Words, 59–60, 107, 116n.23
See also Anthony Trollope
Gosse, Edmund, 217n.9, 218–222
Graham, Sir James, 124n.35
Guthrie, Woody, 2
gypsies, 182–184, 196

Halberstam, Judith, 157
Halperin, David M., 6–7, 49
Hamilton, Rebecca, 7–8
See also blackmail
Hanks, P.C. Lukes, 43
hands, 120–123
lesbian, 121, 123
handwriting, 27n.34, 68
haptics, 30, 142–144
Hardy, Thomas, 18, 36, 186–187, 206
A Laodicean, 99, 101–102, 128–146
H.D., *See* Hilda Doolittle
Heaton, J. Henniker, 23n.29, 159, 168–169
Hegel, G.W.F., 178
Henry VIII (king of England), 10
Henson, Gravenor, 18

Hellenism, 135–137
  Greek antiquity, 134–139, 145, 172, 193
  Greek love, 172, 198
heterosexuality, 8–9, 45, 59, 92–93, 134, 144, 157
  vs. homosexuality, 6–8, 38, 57, 58n.37, 173, 176, 215
  and family structures, 84–85, 157
  in *In the Cage* (James), 215, 218
  in *The Importance of Being Earnest* (Wilde), 63–64
  in *A Laodicean* (Hardy), 133–134, 140, 142–144
  in *The Rebel of the Family* (Linton), 120, 123, 127
  and Trollope, 79, 92, 119
  See also marriage plot *entries*; reproduction *entries*
hieroglyphics, 27, 84, 93
Hill, Rowland, 10–17, 19n.25, 20–22, 26, 33, 90n.34, 93, 118n.27, 156n.10
  and egalitarianism, 10–11, 14, 16–17, 21
  as headmaster, 21
  Post Office Reform,
  See also Penny Post
homoeroticism, *See* homosexuality
homo-sensorium, *See* sensorium
homosexuality, 4–8, 37–38, 57–58, 61, 146, 222–223
  Anglo-American fraternity, 162, 172–173, 179
  and aristocratic degeneracy, 51
  criminalization of, 40–42, 47–48, 58, 62, 66–67
  in *Dracula* (Stoker), 189–191, 201
  in *The Importance of Being Earnest* (Wilde), 63–64
  and empire, 110n.19, 176–177
  in *In the Cage* (James), 218
  "invention" of, 41–42, 48
  and postal system, 44, 53, 65n.48, 98
  public/private distinction, 47–49, 51
  secrecy of, 59, 65, 219
  in "The Telegraph Girl" (Trollope), 126,
  See also Cleveland Street Affair *entries*; Criminal Law Amendment Act *entries*; lesbianism *entries*
homosociality, 57
  of imperial bureaucracy, 37, 157–158, 176–178, 180, 190–191, 198

of Post Office, 44, 102, 110, 117, 126
and racial purity, 173
hybridity, 23, 175, 177n.45
Hyde, James Wilson: *The Royal Mail*, 17, 19

illiteracy, *See* literacy
imperialism, 149–156
  Anglo-Saxon, 157–158, 160, 162, 166 173, 177, 206
  and degeneration, 195, 199
  in *Dracula* (Stoker), 180–181, 183–184, 186–190, 193n.70, 194–198
  and homoeroticism, 110, 157–158, 173, 176–177, 184
  Imperial Conference of 1887, 168
  and the postal network, 12, 17, 19, 22–25, 32, 105, 168, 177, 183, 222–223
  in *The Rebel of the Family* (Linton), 127
  in "A Study in Scarlet" (Doyle), 163–164, 169, 194
  U.S., 186, 188
  in "The White Man's Burden" (Kipling), 171–173, 175, 177
  See also colonialism *entries*; Imperial Penny Post *entries*
impersonality, 42n.7, 79–82, 87, 89, 157, 212–214
infidelity, 2, 87, 90
  authorial, 72, 91, 98
  romantic, 66
  sexual, 91–2
institution,
  See Post Office
India, 29–30, 131–132, 149, 153, 179–180, 184, 204
information, 12, 17, 57, 116, 168, 170, 174, 185n.56, 189n.62, 193, 199, 213
  dissemination of, 20–23, 25, 35, 93, 151n.6,
  and misinformation, 140
  society, 32, 42n.7, 100, 190
interface, 4–5, 98, 100, 103n.5, 102, 131, 146
Iris, Greek goddess, 125
Irving, Henry, 185n.56, 187, 189n.62, 192, 194, 200
Isbister, William, 59–61

Jack the Ripper, 42n.7, 46
James, Henry,

The Ambassadors, 215
"The Art of Fiction," 210
"The Author of Beltraffio," 218–219
"A Bundle of Letters," 209, 214
In the Cage, 9, 33, 37, 208–210, 212–218, 220–221
and letters, 66, 210–211, 219–222
Notes of a Son and Brother, 210–211
Partial Portraits, 37, 71–72, 74n.12, 76n.16, 92
and postal pleasures, 210, 218
A Small Boy and Others, 213n.4, 218n.11, 221n.21
on Trollope, Anthony; 70–75, 76n.16, 80–82, 91, 97–98
James, William, 210–212
Jefferson, Thomas, 148–149, 157–158, 167, 172
Declaration of Independence, 148
Jupiter, Roman god, 74, 118n.27

Kaplan, Fred, 218n.13, 222
Kermode, Anita and Frank, 32
Kipling, Rudyard, 37, 158, 179, 180
"The Deep-Sea Cables," 178–180
"His Chance in Life," 179–180
"The Overland Mail," 180
"The White Man's Burden," 171–173, 175, 177
Kristeva, Julia, *See* abjection

Labouchère, Henry, *See* Criminal Law Amendment Act of 1885, Section 11
Lake Victoria, 161
Lane, Christopher, 83n.24, 110n.19, 176–177, 179
law, 75, 79, 146, 155n.9, 164, 169, 186, 189
contract, 90
in *The Eustace Diamonds* (Trollope), 90
in *John Caldigate* (Trollope), 85, 90–91, 93n.42, 94–95
libel, 116
and postal workers, 113, 115–116
in "The Telegraph Girl" (Trollope), 115
See also Comstock Law of 1873 *entries*; Criminal Law Amendment Act *entries*; Telegraph Act of 1868 *entries*
League of Universal Brotherhood, 151, 153, 168
letters, 1, 40, 82–83, 222

circulation of, 16, 20
democracy of, 6–7, 21, 36
and homosexuality, 5–7, 27, 98, 177, 219
and imperialism, 177
interiors vs. exteriors of, 2, 26, 82, 87, 93, 220–221
inverted, 67n.53
as legal evidence, 66–8, 88
legibility of, 68, 170
lettres de cachet, 125
love-, 64, 88–89, 90, 131, 182, 206
purloined, 67 n. 53, 69
writing of, 43, 61, 181–182, 206
See also body as text *entries*; Dead Letter *entries*; Penny Post *entries*
lesbianism, 36, 92, 99, 101, 111–113, 128, 137n.48
in *In the Cage* (James), 215
"Lesbian rule," 141–145, 215
in *A Laodicean* (Hardy), 129
and marriage, 101, 111, 120, 128–129, 145
and media, 145
as Post Office, product of, 113, 127–128
and public life, 101
in *The Rebel of the Family* (Linton), 120–121, 124, 128, 134, 141–145
in "The Telegraph Girl" (Trollope), 128
spectral, 134
See also duty *entries*; marriage *entries*; women *entries*
libel, 66–68, 84, 93n.42, 115–116
Linton, Eliza Lynn, 36, 99
antifeminism of, 36, 105, 127
The Autobiography of Christopher Kirkland, 36, 122–124, 127
"The Modern Revolt," 126, 128
The Rebel of the Family, 99, 101, 119–128, 140
Linton, William James, 124,
literacy, 17–19, 62
Lloyd, Constance, 8–9
London, Jack, 174–177, 190, 199n.77
The People of the Abyss, 174–176

Macaulay, Thomas Babington, 14
Macleod, Donald, 59
mail coach, 10, 25–6, 35
manifest destiny, 197
Manners, Lady John: *Employment of Women in the Public Service*, 106, 126, 138

maps, 12, 19–20, 166, 181
marriage, 9n.11, 38, 93, 101, 103, 126
   contract, 86–87, 88n.32, 90, 95
   in *Dracula* (Stoker), 191
   in *The Eustace Diamonds* (Trollope), 89–90
   gender transitivity of, 96
   in *John Caldigate* (Trollope), 83, 85–87, 88n.32, 92–96
   heterosexual, 99, 100–101, 108, 120, 122, 128–129, 144–145
   in *In the Cage* (James), 213–214, 218
   in *A Laodicean* (Hardy), 101, 129, 133, 139, 141n.54, 144–145
   lesbian, 108, 111-2, 119, 128
   vs. lesbianism, 120
   as network, 38, 87, 94
   in *The Picture of Dorian Gray* (Wilde), 59
   plot, 9, 83, 86, 91, 99, 101, 122, 126, 129, 145–146, 217n.9, 218
   and polygamy, 86, 169, 217
   in *The Rebel in the Family* (Linton), 101, 120, 121n.32, 122, 126–128
   in "The Telegraph Girl" (Trollope), 101, 108–110, 112, 115, 126, 128
   and work, 102, 108–111, 127–128
   See also duty *entries*; bigamy *entries*; Post Office *entries*
Martineau, Harriet, 16, 21–22, 115, 149
Marx, Karl, *See* Marxism
Marxism, 14n.20, 80, 176, 195n.73
masculinity,
   and civic service, 104–105, 110, 126
   and homogenic love, 172–173, 177, 179, 198
   and imperialism, 110
   in *In the Cage* (James), 37
   in *John Caldigate* (Trollope), 85
   in *A Laodicean* (Hardy), 131
   and nation building, 85, 148
   in *The Rebel of the Family* (Linton), 128
   in "The Telegraph Girl" (Trollope), 108, 112, 126–128
   Trollope's, 75–76, 92, 107n.15
   See also effeminacy
Mazzini, Giuseppe, 124
McIntosh, Walter, 219n.15
McLuhan, Marshall, 132
media, 12, 34n.45, 35, 42n.7, 180
   circulation of, 43, 151n.6
   in *Dracula* (Stoker), 181, 183, 185

   in *In the Cage* (James), 216
   in *John Caldigate* (Trollope), 94
   in *A Laodicean* (Hardy), 143–145
   in *The Rebel of the Family* (Linton), 126
   and Trollope, 71, 79n.18
   queer, 59, 145
medievalism, 134–135, 137, 142
Menke, Richard, 27, 35
Merck, Mandy, 121
Merrill, George, 203
Merrill, James, 57–58
   See also Jeff Nunokawa
mesmerism, 123n.33
messenger, 12, 18, 30, 36, 125
   angelic, 22, 36, 78, 81, 155–156, 192
   as healer, 25
   in *John Caldigate* (Trollope), 36
   as message, 65
   as novelist, 71–72, 79, 84, 96, 98, *See also* Anthony Trollope
   as poet, 21–22, 66
   See also Boy Messengers *entries*; Trollope, Anthony *entries*
Miller, D.A., 58–59, 61, 82
Miller, J. Hillis, 75, 79
Minerva, Roman goddess, 74
Monroe Doctrine, 185–186, 194, 198
Moon, Michael, 40, 201, 218n.11
Moretti, Franco, 182–183, 195
Mulready Envelope, 155–157

nation, 23, 151–153, 164, 178
   and blood brotherhood, 151, 154, 158–160, 164, 169, 187, 195, 205
   in *Dracula* (Stoker), 181, 185, 187, 193–195, 197
   and homosexuality, 173, 176–177
   in *In the Cage* (James), 221
   in *A Laodicean* (Hardy), 139
   in *The People of the Abyss* (London), 176
   postal system's unification of, 14, 16–17, 19–22, 24n.31, 35, 43, 54, 105, 115, 149, 151n.6, 153, 174, 177, 199, 206, 222
   in "A Study in Scarlet" (Doyle), 165–169
   transnational relations, 159, 163n.22, 169, 172, 203
   in "The White Man's Burden" (Kipling), 171–173
   Whitman's vision of unified, 203–206

women's employment and, 101–102, 105, 113, 139
Native Americans, 164, 167n.31, 184n.54, 199n.77, 197
nervous system, 35, 43, 162–163, 169, 174, 177
network, 40, 72–73, 82, 102
   and Anglo-American relations, 149, 155, 158–159, 168, 177
   and communication, 1, 8, 10, 14n.20, 23, 25, 34, 69, 77, 100, 115, 126, 128–129, 132, 139, 147, 149, 157, 162, 169, 177–178, 180, 203
   in *Dracula* (Stoker), 181–183, 189–190, 193, 195–198
   egalitarianism of, 4, 6–7, 38, 45, 105, 146
   erotics of, 25, 36, 203–4
   familial, 155, 163, 175
   homosexuality, alliance with, 4–7, 44, 46, 157
   homosocial, 177, 190, 195
   imperial, 22, 24–25, 32, 153, 157, 162, 168–169, 177, 183, 189, 198–199
   and infiltration, 162, 180–3, 198
   in *John Caldigate* (Trollope), 89, 91, 94
   in *A Laodicean* (Hardy), 131–133, 139, 145
   and nation building, 14, 22, 25, 149, 175, 157, 177–178, 183, 195–196, 198
   in *Post Haste* (Ballantyne), 115
   queerness of, 9, 25, 38, 69, 99–100, 126, 131, 146, 157
   in *The Rebel of the Family* (Linton), 126
   social, 43, 89, 103, 140 n. 51, 146, 204
   in "A Study in Scarlet" (Doyle), 165, 167–170
   unifying effects of, 6, 22, 199, 204
   and universalism, 180
   as web, 8–9, 34–5, 37–8, 90, 97, 155, 159, 170, 178, 210, 222–223
   and women, 100, 131
New Journalism, 49, 51, 52
Newlove, Henry, 43–44
Nicholson, John Gambril, "Your City Cousins," 56
Nordau, Max, 173–174
Nunokawa, Jeff, 57–58

Oliphant, Margaret, 72
Oregon Boundary Dispute, 151, 186
O'Farrell, Mary Ann, 140
O'Sullivan, John L., *See* manifest destiny

Otis, Laura, 35, 162
Oxford University, 57, 62

passing, 62, 64, 123, 128
patrilineal relations, 50, 95, 97, 102, 155, 172
patronage, 45–47, 104
Pears' Soap, 149, 150 fig. 4.1
Penny Post, 11, 23, 87, 149, 174
   Atlantic penny postage, 149
   and class equality, 11, 14, 16–18, 21–22
   economics of, 11, 13–15, 17
   founding of, 10–12, 65n.46
   imperial function of, 12, 22–23, 32–33
   Imperial Penny Postage, 23, 37, 159, 168
   and nation formation, 16–17, 22
   "Ocean Penny Post," 151, 152 fig. 4.2, 153
   "The Penny Post Act" song, 11–12, 13 fig.1.2
   Penny Postage Scheme, 16, 23, 151, 174
   penny stamp, 16, 25n.33, 26, 86, 93, 151, 213
   and racial federation, 23, 149
   and spatial consciousness, 12–16
performativity, 8–9, 58, 64, 80, 91, 147
   in *the Autobiography* (Trollope), 79n.18, 80
   in *Cranford* (Gaskell), 31
   in *The Importance of Being Earnest* (Wilde), 64
   in *John Caldigate* (Trollope), 93
   in *A Laodicean* (Hardy), 147
   and the "periperformative," 101
Philadelphia, 199, 204
philately, 16n.22
photography, 65n.48, 140–144, 219n.15
pillar-box, 52, 70, 70n.2, 77, 82, 89, 90
   See also Anthony Trollope
Pickering, Neville, 162
plague, 35, 180
Plotz, John, 26, 133 n.41
Poe, Edgar Allan: "The Purloined Letter," 67
Polk, James K., 186
polygamy, *See* marriage
Pope, Alexander: "Eloisa to Abelard," 33n.44
Post Office,
   annihilation of time and space by, 13–14, 29, 32, 38, 97, 122, 157, 198–199
   as brothel, *See* Cleveland Street Affair
   and citizenship, 19, 22
   as desiring machine, 34
   as guardian, 51–55, 112
   as heart, 54, 174

and imperialism, 17, 22, 24
as institution, 1, 5, 31, 35
as mother, 26–7
and nationalism,16, 22
as non-familial structure, 44, 113
as pimp, 51
and postcolonialism, 24
queering effects of, 7, 9, 30
as spouse, 102, 110–114
Post Office Protection Act, 219
postage stamp, 1–2, 6–7, 18–19, 35–36, 83, 159
   in *In the Cage* (James), 213
   invention of, 14
   in *John Caldigate* (Trollope), 84–87, 93, 95
   Penny Black, 1, 12, 14–15, 19, 155–156
   "tell-tale," 26, 93, See also Penny Black Stamp
   See also Mulready Envelope *entries*; philately *entries*
postal reform, 2, 10–22, 56, 104–5
Postal Telegraph Clerks Association, 56
postbag, 1–2, 3–4, 10, 45, 71, 162
postcard, 25, 149, 219
postcolonialism, 24, 32
postman, *See* messenger
"postman's knock," 41 fig. 1.1
   as game, 64–65
postmark, 2, 6, 68, 83–86, 90, 93, 182, 222
post-structuralism, 7, 82
Prins, Yopie, 137, 138n.47
prosthetics, 37–38, 100, 145, 179, 207n.95
prostitution, 40, 43, 51, 54, 60, 73, 98n.49, 107, 112–133, 116–117, 217
proxy, 1, 18, 62, 123, 145, 148, 180, 216
psychoanalysis, 80
public, 5, 7, 10, 19–20, 54, 89, 114–5, 174
   imagination, 11, 32, 34, 48 n. 19, 90, 102
   interest, 47, 42 n. 7
   life, 42n.7, 94, 101–2, 110, 146
   morals, 39
   publication, 9, 61–2, 65–8, 90, 115–6
   publicity, 41, 47, 49, 217n.9
   "public facility," 43–46, *See also* water closet
   public vs. private, 31–32, 45–52, 77, 88, 93, 100, 103–4, 110, 113, 115–6, 219–20
   service, 53, 101, 104, 113–4, 126
   space, 6, 45–6, 48, 58, 68, 100, 103, 58 n. 36, 77, 213
   sphere, 126, 46 n. 16, 77, 103, 113, 126

public servant, 31, 42, 47, 51–2, 55–6, 58 n.36, 101–6, 113–5, 124, 181 n.50, 209–10, 234
Punch, 19n.25, 160, 161 fig. 4.5

Queensberry, Marquis of, 33, 66–68
queer,
   effects, 27, 29–30, 36, 71 n. 8, 99, 128–9, 131, 143, 215, 218, 221
   interfaces, 4–5, 8, 69, 98
   in *A Laodicean* (Hardy), 139
   structures of alliance, 9, 25, 37, 82–3, 135, 214–5, 222
   subjectivity, 7, 38, 46

race, 23, 45, 155, 162n.20, 223
   blackness, 12, 179, 199n.77
   and class, 188–189
   and degeneration, 177, 195
   and diaspora, 23, 25, 153–154, 159, 168
   in *Dracula* (Stoker), 188–189, 194–195, 198
   homosexuality, dependence on, 157–158, 162, 173, 177, 204–205
   and hybridity, 45, 106, 175, 177n.45, 178, 180, 205
   and imperialism, 154, 159–160, 187
   in *A Laodicean* (Hardy), 139
   vs. nationalism, 159–160
   and racial brotherhood, 151, 159, 166, 173, 188–189, 195, 204–205
   patriotism, 149, 154, 160, 187, 194
   and racism, 149n.3, 154n.7, 160, 178
   unity of, 149, 158, 160, 163–164, 166, 168, 173, 183, 189, 204–206
   in "The White Man's Burden" (Kipling), 173, 175
   whiteness, 23, 25, 121, 123, 137–8, 149n.3, 154, 159, 163–4, 166, 169, 179–80, 199, 205
   See also alliance *entries*; Anglo Saxonism *entries*
Raikes, H.C., 56–7
railway, 14n.20, 26n.36, 32, 45, 64, 151n.6, 180
   and Carnegie, Andrew, 24n.30
   in *A Laodicean* (Hardy), 129–130, 133
   and sexuality, 46n.17, 64, 203
   and Trollope, Anthony, 71, 76
   and Ghandi, Mahatma, 180
   in "Passage to India" (Whitman), 204
   and postal system, 10, 25–26

"All Red Routes," 23, 37, 148–149, 159, 168–169, 181–182
realism, 35, 72–73, 79n.18
Reform Act of 1832, 17
religion, 20, 23, 156n.10, 60n.40, 135–136, 140n.53, 151, 155n.9, 164
reproduction, 74, 87, 180
 in *Dracula* (Stoker), 157, 191
 heterosexual, 157, 171, 176
 homosexual, 173, 176–177, 189
 in *The People of the Abyss* (London), 174, 177–176
Rhodes, Cecil, 37, 149n.2,
 "Rhodes Colossus," 160
 Rhodes Scholarship, 161–162
Richards, Thomas, 32, 154n.7, 193n.70
Richardson, Samuel, 131–132, 181
Ross, Robert, 65–66
 See also Oscar Wilde
Rowe, Katherine, 121
Rushdie, Salman, 24

Said, Edward, 24n.31, 154n.7
St. Martin's-Le-Grand, 43, 107, 114, 138n.50
Savoy, Eric, 9, 31n.39, 214, 220, 222
Schaffer, Talia, 189, 201
Schivelbusch, Wolfgang, 14n.20
Scudamore, Frank Ives, 105–107, 121
secrecy, 9, 31, 58–59, 61, 68
 and homosexuality, 59, 65, 146, 219
 in *In the Cage* (James), 216
 in *John Caldigate*, 94
 open, 58–59, 61, 94, 220
 in *Rebel of the Family* (Linton), 120, 123–124
 and telegraphy, 117, 120, 130, 216
 and Trollope, Anthony, 77, 79
 See also D.A. Miller; spying
Sedgwick, Eve Kosofsky, 6, 49, 57, 59, 81, 93, 95, 101, 142–143, 190–191, 221
sensorium, 125
 homo-sensorium, 119, 102
Seward, William H., 185n.56
Shakespeare, William: *A Winter's Tale*, 119
shame, 62, 68, 81
 class, 39
 in Dracula (Stoker), 189
 in In the Cage (James), 220
 in John Caldigate (Trollope), 84, 89, 95
 sexual, 39, 79, 89, 201

 and Trollope, Anthony, 71–72, 79, 81–82
Percy Bysshe, 11n.16, 154n.7
Simmel, Georg, 91
Sims, George, 174
 How the Poor Live, 198–199
slavery, 25n.32, 26–27, 51n.25, 197
Smith, Goldwin, 164
Smith, James, 60–61
sociability, 46, 91
social hierarchy, *See* class
socialism, 4, 6, 119–120, 124, 127, 199
Society for the Diffusion of Useful Knowledge, 20
sodomy, 8–9, 48, 66
Somerset, Lord Arthur, 46, 49–50, 52
speed, 10, 13, 21, 25, 33–35, 76–77, 90n.34
 and Trollope, Anthony, 76–77, 90n.34
Spanish-American War, 194
spying, 124, 170, 214
Stafford, Harry, 203
Stead, W. T., 149n.2, 160, 164, 173, 186–187, 192n.68
steamship, 32
Stevenson, Fanny Van De Grift, *See* Robert Louis Stevenson
Stevenson, Robert Louis, 62, 64
 The Dynamiter, 63
Stephen, Leslie, 70
Stephenson, Sir Augustus, 47, 49–54
stigma, 71, 73, 82, 212, 218n.10
Stoker, Bram, 37, 157–158, 164n.24, 180–183, 184n.54, 185–203
 "The Censorship of Fiction," 201–202
 Dracula, 37, 157, 180–198, 200
 and epistolary form, 181–182
 and homosexuality, 199
 A Glimpse of America, 188–190, 194
 The Jewel of the Seven Stars, 190
 Lady Athlyne, 184n.54, 201
 Personal Reminiscences of Henry Irving, 187, 192, 200
 The Shoulder of Shasta, 184n.54, 193n.71
 Under the Sunset, 188n.61
 Walt Whitman, friendship with, 37, 182, 192, 199–203
Story, Waldo, 8–9
Strachey, Giles Lytton: *Elizabeth and Essex*, 65
Swinscow, Charles, 43–44, 56
Symonds, John Addington, 172–173, 177, 193, 198, 219

sympathy, 17, 22, 50, 82, 84, 97, 121, 131–2, 168–9, 201, 212

tailoring, 39, 57–58
"A Tangled Skein," *See* Arthur Conan Doyle, "A Study in Scarlet"
Taylor, Marc C., 178–179
teledildonics, 179
Telegraph Act of 1868, 115
Telegraph Act of 1869, 33n.43, 101–102
telegraph boys, *See* Boy Messengers
telegraph girls, 36, 54, 138
   in *In the Cage*, 208–210, 212–218, 220
   masculine identity, 126–127
   and prostitution, 112–113, 116–117
   queer, 37, 113, 215
   resistance to marriage, 99–101
   See also lesbianism
telegraph wires, 23, 35, 45, 129–130, 139, 141, 143–144, 147, 160–161, 168–9, 180, 204, 206, 215
   as bloodline, 168–169
   resistance to lineage, 139
telegraphy,
   vs. post-letter, 33–34
   queer effects of, 9, 64, 128–129, 131, 139, 143
telepathy, 197
telephone, 32, 180
   as game, 179
temporality, 22, 29, 108, 124n.35, 144, 203
   in *The Autobiography of Christopher Kirkland* (Linton), 122
   in *Cranford* (Gaskell), 29
   futurity, 185–191, 195, 197–198
   trans-generational, 171, 173
   and space, annihilation of, 13–14, 29, 32, 38, 97, 122, 157, 198–199
   in "A Study in Scarlet," 165
   and Trollope, Anthony, 71
   See also delay *entries*; touch *entries*
terminus, 64, 210
Texas, 185–186
   annexation of, 197
Tichborne, Claimant, 83n.27
touch, 30, 142–143, 203–204
   in *Cranford* (Gaskell), 30–31
   in *In the Cage* (James), 216, 218
   in *A Laodicean* (Hardy), 142, 1444

   in *Post Haste* (Ballantyne), 114
   in *The Rebel of the Family* (Linton), 121, 125
   and telegraph girls, 99, 105, 114, 121, 125, 142–143, 218
train, *See* railway
The Treaty of Paris, 171 n.34, 194n.72
Trollope, Anthony, 36, 75–78, 81–82, 84, 95–97, 99n.1, 206
   and anonymity, 79
   the *Autobiography*, 36, 70n.2, 73–82, 84, 86n.31, 92n.41, 95, 98, 104, 105n.9, 118,
   "The Civil Service as a Profession," 104
   and the epistolary form, 71
   The Eustace Diamonds, 89
   "The Gentle Euphemia," 83n.25,
   and homosexuality, 61, 77–78, 80n.19
   and impersonality, 80–81
   John Caldigate, 30, 36, 60n.40, 81n.22, 83–89, 92–97, 117n.26
   as postman, 36, 70–72, 192, 210
   and shame, 71–73, 79, 81–82, 84
   on telegraph boys vs. telegraph girls, 59–61
   "The Telegraph Girl," 50n.30, 99–101, 107–109, 111–112, 115, 119, 126–127, 217
   "The Turkish Bath," 98n.49
   The Vicar of Bullhampton, 73
   and women's rights, 91, 107n.15
   and writing practices, 73–77, 90n.34, 98
   "The Young Women at the London Telegraph Office," 59n.39, 102, 107, 116

uniforms, 34–35, 40–41, 44–46, 52–53, 55–58, 65, 169
uniformity, 7, 11, 14, 56, 87, 135
United States, 7n.8, 33,
   in *Dracula* (Stoker), 159, 180, 184, 186–195, 197
   imperialism, 171, 187, 189, 194–195
   as "lost boy," 37
   postal system, 2n.2, 6, 25n.32, 42n.7, 65n.48
   and relations with Britain, 23–25, 148–149, 151, 153, 158–160, 162–164, 166–168, 171–172, 177, 185n.56, 186–189, 192, 194, 198, 205
   "A Study in Scarlet" (Doyle), 163–169
   in "The White Man's Burden," 177
Universal Penny Postage, *See* Penny Postage Scheme
universalism, 23–24, 105, 132, 146

Uranianism, *See* homosexuality & Edward Carpenter
utopia, 119n.30, 120, 124

vagrancy, 48n.18, 71, 98
Valentine's Day, 12, 200
vampirism, 124n.34, 176, 181–184, 191, 195–198, 200n.79
  See also Bram Stoker
veins, *See* arteries
Venezuela Boundary Dispute, 166n.27, 186–187
Vicinus, Martha, 103n.7, 110, 113, 137n.48
Victor, Prince Albert, 46
  See also Cleveland Street Affair
Victoria (queen of England), 1, 12, 14
  image of, 1, 14, 16, 19, 25n.33, 85, 87, 213
Villarejo, Amy, 145
voice, 53 n.30, 60 n. 40, 73, 78, 92, 108, 117, 149, 183, 206, 221
  as media, 144–5
  thrown, 36, 72, 218

Wagner, Richard: *The Art-Work of the Future*, 5–6, 31, 35
Walpole, Sir Spenser, 23
Weeks, Jeffrey, 42n.6, 48n.19, 49, 66n.52, 173, 176n.44
Wells, H.G., 174n.40, 178
  The Time Machine, 174n.40
West End Scandal, *See* Cleveland Street Affair
Whitman, Walt, 37, 40, 69, 158, 203–207
  "Children of Adam" poems, 202
  and civil war hospitals, 192, 206–207
  "Come Up from the Fields Father," 206
  "Death of Lincoln" lecture, 200
  and homosexuality, 40, 69, 158, 192n.69, 199
  Leaves of Grass, 199, 202
  "The Moral Effect of the Cable," 205–206
  "On the Beach at Night Alone," 204
  "Passage to India," 204
  "Song of the Exposition," 204, 206
  "Song of Myself," 203
  "Song of the Open Road," 207
  "Starting from Paumanok," 204–205
  "Years of the Modern," 204
  See also Bram Stoker *entries*; Edward Carpenter *entries*
Wilde, Oscar, 8–9, 39, 62, 66–69, 134
  and blackmail, 36, 66, 68
  and homosexuality, 39, 59, 62–64, 67, 69, 173, 201
  The Importance of Being Earnest, 63–64
  The Picture of Dorian Gray, 39, 53n.30, 59, 137
  "The Portrait of Mr. W.H.," 219
  Salomé, 65,
  and telegram sending, 9, 63–64, 68
  and telegraph boys, 39–40
  trials of, 28, 36, 40, 48n.19, 50n.23, 57, 62–63, 65–69, 189n.63, 201, 215, 217n.9, 219
  See also alias
Williams, Raymond, 17n.23, 34
Williams, Tennessee: *Auto-Da-Fe,* 65n.48
women, 36, 99, 101, 105–106, 109–110, 126
  and civil service, 102–106, 191n.67
  and class, 36, 99, 102–103, 105–106
  in *Dracula* (Stoker), 193
  in *In the Cage* (James), 214
  unmarried, 36, 99, 103–104, 107, 129, 138
  "woman question," 103
  See also telegraph girls *entries*; lesbianism *entries*
Woolf, Virginia, 70, 179

Yellow Book, 66

www.ingramcontent.com/pod-product-compliance
Ingram Content Group UK Ltd.
Pitfield, Milton Keynes, MK11 3LW, UK
UKHW042006230426
12048UKWH00009B/582